The battle of Britishness

MANCHESTER
1824

Manchester University Press

In memory of Ian Karten (1920–2011), a true *mensch*, and
for Sam Kushner in the year of his *Barmitzvah*

'People don't make the journeys to come and die, they make them
to come and live. And to live you transform the place.'
John Akomfrah

'My soul has grown deep like the rivers.'
Langston Hughes

The battle of
Britishness

Migrant journeys, 1685 to the present

Tony Kushner

Manchester University Press
Manchester and New York

distributed in the United States exclusively
by Palgrave Macmillan

Published by Manchester University Press
Oxford Road, Manchester M13 9NR, UK
and Room 400, 175 Fifth Avenue, New York, NY 10010, USA
www.manchesteruniversitypress.co.uk

Distributed in the United States exclusively by
Palgrave Macmillan, 175 Fifth Avenue,
New York, NY 10010, USA

Distributed in Canada exclusively by
UBC Press, University of British Columbia, 2029 West Mall,
Vancouver, BC, Canada V6T 1Z2

British Library Cataloguing-in-Publication Data is available

Library of Congress Cataloging-in-Publication Data is available

ISBN 978 0 7190 6641 2 *paperback*

First published by Manchester University Press in hardback 2012

This paperback edition first published 2014

The publisher has no responsibility for the persistence or accuracy of URLs for any external or third-party internet websites referred to in this book, and does not guarantee that any content on such websites is, or will remain, accurate or appropriate.

Printed by Lightning Source

Contents

Acknowledgements

I would like to start by thanking a generation – twenty five-years to be precise – of students who have taken part in my second year undergraduate course, The Making of Englishness. Through discussions with them I have been stimulated to think through some of the subject matter of this book in what was a fast evolving historiography and sociology of knowledge, reflecting changes in society as a whole. A much loved feature of this course has been a walking tour of the East End of London and thanks are due to those who have led them, including David Cesarani, David Rosenberg and especially Alan Dein. The individual who was a pioneer of such tours, as well as being the leading scholar of the East End and its migrant history, deserves particular praise – Bill Fishman. It was delightful in June 2011 to celebrate Bill's 90th birthday at Queen Mary College in Mile End where he taught for so many years.

One of the pleasures of being part of the History Department at the University of Southampton is to benefit from the global interests, chronological range and breadth of expertise of my colleagues. For the subject matter of this study this extensive knowledge has been of immense help and I would like to thank in particular John Oldfield, Alastair Duke, Ian Talbot, Jane McDermit, Joan Tumblety, Julie Gammon, Mark Stoyle and Matt Kelly and ex-colleagues Peter Gray, Tobias Brinkmann, Gemma Romain, Greg Walker, Tom Lawson and Gavin Schaffer for advice and information. My colleagues in the Parkes Institute, both full-timers and Honorary Fellows, were of equal importance in providing stimulation, and thanks especially to Sarah Pearce, Joachim Schloer, Mark Levene, Barbara Rosenbaum, Brian Klug, Hannah Ewence, Jan Lanicek, Jane Gerson, Jo Reilly and a friend who continues to inspire, amuse and reassure, Colin Richmond. James Jordan went beyond collegiality and was a source of wonderfully obscure but exciting material. James helped throughout and

Acknowledgements

his interest and enthusiasm helped more than perhaps he realises. I would also like to thank him for his work in helping to forge stronger links between the Parkes Institute and our partners in Cape Town and Sydney.

This book is part of wider work on migration in Britain and I would like to thank those working in this field, including Kathy Burrell, John Solomos and Liza Schuster as well as Paul Gilroy, Bryan Cheyette and others who are providing theoretical perspectives to enable intellectual cross-fertilisation between different areas of study. More specifically within the discipline of history, Bill Williams, Colin Holmes, Ken Lunn and Panikos Panayi as pioneers of British migration studies deserve praise. As part of the next generation of such scholars, I would like to mention especially Nick Evans. Nick was a great guide to Hull and its sites of transmigrancy and, as ever, was fun to be with. It is a source of regret that his remarkable departure from a restaurant in Hamburg at a conference on transmigrancy was never recorded for posterity. His rapid exit goes to show what we humans can achieve even without the aid of alcohol. Equally pleasurable were trips to the Lake District to work with Trevor Avery and the Another Space project on the child survivors who went to Windermere. Trevor and his team are producing outstanding work and it has been a privilege to see it evolve so successfully. Whilst the Windermere experience will feature only briefly in this study, the work of Another Space has been influential on it. I continue to work on the cultural history of the child survivors with Aimée Bunting who jointly gave papers based on the Windermere story. She has seen this overall project evolve and has given wise advice, provided source material and undertaken journeys in search of journeys. More generally she has helped give it shape and direction without which the book would not have been completed.

I gave papers across Britain, Cape Town and Sydney based on some of the material in this book. I would like to thank those who hosted me, especially Milton Shain and Janine Blumberg at Cape Town and to the audiences who gave extremely helpful feedback and criticism. I am indebted to the many archivists, librarians and curators who provided assistance. Karen Robson, Chris Woolgar and Jenny Ruthven at the University of Southampton's Special Collections, as ever, deserve particular mention. I would also like to thank the librarians and archivists of the National Archives (Kew), the British Library, the Imperial War Museum, the Mass-Observation Archive (University of Sussex), the Guildhall Library, Southampton Local Studies Library, Southampton Archives, Hampshire Record Office, Manchester Central Reference Library, Stockport Reference Library, Kendal Local Studies Library, Tower Hamlets Local Studies Library, the Wiener Library, London Metropolitan Archives, St Ives Local Studies Library, Brighton Local Studies Library, Windermere Library, the Museum of London, the Dover Museum, the Manchester Jewish

Museum, the Jewish Museum (London), the Irish Jewish Museum, the National Maritime Museum (Liverpool), the National Maritime Museum (Falmouth), the National Museum of Scotland (Edinburgh), the Butetown History and Arts Centre (Cardiff), Black Cultural Archives, the University of Cape Town archives, and the Australian National Maritime Museum (Sydney).

I have enjoyed a long working relationship with Manchester University Press and would like to thank the History editor, Emma Brennan, for her work on this project. On the Manchester front, thanks as ever to my mother and Mike for their loving hospitality and continued lunacy when making regular visits up north. 2011 was a very mixed sporting year in my particular part of the north-west. On the one hand, there was Manchester City's first major trophy since 1976 and what was a special day spent with my brother Ben and nephew Toby witnessing the lifting of the FA Cup, alongside Lancashire County Cricket Club winning the championship outright for the first time since 1934. On the other, it was also the year that Stockport County lost their place in the Football League – one that they had held for over a century. The differing fortunes of City and County reflect the victors and victims of Mammon that is in danger of destroying the game. In this respect, it is always pleasing to report that the Cavaliers Cricket Club remain untainted by commercialisation in spite of tempting offers from the IPL. Last season (2010) we broke a losing sequence that had lasted over a year. In 2011, while our losing habit has returned, it has been a pleasure to watch Sam join Jack as promising all-rounders in the pursuit of excellence. Sam took his first Cavalier wickets and for this, and also because he has not had a book dedicated to him before (although his wandering feet featured on the cover of my last monograph, *Anglo-Jewry since 1066*), he belatedly gets a special mention. Hopefully he will not grow up to be a mere 'buffet bowler' like Donald Bloxham whose return to the Cavaliers in May 2011 was a joy. Lloyd Gartner in Jerusalem always took an interest in the Cavaliers and I am sad that he is no longer with us to read this latest update. As the first critical scholar of British Jewish history and especially that of modern migration, we later historians will always be in his debt. Mag, Jack and Sam have lived with this book for several years and deserve praise for their tolerance. Thanks also to Jack and Mag for helping to locate sources and to Sybil Lunn for the index. My friends made sure I kept going in what is an increasingly worrying and depressing world – one where migrants are increasingly vulnerable and under threat.

I would like to close by remembering Ian Karten, a man who had carried out his own migrant journey in the dark days of the 1930s and who then contributed so much to his adopted country. Ian sadly died as this book was being completed. I will miss him deeply as a good friend. He was a remarkable and gentle man whose unstinting generosity was an inspiration to us all at the Parkes Institute. I hope that this book is a small way of repaying the huge debt of gratitude we owe him.

Introduction and contexts

Introduction

'The history of the world', it has been suggested, 'includes remarkable stories of migration in every era.'[1] From its origins in Africa, the human story has been one of constant movement.[2] In the new millennium, western nations in particular are desperately trying to control mass movements across their borders. But viewing history long-term suggests the task they are setting themselves will be immense and ultimately futile. In his 'concise [global] summary' of the subject from prehistory to the twenty-first century, Patrick Manning describes 'migratory movement as a human habit'.[3] Here, the focus is also on the long term but the specific emphasis is on the experiences of one country: Britain. As Manning recognises, with the 'rise of nationhood throughout the world, migration remained one of the key factors in the definition of national identity'.[4] To do justice, however, to its complex subject matter the coverage inevitably has to be international. At a basic level 'Migration encourages one to think of connections, at least because every migration connects a point of origin and a destination.'[5] This introduction provides a guide to the theories and methodologies underpinning this book's structure and how the 'global' and the 'local' connect within *The Battle of Britishness*. The aim is to explain the logic of what has, and has not, been included within this study. The following chapters in Part I explore in detail the contexts and meanings associated with the book's key twin concepts of the journey and Britishness.

Ultimately, *The Battle of Britishness* is about twoness. It is about both famous and obscure migrant journeys to Britain. Included are migrants who passed through its ports only briefly and others who were allowed and chose to settle permanently. Rarely does human migration follow a straightforward path from one place (home) to another (the place of settlement). The story of migration to any modern nation state is also one of exclusion. Britain is no exception. There were/are still those deemed so different that they are prohibited from entry. This book also includes journeys in which Britain was intrinsically involved because of its global empire and its extensive role, as a leading maritime nation, in international trade. It thus confronts the 'Middle Passage' of transatlantic slavery as well as migrant journeys to places overseas under its control. Included, therefore, are migrant journeys *to* Britain as well as *away* from it.

There are stories within *The Battle of Britishness* which were once well known, even notorious, and are now forgotten, some that have recently been rediscovered and celebrated and others still that were and remain largely concealed. This study is also, in relation to twoness, about inclusion and exclusion in defining Britishness. Yet across these binaries it is also about *ambivalence* and *ambiguity* in both migrant stories as well as in the making and re-making of national identity over many centuries. It thus follows the work of literary scholars and cultural theorists such as Bryan Cheyette and Homi Bhabha on the nation state and ethnic difference.

Minorities, they suggest, can be perceived as transformable through universalism but simultaneously rejected 'as an unchanging racial "other"'. Cheyette, confronting the place of 'the Jew' in liberal culture, suggests that this constructed figure can encompass 'the possibility of a new redemptive order as well as the degeneration of an untransfigured past'.[6] More generally Bhabha in his seminal collection, *Nation and Narration* (1990) explores

> the Janus-faced ambivalence of language itself in the construction of the Janus-faced discourse of the nation. This turns the familiar two-faced god into a figure of prodigious doubling that investigates the nation-space in the *process* of the articulation of elements: where meanings may be partial because they are *in medias res*; and history may be half-made because it is in the process of being made.[7]

Such 'stark doubleness' will be seen throughout this book.[8] The migrant journey, real or imagined, has evoked especially strong, if often contradictory, responses from state and public alike. Such responses have cut across politics and society and have been made manifest through varied representations from 'self' and 'other' and across many different cultural forms.

To further highlight the centrality of twoness the chapters beyond this section have been organised in pairs, incorporating eight case studies. At one level, this structure, organised chronologically from the seventeenth century onwards, appears simplistic. One journey within each section is famous and those undertaking them regarded positively, while the other is marginalised and pathologised. Yet each case study will reveal more complexity at work. For example, 'disturbing' elements within narratives relating to celebrated journeys

4

have been deliberately ignored or forgotten. They have been shaped to meet expectations of conformity and assimilation, thereby presenting the migrant group as a success story. Alternatively, it is rare to find an utter absence of positive responses to those generally treated in a hostile way. Equally in such 'negative' cases, battles over memory have taken place in which counter-narratives are produced highlighting racism and resistance. Indeed, the phrase 'staying power', coined by Peter Fryer in his landmark history of black people in Britain, will feature throughout this study. It reflects the determination of migrants and their descendants to be a part of the nation. Fryer passionately claimed that his was 'an account of the lives, struggles, and achievements of men and women most of whom have either been forgotten or, still more insultingly, remembered as curiosities or objects of condescension'.[9] His approach will be followed in the Parts that follow. Nevertheless, the struggles and divisions *within* migrant groups and the narratives which might be internally suppressed by 'ethnic brokers' must equally be kept in mind. There is a danger, in attempting to recover the experiences of the downtrodden and marginalised, of presenting celebratory history and heritage as a form of compensation.

By juxtaposing two contrasting stories in each section a rich seam of British migration history is revealed. The objective is to add critical perspectives on stories supposedly already 'known' and to supplement them with those subject to amnesia. Moreover, the evolving and contested nature of Britishness can be explored by analysing which groups have been allowed entry to, and which have been excluded from, the nation's borders. But migration cannot be studied in isolation. This study explores how constructs of race, religion, ethnicity, place, gender, age and class have been employed in selection processes both at the level of immigration control procedures and within the stories Britain tells of itself.

What follows, however, is not a comprehensive history of migration to Britain – many such journeys are *not* incorporated simply through reasons of space. Indeed, this book is the first devoted to its subject matter. It is hoped that it will inspire others to add further to its scope, especially in relation to very recent migrant journeys. In terms of organisation, some journeys covered, such as those relating to slavery, will not have a separate chapter devoted to them. They will, however, feature prominently at certain stages of this study. The generic slave journey as depicted from the Bible onwards has become crucial in constructing the narratives of later migrant movements. The 'Middle Passage' especially will be confronted and re-addressed here within different contexts of time and place. Similarly, the wider global narratives relating to the two most famous migrant movements of the long nineteenth century – the Jews and the Irish – are incorporated into the second chapter of *The Battle of Britishness*. These particular journeys were huge in scale and attracted much attention both at the time and subsequently. A comparison of them enables a close reading of the politics and memory of migrant journeys more generally.

Migration from South East Asia (or of those of that origin including from East Africa) has, since the late 1950s, been the largest of all global movements to Britain. The associated journeys and readings of them will receive attention at key moments in this study. The main focus, however, of *The Battle of Britishness* is historical. While recent and ongoing migrant journeys, including those from Eastern Europe at the turn of the twenty-first century, will not be ignored, the emphasis is on movements up to the 1950s. More attention, therefore, will be placed, for example, on *earlier* Asian journeys to Britain than those since the second half of the twentieth century.

As the heart of this study is the inter-relationship between migrant journeys and Britishness, certain historical moments have received particular attention. The memory of the Second World War and more generally the Nazi era is generally regarded as the most central element in constructing national identity in modern Britain.[10] It is for this reason that two Parts relate to migrant movements (or the suppressing of them) from the 1930s to the early 1950s. Part III includes journeys of escape from persecution in the Third Reich, culminating in the Holocaust. Part IV incorporates colonial and postcolonial journeys made by fighting for the 'Mother Country' during the Second World War and bettering oneself after it. Finally, in terms of chronology, while the coverage of journeys *after* the 1950s is less sustained, they will not be ignored. Such recent journeys will be studied in their own right. They will also be read in relation to the politics of memory relating to earlier movements and contestations of national identity in the late twentieth and early twenty-first centuries.

The Battle of Britishness is thus deliberately selective but even so the coverage is broad chronologically. It starts in detail from the late seventeenth century onwards with the Huguenots, the first 'modern' migrants to Britain and a group now idealised as newcomers. It also includes earlier periods (including prehistory) with regard to the *memory* and *politicisation* of migration in Britain. The major focus, however, is from the nineteenth century onwards, reflecting the intensification of migration at a global level and the point at which permanent structures were implemented to control the entry and activities of immigrants.

This study is also wide-ranging through the types of groups studied who came from (or went to) all parts of the globe. It includes North, South, Western and Central Europe; South, North, East and West Africa; the Middle East; the Far East; South East Asia; the Caribbean; Oceania; North America; and Central and South America. Journeys *beyond* the British sphere of influence are included – especially relating to the wider diasporic experiences of the groups featured within. They are made part of this study in order to provide context and comparison. There are also narratives included that while intimately connected to Britain have gained fame and notoriety elsewhere but not, significantly, at 'home'. Again, such journeys illustrate how any study of migration cannot ultimately be restrained by focusing on one country in isolation.

The Battle of Britishness will thus juxtapose migrant experiences that some will find intriguing but others may well find challenging. It explores, for example, migrant journeys that were both forced and voluntary, as well as those that were colonial, post-colonial and non-colonial. Likewise the confrontation with the nature of Britishness enters controversial and emotionally charged territory. It is, however, increasingly necessary as the forces of globalisation are filtered through the 'local' in a world of fast-changing and increasingly insecure identities.

This book builds on the pioneer accounts of Colin Holmes,[11] Peter Fryer,[12] Rozina Visram,[13] Robert Winder,[14] James Walvin,[15] Panikos Panayi,[16] Anne Kershen,[17] John Solomos,[18] Lloyd Gartner,[19] Bill Williams,[20] and many others. These scholars have started to establish, against the dominant belief in past homogeneity, the importance of immigration in British history. *The Battle of Britishness* also attempts something beyond. It is a study, incorporating history and memory (and the tensions between the two, thereby complicating its chronological progression between sections), of the place of migration in the construction of Britishness. Migration and ethnic minority presence are sadly themes lacking in most studies of Britishness (or more specifically, Englishness).[21] The desire here is to weave such academic work together, or at least to promote much needed dialogue between scholarship on migration and that on national identity. In addition, it is a plea to promote dialogue between post-colonial scholarship and work on non-colonial minorities.[22]

The chapters that follow examine the 'inner lives' of the migrants as well as responses to them from state and public. It is a history from above, but also from below, incorporating many different forms of cultural representation. Wherever possible, the testimony of those involved – both migrant and non-migrant – is utilised to ensure that the human dimension of migration is never forgotten. The absence of the individual is a major lacuna in migration studies as a whole. Yet the use of testimony is not straightforward. There is a need always to deal with testimony critically and to understand the complex dynamics of its construction.[23] In addition, there are many journeys in which the migrant voice is simply absent from the historical record or where certain types of migrants are heard and not others. Such distortions and silences in the archives have always to be recognised.

Because of its overarching ambitions, the sources used are numerous and varied, including government documentation, debate and legislation; political polemic; speeches; SMSs; organisational archives and personal papers; census records; autobiographical writings (published and archival, migrant and non-migrant, written and oral, contemporary and non-contemporary); travel writing; novels and poetry; theatre; carnival; films, television, radio and newspapers; photographs, drawings, paintings and sculpture; music; food and drink; the internet; museums, exhibitions, heritage sites and memorials; buildings and landscape; and many different forms of historiography. In some chapters, particular sources and themes come to the fore, but generally the combination of them is employed to provide a richer, multi-layered cultural history. Within it is the complex study of memory. By utilising the concept of 'memory work' as self-conscious praxis I am emphasising that memory as a whole is socially constructed. Memory work is often carried out by the powerful in order to ensure that their version of the past remains dominant in the present. Increasingly, however, memory work is being carried out from the grassroots in an attempt to empower the dispossessed.[24] *The Battle of Britishness* explores which migrant journeys have been remembered and by whom, asking how such memories have been constructed and contested over time and place. As Jeffrey Olick and Joyce Robbins suggest, 'The fields of social memory studies is clearly vast, the forms of memory work diverse.'[25] It will not, however, ignore the processes and politics of forgetting which, as Jonathan Boyarin notes, is 'sometimes a technique of the dominated, used to enable memory'.[26]

The emphasis in this study is on the importance of the journey itself, an aspect often curiously missing in migration studies.[27] The mechanics of the particular means of journeying will thus feature prominently – especially the ship, and to a lesser extent the railway – as well as the ports and terminals associated with them. Aeroplanes and airports also appear from the 1930s onwards. Yet as the historical focus of this study largely closes in the 1950s, air travel will be less to the fore. It has, however, become the dominant mode of migrant movement since the 1960s. In his official history of immigration control in Britain, *The Key in the Lock* (1969), T.W.E. Roche noted that 'Heathrow is the largest international airport in the world. It is unique: in twenty years it has grown from a collection of tents to this complex which for many months annually handles far more passengers than all the seaports of the country put together.'[28]

Air travel, for all the fears associated with it, has been far safer than other means of mass migration. This is especially true of the ship which has remained a dangerous form of transport – perilous journeys by sea remain a feature of many migrant journeys in the twenty-first century, especially for those escaping persecution. In March 2011, for example, a small boat carrying seventy-two passengers from North Africa, including refugees from the 'Arab spring' uprisings in Tunisia and Libya, attempted to make its way to the Italian island of Lampedusa. Drifting for over two weeks and apparently ignored by

Nato military units, 'All but 11 of those on board died from thirst and hunger'.[29] Thousands more refugees from North Africa on similarly unsuitable vessels drowned in the first few months of 2011 alone.

Air travel is, of course, a far speedier means of transport over long distances. For some migrants, it has been an exciting and liberating form of travel. Nevertheless, as Kathy Burrell notes, it does not always lead to comfortable and happy journeys.[30] Moreover, through the enforcement of ever stricter and systematic security and immigration and asylum regulations, air travel has enabled different types of abuse and mistreatment of migrants. Heathrow airport possesses, for example, extensive and purpose-built immigration facilities, designed initially in the 1950s. It was here in the late 1970s that at least eighty Asian women were subject to 'virginity tests' by British immigration staff. These were implemented to meet new Home Office regulations in order to 'prove' or 'disprove' the marital status of Indian and Pakistani women attempting to join their betrothed in Britain. It was a process, as one of these women later recalled, that was 'embarrassing, and it also felt a little shameful'.[31]

In the world of fiction, Salman Rushdie satirised such immigration procedures in *The Satanic Verses* (1988). It begins with Flight A1-420, a jumbo jet *Bostan* flying from India to London. *Bostan* had 'more than a few migrants aboard, yes, quite a quantity of wives grilled by reasonable, doing-their-job officials about the length of and distinguishing moles upon their husbands' genitalia, a sufficiency of children upon whose legitimacy the British Government had cast its ever-reasonable doubts ... '[32] At a more extreme level, in October 2010, Jimmy Mubenga died on board a plane deporting him from Heathrow on British Airways flight 77 to Angola. Mubenga had fled Angola in 1994 as a student leader who had come into conflict with his country's regime. Mubenga was granted exceptional leave to remain and had lived in London with his wife and five children for sixteen years. Mubenga's death occurred on the runway at Heathrow when he was being heavily restrained by guards from the security firm G4S, operating on behalf of the Home Office.[33]

This study will feature those who have journeyed to Britain illegally by hiding in ships, trains and trucks. While less common, remarkably there are those migrants so desperate that they have attempted to hide themselves in the exterior of aeroplanes. Les Back, in his analysis of European immigration policies in the early twenty-first century in which at least three thousand have died in recent decades at its borders, relates how

> Reckless stowaways are literally falling out of the skies along London Heathrow airport's flight path. In the summer of 2001 a young Pakistani called Mohammed Ayaz fell out of the undercarriage of a Boeing 777, descending thousands of feet only to land in a Homebase car park in suburban Richmond, West London.

Sometimes, as Back adds, 'they drop without trace. In the summer of 2002 a driver on the M25 motorway close to Gatwick saw a human figure fall from the sky. The body was never found; England's "green and pleasant land" ate it.'[34] In this light, the story of the two Indian actors in *The Satanic Verses* falling to earth after the *Bostan* has been blown up over England by terrorists who are then interrogated and abused by immigration officers seems less far-fetched.[35]

For those migrants who have little or no choice, air travel and related immigration procedures may have changed the nature of their journeys, avoiding at least the continuing mass death that still occurs by sea and land in the twenty-first century. It has not, however, necessarily altered the dislocation and humiliation that has accompanied so many migrant journeys since the early modern world. But by focusing on those who have through choice or necessity carried out such movements, it is to be hoped that their individuality and agency will be at least partially restored. From there a more humane response might emerge more generally to this emotive subject in which migrants, past and present, are often treated as an undifferentiated, faceless menace. Returning to Les Back, he notes how 'The 3,000 dead of 11 September are remembered in the exercise of patriotic *Gemeinschaft* and civilised outrage.' He wonders whether perhaps 'the deaths of the unnamed and undocumented migrant workers who were among those 3,000 in the World Trade Centre on that day invite the development of a broader conscience that connects with the plight of today's migrants'. Back asks 'What of the 3,000 and rising numbers who have died invisible, stateless deaths? What of the wretched at the border and those who are literally falling from the sky?'[36] Answering Back's challenge, this book will attempt to name the nameless and remove the concealment and anonymity of the migrant.

This book on migrant journeys will be followed by others which will look further at questions of national identity in relation to migrant *settlement*. Its sequel will do so through the prisms of place, people, material culture, heritage and history, and war and peace – ones that will be anticipated briefly in the chapters that follow. Ultimately the aim of *The Battle of Britishness* is to probe the nature of belonging – it asks who can become part of the nation and on what terms? It is a study of both 'now' and 'then' and how the past is mobilised in contemporary debates. It is about remembering and forgetting and part of an ongoing political and cultural struggle to keep open the borders of Britain – both real and metaphorical.

I

Britishness, entry and exclusion

Introduction

'Barrier, bridge and gateway to the world': this is the subtitle of historian and former diplomat, Peter Unwin's history of the English Channel.[1] The twoness identified by Unwin – consisting of entry and exclusion, opportunity and danger – will be, as highlighted, at the heart of this study. In his thoughtful overview, Unwin notes in passing that such duality relating to the Channel's meanings extends to the reception of migrants and refugees, the subject matter here. On the one hand it stands for 'the sea as defence and demarcation … the obstacle that kept invaders out of Britain and made island and islanders different from the continent and fellow Europeans'. It is, Unwin adds, 'an interpretation to which a certain kind of Briton still clings when he finds himself faced with such continental challenges as illegal immigrants, the Channel Tunnel, the euro or the European sausage'.[2] On the other, the Channel provides an opportunity to be part of Europe. It is a

> saltwater highway that brought the forebears of nearly all today's Britons to Britain and, after millennia of to-ings and fro-ings by Celts, Romans, Angles and Saxons, Vikings and Normans, Dutchmen, Huguenots, Jews and east European refugees, carried the Allied armada to the Normandy invasion beaches in 1944.[3]

The polarity identified by Peter Unwin and suggested by the chapter organisation of this study, while never absent, is, it will be argued, the exception rather than the rule. There have been moments of intense hostility and undifferentiated exclusion in the British treatment of migrants: the experiences of Germans in the First World War subject to deportation, internment, popular violence,

vilification in the press, and expropriation by the state is one of the most striking modern examples of hostility in word and deed, as Panikos Panayi has
amply demonstrated.[4] So great was the anti-alienism of this period that anyone
regarded as 'different' was regarded with suspicion. R.M. Morris, in an official (but unpublished) history of the Home Office's Immigration & Nationality
Department commented that

> xenophobia during the First World War persisted strongly throughout
> and pervaded the whole country to an extent now difficult to recapture.
> Home Office files contain many examples of extreme cases such as the
> London taxi-driver who was hounded as an uninterned alien though
> investigation proved that he merely had a strong Yorkshire accent plus
> an impediment in his speech.

Such local objections to 'strangers' were matched, noted Morris, in a
'Hertfordshire village [where] two "enemy aliens" were rescued from a
hostile crowd only to be found to be Wiltshire labourers whose accent was
unfamiliar'.[5]

It might be argued that there are other 'extreme cases' reflecting not animosity but instead intense generosity and sympathy at the arrival of refugees
and immigrants. These would include the *Kindertransportees* in late 1938/
early 1939 and the West Indians aboard the *Empire Windrush* in June 1948.
Chapters will be devoted to both of these now celebrated migrant journeys:
the positive reactions from state and public to the arrival of these newcomers cannot be denied. Yet there was also contemporary hostility in each case
which has tended to be forgotten over time in the desire to present a 'usable'
past – as was also true with the 'model' migrants, the Huguenots. Indeed, one
of the most powerful (if circular) 'myths of the British' is a supposed inherent tendency towards tolerance and decency towards minorities, especially
those fleeing persecution. According to a poll carried out in April 2011 by
the Refugee Council to mark the sixtieth anniversary of the United Nations
Convention for Refugees, 'Helping others is part of the British DNA ... Most
Britons are proud to be British (84%) and believe protecting the most vulnerable is a core British value (82%)'.[6]

In the Home Office document, *Life in the United Kingdom: A Journey to
Citizenship* (2004), 'To be British seems to us to mean that we respect ... traditional values of mutual tolerance'.[7] Such self-congratulation is manifested
particularly with regard to the entry of refugees. Official proclamations from
politicians of all hues from the late twentieth century onwards emphasise that
'The UK has a long standing tradition of giving shelter to those fleeing persecution in other parts of the world'.[8] A contrary tradition of animosity has been
less easily accepted in self-mythology.

While R.M. Morris, through his working knowledge of his own depart-ment's history of immigration controls and procedures, might have believed that the intense anti-alienism of British society during the First World War was 'commonly known', by the 1960s it is hard to believe that this was the case outside the Home Office.[9] As Colin Holmes has noted in his *A Tolerant Country?* (1991), in Britain 'Hostility is regarded as the property of others; it is difficult to admit to its possession oneself, in a culture which prides itself on the strength of its toleration.'[10] Such projection is often focused on groups outside the 'mainstream', most recently the far right British National Party. Alternatively, it is located beyond the shores of the country – France, Russia, America (in relation to race relations), and most recently and espe-cially Germany fulfilling this role of intolerant 'other' in contrast to the liberal British 'self'.

There persists a strong tendency to deny racism and exclusion – past and present – and therefore a need still to study its impact and importance in British society and culture, especially on the minorities concerned. Such work needs to be carefully contextualised and without moving into the eulogistic sphere, positive responses also require more detailed research rather than glib assertions about their inherent existence. The study, for example, of the many thousands of organisations set up to *help* immigrants and refugees from the Huguenots onwards is still in its infancy as is the study of explicitly anti-racist/anti-fascist organisations in more recent times.[11] Yet what is more fundamen-tal, as noted in the Introduction, is to explore the *ambivalence* and *ambiguity* of responses to newcomers in Britain and also to understand the multi-layered nature of migrant experiences in (re-)creating new homes for themselves. Thus revealed within each section, while the two chapters have been set up in ap-parent opposition to one another, are the complex realities of everyday lives: in reality, their apparent differences are less pronounced. Great emphasis is placed in this study on the importance of story telling in which some narra-tives are emphasised and others silenced. But in no case are these narratives uncontested and static. Through the lens of migrant journeys, it reveals both the stories we tell of ourselves (and the ones that we do not) in constructing and reconstructing a sense of national identity.

In *Life in the United Kingdom: A Journey to Citizenship* the bold state-ment is made that 'We are a nation of immigrants – able to trace our roots to countries throughout Europe, Russia, the Middle East, Africa, Asia, and the Caribbean.'[12] Such an acknowledgement has been a long time coming. At the Evian conference on refugees held in July 1938, the leading British delegate, Lord Winterton, dismissed the idea that Britain should allow any significant number of refugees the right to seek entry because, as it was seemingly self-evident, 'the United Kingdom is not a country of immigration.'[13] Similarly rejecting Hungarian refugees in early 1957, Home Secretary R.A. Butler told the House of Commons that 'The United Kingdom was not an immigration country'.[14] Such denial extends into the academic and popular realm. It is significant that *Life in the United Kingdom* is aimed at those born outside the nation state and aiming to become citizens of it: 'It is more comfortable for those of migrant origins themselves to accept Britain as a country of immigration than it is for those who are not, whether this assertion refers to the historical profession or wider society'.[15] And even *Life in the United Kingdom*, while acknowledging a deep historic tradition of immigration, seems to accept that it is a largely post-1945 development of 'A changing society'.[16]

Until recently the dominant response from those writing 'island stories' has been to emphasise diverse origins in the 'deep' past, but to highlight homogeneity thereafter. Typical of this approach was a contribution to Ernest Barker's much-cited collection *The Character of England* (1947), devoted to 'England and the Sea'. It outlined invasions 'century after century ... until the process became historic with the Saxons and the Danes'. By this point, 'the national stock was fully established'.[17] The editor himself highlighted how the English were 'mixed in their stock and the blood in our veins'.[18] When a rival publication, *The British Heritage* was published a year later, it opened with a similar assertion that its purpose was to 'show how the British way of life is a compound of ingredients derived from the cultures of many races and many peoples'.[19] Such sweeping statements were not forerunners of contemporary multi-culturalism. Instead, they simply confirmed what Barker himself had suggested that 'we' were '"Saxon and Norman and Dane"'.[20] Indeed, in neither of these best-selling volumes was there acknowledgement of later migratory movements to Britain, not even of the fabled Huguenots. Again we are faced with a two-ness – an acceptance of distant migration but an insistence on subsequent homogeneity.

In an earlier study published in 1927, Barker had argued that a 'sound racial basis' was necessary to safeguard the national state. While a nation 'may be enriched by the varied contributions of foreign immigrants', there was a danger 'if the stream of immigration grows unchecked into the volume of a great river' and thereby 'lose the integrity of the solid core which is the basis of its tradition'.[21] Seven years later, Arthur Bryant used the same argument but a different metaphor to describe the role of immigration in the nation's history: 'fortunately for England, this alien inflow has never been too rapid, and she has never suffered as other countries have from racial indigestion'.[22] In such narratives, the county of Kent and especially the port of Dover, its fortifications and, most symbolically, its 'White Cliffs', were perceived as playing a central role.

Kent, according to the prolific writer and populariser of history and geography, Arthur Mee, was the 'wonderful gateway into England ... Far back she takes us into history, for she is Norman, Saxon, and Roman, and Ancient British first of all.' Mee approvingly quoted the popular writer, Hilaire Belloc, on his adopted home. Only two things, suggested Belloc, were as permanent as the shapes of the earth and the sea 'and these two things are the English race and the name of Kent'.[23] Dover, added Mee, was 'the gate of Kent' and he eulogised its significance in relation to (racial) national identity:

> Its white cliffs are the gladdest sight the Englishman from home can wish to see. The loyal Englishman has not been born who can look on Shakespeare's Cliff without emotion. It was here before there was life in these islands. It stood here when our race began. Through all our ancient story it has guarded our island home.[24]

Dover Castle was literally the pinnacle of this fortress place. Roman, Saxon, Norman and English, Mee was quick to point out the wider symbolism of this historic site: 'Something like a genealogy of the English nation is written for us here ... We are made up of them all, and the work of their hands is all about us.'[25]

In the words of medieval chronicler, Matthew Paris, Dover Castle was 'the key of England'.[26] The Dover Straits made her vulnerable, but as cultural geographer Harold Mackinder made clear in his seminal *Britain and the British Seas* (1902), 'England had defeated that channel, and indeed used it to take the best of European culture whilst repelling the worst of continental despotism.'[27] The Second World War, and the epic story of Dunkirk in June 1940, further intensified the mythology of this singular place. It was immortalised further in Nat Burton's *The White Cliffs of Dover* (1941) sung by the 'forces' sweetheart' and subsequent icon of the British war effort, Vera Lynn.

Dover was thus a fortress to protect Britishness (or more frequently Englishness), but it was also, as Mackinder argued, a filter to what was good, and not good, arriving from the continent and beyond. In 1997, the metaphor employed by Mackinder was taken to an extreme and racist position by a local newspaper, the *Dover Express*, in a campaign against Roma asylum seekers fleeing persecution from the Czech Republic and Slovakia. One editorial referred to the Roma as 'human sewage' and in equally inflammatory language stated 'We want to wash the dross down the drain.'[28] Dirt, as anthropologist Mary Douglas noted, is 'matter out of place'[29] – an aphorism to be returned to throughout this study – and all efforts were made by the British state following the Dover lead to keep the Roma asylum seekers from 'soiling' Britain.[30] At a national level, the Conservative tabloid press soon followed this local invective and began a campaign against the Roma that was extended to all asylum seekers, utilising anti-alien discourse that was relentless and unrestricted in its animosity. War metaphors were freely employed.[31] According to the *Daily*

Express, which has been consistently anti-migrant since its creation in the 1900s as will be noted regularly, Dover was 'under siege'. More remarkably, the *Independent*, normally supportive of asylum seekers, produced the headline 'Gypsies invade Dover Hoping for a Handout'.[32]

There are other narratives that can and have been constructed of Dover and the entry and restriction of migrants. Robert Winder's powerful *Bloody Foreigners: The Story of Immigration to Britain* (2004) was written explicitly against such twenty-first century invasion scare stories as those relating to Roma asylum seekers. In covering the Huguenots, Winder brought into play the Minet family who attempted to flee Calais in 1685 following the revocation of the Edict of Nantes. Their first attempt failed as they were caught and tortured but a year later they succeeded in evading the patrols: 'they managed to steal aboard and slip quietly across the dark sea to Dover'. The son, Isaac, set up shop in London, but in 1690

> he returned to Dover, where he helped establish the family insurance firm (and a line that led unbroken to John Minet, a leading light at Lloyd's in the twentieth century). He also, in a poignant tribute to the sea-crossing that had saved his life, set up a packet-boat service between Dover and Calais.[33]

Winder sets up a classic tale of refugee-dom – persecution, dangerous journey, settlement, rebirth, economic success, contribution and gratitude: 'For the rest of his life, 1 August – the date of his arrival [in Dover] – was a sacred festival in the Minet household, observed with fasts and prayers'.[34] Similarly, Isaac and his family feature in both permanent and temporary exhibitions within Dover Museum: 'Through hard work and good management Isaac built up one of the most important private businesses of 18th century Dover. He became a Freeman of the Town in 1698'.[35] Chapter 3 will return to the Minets in more detail.

Just over three centuries later, Bosnian schoolchild, Vesna Maric, experienced Dover at a practical level of immigration controls where she was greeted by an official 'with a face like a scrunched up fist'. But to Vesna, Dover was more than just a port with soulless form-filling procedures – it was a place with the power of myth coming out of an infatuation with Vera Lynn's classic wartime song taped from Yugoslav radio. Escaping Mostar and the Bosnian war as a sixteen-year-old in 1992, she remembers crossing the Channel: 'And though I couldn't see bluebirds anywhere, the white cliffs of Dover were becoming visible on the other side, brooding above the grey water and greeting us as if we were Dunkirk evacuees'.[36] Yet any romance of her vision of England and Englishness was queried by the subsequent bureaucratic intervention:

> We flooded into Dover immigration office, a drab, cold waiting room with tiled walls and bleak lighting. There were orange plastic chairs and a poster reminding us what not to do.[37]

As Vesna Maric notes, 'It's not easy suddenly becoming a refugee.'[38] Nevertheless, her life since settling in Britain has not been defined purely by this status and she is now an award-winning writer and journalist. Indeed, her memoir *Bluebird* gently satirises her fellow refugees and, more particularly, her hosts. It is the latest in a long line of such literary interventions by migrants, whether forced or voluntary, teasing out what it means to be British.

It should be kept in mind that for all the bureaucratic indifference shown to her and her party, Vesna Maric was comparatively fortunate in coming to Britain and passing through Dover in what was an organised (if somewhat chaotic and basic) scheme. Others have endured truly horrific journeys and many have died attempting to come to Britain.[39] One of the most notorious incidents occurred in June 2008 when 58 Chinese migrants were found dead at Dover. They had suffocated in the back of a refrigerated lorry when the air vents had closed. The tragedy prompted sympathy with their loss as well as irritation at the alleged 'tidal wave of displaced people' coming to Britain.[40] In spite of the initial interest, their story, as will be noted in the concluding chapter, was soon forgotten. Even less attention has been given to the anonymous asylum seekers and others who have died attempting to get to Kent's ports hidden underneath Eurostar and freight trains through the Channel Tunnel or who have been run over by or asphyxiated in lorries travelling to Dover.[41]

In the ten years before the Dover tragedy, it has been estimated that there had been 'at least 2,000 deaths on the borders of Europe',[42] a mortality rate that has increased in the new millennium. The appalling reality associated with such desperate migrant journeys and especially the death of the 58 Chinese stowaways prompted Michael Winterbottom to make his harrowing and award-winning film *In This World* (2003).[43] The film focuses on the journey of a young Afghan asylum seeker, Jamal, from a refugee camp on the border of Pakistan through Iran, Turkey, Italy, France (including the Sangatte refugee camp near Calais), the Channel Tunnel, and finally to London. Its title is a euphemism for those who died en route through suffocation in a lorry – they are simply 'no longer in this world'. It is significant that an earlier and ironic name for the film, *The Silk Road*, referring to the lucrative trade route from Asia to Europe, was eventually rejected as too playful by Winterton in light of the bleakness his film portrays.[44]

Dover, then, as both a 'real' and 'imagined' place has been at the heart of the 'battle of Britishness'. In 2001, an Afghan asylum seeker arrived at the port and kissed the ground. He told the BBC that 'I love this land. Fair play, football,

David Beckham, nice police.' To some, this would be a confirmation of all that was decent and noteworthy in British society, re-establishing its tradition of providing a haven for refugees and proof of its fundamentally kind nature. To others, the Afghan's comments and actions reflected that the country was a 'soft touch' for 'bogus' asylum seekers who illegally buy their way in: 'entering Britain with a concocted story is an attempt to obtain public funds under false pretenses, funds that millions have worked to contribute to'.[45]

The two sides to the conflict – on the one side, Winder's biographical sketch of the Minet family alongside that of the Dover Museum, Vesna Maric's account of being part of and contributing to Britain and the Afghan's delight at arrival and the promise of freedom, and, on the other, the 'human sewage' of the *Dover Express* – reflect the intensity of recent debates about belonging and the nation. Indeed, the last years of the twentieth century, and the first of the new millennia (especially in the light of the terrorist attacks on 11 September 2001 and, closer to home, 7 July 2005) have seen anxieties about Britishness intensify, a concern that has been particularly tied to migration and the migrant presence. It is thus not surprising that when the *Economist* in summer 2011 launched a poster campaign on 'key issues of the day' that movement into Britain was one of its first themes. Two rival posters were displayed on the London Underground system, proclaiming that 'slash[ing] immigration' was alternatively a 'good' or a 'bad idea'. Both striking posters employ the White Cliffs of Dover as their dramatic backdrop. In the former, however, they are represented in castellated form, as a gunned fortress keeping out the foreigner and blatantly evoking the Second World War and the myth of 'Britain alone'.[46]

For some, such as Robert Winder and Peter Unwin, the question of whether migration is desirable or not – as outlined in the *Economist* posters – is simply irrelevant. Winder, with endearing honesty, starts his book by admitting that 'I did start with the premise that immigration is a form of enrichment and renewal'. He adds that he had 'changed my mind only to the extent that I now find it pointless even to brood on whether it can be described as a "good" or a "bad" thing'. The movement of people within the global economy is simply inevitable, he argues, and 'It is like wondering whether it is good or bad to grow old'.[47] With perhaps far less conviction about its merits, Peter Unwin predicts that

> Neither Britain nor France will want to cut itself off from the wider world … One of the consequences will be more immigration, more cross-Channel movement, and more squabbles about immigrants and refugees. At the end of the line I guess that there will be yet more dark faces on the streets of London and Paris, more new Frenchmen and new Britons.[48]

Unwin concludes his epic historical overview by stating that 'The Channel never kept new tribes, new races, new religions, new influences out of Britain. It will not start to do so now.'[49] Yet faced with the 'inevitability' of migration in a global economy, British governments – Conservative, Labour and most recently the Liberal Democrat/Conservative coalition – since the last decade of the twentieth century have made a particular effort to limit inward movement, starting with the Asylum and Immigration (Appeals) Act of 1993. This legislation was the first to use 'asylum' in its title. Further acts have followed in 1996, 1999, 2002, 2004, 2006 and 2009 – the most intensive legislative intervention in British immigration history, each attempting to limit entry more than its 'failed' predecessor.[50]

The end of the nineteenth century was marked by intensified political, social and cultural fears about the well-being of the nation and specifically the danger of external invasion and internal decline: the alien menace was perceived to be coming from within and without. As Eitan Bar-Yosef and Nadia Valman suggest, 'The place to which Jews emigrated in the late-nineteenth century was ... already freighted with the most acute of contemporary anxieties.'[51] The new millennium witnessed similar *fin-de-siecle* nervousness. Krishan Kumar in *The Making of English National Identity* (2003) argues that even taking the long historical view, 'There has been a massive and unprecedented inquiry into the national soul.'[52]

The politics of belonging

The world, to many, appears an increasingly frightening place: while accelerated globalisation and technological change produced new opportunities it has also intensified insecurities. In Britain, 2001 was a major turning point in concern about threats to the state from those 'inside' but with 'outside' inspiration. The terrorist outrage of '9/11' was preceded by the so-called 'northern riots' and concern both about Muslim extremism and a 'white' racist backlash. Official reports on the disturbances in Oldham, Burnley and Bradford emphasised the separation of Muslim and white communities within these economically struggling towns. According to the major government enquiry led by Ted Cantle, *Community Cohesion* (2001), 'many communities operate on the basis of a series of parallel lives. These lives often do not seem to touch at any point, let alone overlap and promote any meaningful interchanges.'[53] Efforts were therefore required to integrate the two before such separation led to increasing friction and extremism on both sides.[54]

'New Labour', especially through the efforts of Chancellor and then Prime Minister, Gordon Brown, and the Minister for Public Order and Community

Cohesion in the early 2000s, John Denham, placed great emphasis on the need to construct a sense of Britishness to which all could feel a sense of belonging. For Gordon Brown especially, it was a matter of great urgency and importance. If it was not tackled, the country ran the risk of fragmentation and discord: 'Britishness is not just an academic debate, something for the historians, just for the commentators, just for the so-called chattering classes.'[55] In a speech delivered in March 2002 in the aftermath of the riots and the various reports coming out of them, Denham outlined the purpose, parameters and challenges of future initiatives: 'Without discussion and debate we are not going to be able to articulate common British values and have the confidence that our respect for diversity and our opposition to racism is founded on clear common principles.'[56] Yet while within this vision, 'cultural pluralism' would not only be accepted, but might also 'even' be celebrated, the upper case 'Nation' was to be paramount. As the Cantle report summarised:

> A meaningful concept of 'citizenship' needs establishing – and championing – which recognises (in education programmes in particular) the contribution of all cultures to this Nation's development throughout its history, but establishes a clear primary loyalty to this Nation.[57]

Such concern about cultural fragmentation and division were intensified after the London Underground and bus bombings of July 2005. And although those carrying out the terrorism were British-born, all discussion of national identity was tied to the question of immigration – those migrants here must integrate and strict controls would be placed on those trying to enter. Gordon Brown, as Derek McGhee argues, produced a 'model of civic nationalism with [a] post-7/7 emphasis on loyalty, duty and responsibilities'. In introducing proposals for 'earned-citizenship naturalization processes', Brown wanted to ensure, as he stated in 2008, that 'migration benefits us as much socially and culturally as it does economically'.[58]

During the first decade of the twenty-first century, Britishness became increasingly defined as a club whose membership was conditional. Linked to this growing exclusivity, concepts of multiculturalism came under increasing scrutiny and attack. In February 2011, less than a year after having become Prime Minister, the Conservative leader David Cameron, in a speech to the Munich Security Conference went further, giving critics of the concept official support. Cameron claimed that

> we have allowed the weakening of our collective identity. Under the doctrine of state multiculturalism, we have encouraged different cultures to live separate lives, apart from each other and apart from the mainstream.[59]

Cameron's intervention can be partly traced to a longer Conservative tradition reaching back to at least the post-war era but taking specific shape since Enoch Powell's major speeches from the late 1960s. From that time on, the 'New Right', including Margaret Thatcher, dominated discussions about Englishness through to the 1990s, employing a discourse that highlighted 'culture' rather than 'race' in defining national identity.[60] At Eastbourne in November 1968, Powell infamously commented that 'The West Indian or Asian does not, by being born in England become an Englishman. In law he becomes a United Kingdom citizen by birth; in fact he is a West Indian or an Asian still.'[61] His speech highlighted the blurring of categories between culture and race, and nation and ethnicity, revealing the essentialism behind 'New Right' definitions of Englishness. It reached a climax in the Thatcher regime with new legislation beginning with the 1981 Nationality Act and, on a cultural level, Norman Tebbit's infamous 'cricket test' of 1990, demanding ethnic minorities in Britain to choose national over diasporic loyalties and providing no space for multiple identities.[62] Yet from the first decade of the twenty-first century, debates about national identity and multiculturalism were led by 'progressives' with the emphasis equally focused on culture, identity and belonging. The following section will analyse some key texts, taken from a variety of sources, to explore this new 'battle of Britishness' and especially its relationship to questions of migration. In the process, the key differences, but also some of the shared ground, between 'left' and 'right' in the desperate attempt to define the nation will become apparent. Indeed, so much has been perceived as being at stake that traditional political categories have often become blurred and confusing.

At the forefront of the intellectual debate on Britishness was the left-liberal progressive journal, *Prospect*. As Paul Gilroy notes, its 'treatment of the hot topic of race, diversity and national identity was dominated by the political problems supposedly introduced by unassimilable mass immigration, by intrusive refugees, and, most importantly, by a conflict rooted in the stubborn adherance of settler-descendants to their original cultures, religions and other ethnic habits'. To these commentators within *Prospect*, Gilroy adds, 'increased diversity made solidarity impossible.'[63]

One of the first major contributions to this debate within *Prospect* came in 2003 from Bob Rowthorn, professor of economics at Cambridge University. Describing himself as a 'prominent left-wing economist', Rowthorn claimed that recent large-scale immigration to Britain could not continue 'at current rates without disturbing national culture and identities'. As was the case with much of the debate in the new millennium, history and heritage were evoked regularly in relation to migration. Rowthorn argued that history was a 'central component of national self-understanding' but the 'presence of ethnic minorities has made it more difficult to teach a coherent national history.'[64] Following

Rowthorn, the founding editor of *Prospect*, David Goodhart, has been particularly anxious about the undermining of past 'homogenisation' of Britain's population, one which he assumes without any evidence or knowledge was simply the case until the 1940s. It was followed by 'two big waves of immigration' – first from the Commonwealth in the 1950s and 1960s and second 'by asylum-driven migrants from Europe, Africa and the greater middle east in the late 1990s'. The result, asserts Goodhart, was a loss of common values and assumptions: 'as Britain becomes more diverse that common culture is being eroded'.[65]

Goodhart is, like many recent 'progressive' contributors to the debate about national identity, ambivalent about migration. Immigrants, he concedes, 'come in all shapes and sizes … [f]rom the American banker or Indian software engineer to the Somali asylum seeker'. These are not accidental examples and Goodhart provides a commentary on their respective worth, stating bluntly that his list moves 'from the most desirable to the most burdensome'. Goodhart's use of the Indian engineer was also far from random, it might be suggested, forestalling accusation of blatant racism in his hiearchical ordering of would-be migrants. In terms of integration Goodhart argues that those who want to stay in the country 'should be encouraged to become Britons as far as that is compatible with holding on to some core aspects of their own culture'.[66] What it is to become a 'Briton' is, as with all the debate in the 2000s, elliptical and never fully explained or explored. Indeed, in 2006 Gordon Brown launched a campaign to celebrate national identity and teach 'core British values'. That what was held in common had still to be identified – Brown somewhat wishfully suggested that 'out of a debate, [it would] hopefully lead … to a broad consensus about what Britishness means' – exposed the elusive notion of Britishness, revealing the exercise's circularity and internal inconsistency.[67] As one editorial quipped: 'The notion of trumpeting the gloriousness of Britain feels rather … unBritish'.[68]

Brown contributed to a round-table discussion in *Prospect*, arguing that 'we have not been explicit enough about what we mean by Britishness for far too long'. In his attempt to define the essence of the history and values that 'shape British national identity', Brown wanted 'to stress a belief in tolerance and liberty, a sense of civic duty, a sense of fair play, a sense of belonging to the world'.[69] It is, however, hard to think of a western nation that would not similarly define itself, or do so by upholding their opposites – intolerance, subjection, selfishness, cheating and isolation. As the historian-politician Tristram Hunt noted, these alleged virtues of Britishness 'are neither unique to these isles nor have they always been on display across Britain's long history'.[70]

Returning to the editor of *Prospect*, Goodhart is convinced that there *is* one past and one culture which needs to be maintained and that children should be taught at school 'the broad sweep of their national history'. Tellingly, he adds that 'The teaching of British history, and in particular the history of the empire and of subsequent immigration into Britain, should be a central part of the school curriculum.'[71] That immigration to Britain has a much earlier and intensive history is sidelined by Goodhart, requiring a process of active amnesia. For example, Goodhart, as many others, places great importance on memories of the Second World War which, he believes, are fading, leading to 'less and less loyalty'.[72] That the war effort was fundamentally diverse, relying on those from the colonies and the troops of many allied nations, has to be distorted to maintain the myth of homogeneity and 'Britain alone'. Goodhart suggests that 'Helpfully, Britain's story includes, through empire, the story of many of our immigrant groups', noting especially that 'empire soldiers ... fought in many of the wars that created modern Britain'.[73] Unhelpfully, one might add, an alternative and more informed reading would point to the biological racism that led to the exclusion and marginality of colonial fighting power in both world wars and attempts at their brutal removal at the end of these global conflicts. How this would support Goodhart's model of turning 'immigrant "them" to citizen "us"' is hard to conceive.[74]

Goodhart's emphasis on history and especially the Second World War is not unusual in such debates about belonging. Indeed, the memory of the conflict remains central to constructions and contestations of national identity. In February 2010, during a public lecture entitled 'Cry "God for Harry, England and Saint George!": Celebrating England and Englishness', John Denham emphasised that his vision of patriotism did 'not reject history. Indeed it draws heavily on it ... [a]llowing us to enjoy the strength which comes from sharing a common story'. The two 'most potent stories in our history', according to Denham,

> are of Dunkirk and the Battle of Britain. They speak deeply of two traits in both the British and the English national stories – the heroic national defeat; and standing alone against the world.[75]

'History', therefore, matters, but it is often a narrow and mythical narrative of the past that has been employed by commentators and politicians alike. By arguing, as Goodhart does, that 'immigrants should be encouraged to become part of the British "we", even while bringing their own very different perspective on its [Empire] formation' may appear on the surface to accept plural readings of the nation's heritage.[76] Indeed, he is anxious to differentiate himself from 'the coercive assimilationism of the nationalist right, which rejects any element of foreign culture'.[77] Yet that Goodhart accepts uncritically a homogeneous 'we' British exposes a crude and limited understanding of the diversity and contestation of Britishness over time. As black British radical writer, Gary Younge, noted in response:

His articles are littered with assumptions about 'us' and 'them' and peppered with references to a 'common culture' and 'homogeneity', as though such terms are not only universally agreed but eternally static.[78]

Goodhart's mono-cultural vision of Britishness, past and present, was also challenged, if ambivalently, by Gordon Brown in key speeches on the subject delivered in the mid-2000s. In the annual British Council lecture in July 2004, Brown argued that rather than undermining national identity, past migrations and global connections had helped to forge the nation:

> out of tidal flows of British history – 2000 years of successive waves of invasion, immigration, assimilation and trading partnerships that have created a uniquely rich and diverse culture – certain forces emerge again and again which make up a characteristically British set of values which, taken together, mean that there is indeed a strong and vibrant Britishness that underpins Britain.

The Channel as 'bridge and gateway' rather than 'barrier' was at the forefront of this progressive and inclusive construction of Britishness: 'I believe that because these islands – and our maritime and trading traditions – have made us remarkably outward looking and open, this country has fostered a vigorously adaptable society and has given rise to a culture both creative and inventive.' Indeed, Brown quoted historian David Cannadine approvingly in his statement that the Channel was not a moat but a highway.[79] Here Brown was distancing himself from English nationalists, many of whom have, as noted by Peter Mandler,[80] invoked Shakespeare's John of Gaunt's speech from *Richard II* in supporting their insular vision of the nation:

> This precious stone set in the silver sea
> ·Which serves it in the office of a wall
> Or as a moat defensive to a house
> Against the envy of less happier lands ... [81]

Brown believed that British openness led especially to an intrinsic commitment 'to tolerance and fair play', manifest particularly with regard to newcomers. He suggested 'that it is because different ethnic groups came to live together in one small island that we first made a virtue of tolerance, welcoming and includ[ing] successive waves of settlers – from Saxons and Normans to Huguenots and Jews and Asians and Afro-Caribbeans, and recognising plural identities'. Perhaps relating to his own Scottishness and, by the early twenty-first century, the reality of devolution, the then Chancellor emphasised that the United Kingdom had always been a 'country of different nations and thus of plural identities – a Welshman can be Welsh and British just as a Cornishman or woman is Cornish, English and British – any may be Muslim, Pakistani or Afro-Caribbean, Cornish, English and British.[82]

By January 2006, when discussion, in the light of the London bombings had become more intense and anxious, Brown returned to his theme in a Fabian Society lecture, 'The future of Britishness'. Yet while acknowledging the 'uncomfortable facts that there were British citizens, British born, apparently integrated into our communities, who were prepared to maim and kill fellow British citizens', the tenor of his speech remained optimistic. Integration, Brown believed, could still be achieved by 'giving more emphasis to the common glue, a Britishness which welcomes differences but which is not so loose, so nebulous that it is simply defined as the toleration of difference and leaves a hole where national identity should be'.[83]

In his earlier British Council speech, Gordon Brown acknowledged that there were rival versions of Britishness to the model he was offering. For those commentators on the 'new right' subscribing to a 'view of decline and decay' such as Roger Scruton, Simon Heffer and Melanie Phillips, the 'final nails in the coffin of Great Britain are not just devolution but Britain succumbing to multiculturalism and to Europe'. Such individuals, acknowledged Brown, would be challenged by his more outward-looking vision of Britishness. He did not deny that between them and him there were 'battleground[s]' on particular issues, including asylum and immigration. And yet he was convinced that 'some common ground does exist: it is the recognition of the importance of and the need to celebrate and entrench a Britishness defined by shared values strong enough to overcome discordant claims of separatism and disintegration'.[84] The question remains whether Brown's belief in a shared commitment to Britishness and the 'story of Britain' on both sides of the political spectrum was illusory or not. At the heart of this analysis will be the issue of belonging and the tension between pluralist and essentialist readings of the British past.

To Gordon Brown, 'race' had no place in discussions of Britishness. In his British Council speech there was a clear choice: 'the issue is whether we retreat into more exclusive identities rooted in 19th century conceptions of blood, race and territory', or, alternatively, whether British identity is made open through values, ones 'expressed through our history and our institutions'. Even concerning issues of asylum and immigration and multiculturalism, the 'question is essentially whether our national identity is defined by race and ethnicity – a definition that would leave our country at risk of relapsing into making a misleading "cricket test" or, worse, colour the determination of what it is to be British'.[85] In 'The Future of Britishness', Brown repeated this theme, but, just six months after the July 2005 bombings, warned further about the growing danger of retreating into racial exclusivity at a time when understandably 'people are insecure'.[86]

In September 2000, Barbara Roche, Labour minister with responsibility for immigration, stated that 'This country is a country of migrants and we should celebrate the multi-cultural, multi-racial nature of our society, and the very positive benefits that migration throughout the centuries has brought.'[87] Subsequently Roche has been at the forefront of a campaign to create a national museum that would celebrate the contribution of immigrants to Britain.[88] Her promotion of immigrants as an investment for the present and future, a case made also by Robert Winder in his *Bloody Foreigners*, has not been universally welcomed. David Conway, senior research fellow at Conservative think tank Civitas, denies that such arguments are sustainable, emphasising that a radical shift has occurred in migration to Britain since 1945. Indeed, in utter contrast to Gordon Brown, though following those associated with *Prospect*, Conway argues that Britain's alleged historic freedom from racism and extremism is *because* of its earlier absence of immigration and not the reverse. Britain's tolerant character was enabled, he argues, through possessing 'a relatively homogeneous demographic composition'. Conway warns pessimistically that its 'ability to retain that character could well be under a far more severe threat from current levels of immigration than is made out by those who maintain that substantial immigration has always been a constant feature of Britain's demographic history from time immemorial'.[89] Indeed, Conway argues that disintegration through unregulated migration is not far from happening.[90]

Conway, following 'New Right' politicians and intellectuals from Enoch Powell onwards, places great emphasis on the cultural difference of recent immigrants and their alleged refusal to assimilate. Racial difference is implied but is never openly acknowledged. In another Civitas pamphlet providing a 'brief history of immigration' to Britain, however, an explicitly racialised definition of belonging is provided. In 2003, at the height of the hysteria against asylum seekers in Britain, Myles Harris denied that Britain had ever previously been 'a mongrel society'. His use of breeding metaphor continued with a speedy journey through British history. While there had been immigration in the middle ages and early modern period, Harris argues that it was 'an invasion of close cousins'. Britain was an extreme version of Europe which was, in essence, 'a continent of genetically linked tribes' with males sharing the same 'Y chromosome'. The 'island of Britain ... for nearly 2,000 years remained as racially separate as Polynesia'. But those that came after 1945 from the New Commonwealth and then as asylum seekers were different and the 'aboriginal population' of Britain were never consulted about the invasion of their nation which had been irrevocably and negatively transformed.[91]

The final insult, argued Harris, was the re-writing of history and re-shaping of Britishness to suit the new arrivals:

> While multi-culturalism and ethnic authenticity are welcomed, the word British is either frowned on or demands are made for its meaning to be altered ... Britain should recast its national history as a nation of ex-slavers and exploiters ruling a variety of helots.[92]

Such arguments, especially the use of 'aboriginal' to describe the 'white' population of Britain, are reminiscent of the language of the extremist British National Party with its ex- and not so ex-Nazi supporters.[93] That it has been utilised by a research institute linked to the Conservative Party is an indication that the debates about Britishness have extended across the whole political divide and that Gordon Brown's belief that Britishness could be embraced free of race discourse was optimistic. It might be argued that its usage within Civitas and the BNP was likely if not inevitable given past traditions, but an exploration of concepts of Englishness in the progressive world show that linking race to national identity is far from the preserve of the 'New Right' and neo-Nazis. Indeed, reference to a mystical Englishness, rooted in soil and blood, can be detected in one most unlikely source coming from the world of radical politics and culture.

Billy Bragg, left-wing folk singer and veteran anti-fascist and anti-racist campaigner, was one of the leading forces of 'Rock Against Racism' in the 1970s. His *The Progressive Patriot* (2006) was published in the heart of the debate about Britishness following Gordon Brown's national interventions. The book was Bragg's heartfelt contribution to the discussion.[94] It is significant that Bragg's first contribution to 'Rock Against Racism' was a 'cod reggae song that I had written called "Rivers of Blood"'. It sought, he recalls, 'sincerely yet somewhat clumsily, to refute Enoch Powell's vision of a race war on the streets of Britain'.[95] Powell's vision of Englishness was based on a mystical reading of the country's past. In *The Progressive Patriot*, subtitled ' A Search for Belonging', Bragg challenges exclusive versions of Englishness but he is also anxious to preserve the concept itself, moving away from an earlier position in which he regarded 'the icons of patriotism as symbols of oppression, imperial domination and exploitation'.[96] Even then, 'there was something about England and what it meant to be English that I just couldn't shake off'.[97] With his album *England, Half English* (2002), the title song, 'my paean to Englishness', was greeted with the response: 'You're being ironic, right?' Bragg informs his reader clearly, 'No, actually, I'm not.'[98] His aim was to 'reconcile patriotism with the radical tradition' and to provide a model of Britishness/Englishness so that it was not left to 'the likes of the BNP and the *Daily Mail* [to decide] who does and who doesn't belong here'.[99]

Bragg's book melds family history with a reading of the British past inspired by the English Marxist tradition, especially E.P. Thompson. There is acknowledgement of his great-grandfather, Alphonso D'Urso, who came to

London at the turn of the twentieth century from the Amalfi coastal region, marrying in the Italian church in Clerkenwell. But it is his English descendants that dominate the narrative, albeit one that acknowledges past migration, internal and external:

> The story of how my ancestors worked the land in East Anglia and elsewhere until their children moved away in search of a better life is a constant theme, one that explains not only how my Italian ancestors came to be here, but also why the Angles, Saxons and Jutes left their homelands to find new pastures in Britannia.[100]

Bragg's passport states that he is British. He defines *himself*, however, as 'primarily English, as were three-quarters of my ancestors'. To Bragg, that does not mean denial of 'my Amalfitano heritage. I am, after all, of predominantly English descent.' Does that, he asks, 'make me, ethnically, an Anglo-Saxon? I think it does, albeit one with a bottle of limoncello cooling in the fridge'.[101] Here, the progressive Billy Bragg is not far removed from the Arcadian reactionary Roy Strong. The former director of the Victoria and Albert Museum insists that his 'Vision of England' is informed by being 'English by descent on both sides, with perhaps a smattering of Huguenot'.[102]

Bragg's construction of Englishness is framed as 'ethnic' but in using the phrase 'Anglo-Saxon' he is utilising nineteenth century categorisations based on the language of race – ones that the singer would undoubtedly reject. A similar ambiguity and melding of race/ethnicity can be found in other progressive interventions which attempt to rescue 'English national identity' from abuse. In his 'Celebrating England and Englishness', John Denham, in what was the last months of 'New Labour' in power, stated firmly that his government recognised that people had multiple identities: 'For the centre-left, identity is not about forcing a choice between competing identities … Of equal importance … is our insistence on recognising people's right to enjoy the identity people chose for themselves. We do not impose a "cricket test".' It was still necessary and important, argued Denham, 'to invest energy in developing a shared story of Britishness, and for those within England, a shared English identity'. It was also crucial for those who felt 'English' who were not of immediate migrant origin to feel comfortable celebrating such an identity and to be able to do so without 'slip[ping] back into a racist and ethnically defined view'.[103]

What Englishness consists of is never addressed by Denham who reverts to quoting Bragg that it is time to stop being embarrassed about having it as an identity. More dubiously, he also quotes Morrissey, a singer not known for his subtlety on questions of ethnicity and immigration, in his 'Irish Blood, English heart': 'I've been dreaming of a time when to be English is not to be baneful: to be standing by the flag not feeling shameful, racist or partial'.[104] However well-meaning – and the anti-racist/anti-fascist credentials of both Bragg and Denham are undeniable, especially the former who has been at the forefront of local campaigns to defeat the BNP – leaving Englishness as something that exists but cannot be pinned down carries inherent risks. At best, such romantic patriotism, even if filtered through a radical tradition, can provide some space for pluralism: ethnic minorities are not *necessarily* excluded. Nevertheless, it starts from the premise, as with any form of national identity, of defining the self through the exclusion of others – Englishness is not Welshness, Scottishness or Irishness. Moreover, Englishness is *not* being utilised to validate those who are recent arrivals (or their offspring) with their transnational and often other religious loyalties; it is about providing the 'indigenous' population with an identity. In the case of Bragg, ethnic Englishness is put forward as an alternative to a racially defined version. In the case of Denham, both race and ethnicity are rejected in constructing Englishness, and it is left without content other than an assertion of its very existence. With the historic reality of English dominance over the United Kingdom and the British empire, with longlasting assumptions of superiority over former subjects, this is a dangerous game. The tendency ultimately to exclude within such constructions of Englishness is revealed in a final case study of progressive intervention, again dating from the first decade of the new millennium.

Stuart Maconie has emerged as one of the leading social commentators in popular culture and more generally as a 'national treasure'. His *Adventures on the High Teas* (2009) as with 'New Labour' and Billy Bragg, attempts to rescue Englishness. Maconie wants to query assumptions that it is by nature prejudiced and exclusionary, representing the narrow-minded vision of the *Daily Mail*. His 'search for middle England' ends as a (qualified) love letter.[105] But one place Maconie did not fall for in his quest is the much-maligned town of Slough. Indeed, it is its *unEnglish* nature which alienated him: 'As I was to find out, diverse does not even begin to describe the town now. It is so kaleidoscopic as to be bewildering.' It was the disorientating 'array of races and styles of dresses displayed by the townsfolk', alongside its 'ghastly' and 'gruesome' architecture, that gave Slough 'the feel of a post-apolocalypse shanty town for the displaced refugees of the world'. The ethnic diversity of the town, adds Maconie, is 'mind-boggling'.[106]

There is no escaping modern Slough's migrant presence. Further along the high street from the Asian superstore is a Portuguese café on the high street – 'a little piece of back-street Lisbon transplanted to Berkshire'. Here, the exclusionary potential of Englishness is revealed, even by a proponent with a gentle, humane and humorous perspective:

> I fall into a broken conversation with [the staff] – about football natu-
> rally – but what I really want to say is, before you leave England, visit the
> Lake District or the Cotswolds or Bath. Please don't go home thinking
> that Slough was England.[107]

Here Maconie employs a circular process to construct 'true' middle England:
the Lake District cannot be diverse because it is English and Slough cannot be
English because it is so multi-ethnic and transnational. And yet in later writings, Maconie, proud of his northern English roots, has written of how a

> Lake District head teacher once told me of 'offcomers' in the area while
> saying that in his school there were still some true Viking names that
> reflected ancient stock. I told him I was pretty sure the Vikings were
> offcomers too.

He has also noted that 'In Keswick, you will find many a German surname, evidence of the intermingling with the *locals* [my emphasis] by German copper
miners who came to work on the northern fells of the Lake District half a millennium ago'.[108] We will return to Maconie and his ambiguity about the nation,
diversity and belonging in the final chapter of this study.

While 'left' and 'right' approach Englishness with different perspectives and
objectives, its elusive nature forces common ground. Thus Gordon Brown in his
British Council speech praises Conservative philosopher, Roger Scruton, and
his 'highly challenging study of Englishness'. Indeed, Brown later quotes with
approval from Scruton's *England: An Elegy* (2000) that 'When people discard,
ignore or mock the ideals which formed our national character then they no
longer exist as a people but only as a crowd'.[109] It is telling that in the *Prospect*
round table in April 2005 on Britishness, Scruton, intellectual leader of the
'New Right', could note with approval the contribution to the debate of Billy
Bragg, populariser of a radical patriotism on the Left: 'I would like to go back
to what Billy Bragg said. People don't seem to have a clear picture of the past
any more. It is not a question of the actual history, but rather the history that
is required to create a national loyalty'.[110] And with regard to practical policies,
although Brown argues that on issues of migration he was at odds with those
like Scruton, in power 'New Labour' waged war against asylum seekers. The
Blair Government legislated again and again to ensure that entry into Britain
would become extremely difficult. Furthermore, life for those who had got here
was made increasingly intolerable including the removal of benefit entitlement
and the use of lengthy detention. In *England: An Elegy*, Scruton, like Brown,
praises the treatment of Huguenots and other earlier migrants as 'newcomers
to the home, entitled to hospitality while they found their feet'. Like Blair, he
defends in a tokenistic way the right of asylum but attacks its 'widespread and
criminal abuse'.[111]

During the 2005 General Election campaign the Conservative Party used immigration scares as one of their major tactics to garner popular support. Rather than confront such views, then Prime Minister, Tony Blair, simply accepted the veracity of anti-alien arguments, refusing to accept that they might be motivated by racism. 'Instead,' writes Blair in his memoirs, *A Journey* (2010), 'I visited Dover, where unfounded asylum claimants were often lodged, and made a speech that directly took on the issue'.[112] This, as has been noted, was a place with such powerful resonance that Blair's intervention was deeply symbolic. A dilemma remained for 'New Labour' – how to square the clamping down on asylum seeker entry with the country's alleged role of hospitality to refugees, one of the core foundations of Britain's myth of tolerance and fairness. *A Journey* provides a narrative superficially enabling this contradiction to be solved.

Blair argues that Britain 'had inherited the post-war, post-Holocaust system and sentiment on asylum'. He even allows for the possibility that past policy might not have been as generous as was once assumed: 'The painful stories of refugees fleeing from Hitler and the Nazis and being turned away produced a right and proper revulsion'. But if the presumption was that 'someone who claimed asylum was persecuted and should be taken in' was thus understandable 'in the aftermath of such horror', it was now 'completely unrealistic'. If that appeared morally dubious, then consciences could be salved: 'The presumption was plainly false; most asylum claims were not genuine'.[113] And this was not simply the perspective of Tony Blair. Asylum seekers never had a place within Gordon Brown's vision of a more inclusive Britishness – they were regarded as too lacking in rootedness and integrity to be part of the nation. The result were procedures that have received international condemnation from international human rights organisations.

In 2010, a Ugandan, 'Francis', who had suffered torture and rape before fleeing to Britain in 2006 was awarded £110,000 by British courts for ten months of unlawful detention. As his lawyer commented:

> It is nothing short of scandalous that we are causing serious harm by detaining people, sometimes for long periods of time, who have done nothing other than seek a place of sanctuary from the horrors they have escaped from, in the mistaken belief that Britain is a just and tolerant society.

As 'Francis' added, 'My experience of detention was terrible. The officials were rude and it felt as though they had been trained to refuse all asylum seekers'. He told them 'again and again that I had been tortured ... but they did not seem interested'. In contrast to Gordon Brown's construction of Britishness as essentially decent, 'Francis' concluded that he thought 'this was a country that would protect me and would respect human rights and human dignity, but I have seen something different'.[114]

Asylum seekers have not been alone in suffering from the narrowing agenda of debates about Britishness. Muslims too, whether established or of recent migrant origin, have become increasingly the subject of political concern. The perceived threat from 'without' and that from 'within' have leaked into one another and reinforced a sense of insecurity. Nevertheless, it has been *British* Muslims especially who have been problematised, monitored and subject to measures designed to render them harmless. In the words of Paul Gilroy, 'since the New York towers fell' and the concept of a 'global clash of cultures' grew, there has been a 'clamour for more difficult citizenship tests and … attention [turned] towards a cavalcade of terror mosques, veiled women and maimed imams'.[115]

9/11 undoubtedly increased the pressures on Muslims in Britain through their representation as an 'alien wedge' and a danger to the well-being of society. But earlier the 'Rushdie affair' from the late 1980s onwards had already emphasised their marginality. Muslims had to 'conform' – but what to was not clear. The political theorist and sociologist, Tariq Modood, came to London as a nine-year-old in 1961 with his family from Karachi, Pakistan. As he emphasised in a volume published in 1992, it was 'not easy being British'.[116] Introducing and summarising Modood's early collection of essays, Robin Richardson, director of the Runnymede Trust (the independent think-tank devoted to the cause of promoting racial justice in Britain), outlined how it was

> not easy to identify the values, processes and customs which are dis-
> tinctively British; not easy, having identified them, to be in all respects
> proud, grateful and loyal; not easy to be recognised and accepted fully
> by other people who are British; not easy to establish and protect public
> policies and laws which recognise and rejoice that there are many differ-
> ent ways of being British, with sources of strength in different continents,
> religions, histories, languages.[117]

With the coming to power of 'New Labour' in 1997, there was hope that a more inclusive form of Britishness might be promoted. It was an optimism articulated most clearly in the Runnymede Trust commission set up in 1998 and led by Professor Bhikhu Parekh which published its report, *The Future of Multi-Ethnic Britain*, in 2000. Its authors argued for an inclusive approach to national identity based on pluralism and recognition of the country's diversity, past and present.[118] As Tariq Modood, who was advisor to the commission, noted, it made the case strongly that there was no incompatibility between political multiculturalism and the promotion of national identity.[119] Yet even when it was published, just three years into the 'New Labour' project, the

'Parekh report' created a strong reaction. One of the commissioners, Yasmin Alibhai-Brown, related that 'Outrage exploded, orchestrated by apoplectic right-wingers and they were followed with indecent haste by … many on the so-called left and even intelligent publications like *Prospect*'.[120] Alibhai-Brown's own studies, *Who Do We Think We Are?* and *After Multiculturalism*, were published in the same year and received an even more hostile reception, again from across the political spectrum. Alibhai-Brown's desire to 'imagin[e] the new Britain' and to create 'New narratives to unite – stories to connect and to liberate', provoked both the right – which accused her of being 'impertinent and ungrateful ('I should remember, they say, how kind this country was to let me in when Uganda threw us out …') – but also some on the left-liberal world uneasy with her insistence on the particular problems faced in the cultural and religious realm by ethnic minority groups.[121]

The moral panic stimulated by 9/11 thus had strong domestic roots exposing a lack of confidence with regard to the ability of Britain to cope with difference – especially that of its post-war Muslim migrants and their descendants. If 'New Labour' initially emphasised 'the plural and dynamic character of British society', the events of 2001, including the 'northern riots', was, as Tariq Modood emphasises, 'a turning point for the idea of multiculturalism in Britain'.[122] The terrorist bombings at home in July 2005 merely confirmed what many politicians and others feared about Muslims. The outrages were seen as due to the failure or the even the *fault* of multiculturalism.[123] Subsequently such concerns have not disappeared. As Modood again noted in a 2010 sequel to his 1992 collection, while 'Much had changed in relation to Britishness', for Muslims especially it was 'still not easy being British'.[124]

Popular responses

So far the discussion has focused largely on political and cultural interventions on national identity in the first decade of the twenty-first century. In his Fabian Society speech in 2006, Gordon Brown argued that it was a subject that met also with popular anxiety, quoting an opinion poll that suggested that 'as many as half of British people said they were worried that if we do not promote Britishness we run a real risk of having a divided society'.[125] Mass-Observation was initially set up in 1937 to provide a social anthropology of Britain by the British and using ordinary people to carry out its research. The organisation was revived in the 1980s with an emphasis on literacy practice to understand everyday life. Through a close reading of a Mass-Observation directive carried out in summer 2006 in response to Brown's intervention, it is possible to test the extent and nature of the concern outlined by the Labour politician. More specifically, it will explore whether racism has been a major factor when ordinary people articulate their views on national identity.

More than two hundred people responded to the Mass-Observation directive asking them about 'Core British Values', whether they should be taught and what these might or should be.[126] Statistically, the Mass-Observation respondents do not accurately reflect the whole of the British population – there are more women than men and the sample is biased towards the elderly and those from a professional background. It is the *qualitative* richness, however, of the material created that makes it a valuable source. And whether progressive or conservative, its writers tend to take an independent and critical stance on the world around them. Moreover, the autobiographical approach encouraged by the organisers enables the multi-layered and complex responses of ordinary people to be expressed, rather than the crude binary yes/no answers generated by opinion poll data.[127]

The Mass-Observation responses, because of their lengthy life history approach, do not lend themselves to simplistic numerical analysis. Nevertheless, some generalisations can be made about the 'Core British Values' directive which revealed three major tendencies, each of roughly equal size. The first category consisted of those who agreed with Gordon Brown that the issue needed to be confronted and to be done so particularly through education. For most of these, the tone was inclusive with regard to ethnic minorities. A young male factory worker in Shropshire started off in critical fashion, suggesting that 'Core British values sounds like something archaic', belonging perhaps to the 1940s or 1950s. Britain now was 'multiracial and will include people from other countries in the majority of towns and neighbourhoods'. He was aware that the 'tabloids overstate this [presence of Eastern European, African and Caribbean migrants] hysterically', but the introduction of such core values 'should not isolate these groups – it should be tolerant, show willingness to adopt or learn to the ways of modern immigrants, and help them to feel welcomed – in turn helping them to integrate into society'. He was optimistic this would happen as Britain 'has always been a place where foreigners have come, whether to invade (such as the Romans or Normans) or to flee persecution (the Huguenots, Jews and many more)'.[128]

Nevertheless, the belief of this Observer that the British population had *always* been mixed was not shared by other supporters of Brown's initiative. Nor was this factory worker's conviction that such education should be for everyone, regardless of background. A middle-aged civil servant argued that teaching these values was only appropriate to people of immigrant background and especially those 'who've resolutely refused to "integrate" since their arrival'. These values had to have foundations which would be based on 'history' and 'culture', without which 'They won't create that sense of *us*, living in *our* country, doing things *our* way'.[129]

The sense of 'them' needing to assimilate to 'our' culture was even more pronounced in the writings of a mature male student who believed that the loss of identity was 'because of the increased ethnic passage into our society or the Political correct brigade stopping us being too British, citing it as racial or xenophobic [towards] those of different ethnic origin'.[130] In short, even within those who welcomed Brown's progressive opening up of Britishness, determin- istic constructions of national identity were prominent, responding more to David Goodhart's mono-cultural model.

For the second category of Observers, there was not even cautious optimism about the future. Not only were immigrants 'getting preferential treatment', but those who were white, British and proud of 'wanting to keep our country as it was before' were, as a 59-year-old woman from Derbyshire concluded, forced to feel ashamed: how long, she asked, before it will 'become illegal to call oneself British?'[131] A retired engineer from Derby was even more cynical. Immigrants were coming to Britain 'not for the core value of the country but for the ease of obtaining benefits and housing for virtually nothing'. He fin- ished despairingly:

> we fought two world wars to stop invaders taking our land and now they are taking over whole towns and cities, and we are being threatened by the government that we must not object to this invasion. Life gets tedious, don't it?[132]

Another retired Observer was racially explicit about his opposition to newcom- ers, claiming himself to be descended from the 'Iceni, the original inhabitants of Norfolk'. Muslims, he believed, could never become British, as was exposed by the 'broad Yorkshire accent' of the youth in Bradford, part of a second gen- eration that had carried out the 7/7 bombings. Superficial indications of local belonging hid the alien loyalty of Muslims in Britain.[133] More self-reflexive, and revealing in this respect, were the comments of a middle-aged translator in Yorkshire who acknowledged that he felt 'profoundly uncomfortable discussing this sort of thing'. His discomfort came out of his earlier political outlook:

> Having previously been in the 80s a student with sound socialist princi- ples, I now find myself edging towards a position that I would previously have called racist. No, not edging – I feel I am being dragged there, and with great reluctance.

This unease, he added, was 'the problem of discussing something as apparently innocent as the tuition of core British values, since in the end it comes down to race, and that is a subject that is fraught with difficulty'.[134]

The fragility of Gordon Brown's faith that issues of national identity and belonging could be confronted at a popular level *without* reference to 'race' are thus exposed. It was a concern that was articulated by the third and slightly largest group within the Observers – those that believed that 'traditional British values' in the past were 'rather undesirable' and that the attempt to revive them now, in the words of a retired female auditor, carried 'a hint of racism'.[135] Some British people, added another Observer, a university administrator in his late thirties, 'are characteristically intolerant of foreigners and suspicious of other cultures – where does that fit in with the way we like to see ourselves as exemplifying tolerance?'.[136] A retired technical writer in his eighties was candid about the values he grew up with and which now would be rejected as offensive: 'We thought the British Empire was the most wonderful and correct arrangement of matters, with the Englishman deservedly supreme and certainly superior to all other "lesser breeds"'. The latter, he added, 'included Germans and Frenchmen as well as negroes and Asiatics'. The belief in such a racial hierarchy extended to the 'races' at home: 'Even Scotsmen and Welshmen were regarded as a lower form of Englishman, and the Irish were beyond the pale.'[137]

There was also a strong feeling amongst many more progressive Observers that so-called British values – such as tolerance, belief in freedom of speech, and commitment to democracy – were, in fact, universal. 'Good values', according a bank manager in Kent, 'are international'. Why, he asked, 'do we have to put a British slant on them?'. Instead, there was a need to learn from and appreciate 'the wide diversity of music, literature, painting, sculpture, architecture and the performance arts available to us today'. If there were common values, they 'were human ones [and] not particularly British'.[138] Other Observers were similarly sceptical. One stated that he had 'absolutely no idea what these values might or should be',[139] and another believed that the 'nebulous nature of "Britishness"' made it a futile exercise.[140]

Not only Britishness, but also the necessity of defining Britishness was debated by the Observers with accusations of racism and expressions of racism complicating the responses further. Throughout the directive, almost all the Observers (the vast majority of whom are white), following Gordon Brown and other politicians and commentators, linked 'core British values' to questions of ethnicity, multiculturalism and migration – even if there was no consensus of whether either diversity was a good or a bad thing. Equally there was both optimism and pessimism about the future. If a small majority of the Observers believed in the concept of Britishness, few did so uncritically. The response of a young medical student at Durham University that 'Britain is a free thinking country, and to tell people what they must do to be British is so ... unBritish' reveals the complexity, contradictions and fundamental ambivalence of the majority of the Observers when attempting to define national identity.[141]

The summer 2006 directive thus revealed similar tendencies to the debates in the political sphere, but with the Observers providing further layers of complexity to the question of national identity through the insertion of their life stories. Most attempted, but rarely succeeded in trying to itemise Britishness, to make it concrete. But lists of behaviour patterns, individuals or objects perceived as quintessentially 'British' (and even more so 'English') can be revealing. Many such items had 'foreign' roots – often ones with relatively recent histories. Food is a particular case in point. Migrant groups have regularly been accused of cooking and eating food that is 'smelly' and fundamentally unEnglish. Yet fish and chips, until recently regarded as the favourite national dish, has origins in the cuisine of Spanish and Portuguese Jews and Irish migrants and came together as a meal only in the mid-nineteenth century. At the turn of the twentieth century, East European Jews in the East End of London were criticised for their cooking of fish and the alienness of the olfactory 'offence' thereby caused. By the inter-war period 'Jewish' food had been appropriated as quintessentially 'Cockney'.[142] The ability to appropriate 'foreign' imports as one's own is ongoing. Thirty per cent of British schoolchildren in a 2009 survey thought that Indian curry, now regarded as the new national dish, was 'native to this country'.[143] The concept of 'queuing' is also now perceived as inherently British/English. As with food, its origins are equally 'alien' and have also been acutely politicised.

After the war, when British-Jewish tensions over Palestine were growing, Foreign Secretary Ernest Bevin notoriously criticised Jewish immigrants – in reality survivors of the Holocaust – for trying to jump to 'the head of the queue' by attempting to leave the continent's Displaced Persons camps.[144] In his *Identity of England* (2002), Robert Colls links the cult of the queue in Britain to the Second World War and the idea of patriotism and the notion of equal sacrifice. From then on, he notes, 'if the nation queued, the state would serve'.[145] Before then, however, it has been noted that the English pursuit of individualism mitigated against the idea of the queue which was seen as essentially foreign. Indeed, its otherness was confirmed by its origins in France, the nation's bitter rival. The queue, comments Paul Langford in *Englishness Identified* (2000), 'was a French phenomenon, unknown across the Channel before the late nineteenth century'.[146]

In 1946, the Hungarian Jewish refugee and humorist, George Mikes presented a guide book *How to be an Alien* which in fact was an affectionate parody of Britishness – it was a forerunner of Vesna Maric's later autobiography. Queuing, he noted, was 'the national passion of an otherwise dispassionate race'. On the continent, he claimed, it was unheard of whereas 'An Englishman, even if he is alone, forms an orderly queue of one'.[147] Already established, Mikes could afford to poke fun at his hosts, but in the post-war world of rationing and shortage of goods, those who 'jumped the queue' – a symbol of fairness and waiting one's turn – were regarded as unpatriotic.

Concepts of Englishness have never been static or uncontested. Amongst his '*characteristic* fragments' making up national identity, George Orwell's classic essay, 'England Your England', written late in 1940, famously listed 'the rattle of pin-tables in the Soho pubs [and] the old maids biking to Holy Communion through the mists of the autumn morning'.[148] The latter 'fragment' was later evoked by Conservative Prime Minister, John Major, who in 1993 appropriated and re-directed Orwell's progressive patriotism. Major emphasised the rustic to construct an essentialist vision of Englishness which would act as a defence against foreign influences and especially the European Union.[149] But Orwell, uncomfortably for conservatives, also included 'the queues outside the Labour Exchanges' as another of his 'fragments'.[150] The concept of the queue is thus not a trivial matter – it is about the rules of the game and who belongs but also about the possession of power, authority and justice. Not surprisingly, much debate about entitlement and belonging in the post-war world has used the metaphor of the queue either directly or undirectly. For migrants in particular, their place in the queue, or whether they are entitled to be part of the queue in the first place, has been bitterly contested. In the process, the queue has been utilised as part of the rhetoric of exclusion.

The cultural critic and former Artistic Director of the Institute of Contemporary Arts, Ekow Eshun, whose parents were from Ghana, was born and brought up in London. When his mother was struggling to bring up her children on her own, he relates the spitefulness of strangers:

> At MacFisheries on Wembley high street, she waited her turn at the counter. Waited and waited while the white women behind her were served first. When she complained, the fishmonger affected to notice her for the first time. 'In this country,' he said, 'we prefer to queue.'

Eshun adds that 'She left, trying and failing to hold back tears.'[151] Similarly, Pauline Black, later a pop star, whose origins were part Nigerian, part Anglo-Jewish, recalls shopping as a youngster in Romford market during the 1960s: 'Often, I found myself subjected to undisguised curiosity and rude remarks and deliberately ignored when it was my turn in a queue.' She adds 'I knew enough about the consequences of racial prejudice by now to know that such slights were intentional, but it was a profound discovery at first hand.'[152] While Gordon Brown and other progressive politicians hope that Britishness can be inclusive, some of its treasured manifestations have often been used to define the newcomer as essentially alien.

Not surprisingly, given the symbolic quality that the queue has achieved in post-war Britain, it comes up regularly within the Mass-Observation directive on 'core British values'. In some cases, it is evoked to highlight the need to maintain cohesion and a sense of shared identity 'given the much more fragmented nature of Britain and to help those from different backgrounds assimilate'. Values to be taught would include 'the ability to queue' as well as a love of animals and complaining about the weather.[153] To others, the idea of British values was 'misleading and arrogant' and anything that was unique was of no major consequence. The concept of queuing was used, following Mikes, as a parody:

> here's to our one core value that other nations should consider adopting
> – hurray to that singular trait of Britishness: the British queue!![154]

But there were also some Observers who used the importance of the queue to reveal what they thought was the ultimately foreign nature of Britain's ethnic minorities, especially those who were Muslims. According to one, while it was encouraging that 'some British Muslims immediately queued up to donate blood' after the July 2005 London bombings, 'others expressed an "understanding" of the bombers' motives and seemed reluctant to condemn them'. The outsider status of minorities and how they are tolerated, or conditionally accepted, rather than fully integrated, was further exposed in this Observer's comments: 'if such an attack is carried out in an adopted country, this surely offends against one of the most sacred core British values: that of being a gracious guest, of behaving yourself when you're in someone else's house'.[155]

That the subject was being taken seriously at a political level was shown in the dying months of 'New Labour' when the Immigration Minister, Phil Woolas, confirmed in February 2010 that the 'art of queuing' was to be made part of the formal test for new British citizens. It was reported that 'While the idea may seem like a joke, ministers insist they are entirely serious and want to indoctrinate migrants more effectively on the British way of life'. Woolas was quoted as stating that 'The simple act of taking one's turn is one of the things that holds our country together. It is very important that newcomers take their place in queues whether it is for a bus or a cup of tea.' Woolas added that queuing was 'central to the British sense of fair play and it is also better for everyone. Huge resentment is caused when people push in.'[156]

Woolas's intervention was supported by those who needed an excuse to complain that because of recent mass migration, Britain was full and that the newcomers were putting unfair pressure on essential public services such as schools and hospitals by queue-jumping.[157] There was also criticism of this argument: migrants were contributing far more than they were taking from Britain which, as young and active people, was far less than the population as a whole.[158] It was also noted that the idealised British queue of Woolas's imagination was somewhat mythical. Here, argued one commentator, was 'a man who has apparently not stood at a bus stop for some time'.[159]

The queue is emblematic of many similar debates about Britishness. To some, it is a crucial part of British identity and newcomers have to adopt it as part of their everyday life if they are to be accepted – formally so if they want to become citizens. To others, the queue is so closely tied to national characteristics which are inherited and not learnt that foreigners simply cannot be expected to understand its underlying ethos of fair play and decency. They must therefore be kept out because they will not or simply cannot play the rules of the game. Finally to some, 'forming an orderly queue' is, like Britishness itself, a creation of the heritage industry and as redundant as keeping a 'stiff upper lip' and 'being "gung ho"' given the diversity of the nation past and present.[160]

The migrant in such debates about belonging is thus conditionally accepted, beyond the pale or an integral and inseparable part of the nation. Such contestations will feature throughout *The Battle of Britishness* – who is allowed entry and at what price? But in order to confront these questions through the historic and chronologically organised case studies that form the core of this study, it will be necessary first to explore the nature and significance of the migrant journey. How has the migrant journey (or non-journey) been constructed and represented, and by whom? In a world in which identity politics is playing an increasing part and where we are all, allegedly, on a 'journey' of discovery, how do we remember and forget those that have actually – by choice or necessity – moved from one physical place to another?

2

Constructing migrant journeys

Theorising journeys

Yasmin Alibhai-Brown begins her memoir of 'love, migration and food' lamenting that 'Our family tree is puny, barren in large part'. She notes in *The Settler's Cookbook* that the 'human urge to trace long, biological bloodlines is strong'. In the case of her ancestors, however, 'our far past was swept away by careless fate impetuously carrying off my folk across the seas, away to new beginnings'. This is true of many migrant stories, especially those whose journeys were forced through persecution and economic exploitation. Alibhai-Brown adds

> Like many other East African Asians whose forebears left India in the nineteenth century, I search endlessly for (and sometimes find) the remains of those days. Few maps mark routes of journeys undertaken by these migrants; hardly any books capture their spirit or tell the story.

With those such as the family of Yasmin Alibhai-Brown, the process of dislocation was intensified by their expulsion from Africa in the last quarter of the twentieth century: 'here we are, people in motion, now in the West, the next stopover. There is no place on earth we can historically and unequivocally claim to be ours, and so we have become adept wayfarers who settle but cautiously, ready to move on if the winds change.'[1]

Diasporic minorities – whether at an individual, family or group level – when constructing a usable past often face the problem created by the absence of the archive record. Such a vacuum can promote either romanticisation of or indifference towards roots, becoming a substitute for critical engagement with history. In the process, amnesia and, alternatively, mystification come to the fore. These are tendencies that are especially noticeable concerning the physical journey of migration. With some important exceptions, there are few detailed accounts of migrant journeys and many that do exist have tended to conform, as will become apparent within this study, to a heroic or pitiful model with emphasis placed on the persecution and exploitation that were escaped from and survived. Migrant journeys that do not fit within this template prove particularly difficult to become part of collective memory. As a result, they are confined either to oblivion or to alternative, marginalised narratives.

A wide range of experiences, responses, memories and histories are included within *The Battle of Britishness* and the overarching term 'migrant' requires some consideration and, indeed, problematisation before proceeding further. There is consideration, for example, given to journeys of the 'Middle Passage' in which the enslaved literally had no choice over their departure and destination. While the treatment in this study of the slave trade is far from exhaustive, as noted in the Introduction references to slavery from the Bible onwards inform many narratives of migrant journeys. The same is true of redemption from 'slavery' with regular evocations of 'Exodus' and the 'Promised Land' in much personal and collective testimony. Anne Kershen in her study of London as a centre of migrant movement, comments that whether Hebrews searching for a 'land flowing with milk and honey' or Hittites, Kassites, Romans, Goths and Mongols later, 'All were looking for "the promised land", though its form differed from group to group.'[2] Nor has it been simply the metropolis viewed in such visionary terms. In 1945 and 1946 more than 700 Jewish child survivors were flown to Britain for them to recuperate. Roughly 300 were temporarily housed in the Lake District which was regarded as *ganeydn* (Yiddish for paradise) and the 'promised land'.[3] As one of the former children, Michael Perlmutter recalls, 'I was reborn in Windermere in 1945. The promise of England was a dream to a teenage boy who no longer believed he could believe in dreams.'[4]

Alongside slavery at the extreme of forced migration were those deported to their deaths as part of the Nazis' 'Final Solution'. It was part of the process of what Lawrence Langer calls the victims' 'choiceless choices … shorn of dignity and any of the spiritual renown we normally associate with moral effort'. For the Jews, in the face of overwhelming power of the perpetrators and their isolation within the world of the bystanders, 'whatever you chose, somebody loses'.[5] Again, as with slavery, the Holocaust has had a lasting impact on the description and nomenclature of particular migrant stories beyond its specific chronology and place.

At the other pole of journeying were those for whom individual choice played a major role, such as post-Second World War British migrants to the 'white' colonies. While their special treatment was unusual, the huge variation in the nature of migrant journeys was outlined on a BBC Home Service radio programme in September 1947 when reporting the arrival of British emigrants to Canada. Earlier the programme had provided eyewitness reports of the forced removal of Jewish refugees who were being sent from Palestine to Germany. Noting the gulf between the two journeys, the BBC presenter attempted to provide a bridge:

> And now after the distressing scene at Hamburg, here is some brighter news. Last Monday under the Government of Ontario scheme to fly seven thousand emigrants from the United Kingdom to Canada, the thousand emigrants landed at Toronto.

Its reporter in Canada noted that he had 'always disliked the word emigrant conjuring up as it does visions of under-nourished people with shawls and straw-suitcases coming out of the holds of liners' – imagery that could indeed have been used to describe the contemporaneous scenes in Hamburg. Here, in Toronto, however, was a marked contrast: 'But this is 1947 with modern travel by air offering speed and luxurious comfort.' The British emigrants were taken by limousine from the airport to the centre of Toronto and treated to a good meal and a clean dormitory where the 'settlers are free to do just as they please'.[6]

In between such contrasting poles of compulsion and liberty were economic migrants from poverty and lack of opportunity, such as the Caribbeans coming to Britain after 1945. The nature of migrant journeys, however, was not and is not static. While choice played a significant role in Irish migration to the 'new world' before the 1840s, by the time of the Famine, for 'many who left Ireland, [they did so] more as refugees than considered emigrants'.[7] Frank Neil's powerful study of Irish journeys by cross-channel steamers to British ports such as Liverpool, Glasgow and Cardiff in the dire year of 1847 is simply labelled 'Escape'.[8] Indeed, refugees are another category of migrant. Even so, it will become apparent that persecution has to be placed alongside other reasons for leaving. But it is fear for life at home which tends to be emphasised in refugee narratives. Moreover, the process of escape and its inherent danger is given particular symbolism in the desire to promote sympathy and understanding in often hostile receiving societies.

Some of the most traumatic refugee journeys in recent history have included the Vietnamese in the 1970s and beyond who were faced with appalling dilemmas. For La Thann Xuan, a schoolteacher of ethnic Chinese background, it meant either imprisonment in Vietnam or 'putting out to sea [and] undertaking a perilous journey in which the chance to survive and find freedom due to rescue by a foreign ship was only 10%. I chose the second course, that was "freedom or death".'[9] La Thann Xuan slightly overstates the risk of the journey, but only relatively so – the survival rate was horrendous but closer to 50 per cent. In reality this meant that 250,000 refugees still died 'in unseaworthy small fishing boats or ancient cargo ships' through drowning, starvation or attacks by pirates.[10]

Why refugees highlight their powerlessness and victim status is revealed with the Vietnamese. In spite of the overwhelming evidence of the appalling treatment of the ethnic Chinese and the danger of their journeys, the new British Prime Minister, Margaret Thatcher, was unwilling to single out the survivors for special treatment. In a 'Note for the Record' (June 1979), Thatcher dismissed the most recent official figures which revealed that Britain had taken fewer than 2,000 of the half million-plus Vietnamese refugees across the world. She stated that

> comparisons between the UK's record in receiving refugees and the records of other countries were invalid, since the UK had a much larger merchant fleet than most and, more importantly, had already taken in, with full UK citizenship, nearly 2 million immigrants.

Indeed, her Private Secretary emphasised that the Prime Minister 'could not accept the distinction between refugees and immigrants'. Thatcher agreed with her Home Secretary, William Whitelaw, with regard to any future refugees picked up by British ships that 'the UK could not go on taking them in' and warned there would be 'riots in the streets if the Government had to put refugees into council houses'.[11] Since the First World War, and especially since 1945, refugees have been given international protection and recognition. Nevertheless, they have often continued to be treated as unwanted migrants. The importance of labelling in both the public and private sphere has to be recognised not simply as an intellectual exercise but because it reflects the power politics that underly such classifications.

The grouping together of diverse groups under the heading 'migrant' is thus not to imply an equivalence of experience, especially of suffering on the one hand and self-determination on the other. Nevertheless, as Simone Gigliotti suggests in her study of trains, space and the Holocaust, 'deportation journeys … are prismatic and suggestive for engaging with these historical and ongoing examples of the displacement of colonized, indigenous, and oppressed populations'. She refers particularly to early modern colonialism and the transatlantic slave trade. Gigliotti concludes that the 'possibilities for future comparative and interdisciplinary research on other transit experiences are rich'. This study aims to show that potential.[12]

Lastly, with regard to problematising the term 'migrant', is the necessity of remembering the individuality of those involved in the process of movement, whatever the level of choice and freedom at play. As James Hathaway argues in relation to refugee studies, such scholarship 'is centred on studying particular persons ("refugees"), [whereas] forced migration studies scholarship focuses on analysis of a phenomenon ("forced migration" – notably, not "forced migrants")'.[13] More broadly, even Stephen Castles, a leading proponent of the need for a sociology of forced migration at a macroeconomic level, acknowledges that 'It is vital to investigate the *human agency* of the forced migrants and of the sending and receiving communities'.[14] Power relations – whether economic, political or cultural – at a local and global level will be crucial in understanding the wider significance of the case studies within *The Battle of Britishness*. As Castles adds, the national context is especially important: 'Fundamental ideas on the nature of migration and its consequences for society arise from nationally-specific historical experiences of population mobility and cultural diversity'.[15] Nevertheless, here the individuality of 'migrant journeys', refugee-linked or otherwise, and of those responding to them is of equal importance to the 'structural dimensions'.[16]

Raphael Samuel and Paul Thompson emphasise how 'national myths and the sense of national history which they help to build ... raise fundamental questions of just who belongs and who does not. Time and again, in rallying solidarity they also exclude, and persecute the excluded'. In response, for minorities and other less powerful groups, memory and myth become 'more salient: constantly resorted to both in reinforcing a sense of self and also as a source of strategies for survival'.[17] The previous chapter explored concepts of Britishness, its porousness (or impermeability) and the availability and the price of belonging for Britain's newcomers. For many migrant groups, the journey itself has been particularly traumatic – most violently and murderously in the form of the 'Middle Passage' but for other groups as well – we have already noted the Vietnamese refugees and will explore the horrors of Irish famine emigration shortly. For many groups it is not surprising that the journey itself has been subject to forgetting which as Jonathan Boyarin reminds us 'is a process, an act'.[18] This amnesia is particularly true for first-generation migrants. Such silence is then continued by their children and grandchildren either through an absence of information or for their own particular reasons in the struggle to belong in the place of settlement. And, as noted at the start of this chapter, if details of journeys become lost or obscure for particular migrant groups, powerful collective mythologies often act as a substitute for them.

The next section will juxtapose the memory processes for two groups – one an ethno-religious minority (the Jews) and the other national (the Irish) – to whom migration in the nineteenth century and beyond has been crucial in determining their experiences and in constructing their identities. Indeed, together they represent the largest European migrations in the 'long' nineteenth century. From 1820 to 1914 it has been estimated that '60 million souls left

Europe for destinations overseas', including roughly two-and-a-half million Jews and around six million Irish.[19] For the Jews and the Irish, the proportion emigrating was by far the highest within Europe for either a national group or an ethnic minority. Its impact was even more significant as the emigration was especially pronounced at moments of crisis – from the 1880s with the Jews and from the 1840s with the Irish. In one case the journey has largely been forgotten both at the time and subsequently and in the other it was recorded immediately and remembered and re-remembered thereafter. Yet in spite of recognition that the 'emigration of Jews from the Russian Empire exceeded in intensity any other nineteenth century emigration except that during and in the wake of the Irish famine',[20] there has been very little work comparing the two. What follows is thus a first tentative move towards a comparative approach of the history and memory of these traumatic and momentous migrant journeys.

Jewish journeys from the 'East'

The BBC's immensely popular genealogy series, *Who Do You Think You Are?*, first broadcast in 2004, has devoted a very high percentage of its programmes to those of migrant background.[21] At times, it has reinforced general mythologies that can be shown to be based on historical inaccuracies, as was the case with the comedian and writer, David Baddiel, and the exploration of why his (Jewish) paternal grandparents came from Latvia to the Welsh port of Swansea. Baddiel relates the family legend that when his ancestors arrived in Swansea they thought they had come to New York. In this particular case, the story is demonstrably false, as no immigrants from Eastern Europe actually came direct to Swansea.[22] Nevertheless, the narrative that these naive people were tricked into believing that they had been sold tickets to America is frequently told within the various genres of life stories constructed by those of East European Jewish origin in Britain.[23]

An early and extensive example was provided in the memoir of comedian Bud Flanagan (Chaim Weintrop/Robert Winthrop) whose parents left Radom in Poland in the 1870s. In his romanticised memoir, first published in 1961, his father escaped Poland by swimming across to Germany, while his mother went over on the ferry 'smuggled in a haycart'. From the border, the 'journey to Hamburg was hard going but they were young and in love. Arriving there, they found an immigrants' hostel for Jews, happy in the thought that Poland was behind them'. Sold a ticket to New York with most of their remaining savings, the 'New World lay ahead, safe and golden'. The ship left at night and 'soon they fell asleep in each other's arms':

> Next morning they could still see the coastline and decided they were
> heading for another German port of call to pick up more cargo and
> passengers. They soon realized that they were steaming for the mouth
> of the Thames, their journey's end. The shipping agent in Hamburg had
> taken their £2 10s and given them a 7s 6d ticket to London. With tears
> in their eyes, and still unable to believe they would never see America,
> they said a little prayer and hoped their luck would change.[24]

Flanagan's narrative of the pathos of the tricked Jewish migrant to Britain repeated that of Samuel Chotzinoff whose family *did* eventually settle in America.
Chotzinoff's memoir was published a few years earlier. *A Lost Paradise: Early
Reminsiscences* (1956) provides a rare first-hand account of the Jewish journey
from Eastern Europe – albeit written half a century after it had taken place
and one that was based on his parents' recollections rather than his own as a
five-year-old. Leaving their home town of Vitebsk, Belarus, a centre of ortho-
dox Judaism, they travelled by paddle-boat on the Dvina to Riga and from
there to Stettin in Germany where they 'boarded the ship for America'.[25] The
journey was unpleasant and disorientating: 'We crawled into our bunks and
remained there fully dressed for two days, groaning, vomiting [and] dozing'.
It was, however, remarkably short and they were quickly assembled for disembarkation. Left 'quite alone on the eerie wharf' after their 'record-breaking
journey', a man emerges from the gloom from what is vaguely described as a
'British Immigrant Aid Society' (most likely the Jews Temporary Shelter) and
informs Samuel's father of their true location. 'My father's face was white. "This
is *not* America!" he at last brought out. "We are in *London!*"'.[26]

Such stories could be repeated many times over. Nick Harris's parents
left Lithuania in the early 1900s and they eventually settled in 'Dublin's Little
Jerusalem'. Harris relates in his autobiography that their intention had been to
join his father's brother in America: 'In actual fact my parents, like thousands
of other Jews fleeing from Russia, were dumped in England or Ireland by the
captain of the ship. When my parents first set foot in England, they thought they
were in America.'[27] David Cesarani asks why has the 'myth of accidental arrival
… been installed in Anglo-Jewish "popular memory"?', further enquiring why
'should Jewish individuals and entire communities have cultivated such a self-
denigratory myth of origin?' He argues that the idea of accidental arrival was,
in part, an 'alibi for opportunistic migration. It was hard enough to carp at the
arrival of a "refugee", let alone one who found himself stripped penniless by
a land-shark upon his arrival'. He adds that the emphasis on haplessness and
poverty was to undermine contemporary discourse which emphasised the un-
fettered capitalistic and selfish culture of the Jewish immigrant in Britain.[28]

With Baddiel, Flanagan and Harris, family mythology emphasises that
Britain was a place of haphazard migration, whereas America was the favoured

destination, the *golden medinah*. In the case of Samuel Chotzinoff, the family did after several years make its way to America. The British interlude is treated as no more than years lost through accident, rather than the very common practice of step migration in which the final destination would be determined by chance, ease of settlement and, more than anything, finance.[29] Such auto-biographical practice reflects the dominant national narrative of the British (in contrast to the American) past in which immigration is either seen as marginal and alien or dangerous and undesirable. The reality is that Britain *was* the choice of many East European Jews for a variety of reasons including the well-established presence of a Jewish community (including, for some, existing family networks) and the country's economic opportunities as a leading industrial nation. While not as strong as the mythology associated with America, it also had a reputation – deserved or otherwise – for fairness and tolerance. Wolf Benninson's father came from Mariampol in Lithuania. According to Wolf, he chose England as it was viewed as a 'free country and they imagined it was a sort of paradise compared to Russia where there were so many restrictions against Jews'.[30]

For some, Britain was also closer – geographically and emotionally – than America. Miriam Field's grandmother came to Manchester from Riga as a young woman. Already widowed, she left her children with her parents: 'she always said she was afraid to go to America, she thought England was a more stable quiet country for a woman to come to on her own'. America, in contrast, 'was just this great big country and you had to be tough you know to make your way there … and she thought she'd have a better chance of retrieving her children from Russia to England'.[31] It remains that the dominant note in later testimony is that Britain was *not* a place to be chosen for settlement. Samuel Chotzinoff's father suffered through the 'recurrent fogs' of London which impacted seriously on his health. Yet rather than accept at face value this medical reason for why the family moved on, Samuel in his autobiography sought a deeper meaning relating to the respective place of Britain and America in his father's world view: 'In the light of modern psychiatry, the neuralgia that he suffered could have been brought on by his impatience to continue his interrupted journey'.[32]

But if ethnic history in the form of autobiography or popular genealogy including programmes such as *Who Do You Think You Are?* has reinforced some myths of Jewish migrant arrival, it has also questioned others and revealed stories that have been repressed within family memory. The actress Zoe Wanamaker, born in America but brought up in Britain by her parents who were fleeing McCarthyism, was shocked to find out on the programme that her 'great-grandmother actually died only two weeks after arriving in America. The physical journey from Ukraine to Antwerp and then the conditions on the boat were something you just can't imagine'.[33] The irony that the 'promised land' of

America turned out to be the place of almost instant family tragedy due to the trauma of moving from one world to another was not lost on Wanamaker.[34]

Not surprisingly, few have recalled the physical or mental grimness, dislocation and hardship of such journeys, whether within Europe or beyond it. Samuel Chotzinoff's family lasted over a year in London before travelling to New York from Liverpool on the S.S. *St Paul*. Although not as traumatic as the journey from Stettin, he related that the seven days on board

> introduced us to an olfactory phenomenon known to all transatlantic travelers of those days as the smell of 'ship'. This pervasive, insidious odor, a distillation of bilge and a number of less identifiable putrescences, settled on one's person, clothes, and luggage and stayed there forever …

He adds that it was only much later in his life that he realised that 'only steerage passengers smelled of "ship"'. It was to Samuel, growing up in New York, something that became familiar: 'One *expected* arrivals from Europe to smell of "ship"'.[35] Even the immigrants were aware of the lingering disability resulting from the sea voyage and some self-consciously attempted to avoid being tainted by it. Lew Grade (formerly Winogradsky), the television and film impressario, recalled that his mother managed the 'arduous journey [from Tokmak near Odessa] to England, via Berlin and Hamburg' arriving in London 'looking much smarter than most of the other women on the boat'. Grade adds 'She didn't want to look like a "greener" – someone from the outback'.[36]

Discomfort and the loss of individuality were not the only problems faced by those journeying from Eastern Europe: travel by ship itself was far from safe. As the *Jewish Chronicle* noted when confronting news of the sinking of the *Titanic* in April 1912, the 'vessel rode to its doom along a track over which Jewry has been impelled by destiny to pass in increasing numbers during the past generation'.[37] Just eight years earlier, the *Norge* sank in the Atlantic with the loss of more than 200 Russian Jews on board, only 35 surviving. There were lifeboats for 250 of its 795 passengers – a mixture of migrants from across Europe – and crew.[38] Yet following the *Norge* disaster, no action was taken by the shipping companies to stop such abuses at a time when their profit margins were being squeezed by international competition. It took the trauma of the *Titanic* with its loss of the rich and famous to promote radical change through state intervention. The potential danger of the journey by sea was not lost on the Jewish migrants and their families. Samuel Chotzinoff recalled the emotional scenes as his grandfather, a rabbi, prayed as his daughter departed from Vitebsk that 'The Almighty will guide you safely over the great waters … Lord take them under Your mighty wing'.[39]

The journey from Eastern Europe, with its inherent risks, hardships and the lingering presence of 'ship' and the poverty and low status it reflected were thus better forgotten by all concerned. In the 1970s and 1980s, the Manchester Studies Unit interviewed roughly 300 people of Jewish Eastern European background who were mostly second-generation. Of these, only 3 per cent mentioned their parents' journeys in any detail.[40] When Sidney Epstein was asked about the route taken by his parents from Locklavik in Poland, he responded 'I don't know these things, I was born in England.'[41] Similarly, Lew Grade recalled his mother speaking about the journey from Tokmak to London very rarely and only then to emphasise 'the hazards involved and how unpleasant it had all been'.[42] Significantly, when the journey *was* recalled within the Jewish migrant family, its dangers and misery were sometimes over-stated, becoming part of the escape narrative from Russian persecution. Interviewed in the 1980s, Rebecca Lasky remembered her parents, who settled in the East End, telling her that

> The Pogroms were terrible because not only were Jewish people murdered, but children would be sent away from their parents … [T]he Jewish people had to get out of Russia to survive. The journey was very bad, conditions were terrible and the boats were very, very poor, and many died on the way. The people that brought the Jewish people over took everything, jewellery, money, rings and anything they had of value; they robbed and threatened them the whole journey.[43]

But for all the fragments of memory work that were constructed relating to the East European Jewish journey in Britain, a major difference is apparent with autobiographical practice in America. Put boldly, there are simply no published *contemporary* accounts by Jewish migrants in the former country in contrast to several celebrated autobiographies in the latter. The most famous and significant of these is Mary Antin's *The Promised Land* (1912).

Antin was born in Polotzk, not far from the Chotzinoff family, in the Vitebsk region. They too emigrated in the early 1890s, although in a different pattern – Mary Antin's father went ahead and it was several years before the rest of the family joined him. Moreover, there was no interlude in Britain – Antin's father and then his wife and children went direct to America, settling in Boston. Indeed, what makes Antin's memoir, which had been serialised a year earlier in the *Atlantic Monthly*,[44] especially notable is the clarity of its narrative structure. It is bifurcated into 'old world' and 'new world', the difference between them reflecting the biblical certainty that its title would suggest. As Oscar Handlin noted, in Antin's account, 'To travel from Polotzk to America was to discover one's self by a move from medieval to modern times'.[45] Similarly, Werner Sollors suggests that the book's 'sense of space is related to its sense of time: Polotzk is Antin's past, hence *the* past'.[46]

There is an element of nostalgia present in *The Promised Land*, especially in relation to nature and the culinary delights of Polotzk which taken together represented 'the fragrence of all my childhood's summers'. Here Antin fondly recalled the joys of Polotzk cheesecake, predicting Proust and his legendary madeleines:

> [it] has in it the flavor of daisies and clover picked on the Vall; the sweetness of Dvina water; the richness of newly turned earth which I moulded with bare feet and hands; the ripeness of red cherries bought by the dipperful in the market place ... [47]

Nevertheless, whilst the power of such memories is such that Antin cannot totally forget the 'Old Country',[48] the emphasis within her narrative is on the backward nature of Christian *and* Jewish life in Polotsk. Both are ruled by superstition and prejudice. In the former it led to violence against the Jews made manifest through pogroms and ritual murder accusations. In the latter, it resulted in belief in 'lucky signs, lucky dreams, spirits, and hobgoblins, a grisly collection, gathered by our wandering ancestors from the demonologies of Asia and Europe'. It was also, for the Jews of Polotsk, a restrictive world defined by a 'caste system with social levels sharply marked off, and families united by clannish ties'.[49]

The journey from Polotsk to America is thus more than a physical one: *The Promised Land* is a 'tale of emancipation from the benighted customs, language, and religion of the Old World'.[50] And in order for the spiritual, intellectual and emotional transformation to 'American' to occur, Antin places special emphasis on the journey's intense physical hardship across land and sea. Its trauma is presented as a ritual necessary so that a 'second birth', as she termed it, can take place.[51] But if *The Promised Land* is a 'text *between* worlds',[52] the journey between the two has a crucial transformative function and is given a chapter and title of its own by Antin: 'The Exodus'. Much attention is given in it to the immigration procedures on the Russian–German borders and the harrowing, mechanised health inspections experienced at Hamburg, including two weeks of quarantine. Here they were in limbo 'with never a sign of the free world beyond our barred windows; with anxiety and longing and homesickness in our hearts, and in our ears the unfamiliar voice of the invisible ocean, which drew and repelled us at the same time'.[53]

In contrast, for the sixteen days at sea across the Atlantic, when 'the ship was our world',[54] Antin relies on short extracts from her earlier published account *From Plotzk to Boston* (1899). Indeed, in *The Promised Land* the ocean journey is dealt with briefly and without the photographs that accompanied the earlier and later chapters.[55] The emphasis was more on personal metamorphosis rather than the details of the crossing itself. In this respect, *From Plotzk to Boston* provides much more information and was based on a description of the journey written in Yiddish by a then eleven-year-old Antin to her uncle.[56]

From Plotzk to Boston was originally serialised, as was her later account, by the *Atlantic Monthly* reflecting Antin's status as an 'infant phenomenon' in the world of American letters. It also revealed a demand to understand the world of the immigrant from within. As the Anglo-Jewish novelist, Israel Zangwill, wrote in its foreword, 'we still know too little of the inner feelings of the people themselves, nor do we adequately realize what magic vision of free America lures them on to face the great journey to the other side of the world'.[57] The young Antin certainly provided such an understanding in a manner designed to evoke the reader's sympathy:

> imagine yourself parting with all you love, believing it to be a parting for life; breaking up your home, selling the things that years have made dear to you; starting on a journey without the least experience in travelling, in the face of many inconveniences on account of the want of sufficient money; being met with disappointment where it was not expected; with rough treatment everywhere … ?[58]

In contrast, the journey in *The Promised Land* is far more focused on arrival than on departure. In this text, evoking the memory of the *Mayflower*, Antin describes her family embarking for America as 'five frightened pilgrims … on the deck of a great big steamship afloat on the strange big waters of the ocean'. The misery of seasickness and the 'perils of the sea' to inexperienced and frightened emigrants 'await[ing] our watery graves' was highlighted by Antin but so were the moments of quiet reflection in 'fugitive sunshine'. Yet through all the 'suffering, brooding, [and] rejoicing' the wider significance of the journey is never lost sight of: 'we crept nearer and nearer to the coveted shore, until, on a glorious May morning, six weeks after our departure from Polotzk, our eyes beheld the Promised Land, and my father received us in his arms'.[59]

The propagandist purpose of *The Promised Land*, written by a now-established author, was more intense than her earlier published account of the journey. Even the naming of the book was carefully chosen and negotiated with *The Heir of the Ages* rejected by the publisher. It was eventually a choice between the eventual title and the similarly Biblical *Out of the Land of Egypt*. *The Promised Land* was agreed because it had a 'challenging sound'. As Antin wrote to her publisher in 1911, 'I want to find a phrase that directly in a word tells what America does for the immigrant'.[60] In the period between the publication of her two accounts of her migrant journey – from 1899 to 1912 – the move to restrict immigration to America, especially from 'undesirable races' from Eastern and Southern Europe and, with a particular animosity, China, had grown in intensity. While Antin's *The Promised Land* was a deeply personal narrative, it also possessed a collective purpose to show the humanity and worth of the new immigrants. Its 'chief interest', she noted in the book's introduction, 'lies in the fact that it is illustrative of scores of unwritten lives. I am only one of many whose fate it has been to live a page of modern history.'[61]

By 1912, American nativism was in the ascendant.[62] Antin was determined, at least in the context of 'white' migration, to prove that the East European Jews could, through education, assimilate fully into American life. Thus Antin 'places her story in the context of a nation that was founded by immigrants, making her heir to a tradition that goes back to the Pilgrims and that encompasses the ancestors of all Americans of European descent'.[63] Again, in this respect *The Promised Land* is in effect a *collective* autobiography: 'We [my emphasis] are the strands of the cable that binds the Old World to the New.'[64]

The journey to Antin represented equally a real struggle over physical landscape *and* a metaphor for the transformation that is about to occur:

> As the ships that brought us link the shores of Europe and America, so our lives span the bitter sea of racial differences and misunderstandings. Before we came, the New World knew not the Old; but since we have begun to come, the Young World has taken the Old by the hand, and the two are learning to march side by side, seeking a common destiny.[65]

Polotzk, she concludes, 'was not my country. It was *goluth* – exile.' Yet rather than the Biblical Jerusalem, it is in fact America that is 'My country' and 'The Promised Land'.[66] Antin describes herself in the last paragraph of her migrant journey as 'the youngest of America's children', ending with ultimate optimism that 'Mine is the whole majestic past, and mine is the shining future.'[67]

It has been suggested (with a little overstatement) that in America *The Promised Land* 'launched a vogue for ethnic autobiography, of which *Out of the Shadow* is a prime example'.[68] Published in 1918, when its author, Rose Cohen, was in her late thirties and previously unknown, it is the 'moving story of a young immigrant's efforts to navigate the cultural distance from the Russian countryside to the tenements of the Lower East Side'.[69] As with Antin's *The Promised Land*, Cohen's autobiography emphasises the limited world of the former compared to the latter, especially in relation to literacy. The journey between them was hard and the 'New World' was tough and required time to adjust to its modernity. Nevertheless, America provides the opportunities, especially for females, previously denied.[70] Yet while the work of Antin and Cohen could not stop the triumph of restrictionism in the form of the racially motivated 1921 and 1924 quotas that blatantly discriminated against 'non-Nordics', both writers could at least claim that they were part of America's foundation myths of a nation made up of immigrants. Their move from 'Old' to 'New' world could thus be seen to be part of a tradition beginning with the epic journey of *The Mayflower* and the Pilgrim Fathers.

In Britain, there was only a tentative acceptance, and even then amongst a sympathetic minority, of the nation's migrant past. Immigrants, if referred to at all, were exceptions that proved the rule of 'native' homogeneity. Lacking such a 'usable past' as was the case in America at the level of collective memory, none of the Jewish migrants to Britain at the *fin de siècle* produced work such as Cohen's, let alone the iconic account of Antin's. It was left to a few from the second generation, and even then normally those who had become successful and prominent, such as Bud Flanagan, to refer to the journey and tellingly to do so by reference to the myth of accidental arrival. It is a biographical practice now perpetuated and institutionalised by third and fourth-generation Jews of East European origin as has been demonstrated by the example of David Baddiel.

Whereas nativism in America prompted the self-confident writing of Mary Antin, in the United Kingdom anti-alienism led to silence and the search for invisibility. In Dublin, Nick Harris recalls that his 'parents never spoke about their life in Russia when they were young. They never even mentioned their own parents and I never knew of any aunts or uncles'. Significantly, there was one exception to this family silence. It related to his father's brother 'who went to America'.[71] And where families of East European Jewish origin *did* admit to choosing Britain, as was the case with Isaac Winogradsky, the father of Lew Grade, there is a tendency to highlight parents' lack of menace through their incompetence. Lew Grade concludes that whilst his father 'was a well-intentioned man … from the time he arrived in England he was what you'd call a loser'.[72] Furthermore, in prominent second-generation accounts such as those by Grade and Flanagan, while immigrant roots are not denied, they are dealt with cursorily at the start of their autobiographies before the 'real' story begins.

Bud Flanagan's parents arrived in Britain before the large-scale migration of East European Jews from the 1880s onwards. They soon had ten children, of whom Chaim (Bud) was one of the last. To eke out a living his father, Wolf, ran a grocer's shop and was also described in the census as a 'bootfinisher'. A lodger – an elderly widower – further supplemented the family income.[73] His parents came to Britain before Jewish immigration was an issue even at a local level. Yet by the time Chaim was born in 1896 there was the beginnings of an anti-alien campaign that would culminate in the first permanent piece of legislation in Britain with the purpose of restricting mass immigration.[74] As will be explored in the conclusion of this study, hostile representations of migrant journeys played a key role in the aliens debate and the battle for restricted entry.

The Aliens Act, 1905, was aimed particularly at poor East European Jews who were perceived as diseased, subversive and essentially unEnglish and un-assimilable.[75] The Act did not fully stop movement to Britain but it did make coming to it carry the risk of rejection at its major ports. Even so, from the 1880s through to 1914, roughly 150,000 East European Jews settled perma-nently in Britain, with perhaps more than three times that number spending two years in the country. While this was only a fraction of the two million-plus Jews who left the Russian empire in the same period, the majority heading to America, there is still a notable difference between the two receiving countries when it came to autobiographical practice in the age of mass migration. In Britain it led to the void in ethnic memory that was referred to at the start of this chapter. Its impact could be long lasting. In his *Roots Schmoots: Journeys Among Jews* (1993), third-generation British Jewish writer, Howard Jacobson, recalls that growing up in Manchester during the 1950s, there was neither in-terest in nor knowledge of migrant origins:

> Our grandparents, or our parents' grandparents, had come over with chickens in their baggage fifty years before, fleeing the usual – some libel or pogrom or another, brewed up in some Eastern European *shtetl* or another – that was as much as they cared to remember or to tell us.

Jacobson adds that 'in truth that was as much as we cared to know … Roots we didn't think about; tendrils we needed [to become English]. You don't look down when you're climbing.'[76]

Irish famine journeys

At a basic level, there is a similar pattern with regard to Irish autobiographical practice and the mass migration of the mid-nineteenth century and that of the Jews some fifty years later. The vast majority of both poor Irish and Jewish migrants were either illiterate or unable to write fluently in English. Economic survival on a day-to-day basis took most of their energy and not surprisingly neither group left much in respect of contemporary letters, diaries or memoirs that describe their journeys. But there are subtle differences – in the case of the Irish fleeing the famine, the journey itself became politicised and publicised at the time. If such accounts were rarely produced in the public domain by ordi-nary migrants, they were recorded by a variety of observers and campaigners on their behalf.[77] Moreover, in contrast to the Jewish migratory experience half a century later, a relatively large number relating to the Irish tragedy were con-temporaneously published. Significantly, many were in diary format reflecting the instant nature of their polemic and their desire for justice as well as, in some cases, to expose the cruelty of the British government.

Just as Mary Antin's *The Promised Land* was as much an intervention into American politics as it was literary masterpiece, so this was true with a classic contemporary account of the famine. Antin's autobiography was an unqualified paean to the ability of America to assimilate immigrants, regardless of race and religion. In an equally striking way, but with the reverse intention, John Mitchel's *Jail Journal* was a demolition of any claim of Britain and its empire to the reputation of fairness and decency. While extreme in its politics, Mitchel's polemic set the tone for later memory work, including within the realm of autobiography and historiography. Indeed, as Peter Gray notes, the 'Mitchelite' perspective 'derived its power (especially in the diaspora) from its ability to give a coherent structure of meaning to the often horrific and alienating individual experiences of survivors'. He adds that

> its influence from the mid-nineteenth century was considerable; the narrative told a tale of a people subjected to an artificial famine at the whim of a genocidal government, the victims of a great injustice that could only be redeemed through the victory of the nationalist movement in removing British rule in Ireland.[78]

As with Antin's *The Promised Land*, the *Jail Journal* was initially serialised in an American periodical before being published the same year (1854).[79] Mitchel was a radical and charismatic leader of the 'Young Ireland' movement, advocating rent and rates strikes against landlords as a way of freeing the Irish population from what he saw as English tyranny. In 1848, Mitchel was arrested by the British authorities fearing a rebellion in Ireland following the revolutions in France and elsewhere on the continent. After a dubious trial, he was found guilty of treason and sentenced to fourteen years transportation to Van Diemen's Land (Tasmania) from where he escaped to America.

Jail Journal is not a famine journey diary per se.[80] Mitchel was transported on board British convict ships. The conditions on such vessels were subject to greater control than those belonging to commercial ventures exploiting the Irish migrants. The so-called 'famine ships' were often sprung into action at short notice to meet the desperate demand of Irish migrants to leave for the new world. It enabled the shipping companies to make a quick profit.[81] Even if the convict ships were less subject to abusing their human cargo, Mitchel encountered many poor Irish en route. He described in his diary their pitiful state on his journey from Bermuda to South Africa. Numbering nearly two hundred, most of them, he stated, were 'so shattered in constitution by mere hunger and hardship, that all the deaths amongst the prisoners, ever since we embarked, have been Irish'.[82] Furthermore, the anger that powers Mitchel's account was motored by the misery inflicted upon the Irish people as a whole culminating in the famine. His account of the journey was used to expose the exploitation that preceded it.

Mitchel's published diary is unrestrained in its language and political invective. The success of the *Jail Journal* in constructing later memory work in representing the leaving of Ireland reflects the wider underlying resentment towards England. It has been suggested that for 'those readers who were part of the great tide of emigration ... Mitchel's abruptly terminated history of Ireland [in 1848] would duplicate the experience of emigration', presenting as it did history as 'unfinished business'.[83] Such lingering hostility was present not only amongst many of the 1.8 million emigrants from the late 1840s to the late 1850s but also persisted and in many cases intensified with their descendants.

The *Jail Journal*, as Thomas Flanagan suggests, 'is carefully composed', revealing Mitchel as 'a rebel with a savage wit, the constant and deadly enemy of English rule, but the enemy also of cant, sentimentality and false humanitarianism'.[84] To Mitchel the 'English' system was deliberately used to create famine in order to clear the land of a surplus population in what would be a 'final conquest' of Ireland. From the start of his journal, Mitchel describes himself as being in a state of exile, he is a 'banished man',[85] later noting at a more collective level that America 'swarms with our refugees of "48"'.[86] There is thus no choice for the Irish migrants, whether they be leaders such as himself or the ordinary men and women escaping starvation. The situation in which the Irish find themselves he likens only to slavery, but in the form of servitude that is itself unprofitable.

Off the coast of Brazil, Mitchel comes across 'real' slaves of African origin and compares their lives to those of the Irish. A slave in Brazil was a 'merchantable slave, a slave of real money-value, whom a prudent man will, in the way of business, pay for and feed afterwards'. In contrast, notes Mitchel at his bitterest, ironic best:

> The poor slaves I have been accustomed to see are not only of no value, but their owners will go to heavy expense to get rid of them – not imported slaves, but surplus slaves for export – slaves with a Glorious Constitution ... a Habeas Corpus to be suspended, and a trial by jury whereby they may have the comfort of being routed out of house and home, transported, and hanged at the pleasure of the 'upper classes'.[87]

The English, argues Mitchel, had inflicted 'three seasons of famine-slaughter in the midst of heaven's abundance'.[88]

Mitchel's legacy in representing the origins of the famine was to lie in the future. Aside from within the Irish nationalist press, most contemporary accounts of the mass migration were less conspiratorial about their portrayal of

British misrule and the resultant famine. Instead, they were more concerned with averting the horrors of the journey itself, as will become apparent in the four key narratives which will now be analysed. This was certainly the case with two leading campaigners against the abuses of the famine ships, Stephen de Vere and Vere Foster. The former was a landowner in Limerick who wrote an extensive report in 1847 having travelled steerage from London to Quebec that year in a three-month journey. It was utilised by the House of Lords Select Committee on Colonization from Ireland in 1848. De Vere was horrified by what he had experienced and witnessed:

> Before the Emigrant has been a Week at Sea he is an altered Man. How can it be otherwise? Hundreds of poor People, Men, Women and Children of all Ages from the drivelling Idiot of Ninety to the Babe just born, huddled together without Light, without Air, wallowing in Filth and breathing a fetid Atmosphere, sick in Body, dispirited in Heart ...[89]

His intervention at a parliamentary level was important and it 'weighed much with the Government'.[90] While new regulations controlling the shipping of migrants were to be painfully slow in coming, it was still 'the first time that an educated observer had made the voyage between the decks, and described exactly what he saw'.[91]

Even more sustained was the input of Vere Foster, educational campaigner and philanthropist who devoted much energy from the late 1840s to improving conditions for Irish emigrants. Indeed, he was the author of a successful 'Penny Emigrant's Guide' which sold in the hundreds of thousands. It advised those embarking on the journey across the Atlantic about the problems they might encounter in leaving Ireland, in Liverpool as the port of transmigrancy, and finally concerning their early days in North America. It was based, as he told his reader, on two journeys travelling steerage, first from Liverpool to New York on board the *Washington* and then from the same port to Quebec on the *Cleopatra*.[92]

Foster travelled on the *Washington* in October 1850 bound with its 900 Irish migrants for New York. He was, like de Vere before him, incensed by the conditions endured by the passengers and the abuse on board. A year later he presented his evidence to the Colonial Office in the form of a detailed diary and this was then published as an official paper. Foster noted that the Irish passengers travelling steerage were, from the start, treated roughly 'like so many bundles'. Any attempts to protest about the conditions and lack of food were met with violence by the crew. On 25 November 1850, Vere Foster recorded that 'Another child, making about 12 in all, died of dysentery for want of proper nourishing food and was thrown into the sea sown up, along with a great stone, in a cloth'. He added that no funeral service had yet been performed 'over anyone who has died on board'.[93]

Foster noted that 'Many of the passengers have, at different times during the voyage, expressed to me their intention of making a public complaint respecting their ill-treatment on board this ship'. On 2 December 1850 as they moved close to New York, Foster drew up a statement to this effect, signed by thirty-four women and ninety-five men and headed by himself, attaching it to the diary of his journey:

> We testify as a warning to, and for the sake of future emigrants, that the passengers generally, on board this noble ship the 'Washington' ... have been treated in a brutal manner by its officers, and that we have not received one-half the quantity of provisions allowed by Act of Parliament and stipulated for by us in our contract tickets.

He emphasised that the shipping company, Black Star, had other equally appalling packets operating with the same problems. In contrast, he noted, rival companies were completing the transatlantic run without such misery and death. In short, his complaint was with the unnecessary brutality and suffering caused on board certain emigrant ships and not with the underlying causes of the famine movement.[94] Indeed, Foster was at pains to inform the Colonial Office that 'my desire of proceeding against the owners of the "Washington" arises solely from a wish to take a part towards obtaining better treatment [in the future]'.[95]

Our third account – and one that was halfway between de Vere and Foster in explaining the unnecessary suffering of the Irish transatlantic experience – was provided by Robert Whyte's *The Ocean Plague* (1848) and published in Boston. While Whyte's emphasis was on the journey itself, the author was still critical of the reasons behind the 'violent rush of famished, reckless human beings, flying from their native land to seek food in a distant and unknown country'.[96] In its introduction Whyte queried the policy of emigration as a solution to 'alleviating the grievous ills under which the Irish peasantry labour'. He added that while it was not 'our province to enquire into its expediency', through the 'single eye of common-sense ... it is difficult to see the necessity of expatriating the superfluous population a country wherein hundreds of thousands of acres of land susceptible of the highest culture, lie waste'.[97]

Whyte was a middle-class migrant who travelled from Dublin to the notorious Canadian quarantine station of Grosse Ile in 1847 on what would soon be referred to as a 'coffin ship'.[98] Little is known of Whyte but his account was, as with Mitchel, carefully constructed, suggesting that he was an experienced writer and intended his account to be placed in the public domain as a collective version of the Irish journey. In his narrative Whyte quickly introduced the poor Irish migrants whom he presented as innocent and naive:

> many … had never seen the sea nor a ship until they were on board. They were chiefly from the County Meath, and sent out at the expense of their landlord without any knowledge of the country to which they were going, or means of livelihood except the labour of the father of each family. All they knew concerning Canada was that they were to land in Quebec and to go up the country.[99]

All starts off calmly as the ship left in late May. Whyte states that the passengers had 'a settled conviction that the voyage was to last exactly three weeks'.[100] Two weeks after leaving Dublin, there were already intense problems with contaminated water. Severe cases of dysentery and fever were occurring. Without medicine and water, Whyte's tone was now sombre. For the 110 people on board 'The prospect before us was indeed an awful one and there was no hope for us but in the mercy of God.'[101] The first deaths occurred and Whyte highlighted the menace of the sharks, waiting for the disposal of dead bodies and other 'waste' from the ship. As with accounts of the 'Middle Passage', the shark evoked particular fear amongst all those on board: 'If the shark was the dread of the sailors, it was the outright terror of the enslaved.'[102]

By 8 July, apart from the increasing number who had died, half of the survivors on Whyte's ship were sick. By the end of the month, it had arrived at Grosse Ile, 'the Isle of Death', and the passengers and crew prepared themselves for medical inspection. Even then, there was no relief:

> I could not believe it possible that here, within reach of help, we should be left as neglected as when upon the ocean. That after a voyage of two months' duration we were to be left still enveloped by reeking pestilence, the sick without medicine, medical skill, nourishment or so much as a drop of pure water.[103]

Whyte opens and closes his book with an account of the abuses of the Irish migrant trade and a plea for them to be addressed – the regulations that existed had 'proved quite ineffectual'. Struggling to find a way of 'convey[ing] my sentiments in my own language', he turned to Charles Dickens in *American Notes* to relay the horror of the journey and the necessity of reform. And as with Vere Foster, Whyte used the example of other shipping companies to show that the suffering was unnecessary. In this case, he pointed to the example of the ships for German migrants who 'underwent none of those heartrending trials reserved exclusively for the Irish'. Ultimately, although Whyte utilises a religious discourse throughout his narrative, there is no redemption for those 'quitting their poverty-stricken country for "a land flowing with milk and honey" – poor creatures, they thought that any change would be for the better'. The only hope for Whyte was to ensure that there would be no repetition of the 'fatal scenes of the awfully tragic drama enacted upon the wide stage of the Atlantic Ocean in the floating lazar houses that were wafted upon its bosom during the never-to-be-forgotten year 1847'.[104]

De Vere, Foster and Whyte shared the same space as the poor Irish emigrant but all three were removed from them by class. In the last contemporary example describing the transatlantic journey to be examined here, it was not class but national origin that separated the author from the Irish – he was an English radical. William Smith's account, self-published in New York, was entitled *An Emigrant's Narrative or a Voice from the Steerage* (1850). It described the journey of the *India* which sailed from Liverpool to New York in the winter of 1847/48. That most of those in steerage were Irish was not denied by Smith but his was a universal account aimed at showing the ill-treatment of all such emigrants bound for America. When they left Liverpool in November 1847 there were '300 souls confined below', all

> breathing the close, polluted, and unhealthy atmosphere constantly in all ships, especially immigrant ships, where large numbers of human beings are crowded together in a small space.[105]

As with De Vere, Foster and Whyte, Smith's emphasis was on illness through 'ship fever' and then dysentery and the resultant deaths on board. By the fifth week, fifteen had died and forty-two were confined to bed and by the time of arrival in New York in mid-January 1848 the figure had reached 26 dead with 123 sent to hospital, many beyond hope of recovery.[106] The misery of Smith's narrative did not end with the arrival in New York but extended to his treatment in the Staten Island Hospital. Smith initially described his account as a 'plain narrative of the prominent events of the voyage', and most of the description is devoted to the suffering on board. Nevertheless, it is not void of politics – Smith was a republican who saw America (in contrast to Britain) as the 'glorious land of freedom'.[107] The animus in his short published account, however, is aimed at the harsh and unfeeling treatment he received in the Staten Island Hospital.

William Smith, writing two years after his journey, was still bitterly disappointed about his first experiences of America. Rather than the 'Promised Land', Smith leaves the cruelty of the hospital as he was 'willing to risk anything rather than remain here in worse than Egyptian bondage'.[108] Nevertheless, Smith's belief in American ideals was not fully tarnished. He concluded his account imploring the American reader to

> let your sympathy be extended to the honest immigrants, when tyranny, overpopulation and taxation has forced upon your shores, and may the star-spangled banner protect your noble institutions, and triumph over liberty'd foes till time shall be no more.[109]

None of the four famine journey diaries and accounts analysed here come close to the message of Mitchel that the Irish famine and subsequent migration was deliberately fostered by the British government to remove the poor Irish presence. It is significant, however, that including Mitchel, three of the five were published in America and that it was within North America, with its large Irish diaspora, that a conspiratorial model of deliberate neglect and ill-treatment on board the 'coffin ships' would take hold. It became part of a wider narrative that implied a genocidal imperative behind the British government's policies. A usable past, both for the individual migrant and the wider Irish diaspora, demanded stories of the migration journey that were fundamentally Anglophobic.

In popular memory in both Ireland itself and within the Irish diaspora, the element of choice in leaving the homeland was largely removed. In John Denvir's *The Irish in Britain from the Earliest Times to the Fall and Death of Parnell* (1892), the 'panic-stricken people fled from their country, literally in millions, to America, to England – anywhere to escape from what seemed a doomed land'. There was, argued Denvir, enough food for the whole people: 'The British government then, *ruling in spite of them*, stands charged with their murder'.[110] In an account published just over one hundred years later but with a similar message, *A Farewell to Famine* (1994), the author contrasts earlier Irish migrations with those in the 1840s: 'These people did not leave Ireland with money jingling in their pockets or hope in their hearts. They did not sail *to* anywhere, they simply sailed *from* Ireland'.[111] Again, personal choice and variation is totally removed.

There were English newspapers such as the *Illustrated London News* that presented the plight of the Irish famine victims and their journeys in a sympathetic manner.[112] More common, however, was the response of *The Times* which blamed the Irish for their own misfortune as feckless, stupid and lazy.[113] Such insensitivity and antipathy even extended into descriptions of and responses to Irish migratory journeys. In 1848, the *Londonderry*, travelling from Sligo for Liverpool hit a storm. The steerage passengers were locked in and 72 of the 174 suffocated to death. Rather than blame the captain and crew, initially the focus was on the Irish migrants who were accused of panicking, fighting, rioting and of stealing from one another.[114] Such derogatory images of migrants as selfish, cowardly and unruly would be repeated in other journeys, including most infamously the *Titanic*. Nevertheless, and as was the case with the luxury liner in 1912, subsequent investigations concerning the *Londonderry* 'set off an outcry against conditions on the steamers', especially accommodation for the 'poorer class of passengers'.[115]

Not surprisingly, given the trauma of the famine and the desire to counter lingering negative perceptions of the Irish, Mitchel's narrative presenting the migrants as exiles who left because they had no choice has, at a popular level, become dominant. As Graham Davis notes, 'Historically, the importance of the Mitchel thesis lay not only in its early acceptance among Irish emigrants, especially in North America, but also in the influence it was to exercise over later historians and in popular fiction.'[116] The clarity of Mitchel's political analysis has also extended into memory work associated with migration. As Davis adds, in recent years 'popular understanding of the impact of the Famine on Ireland's population and on emigration from Ireland has not kept pace with the work of scholars'.[117] Such academic work has not underestimated the scope of the disaster, but it has highlighted how emigration did not correspond directly to poverty – the poorest counties in the south had some of the lowest rates of leaving. In short, the very poorest did not have the means to leave. Chain migration, often with support from American relatives, as well as wealth, skills and opportunity, politics and religion, explain why some journeyed across the Atlantic, others left for England and Scotland, and the majority stayed home during the years of intense famine.[118] Thus Miller notes, although

> witnesses in North America frequently described all Famine emigrants as the dregs of humanity, their universally wretched appearance after long, often disease-ridden voyages disguised the fact that many were no more impoverished or unskilled than their immediate pre-Famine predecessors.

As he adds, 'Craftsmen and petty entrepreneurs constituted a sizable minority.'[119] Similarly, in her study of Irish migration to Scotland, Brenda Collins highlights how 'The heaviest emigration during the 1840s was not from the most destitute areas. The poor in the west could not afford to go themselves and the common landlord response was eviction rather than help with emigration.'[120]

But folk memory of the Irish journey requires a more straightforward analysis of this traumatic movement. It is thus not surprising that rather than the four complex narratives analysed here, it is an account that is now regarded in the academic world as a literary construction – Gerald Keegan's *Famine Diary* – that has gained interest in the late twentieth century and the 150th anniversary of the Famine.[121] First published in a re-worked, fictionalised form in 1982 by James Mangan, it was republished in 1991 to popular acclaim and widespread success, including radio and newspaper serialisation. Mangan claimed the account was based on an original manuscript but it is now popularly accepted as being closely based on Robert Sellars' novel, *Summer of Sorrow* (1892). In turn, this late nineteenth-century version of a famine journey, rather than being based on Keegan's diary, borrowed heavily from contemporary newspaper reports which utilised material from the House of Lords Select Committee in 1847/48.[122] From the perspective of memory work, what is intriguing is that Keegan's 'diary' is now included as authentic source material on the famine ships. In it, a clear 'Young Ireland' narrative is imposed with British guilt and the involuntary nature of exile emphasised throughout.[123]

In the case of Irish famine journeys, in which 'at least five per cent of trans-Atlantic passengers perished en route',[124] and up to 20 per cent or 40,000 in 1847 alone,[125] a decisive anti-British political underpinning is now popularly imposed. It has led to a growing gulf between nuanced scholarship, which emphasises regional variation in migration, and folk legend which standardises the narrative to a single Irish experience. In the process, there is no consideration given to those whose journeys were less horrific, or to the variations between journeys that were voluntary, assisted by landlords or on convict ships.

One exception is the now celebrated *Jeanie Johnston*, 'a proud Irish emigrant ship' in which it is claimed that from 1848 to 1855 in sixteen journeys across the Atlantic, over 2,500 Irish migrants arrived in Canada and America without any loss of life. The ship in replica form is now a major tourist attraction aimed at presenting a more positive example.[126] As with the Yad Vashem Holocaust museum in Jerusalem, however, and its 'Avenue of the Righteous Gentiles', it must be suggested that famous counter-examples such as Oskar Schindler and here, the *Jeanie Johnston*, are being instrumentalised as exceptions to show the norm of Holocaust bystander indifference in one case and the horror of the normal Irish 'coffin ship' journey on the other.[127] They are also utilised as stories with redemptive endings – with the former, the creation of the Jewish state and Jewish survival and, with the latter, the success of the Irish diaspora in north America with pride of place given to John F. Kennedy.

Furthermore, change over time – before, during and after the famine – is smoothed over (in fact most of the seven million departures from Ireland from the seventeenth century to 1922 took place *after* the famine).[128] Instead, with folk legend there is a conformity with the expectation of exploitation and death. Cathal Poirteir's *Famine Echoes* (1995) includes second and later generation testimony which produces a undiluted picture of misery relating to 'The Coffin Ships and Going Away'. It includes the story of James Annesley who was in a workhouse in Ross: 'the English were shipping young people [like him] and selling them into slavery in America' and a short account that summarises the transatlantic voyage in two sentences:

> A ship which came to Killybegs to take off emigrants sold the provisions which were to be used on the journey. Before the boat reached America there was starvation on board and many deaths resulted.[129]

In the case of Jewish migration from Eastern Europe some half a century later, an equal mythology has grown up, one that is at increasing odds with recent and critical historical scholarship. In the Irish and Jewish examples in popular memory, refugee status is emphasised – the journey is involuntary and the result of persecution, Russian in the one case, British in the other. Kerby Miller has emphasised that personal guilt at leaving family behind is a major factor in explaining the desire to be labelled as exiles amongst the Irish migrants.[130] The decision to emigrate to the 'New World' is rendered choiceless through English persecution and the desire for self-improvement is thus marginalised in subsequent memory work. The same tendency is apparent also in East European Jewish autobiographical practice although without the nostalgia for a lost 'home'. Instead, there is greater emphasis on America as the 'Promised Land' and hence the idea of accidental arrival in Britain. The major difference between the Jews and the Irish is that at the time, amongst the former, little was written (or talked about) concerning the journey. That would be left to Jewish migrants who went to the 'Promised Land' of America and assimilated quickly – it is perhaps not accidental that some of the leading accounts there were written by women and were thus perhaps less threatening to nativists. With Antin, the emphasis was placed on her educational experiences in America. These enabled a move from the personal – a Boston schoolgirl – to the collective: 'the school success of the autobiographical "I" becomes a metaphor for the potential success of all immigrants'.[131] Gender also played a role in the descriptions of the Irish famine journeys studied here – concepts of masculinity infused the narratives of all five (male) accounts, especially that of Mitchel. The 'battle of Britishness', of inclusion and exclusion, and of arriving and departing, necessitated different narrative strategies both then and now. In one case it led to amnesia of the journey, and in the other to a surplus of memory. This theme will be returned to in the Conclusion and why it is that the journeys of the 'coffin ships' have gained iconic status in subsequent memory work, thereby joining a very select club of migrant vessels that have not suffered from oblivion.

Irish migratory journeys to Britain did not end in the early 1850s and ironically continued at a not dissimilar rate of settlement to those of East European Jews in the period from the 1880s to 1914.[132] But it was rare, apart from areas of sectarian tension in Britain such as Liverpool, Glasgow and Edinburgh, for anti-Irish migrant sentiment to be politicised in the late nineteenth century in the form of national debates on immigration. While anti-Irish sentiment did not disappear in society and culture, the focus was on the 'alien', a shorthand for the East European Jews. If referred to at all in the aliens debate, the Irish migrants were regarded as being in the past. Thus in one of the first Cabinet discussions of the aliens question in 1891, Sir James Fergusson, Parliamentary Under-Secretary of State for Foreign Affairs, thought it unwise that Britain should protest to the Russian government about its treatment of Jews as it could be accused of hypocrisy. Fergusson noted that only fifty years earlier, 'The flight of Irishmen from these islands ... has been in excess of anything which has ever been witnessed in the case of any other country.' He added that there were some people who were of the opinion that this Irish emigration was 'at least partially, due to the operation of laws and administrative acts in this country.'[133]

In 1891, there was little desire to legislate and end the traditional policy of free entry of aliens. A year later, Robert Giffen, head of the Commercial and Statistical Department of the Board of Trade, reviewing the state of immigration to Britain, concluded that

> Apart from poverty and strange language, and difference of race and traditions, these poor Jews have a good moral and other citizen qualities as a rule. They are not a bad lot.[134]

Less than a decade later, the balance had changed. It reflected a shift in mood that was not simply a result of increased migration. Self-confidence was in decline and the eventual success of anti-alienism was as much a result of the 'question of England' and fears of national deterioration as it was of immigrant numbers.

Simultaneous with the 'aliens question' and not unrelated to it, the idea of Britain as an 'island race' became powerful in late Victorian and Edwardian Britain.[135] It was typified in the works of geographer H.J. Mackinder, whose contribution, including his *Britain and the British Seas* (1902), has already been noted in Chapter 1. One of the 'essential qualities of the British environment', argued Mackinder, was 'insularity, which has tended to preserve the continuity of social organisation.'[136] The sea acted as a barrier to mass movement and earlier migrations racially melded so that 'One of the most surprising facts in connection with modern Britain is the uniformity with which, in all parts of the country, the long-skulled type predominates. No distinction whatever can be drawn in this respect between the most thoroughly Teutonic and the most completely Celticised districts.' Mackinder continued that 'The Neolithic peoples of ancient Britain were of the long-skulled group.'[137]

In Mackinder's and other such writings, the emphasis was on continuity of presence and stability: 'Until recent times most men lived their lives in the neighbourhood of their birthplace' and the population of 'each district was recruited in the main from an ancestry locally restricted'. Mackinder did not deny the arrival of newcomers penetrating Britain's shoreline. Their racial and overall significance was, however, minimised: 'Fresh strains of blood were occasionally introduced by an invasion, as of the Normans, or by some great pacific immigration amd settlement, as of the Jews, the Flemings, or the Huguenots, but the influence even of these was confined to certain spots.'[138]

To Mackinder, the navy was central to Britain's greatness in the past and present and the 'whole course of future history depends on whether the Old Britain beside the Narrow Seas have enough of virility and imagination to withstand all challenge of her naval supremacy'.[139] Given the centrality of maritime defence and victory in the construction and reconstruction of British identity,[140] it is not surprising that historians of minority groups such as Jews and Afro-Caribbeans should have made attempts in recent years to show the long-standing diversity of the navy. Indeed, they have shown that the Royal Navy has relied on those of foreign origin throughout its history.[141] Of 663 officers and men on board Nelsen's *Victory*, for example, there were 'two Indians, one African, nine West Indians, twenty-two Americans ... and one Maltese woman disguised as a man'.[142]

Attempts at creating a more inclusive 'mainstream' British history with regards to epic journeys such as that of the *Victory* are difficult given the hegemony of mono-cultural interpretations of the past. The efforts of bodies such as the Black and Asian Studies Association and the Jewish Historical Society of England, as well as that of individual scholars and activists, alongside the greater commitment to pluralism and diversity, have at least made this feasible. Harder still, however, has been the consideration and incorporation of more challenging journeys such as those linked to transatlantic slavery with which this second introductory chapter will conclude.

The Middle Passage

As Marcus Wood highlights, in the world of heritage 'England has saved its fastest clipper, the *Cutty Sark*, as a tribute to its East India trade, and it has preserved HMS *Victory* as a tribute to Nelson and the British naval defeat of Napoleonic France.' In contrast, Wood states simply how 'No slave boats were preserved: they were adapted to other trade and sailed on, and when they wore out they were scrapped. Not one plank survives to bear silent witness to the suffering they contained.'[143] Black British artist, Lubaina Himid, has directly confronted this problem of representation and how 'when something is there you can talk about it, write about it, paint about it, but when something isn't there what can you say, how can you make something of it'? Himid was particularly concerned with those 'potential slaves [who were] thrown into the sea' and the dilemma, as an artist of 'How do you talk about something that can be seen and be thought of as not being there? Inside the invisible, if you like.'[144]

Lubaina Himid's focus was that 'vast expanse of water between yesterday and tomorrow, Africa and the New World and ... the place where all these people are now in the water. They are the body of the water now, they are it.'[145]

More prosaically, and 120 years earlier, 'Dicky Sam' attempted to re-connect a more fixed point – Liverpool – to its crucial role in the slave trade. In the process, he outlined what was, and was not, a 'usable past' in local topography. He imagined Liverpool's docks in 1760 and how it was 'here many of the fine and noble ships for the Royal Navy were built, and here, also those fast sailing slavers which were destined to traffic in human blood, and to make rich the Liverpool merchants, traders, and others concerned'.[146] 'Dicky Sam' was, however, generations ahead of his time in making such linkages through place and history.[147] As was noted in a centenary reprint of his account, the author 'chose to disguise his identity ... for a good reason: when he wrote it [1884], many of the former slave merchants (or at any rate their sons) would still have been alive, deprived of a lucrative living not many decades earlier through the efforts of the abolitionists'.[148]

In *The Black Atlantic* (1993), Paul Gilroy explains why he settled 'on the image of ships in motion across the spaces between Europe, America, Africa, and the Caribbean' as his starting point. 'The image of the ship – a living, micro-cultural, micro-political system in motion – is especially important for historical and theoretical reasons', states Gilroy:

> Ships immediately focus attention on the middle passage, on the various projects for redemptive return to an African homeland, on the circulation of ideas and activists as well as the movement of key cultural and political aretefacts: tracts, books, gramophone records, and choirs.[149]

Gilroy's postcolonial and innovative reading of the diasporic black experience acknowledges both the horror of the 'Middle Passage' and gives agency and multi-layered complexity to its victims.

Gilroy's *The Black Atlantic* and the work of Zanzibar-born Lubaina Himid is thus part of a black cultural, artistic and intellectual reaction to an abolotionist discourse which, from the late eighteenth century onwards, presented the African victims of slavery as placeless and passive – as 'things', albeit deserving sympathy and support. In terms of the concept of the journey, the most iconic abolitionist image was that of the Liverpool slave ship *Brookes*. Representations of the *Brookes* was first circulated in 1789 as an engraving – the 'Description of a Slave Ship' – and then disseminated widely by the Society for Effecting the Abolition of the Slave Trade formed two years earlier.[150] Thereafter, it appeared in many different publications and artefacts in Britain, France and America and still remains iconic in representations of slavery across the world.

Not surprisingly, given his Liverpool focus, 'Dicky Sam' devoted a chapter to a 'description of the Slave Ship "Brookes"'. He commented that so 'small was the place allowed to each, they had not so much room as a man in a coffin. They were placed lying on their backs, and sometimes were packed spoonways, one on the other; so close were they, you could not walk without treading on them, but then they were only slaves.'[151] As Wood suggests, the image of the *Brookes* supported 'an abolitionist cultural agenda which dictated that slaves were to be visualised in a manner which emphasised their total passivity and prioritised their status as helpless victims'. Indeed, in one engraving developing the concept of the 'Description' further, 'Plan of Slave Ship' (c. 1800) the slaves 'have literally disappeared as a human representation to become pure geometric form'.[152]

Such tendencies towards anonymity are revealed in the small number of memorials to enslaved Africans in British grave sites, including Scipio Africanus in Henbury, Bristol, servant to Charles William Howard, 7th Earl of Suffolk.[153] In response, black British poet, Fred D'Aguiar, of Guyanese origin and upbringing, restores a sense of belonging and history to Scipio, anticipating the art of Lubaina Himid when confronting the memory of slavery in Britain:

> African slave without a name, I'd call this home
> by now. Would you? Your unknown soldier's tomb
>
> stands for shipload after shipload that docked,
> unloaded, watered, scrubbed, exercised and restocked[.]

D'Aguiar politicises the dangers inherent in such anonymity by contextualising it in regard to black urban unrest during Thatcherite Britain:

> St Paul's, Toxteth, Brixton, Tiger Bay and Handsworth:
> petrol bombs flower in the middle of roads, a sudden growth
>
> at the feet of police lines longer than any cricket pitch.
> African slave, your namelessness is the wick and petrol mix.[154]

Returning to the specific representation of the slaves on the *Brookes*, on one level it was deeply problematic in denying the individuality and past history of the Africans on board. On another, the 'Description' was deeply challenging to contemporaries. By 'adopting a style of draftsmanship used to describe the abstract beauty of ships', it related 'directly to a discourse of British naval power'. Yet as Wood suggests, 'in suddenly inundating the clean lines, which describe the ship, with rows of human bodies printed in wedges of black ink, the print simultaneously questions the relation of the slave trade to British maritime history'. It remains, however, that for all its success as an image, 'it was the only eighteenth-century representation of the middle passage that took one not only on board, but inside the hold of, a slave ship'.[155] And as John Oldfield reminds us, post-abolition (1807) and emancipation (1834), 'Britons – and Britain's colonial subjects – were taught to view transatlantic slavery through the moral triumph of abolition, thereby substituting for the horrors of slavery and the slave trade a "culture of abolitionism". He comments also that what is 'so often striking about this specific "history" is its silencing of African perspectives, and, in particular, the suffering of the millions who were sold into slavery'.[156] Such tendencies are apparent in another grave site – that in Windermere's Parish Church – St Martin's, Bowness. There a headstone is inscribed 'In memory of Rasselas Belfield a Native of Abyssinia who departed this life on the 16th of January 1822, Aged 32 Years':

> A Slave by birth I left my native Land.
> And found my Freedom on Britannia's Strand.
> Blest Isle. Thou Glory of the Wise and Free!
> Thy touch Alone unbinds the Chains of Slavery.[157]

Marcus Wood contrasts the 'Description' of the *Brookes* with the 1846 water-colour drawing by English naval officer, Francis Meynell, depicting 'the state of slaves on the captured Spanish slaver, the *Albanoz*'. Made some thirty-nine years after the abolition of the British slave trade, it was a 'period when national self-doubt and self-loathing over British domination of the slave trade had been effaced and a self-aggrandising mythology reinscribed'. Such comforting narratives now had a different nautical discourse: the 'British Navy's African slave patrols were presented as the glorious product of the 1807 abolition bill'.[158] Turner's *Slavers Throwing Overboard the Dead and the Dying* (1840) was an exception. Inspired directly or indirectly by the appalling incident in 1781, when the captain of the Liverpool slave ship *Zong* threw overboard 132 Africans in the Caribbean to enable an insurance claim, Turner's work opened up the possibility of later postcolonial interventions such as the work of Fred D'Aguiar and Lubaina Himid.[159] In the painting the 'slaves are to be dissolved in the waters of the ocean, forever inextricably mixed with the element of their destruction'. Wood suggests that Turner 'enacts a powerful reversal of the biblical myth. The greed of slavery has turned the interior of the ark from a place of rebirth into a living hell.'[160]

Yet the rejection of *Slavers* by most of Turner's contemporaries on artistic and moral lines reinforced the uniqueness of his independent vision. Slavery was now being presented as essentially unBritish, or, in celebrations of iconic figures such as William Wilberforce, as more specifically unEnglish.[161] The detail that 'Between 1662 and 1807 ships of the British Empire carried approximately 3.4 million enslaved Africans from Africa to America, about 50 per cent of all slave exports during the period' was conveniently forgotten.[162]

Any reference linking Britain to slavery – as opposed to abolition – was a source of embarrassment as was exposed during the Second World War. In 1940, Britain deported several thousand 'enemy aliens', including Jewish refugees from Nazism, to Canada and Australia. The treatment of the internees on board the ships taking them from Britain was the subject of scandal – they were robbed of their possessions, treated like criminals and faced antisemitic taunts. One refugee diary of such a journey – on board the SS *Ettrick* (a troop transport ship, formerly owned by P&O) which left Liverpool in July 1940 for Quebec – was censored and confiscated by the War Office. Offence was caused by one specific entry: 'Inhuman treatment – like a slave ship. Two large rooms, perhaps sufficient for 500 soldiers occupied by 1,000 people.' At a sensitive time, Britain did not want its reputation for decency challenged by the evocation of such a troubling part of its history.[163] Accusations of slavery were also part of the vicious propaganda wars between Britain and the Jewish world in post-war conflict over migration to Palestine. In summer 1947, the *President Warfield*, renamed *Exodus 1947*, carrying 4,500 Jewish passengers who were mostly Holocaust survivors, sailed from France to Palestine only to be intercepted by the British navy. The passengers were sent back to Europe. Responding to what they called 'evil propaganda' which labelled those organis- ing these desperate journeys as 'slave merchants', those on the ship broadcasted that it was the British who were 'the damned slave merchants. You traded with Jewish blood during the war and you are continuing to do so now.'[164]

Not until the late twentieth and early twenty-first centuries would a more self-critical perspective emerge and the 'Middle Passage' become central to discussions of Britain, Britishness and the transatlantic slave trade. Indeed, while the treatment of the slave journey has deliberately been left brief here, it will be returned to throughout this study. If the 'Middle Passage' has especially provided the basis for much memory work of Africans and Afro-Caribbeans in post-war Britain, it has also become part of wider consciousness in culture and society as a whole.[165]

Conclusion

Migrant journeys are, as emphasised so far, far from straightforward or un- contested. They incorporate suffering as well as escape, trauma and loss alongside opportunities for economic and social advancement. It is for this reason that the word 'journey' has been deliberately chosen to head this study rather than alternatives such as 'travel' or 'voyages'. The black American critic, bell hooks, has criticised James Clifford for 'playfully evok[ing] a sense of travel'.[166] Clifford himself is aware of the problems associated with the word, but states that he 'hang[s] on to "travel" as a term of cultural comparison pre- cisely because of its historic taintedness, its associations with gendered, racial bodies, class privilege, specific means of conveyance, beaten paths, agents, frontiers, documents and the like'.[167] Nevertheless, to hooks, 'Travel is not a word that can be easily evoked to talk about the Middle Passage, the Trail of Tears, the landing of Chinese immigrants at Ellis Island, the forced relocation of Japanese-Americans, the plight of the homeless.' Instead, hooks proposes 'a theory of the journey that would expose the extent to which holding on to the concept of "travel" as we know it is also a way to hold on to imperialism [and one might add ethnic cleansing and genocide]'. And it is with her suggestion that the *Journey* could 'become the rubric within which travel as a starting point for discourse … associated with different headings – rites of passage, immigration, enforced migration, relocation, enslavement, homelessness' that the term will be utilised here.[168]

Jeremy Leigh has argued that 'The "journey" is at the heart of the Jewish experience'. There are many types of Jewish journeys – including those of fixed point, those of choice and those of compulsion. There are also individual and collective Jewish journeys. Throughout them all, Leigh suggests, 'is a consistent tension between the physical and the spiritual dimension of the journey'.[169] Not denying the particular history of the Jews, Leigh's comments have a wider application, especially to other groups for whom migration has played a major role in their history. Thus Shabnam Grewal, Jackie Kay (whose poetry and prose will be explored in Chapter 8), Liliane Landor, Gail Lewis and Pratibha Parmar in their collection of writings by 'Black and Third World Women' in Britain, comment that

> Ours … is a journey – a geographical, social and political journey from the present to the past, from the past to the future – shifting in space and time as required – in the hope that the material reality which is the substance of the 'idea' may be preserved and transcended for, and by, our future development. It is a migrants' journey not simply in the commonly accepted sense, but also in the sense of migrations from past to future lives. It includes that other form of migration – movement across the frontiers of life into new, uncharted territories of the self.[170]

Ziauddin Sardar's *Balti Britain: A Provocative Journey Through Asian Britain* (2008), also insists that 'Migration is a disruptive process. It scoops up lives, traditions and histories, and deposits them somewhere else.' The resultant 'quest for identity', he adds, 'is a journey that unravels relationships spun in the web of history'.[171] It is for this reason that it has been argued that for black writers in Britain, but one can broaden this to many other groups of migrant origin, a 'linear narrative would be too tidy, making their journeys seem bogusly inevitable; in fact, [they] were leaps into the unknown, anything but expected'.[172]

Throughout the case studies that follow, the revealing interplay that Leigh, Grewal *et al.* and Sardar locate between the physical and the non-physical in embarking upon, experiencing and remembering journeys will become apparent. It again emphasises the importance of mythology in the story-telling process. In a posthumous collection of essays, Raphael Samuel argued that 'As with other classes of legend, arrival myths are more interesting for the meanings they subsequently take on than for those which they carried at the time.'[173] This book charts the evolution of such mythologies, and more fundamentally explores the politics underpinning the memory and history of migrant journeys. Indeed, it must be emphasised that memory work is both dynamic and constantly contested. James Young notes with regard to Holocaust memorials that 'national memory comprises many, often competing recollections'.[174]

Similarly in this study of migrant journeys the battle over what is remembered/forgotten – and how – will feature throughout. As this chapter has highlighted, the details of physical journeys and modes of transport are particularly subject to amnesia and oblivion, including within the field of historiography. Marcus Rediker's *The Slave Ship: A Human History* was published as late as 2007. In this respect, his comments in justifying his study are worth quoting at length:

> Curiously, many of the poignant tales within the great drama have never been told, and the slave ship itself has been a neglected topic within a rich literature on the Atlantic slave trade. Excellent research has been conducted on the origins, timing, scale, flows and profits of the slave trade, but there exists no broad study of the vessel that made the world-transforming commerce possible.

As he summarises, until his work, there existed 'no account of the mechanism for history's greatest forced migration, which was in many ways the key to an entire phase of globalization'.[175]

The chapters that follow will provide analysis of both the history and memory of migrant journeys, but they will not avoid descriptions of the detailed 'mechanisms' to which Rediker refers. They will do so inclusively alongside the more nebulous area of migrant mythology, notable most clearly with the concept of 'arrival'. Exploring the concept of 'arrival myths', Raphael Samuel emphasises that:

> Just as, in the legend of Hengist and Horsa, the duo who supposedly established an Anglo-Saxon presence in England, lifelike details were added *retrospectively*, so in the case of the *Empire Windrush*, the boat whose arrival in Britain in 1949 [*sic*] supposedly inaugurated the epoch of New Commonwealth immigration, the processes of projection, amplification and displacement seem inconceivably more important than the original event.[176]

This chapter has highlighted especially groups such as the Irish and Jews whose dominant memory work is that their migration was essentially forced and in-voluntary – a reality so blatant in the case of the transatlantic slave trade that it needed no such reinforcement. In the next section, the processes of con-structing migration myths identified by Samuel will be developed further. As will emerge, some pre-twentieth-century movements were made to fit within expectations of a wider, comforting, national narrative. Others, however, have remained too challenging to be incorporated into what Samuel dubbed our 'island stories'.[177]

Early journeys, 1685–1880

3

Huguenot journeys: constructing the *réfugiés*

Journeys of escape

Albert Vajda, the Hungarian humourist, came to Britain late in 1956 after the failed uprising against Soviet domination of his homeland. In his memoir, Vajda presents an ironic and idealised vision of refugee arrival in Britain, following in the footsteps of George Mikes's *How to be an Alien*. On the plane journey he dreamt of being asked by the stewardess to lead his fellow refugees off the plane where he was greeted by Sir Anthony Eden, the Prime Minister, the Chancellor of the Exchequer ('He will look after your financial requirements') and the Minister of Transport ('He will place a car and chauffeur at your disposal').[1] In reality, they were met by the police and sent by bus to a large, disused military camp surrounded by barbed wire near Colchester.[2] There they were given alien identity papers: 'As a refugee I expected that in my new country I was going to live in the enchanting forest of Shakespeare's "A Midsummer Night's Dream" only to find out later that in the life of a refugee there are more "Madsummer Nightmares".[3]

To Vajda, the initial treatment was resented because 'we had a seven-hour journey and twelve years of terror behind us'. In Britain 'people simply ignored us', not able to comprehend what had happened to force them to leave home.[4] In fact, there was a strong body of opinion in Britain that was sympathetic to the Hungarian refugees even if Vajda did not immediately experience it. Initially the government was opposed to the entry of the Hungarians but it was recognised by some senior civil servants that it would be difficult both domestically and internationally to turn away these victims of Soviet oppression. As one Home Office official noted, they had been 'crushed by brute force after a desperate resistance, and public opinion is entirely dominated by admiration for their heroism. We shall be expected to do something for them, and have no chance at all of being allowed to refuse.'[5] Eventually Britain accepted just under 22,000 of the 200,000 Hungarians who had fled their country.[6]

Nushin Arbabzadah, who grew up in Afghanistan during the Soviet occupation and now works in the British media, emphasises how most refugees are simply ordinary people. Their very ordinariness and normality, however, make it hard for people to perceive them as genuine refugees and instead label them as '"illegal immigrants in disguise" or "bogus asylum seekers"'. As she perceptively notes, 'they simply don't fit into the heroic image of the refugee'. Instead most are 'victims of proxy wars, dictatorships and forms of intolerance accepted as the local status quo'. She links their experiences to that of Victor Hugo on becoming a refugee in Britain in the mid-nineteenth century: 'one does not even have the satisfaction of having been oppressed by something great'.[7]

Even in the case of the Hungarian refugees, where a strong Cold War, anti-Communist narrative existed at a popular level explaining their plight (and reasons for their flight), sympathy and understanding soon waned. In November 1956, the liberal newspaper, *News Chronicle*, implored its readers to 'Remember Hungary!'. Its appeal for support was accompanied by a photograph of an elderly refugee in a temporary camp with the caption 'Once he was somebody … Now he's just a refugee.'[8] Such appeals brought forth many offers of financial support and practical help for the refugees arriving in Britain. Yet once the initial support had faded, the Hungarian refugees in Britain were treated increasingly as problematic aliens who were encouraged to disperse and find work (for the men, largely as coal miners) or to re-emigrate to North America. Eventually one-third would move on or return home.[9] It was in the context of empathy as well as lack of understanding and indifference that young film-maker Robert Vaz made his autobiographical *Refuge England* (1959). It was a powerful portrait outlining the dislocation and alienation of arriving in London from Hungary. While Vaz's film has a happy ending – he finds the person whose address is the only contact in his place of refuge – the picture he presents is of the loneliness of the individual refugee and the loss of family, friends and language. In the film, Vaz is at pains to emphasise that he left because he had no choice, not because he wanted to leave.[10] Yet in spite of the efforts of Vajda and Vaz, and the hundreds of volunteers who looked after the Hungarian refugees, their story has largely been forgotten in the wider narrative of migrant settlement in Britain and more generally in the worlds of history and heritage.[11] Such amnesia has political resonance beyond this specific group of refugees.

In the battle to limit the number of asylum seekers granted refugee status in Britain, the barriers that have been erected consist not only of those constructed legally by a narrow interpretation of the 1951 United Nations Convention Relating to the Status of Refugees, but also cultural ones through comparisons drawn with past such arrivals.[12] As noted, the official and standard narrative is that 'The UK has a long standing tradition of giving shelter to those fleeing persecution in other parts of the world, and refugees in turn have contributed much to our society and culture.'[13] Meeting this criteria particularly are Huguenot refugees escaping French persecution following the revocation of the Edict of Nantes in 1685 and Jews finding refuge from the Third Reich. Even if the individuals involved were not famous or prominent, these groups of refugees are now perceived as having been, to return to Hugo's expression, 'oppressed by something great'.[14]

Yet it is only with hindsight that the Huguenots and Jews are viewed as being genuine and deserving refugees. In reality, at the time they had to fight hard to gain recognition and respect and the term 'refugee', used first in the English language to describe the Huguenots and to evoke sympathy, had become tainted by the Nazi era. The German Jewish philosopher, Hannah Arendt, who had fled first to France and then to America, started her forceful statement 'We Refugees' (1943) by stating

> In the first place, we don't like to be called 'refugees'. We ourselves call each other 'newcomers' or 'immigrants' … A refugee used to be a person driven to seek refuge because of some act committed or some political opinion held … With us the meaning of the term 'refugee' has changed. Now 'refugees' are those of us who have been so unfortunate as to arrive in a new country without means and have to be helped by refugee committees.

Arendt wrote against the lack of agency associated with being a refugee and also the stigma attached to the term. With regards to the latter, she noted that 'Our newspapers are papers for "Americans of German language"; and, as far as I know, there is not and never was any club founded by Hitler-persecuted people whose name indicated that its members were refugees.'[15]

In contrast, today a high and increasing percentage of the members of the Association of Jewish Refugees in Britain, formed in 1941, are the children and grandchildren of those who came during the 1930s. In this particular case, family connections to this now celebrated refugee movement bring honour and recognition, just as there is pride in having Huguenot ancestors (or as is somewhat dubiously promoted, a 'Huguenot pedigree'),[16] no matter how distant and obscure. Indeed, it has been noted by Ruth Whelan that in Britain and Ireland, the 'only remnant of their original social identity that descendants of Huguenots retain today is their genealogies and their foreign names, and in many cases, even their names have been assimilated to the naming processes of the receiving society'.[17] As Whelan comments, that is to 'tell the story from the end, rather than beginning'. Constructing a linear history 'from being foreign to being assimilated' does not do justice to the complexities of Huguenot experiences – including that of rejection from the host communities – away from France.[18]

It has been possible, once the initial xenophobia and distrust has been overcome, to construct a narrative with these two particular groups that meets wider expectations, a process facilitated by the ongoing antagonism in British cultural memory to their places of origin. In the case of the Huguenots, it reflected the power of anti-French and anti-Catholic rhetoric in defining Britishness. The Huguenot refugees were thus 'living reminders to their new countrymen of the enduring threat of Catholic persecution'.[19] In 1824 one of the first memoirs of a Huguenot refugee – Jean Migault – appeared in English. Its publisher informed the reader that it was an account of

> foreign despotism – a despotism which it is apprehended there exists a disposition to perpetuate in neighbouring nations [which] may tend to quicken in the breast of every Briton, a sense of gratitude to the Disposer of events, for having cast his lot in this free and Christian country – free because she is Christian.[20]

More recently such tendencies have been apparent concerning memories of Jewish refugees from Hitler. The Second World War and Britain's anti-Nazi struggle, alongside a cruder anti-Germanism, have been of central importance in constructing post-war identities.[21]

In both the Huguenot and Jewish cases, however, the process of nationalistic 'othering' could be so virulent that it would impact even upon those who had come to Britain as victims of persecution. The Huguenots were seen by some contemporaries as Papists in disguise.[22] At the end of the Second World War an attempt was made to remove 'alien' Jews from Hampstead, a campaign that was notable for both its virulent anti-Germanism *and* its antisemitism.[23] There was a particular need therefore to emphasise in the discourse created by these two groups and their supporters that they were genuine *refugees*. That, in the twenty-first century, this is now largely taken for granted should not disguise the earlier struggle to establish their 'deserving' status in places of asylum. But that it *is* now accepted, especially in the case of refugees from Nazism, can be illustrated by the twenty-first century instrumentalisation of such memories by British politicians of very different perspectives.

In September 2010 Ed Miliband became the first Jewish leader of the Labour Party. In his first speech as leader, Miliband began and put great emphasis on his family background and especially his parents' escape from the continent during the war:

My love for this country comes from this story. Two young people fled the darkness that had engulfed the Jews across Europe and in Britain they found the light of liberty. They arrived with nothing. This country gave them everything ... And they took hope and opportunity. They worked hard; they got on.[24]

Seven years earlier, Michael Howard had become the first (non-converted) Jewish leader of the Conservative Party. He, too, emphasised his family origins: 'Britain has always offered a home to genuine refugees and to families who want to work hard. I know – my family was one.'[25] At the Conservative Party conference in 2004 he made even more explicit his refugee roots, emphasising the murder of his grandmother during the Holocaust and, in contrast, the entry granted to his father and grandfather by Britain: 'everything I have, and everything I am, I owe to this country.'[26]

In both cases, such heartfelt re-telling of family history conformed to the classic refugee narrative – that is of persecution–flight–asylum–integration–contribution. In typical ambivalent fashion, however, it was accompanied by justifications for the control of contemporary migration to Britain – shrill in the case of Howard and restrained with Miliband. Indeed, utilising such family stories can work in two directions. In 2010, Donna Covey, Chief Executive of the Refugee Council, responded that 'We are delighted that in Ed Miliband's first speech as Labour leader he acknowledged his parents' refugee background as having a having a significant influence on his values and strength of character.' This, she added, was 'testament to the outstanding contribution refugees have brought to the UK over the years'.[27] In the same year, however, as noted in Chapter 1, Tony Blair's memoir, *A Journey*, made clear that making such linkages between 'then' and 'now' was simply wrong and the result of either naivety or wilful distortion on behalf of pro-asylum activists in the late twentieth century. Those claiming asylum, argued the former Prime Minister, had no real basis for doing so, unlike those deserving refugees fleeing from Hitler and the Nazis.[28]

The reality, as Blair indirectly acknowledged, was that it took time, effort (and hindsight in the form of post-war knowledge of the Holocaust) to accept the 'genuineness' of Jewish refugees from Nazism. Indeed, one irony of Michael Howard's polemical discourse aimed at asylum seekers and other migrants in the 2005 General Election was that it was exposed in the preceeding months that his grandfather had come to Britain 'illegally'. It was a reflection not of his dishonesty but the prejudice against East European Jews – his father and grandfather were Romanian – operating in British immigration procedures during the inter-war years.[29] The details of Howard's family story will be pursued more thoroughly in Chapter 6 of this study. Much earlier, similar dilemmas faced the Huguenots in establishing their authenticity as refugees when arriving in

Britain. Jean Migault, for example, stated firmly at the beginning of his memoir that he was a 'wretched victim of a tyranny as cruel as it was unprovoked'.[30] And as part of this strategy of gaining acceptance, descriptions of the journey have played a crucial role.

The nature of Huguenot journeys

Anywhere between 35,000 to 50,000 Huguenots came to Britain in the last quarter of the seventeenth century. Along with the thousands who had settled beforehand, they totalled roughly 1 per cent of the country's population. As with many migrant groups, they concentrated in specific areas of Britain, the largest number – 20,000 – being located in Spitalfield in the East End of London.[31] Roughly one-quarter of all the Huguenot refugees who left France in the last decades of the seventeenth century came to Britain. More gener-ally 'A fifth or more – 150,000 to 200,000 – of all French Protestants went into exile to the Swiss cantons, various German principalities, the Netherlands, the British Isles, and eventually to North America, South Africa, Scandinavia and Russia.'[32]

There is no doubting the scale of persecution the Huguenots were fleeing from. It included mass and gendered violence from the *dragonnades*, forced conversions, and discrimination including removal from state positions. Punishment included working as galley slaves as well as the use of instru-ments of torture and humiliation. The galley ships in particular were used to expose the horror of the Huguenot situation. Jean Marteilhe, from Bergerac, was condemned to the French galleys operating from Dunkirk to Ostend. His autobiography, outlining the misery of this slavery, was published in different editions during the eighteenth and nineteenth centuries in Holland, Britain, America and France. With graphic descriptions, Marteilhe explained to his readers that

> In truth, it is a terrible thing to see on each galley three hundred naked men, who all row in good time and shake their chains, the noise of which is mingled with their yells and shrieks, and makes those who have never before witnessed such a sight shudder.[33]

It remains that 'In the countries of refuge, narratives about the "poor refugees" proved helpful in negotiating privileges that would have been closed to normal immigrants.' Internally, in family and collective memory, emphasising perse-cution reinforced the 'Huguenots' exclusive identity [which] also served the survival of the refugees as a group'.[34] Underlying their narratives of suffering and refuge was the strong Calvinist conviction of the Huguenots that they were amongst the 'chosen'. It was reflected in a sermon preached during 1682 in the Huguenot temple of the Savoy in London addressed to Charles II. Referring to 'your colony of French Protestants whom the Tempest casts ashore every day in our harbours', their journey was given Biblical significance: 'They are Israelites crossing the sea to retire into Canaan; they are merchants of the Gospel who have come to seek in our kingdom the Kingdom of Heaven.'[35]

Not surprisingly, as Bernard Cottret muses in the conclusion to his history of the Huguenots in England, the 'figure of the Jew – an often mythical figure, indeed – constantly appears in my records: along with the related theme of dispersion or the crossing of the Red Sea.'[36] Illusions to the Biblical Exodus, as has become apparent already within this study, were never far from being utilised within the self-narration of migrant journeys. This tendency was almost inevitable within a group such as these Protestant refugees with their strong religious faith and recourse to Biblical analogies. Yet Huguenot journeys away from persecution were also experienced in the secular realm, and their accounts and those of their historians emphasise the real physical dangers inherent in escape from France alongside their spiritual dimension. If, as Jeremy Leigh suggests, the tension between the physical and spiritual journey is represented in the drama 'that defines the meaning of being Jewish',[37] this is equally so within Huguenot narratives.

Yosef Yerushalmi has highlighted the paradox that 'although Judaism throughout the ages was absorbed with the meaning of history, historiography itself played at best an ancillary role among the Jews, and often no role at all'. He adds that 'while memory of the past was always a central component of Jewish experience, the historian was not its primary custodian.'[38] Modernity changed that balance between history and memory from the early nineteenth century onwards. A similar process can be detected within Huguenot historiography and wider memory work. As Carolyn Lougee Chappell highlights, the Calvinist doctrine entailed a denial of history and an emphasis on predestination. And like many of the groups in this study, the Huguenot refugees left few personal accounts – Chappell's extensive research has only located fifty-one narratives, a good sample of which will be explored in this chapter alongside other sources. Moreover, these surviving accounts are hardly representative of the Huguenot refugees as a whole: 'A minute swath of the social hierarchy finds voice through them: almost exclusively ministers and nobles, from time to time a rare artisan.' Chappell also observes that 'female voices are nearly absent' – just eight were written by women.[39] Further limiting is the detail that the majority of these sources are what she labels 'escape memoirs' and not full autobiographies.[40]

These accounts of escape often utilised Biblical analogies. They were used to garner group solidarity and the continuation of family Huguenot identity across the generations. Chappell shows this at work in the case of Marie de La Rochefoucald, dame de Champagne, who wrote a short account of her refugee journey within her account book between the years 1690 and 1717.[41] The narrative begins by highlighting the reasons behind her family's flight. Persecution in France with dragoons quartered at her house and the threat of forced conversion is dealt with clearly but briefly. More attention is given to the escape and the perils entailed. First, the family moved from their home in Saintonge to La Rochelle where she placed her four daughters and two youngest sons in a ship bound for England: 'A cask was emptied of wine, which was thrown into the sea, and they were hidden in its place … The departure of my children was very secret'. Several months later, Marie with her eldest son went on another vessel bound for south-west England:

> We were put down in the hold on some salt, where we stayed hidden away for eight days at anchor. The ship was searched without our being found. We set sail and arrived at Falmouth eight days later, not without fear and many perils.[42]

As with most accounts of refugee journeys, especially those who have suffered forms of religious persecution, the contrast between the place of persecution and the place of asylum is given particular meaning by Marie: 'The English and refugees in the locality received us wonderfully, coming out to meet us and offering us their help. We felt as if we had left what is called purgatory and arrived in paradise'. Gratitude was given further emphasis by highlighting religious freedom in England: 'The liberty to worship God openly, no longer to fear the dragoons and churchmen, seemed to us a great happiness'.[43] Likewise, Isaac Dumont de Bostaquet, Huguenot nobleman and soldier, who eventually settled in Ireland, wrote in his memoirs that he 'felt a profound sense of peace during my delightful stay in The Hague. My family and I needed nothing and life seemed sweet to us even though we were refugees'.[44]

Chappell argues persuasively that Marie de La Rochefoucald's memoir is 'so close to orality because, rather than composing the escape account as she wrote, [the author] actually composed it orally as she told it and retold it to live audiences'. The audience was likely to be fellow Huguenots as 'Telling their escape was the Huguenot fugitives' rite of passage: the passage being the escape, the rite the telling'. The giving of testimony itself was a semi-religious act, outlining 'the circumstances of their lives and faith before, during, and after their flight. On the basis of their narration, they would be formally accepted, or not, back into the fold'.[45] Silences – in this case the leaving behind of a baby and the failings of Marie's husband – would have been enforced by communal expectations so that a standardised 'genre of the escape account' was constructed by repetition and remoulding the story. Beyond these oral versions, adds Chappell, 'published accounts would become well known and may have served as models for escapees who wrote their memoirs later in their lives, at some distance from the escape'.[46]

Marie was not alone in obsessively narrating and re-narrating the Huguenot's forced leaving of France. Isaac Minet, whose experiences were related in Chapter 1, wrote two such accounts – first in 1722 and then a longer version fifteen years later. As his direct descendant, William Minet (a leading early scholar of the Huguenot refugees) noted in 1892, the fullness of detail 'with which Isaac Minet has told us of his escape to England ... make us regret the slenderness of the information he gives us respecting his parents and his own early life in France'.[47] For Isaac Minet, such painful re-telling must have had a strong impetus. Writing in 1737, some 'fifty years since we landed at Dover', while 'time doth wear out matters', the 'terrible thing' 'of our being in prison and per[s]ecuted by dragoons' was still clearly remembered, as was the need to make sense of the trauma to himself, his descendants and those around him.[48]

In his first narrative, written in 1722, the description of the journey is extremely brief:

> After having tryed severall times before our imprisonment and since to gitt away we did at last embarque at night [the] 1 A[u]gust 1686 and gott to Dover at 8 in [the] morning, for w[hi]ch I shall ever praise the goodness of God whom I begg to forgive me my faults for [the sake] of Jesus Christ.[49]

The second narrative of 1737 and perhaps with a larger audience in mind, was far more detailed and considered. The *danger* of the escape journey was especially highlighted, beginning with the departure two miles from Calais when boarding the boat to take them to England:

> I went to [the] harbour & there saw a vessell w[hi]ch was come from dunkirk & was to goe to sea the next tide ... I saw a detachment made of 25 soldiers & an officer to goe along the sea side to guard [the] coast & prevent protestants from going away.[50]

Managing to avoid detection, the extended Minet family, twenty-three in total, managed to leave France. The risk of detection, however, had not disappeared: 'about 2 [hours] after we left [the] shore we spyed a Sloop & fearing [the] dunkirkcruser, [the sailors] spread a saile over over all [the] passengers heads who layd down in [the] boat'.[51]

The mood of the testimony then shifts to a redemptive tone and the description of the journey thereafter was brisk: '[the] fine wind & w[e]ather being favorable we landed at dover on [the] shore about 8 of the clock [the] same morning for w[hi]ch mercy I shall ever give thanks to God, it being a very great deliverance'. The party were met 'full of tears of joy' by Isaac's family who had come to England earlier. Also greeting them were 'many more of our friend[s] who rec[eived] us as brethren saved from [the] great persecution'.[52] Isaac soon established himself as a leading member of Dover society, becoming a freeman of the town in 1698. He never, however, forgot his roots and particularly his journey to England: the family coat of arms 'depicts their escape from Calais in a rowing boat'.[53] The same image was used in the family 'Seal of the Town of Dover'. Reflecting pride in 'pedigree' as well as their new local patriotism, it was modelled on the Minet 'Seal of the Town of Calais' from 1225 which also portrayed a small boat.[54] Finally, his tombstone in St Mary's Church, Dover, confirmed this narrative of refugeedom: 'Here lieth the Body of Mr Isaac MINET Merchant. He was born at Calais the 5th of September 1660, From whence being persecuted for the sake of the Protestant Religion, he fled to this Place for Refuge 1686'.[55]

Chappell rightly highlights the internal Huguenot readership of such memoirs and escape accounts (and one could add memorials such as that to the Minets), whether they be at a communal or family level. It might also be suggested that they had a potential audience *outside* the Huguenot sphere as with the detailed description of persecution and flight in Isaac Minet's second narrative. This might be to elicit sympathy and thereby to aid integration in places of refuge, especially beyond the early days of settlement, or, alternatively, to present the Huguenots as an example that others might want to follow. As noted, one of the earliest accounts published in English was that of Jean Migault, a village schoolmaster at Mougon and a lay reader at the local chapel. Because he lacked literary fluency, it has been suggested that his memoir, written soon after his arrival in Holland, 'was intended solely for the eyes of his own family'. A different reading, however, is also possible.[56] His emphasis is on persecution and the difficulties and dangers of escape and the impossible dilemmas facing the Huguenots: 'Could any oppression be more intolerable than that which we endured? [G]oaded to distraction if we remained, and punished as malefactors if we flew!' Migault then dealt very briefly with the re-establishment of family life in Holland.[57]

Migault's 'narrative of sufferings' thus conforms to the 'escape account' genre proposed by Chappell. He died in Emden in 1707 but his memoir appeared in various editions across the nineteenth century.[58] Its successful publication history suggests that there was a lively market for Huguenot autobiographies dealing with persecution and refugeedom and that the author may have had this in mind, even if subconsciously, when writing his account. A similar tendency is apparent in another memoir that was written in the early eighteenth century and then published and regularly re-published from the

1830s onwards. Indeed, it could be argued that although it took more than a century for his memoirs to appear in print, its subsequent iconic status in Huguenot refugee historiography puts it alongside the migrant autobiographical works of Mary Antin and John Mitchel studied in Chapter 2.

The Reverend Jaques Fontaine (1658 to 1728) was a minister from Saintonge. From a fourth generation of French Protestants, he was of noble origin. His memoir was ostensibly published at the request of his children across the Atlantic so that their offspring would be inspired and thereby continue as practising Huguenots. Yet the detailed and crafted nature of his autobiography suggest that Fontaine was thinking beyond his family and future descendants as potential readers. Written in 1722, they were published for the first time in 1838 in America as *A Tale of the Huguenots* and then throughout the twentieth century in various editions on both sides of the Atlantic.[59]

While much quoted within histories of the Huguenots, the approach taken to them has often lacked critical distance, marginalising their constructed nature. As Chappell notes more generally in her astute close reading of the Champagne family memoirs – a second was written by Marie's daughter, Suzanne – 'Previous studies of Huguenot memoirs have understood them as more or less straightforward descriptions of the events they recount.'[60] An example of this tendency is found in the case of Jaques Fountaine whose autobiography has rather simplistically been described as 'almost unassailable in its accuracy'.[61]

The thirteenth chapter of his memoirs was devoted to the intensification of persecution in 1685: 'There was no pretence of justice. The dragoons raided and pillaged every Protestant. There is no example in the past ages of such unchecked cruelty.'[62] Fontaine attempted to stir physical resistance but, realising he had little support, he justified the mass departure of the Huguenots by Biblical analogy: 'They forced the true people of Israel from their spiritual Egypt … [T]he ark of God has been driven from France, their house is no longer glorious, and death and dishonour have taken its place.' There could be no regrets at leaving their physical homeland: 'We are happy that we have left this cursed Babylon, for we have not shared her plagues.'[63]

The next chapter of Fontaine's memoirs then focused on the journey of escape following the revocation of the Edict of Nantes: 'I saw that it was necessary either to die or to leave France.'[64] After several failed attempts to leave by boat in which the author thanks God for their failure to be found by the French authorities (had they been so, 'Those they captured were sent to the galleys, the women to convents'),[65] Fontaine and a group of fellow Huguenots managed to leave on a small vessel from La Rochelle. Eventually they caught up with an English frigate, the captain of which had promised them safe passage. Despite the risks, Fontaine had no fear: 'As always, prayer was my resource. I was sure that God would deliver me from this danger. Suddenly I thought of a scheme to which God in His infinite mercy gave success and which achieved our deliverance.' The English frigate took them on board on 30 November 1685, which was a 'memorable day for us who escaped our enemy, who had the power not only to kill our bodies, but also to damn our souls'.[66]

After eleven days on board, they arrived at Appledore in the Bristol Channel, near Barnstaple, hungry, thirsty and almost penniless. Again, his narrative melded the everyday with the spiritual to explain their survival:

> God, who had not brought us to a safe country to have us die there of hunger, touched the hearts of the foremost residents of Barnstaple, who sent for all 12 of us, took each of us into their homes, and treated us with incredible kindness and friendship. God provided us fathers and mothers, brothers and sisters, among strangers.[67]

Immediately, Fontaine saw an opportunity for economic advancement, recognising the cheapness of wheat in Britain compared to France. Thereafter, his memoirs outline not only Fontaine's triumphs in promoting the Huguenot Protestant faith as a minister in England and then in Ireland but also his entrepreneurial acumen and commitment to hard work through a series of business ventures.[68]

Such virtues were later perceived as 'inherently' Huguenot characteristics and were extolled especially in the mid-Victorian era by the apostle of self-help, Samuel Smiles, in his detailed and much reprinted history of the group.[69] This positive representation has continued until what has been recently the largely celebratory historiography of Huguenot refugees and their descendants. Thus in a major publication to mark the tercentary of the revocation of the Edict of Nantes, it was suggested that Jaques Fontaine's 'career in exile demonstrates Huguenot enterprise and perseverence'.[70] While it has been noted that 'Jaques' many adventures … at times seemed like fiction',[71] the dominant use of his memoir has been to accept 'its realism and truthfulness'.[72] In fact, the memoirs of Jaques Fontaine are a classic example confirming the analysis of Samuel and Thompson that 'Any life story, written or oral, more or less dramatically, is in one sense a personal mythology, a self-justification. And all embody and illustrate character ideals'. Such stories, they continue, 'very commonly serve as parables, exemplifying courage or kindness or strength'.[73]

To summarise: Fontaine's memoirs and those of other Huguenot refugees had an 'internal', Huguenot and family purpose – that of showing the importance of faith, continuity and family/group loyalty. They were also part of a discourse for wider consumption in which the Huguenots were seen as deserving refuge and of benefit to the receiving society. Indeed, the *usefulness* of the Huguenots was emphasised by their supporters following 1685. In 1708, for example, a supporter of the campaign to grant a 'General Naturalization' to the Huguenots stated that it was 'very evident to the Commerce of Great Britain has been much increased by the manufactures of the French Refugies have established there'. Naturalisation would be 'not only very usefull, but very necessary'.[74] The narrative of a miraculous escape to England, followed by exceptional economic contribution was even more pronounced in the case of Henri de Portal, a story that is now firmly established as part of local – though significantly not of national – heritage in Britain.[75]

Much retold within Hampshire folklore since the Victorian era, it has been suggested that 'The history of the Portal family ... reads like a romance'.[76] A prominent Protestant aristocratic family from Poitiers in the South of France, the Portals faced increasing persecution from the sixteenth century onwards, intensifying following the Revocation. In the words of Samuel Smiles, Henri's father, Louis, 'to escape the horrors of the dragonnades ... set out with his wife and five children to take refuge on his estate in the Cevennes'. There was to be no safety here as the dragoons 'pursued the family to their retreat, overtook them, cut down the father and mother and one of the children, and burnt to the ground the house in which they had taken refuge'.[77] The story of the surviving children is then told succinctly, if not fully accurately, by Stephen Terry, squire of the small Hampshire village of Dummer, and a prolific diarist in the Victorian era. It reveals how the Huguenot escape narrative genre had now gained wider currency outside this religious minority:

> an old nurse hid the children in an oven, and baffled the soldiers. They were then concealed in wine flasks and smuggled by faithful friends and servitors on a lugger. They were eventually naturalized in England, and with French workmen started a paper mill here.[78]

Smiles took his information from a family memoir written by one of the descendants of the youngest brother, Pierre (who had remained in France), published in Paris in 1860.[79] In England, Sir William Portal, a prominent political and military figure in Hampshire, and grandson of Henri, produced in the early twentieth century a broader study of the settlement of Protestant refugees in Southampton since 1567.[80] It was that year when Queen Elizabeth I granted these Huguenots the use of the Chapel of St Julien as 'L'EgliseWallonne', later known as the French church and part of the medieval complex of God's House in the town's Winkle Street.[81] In fact, the Walloons were actively encouraged to come to Southampton to revive the trading fortunes of the port. Sir William's book included an additional section on 'the papermaking industry as practised by the Southampton refugees' within which, not surprisingly, the Portals featured prominently.[82]

Such family histories reflected a wider tendency within the Huguenot diaspora: 'The more Huguenots lost their privileges and their distinctive characteristics of language and culture within a host state, the more they had to rely on the fostering of memory and heritage as a means of salvaging something of a "Huguenot identity" within a community into which they had been assimilated.'[83] For example, during the mid-nineteenth century a series of historical novels on the Huguenots were published in Britain by those of French Protestant descent.[84] Contribution and loyalty to the country of refuge were particularly emphasised in informal family histories but also in the work of national bodies including the Huguenot Society of America (1883), the Huguenot Society of London (1885) and the German Huguenot Society (1890).[85] Like the Jews, a more secular generation of Huguenots (or individuals of Huguenot origin) were vigorous in their pursuit of history from the late nineteenth century onwards. The Jewish Historical Society of England was formed in 1893 and the American Jewish Historical Society a year earlier.[86]

In both the family accounts of those of Huguenot background, including the Portals, and those who saw them as an example to others, such as Samuel Smiles, explicit descriptions of persecution and of the subsequent miraculous escape were highlighted. The aim was to establish the authenticity of Huguenot flight, their innocence and their deserved refugee status. The Revocation, fumed Smiles, 'was a proclamation of war by the armed against the unarmed – a war against peaceable men, women, and children'. Smiles utilised universal terms to appeal to his Victorian readership. The assault on the Huguenots was 'a war against property, against family, against society, against public morality, and, more than all, against the rights of conscience'.[87] Listing 'these horrors of the past, these tortures inflicted upon innocent women and children', was necessary, argued Smiles, because without that knowledge it would be 'impossible to understand the extraordinary exodus of the French people which shortly followed, and which constituted one of the most important historical events of the seventeenth century'.[88]

The dangers and suffering of the Huguenot journey played an important role in such narratives, especially in accounts published in the mid-nineteenth century in Britain and America. At a time of strong anti-Catholicism in both countries, as well as economic growth and transformation, the Huguenots and their persecution could be exploited at a popular level as a usable past. In 1854, the English translation of Charles Weiss's *History of the French Protestant Refugees* was published in New York. His account highlighted how the fear of the galleys caused the Huguenots to take great risks 'in the hope to escape from their persecutors: 'They trusted themselves sometimes to open boats, and attempted sea voyages, the very thought of which at another time would have made them shudder.'[89] Weiss thus highlighted the story of the Count de

Maranie [or Marance] who 'crossed the British Channel, in midwinter, in a boat of seven tons, with forty persons, among whom were several pregnant women'. A storm occurred and they

> remained long at sea, without provisions, and with no hope of succor, tortured by hunger … reduced for their sole nourishment to a little melted snow, with which they quenched their burning thirst, and moistened the parched lips of their weeping children, until, half dead, they landed on the shores of England.[90]

This account was then reproduced in the preface to the American version of Jean Marteilhe's galley slave narrative and in Samuel Smiles' *The Huguenots*, both published in the 1860s.[91] Smiles added further to this picture of misery and suffering, noting that the 'lord of Castelfranc … was less fortunate than the Count de Marance. He was captured at sea, in an open boat, while attempting to escape to England with his wife and family. Three of his sons and three of his daughters thus taken were sent to the Caribee Islands as slaves.'[92]

The Huguenot 'escape account' hidden in a wine barrel has already been noted with regard to the autobiographical writings of Marie de La Rochefoucold. Similarly it features promonently within Hampshire and stories of Henri de Portal. So common is this trope representing the dangers of the Huguenot journey that it has been parodied by Richard Bean in his satire of English xenophobia, *England People Very Nice* (2009). De Gasgoigne, the stock Huguenot character, explains that 'The barrel stories are exaggerated. I paid passage from Dieppe.' Another character is disappointed to hear the reality, responding 'How prosaic.'[93] Bean might be accused of insensitivity towards the Huguenot journey but he is right to point out the role of mythology in this particular refugee flight. The Courtauld family have become one of the most famous examples of Huguenot economic success stories, in this case as goldsmiths and silversmiths and then in textile manufacture. Augustin Courtauld, a merchant of Saint Pierre d'Oleron, left France for England in 1686. The particular timing was linked to the death of his wife that year, possibly giving birth to their son. 'The baby was left behind with his grandfather … despite the romantic story that he was smuggled over in a basket of vegetables. The boy … only joined his father in 1696 after his grandfather was taken seriously ill and feared he might die.'[94] This reality was somewhat 'prosaic' – in Bean's terminology. To work at a popular level, however, the Huguenot escape narrative requires drama, excitement and danger. In this respect, the wine barrel is as emblematic of the migrant journey and its horrors for the Huguenots as the coffin ship is for the Irish. Applied to Henri de Portal, it adds pathos to his 'rags to riches' fairytale romance.

Memory works

Narratives of Henri's life story also incorporated those Huguenots who had supported him at the French church when he first arrived in Southampton 'penniless and without friends'. In the south coast port, Henri de Portal (later anglicised to Henri Portal or Henry Portall) learnt the skill of papermaking from a fellow Huguenot, Gerard de Vaux, who had left France much earlier.[95] Henri's integration and economic success were speedy. In Winchester during 1711 he took an Oath of Allegiance 'required by an Act for Naturalizing foreign Protestants' and he set up his own mill in Laverstoke, Hampshire.[96] The popular local historian, Elsie Sandell, incorporated his subsequent success in her account of *Southampton Through the Ages* (1960):

> Such was his skill that in 1724 he obtained the monopoly for manu-
> facturing the special paper for the Bank of England notes, a privilege
> which his descendants, who carry on the mill, still hold. The Portals
> have indeed served their adopted country well, not only in Hampshire
> but in a national way in war and peace.[97]

Sandell was deeply attached to the memory of these French Protestants, suggesting that 'It requires but little imagination to see those Huguenot refugees wending their way along our old High Street to Winkle Street and their quiet church whence they drew spiritual help and encouragement.' Hers was a mutually comforting narrative: 'They had reached a safe haven here and they wrought industriously for the town of their adoption.' She concluded her brief study of these refugees by listing their achievements as 'School teachers, ministers, serge-makers, silk weavers, paper-makers, merchants, soldiers, sailors and government officials', adding evocatively that 'the pattern of their lives is woven for ever into the story of Southampton'.[98] Yet if inclusion of this romantic narrative is increasingly acknowledged within memory work on the history and heritage of Hampshire (where a recent walking guide simply describes Henri Portal as a 'Huguenot success story', the walk around the River Test 'showcasing an entrepreneurial Huguenot paper-maker'),[99] it has not happened much beyond the county.

It is true that there were some prominent nineteenth-century British historians, especially Thomas Macaulay, who emphasised the '"heroic, empire-building" character of the Huguenots'.[100] Unlike in America, however, this role was rarely acknowledged, other than tokenistically, in general British historiography which largely ignored the professional and popular writings on Huguenot refugee movement and settlement. It reflected the lack of acceptance of immigration (albeit, in the American case, of the right kind – that is white, Anglo-Saxon and Protestant) as part of the nation's story. And such marginalisation has continued until recently: 'there has been almost a void in historical writing on the Huguenots in Britain' since the 1890s. In 1985, Robin Gwynn complained that 'The contribution and assimilation of England's first "réfugiés", indeed their very existence, has ceased to interest historians concerned with the mainstream of English history.'[101]

Gwynn explained this lacuna by the failure in the twentieth century to take earlier religious devotion seriously, yet it can be equally explained by the unwillingness of historians and society as a whole to accept that immigration, and within it the movement of refugees, has long been a feature of the British past. In anger at the denial of the 'intricate intertwined history' of Britain and India, and the construction of British Asian migrants of the 1950s and beyond 'as new people', Ziauddin Sardar comments that 'Forgetting is no accident'. He then rehearses the long-standing history of and loyalty of Asians to Britain.[102] Similar to British Jewish historiography and more recently Afro-Caribbean and Asian historiography, the need to initially explain and justify presence, and then to find a place subsequently in the 'island story' – in spite of widespread indifference or ignorance – has led to a defensive and apologetic construction of Huguenot heritage in Britain. The emphasis has been on persecution in and flight from France and contribution, gratitude and loyalty to Britain. That Huguenot motivations for leaving, and who stayed and who left, were often complex, as were Huguenot identities in the place of settlement, has been obscured, as has the experience of those who were less prominent and successful.

Only in the last quarter century has a more sophisticated analysis emerged, prompted in part by the tercentenary commemorations of 1985 which 'encouraged an outpouring of research and scholarly writings about the Walloon and Huguenots in Britain'.[103] At its best, it has enabled a close reading of Huguenot refugee memoirs in which their internal dynamics and emphasis on certain narrative devices have been revealed. Yet such work also has an impetus beyond the internal dynamics of Huguenot historiography. The desire to promote multiculturalism has led to an instrumentisation of history, and the Huguenots have proved to be a success story in which the nuances of past migration patterns are obscured. In 1996, for example, the Commission for Racial Equality produced a lavishly illustrated book and travelling exhibition: *Roots of the Future: Ethnic Diversity in the Making of Britain.* A section was devoted to 'Protestant Refugees' in which a standardised narrative was provided: 'The Huguenots brought with them the arts of making crystal, fine paper …, dyes, watches and clocks, spectacles and scientific instruments, boots, hats and wigs, and silk.' In addition they were 'distinguished writers, scholars and artists … who broadened the nation's intellectual life' as well as playing a 'vital role in the development of banking'. And while initially setting up their own schools, churches and charities, 'in time, both newcomers and natives changed, learning from each other and gradually becoming part of a new and richer culture.'[104]

Recent heritage work, including that at the Museum of London's new £20 million galleries (2010), further emphasises the skill and magnificence of the Huguenot contribution through the display of eighteenth-century silk costumes and the precision of its watch-making.[105] It builds on an earlier landmark temporary exhibition, 'The Quiet Conquest: The Huguenots 1685 to 1985' which, according to the Museum's director, 'celebrate[d] their rich contribution to all aspects of the nation's life: the arts, crafts, commerce, science and industry.'[106]

In 2000, a conference was held to mark the 450th anniversary of the charter granted by Edward VI to give 'strangers' the right to hold Reformed services in their own place of worship in England. Prince Charles, in a foreword to the conference volume, was even more explicit about the potential of the Huguenot experience to provide a present-day model:

> Even those of us who rejoice in the multicultural character of today's United Kingdom often forget that this character – and our tradition of tolerance, of which Britain can be proud – are not new phenomena. It helps to be reminded that today's waves of refugees are only the latest of many.

He noted that 'our understanding of contemporary opportunities and challenges … can be enormously enhanced by a better grasp of our own history', suggesting an exploration of East End topography as a prompt: 'A walk through Spitalfields, past weaver's house, synagogue and Bangladeshi grocer's, is a good start.'[107] The use of Isaac Minet's story as a young Huguenot made good within Robert Winder's pro-immigration *Bloody Foreigners* (2004) has been noted earlier. Winder's study of migration to Britain written at the height of anti-asylum seeker 'madness' also briefly mentions Henri Portal's similar rags to riches story and others in which young Huguenots were smuggled into England in wine casks.[108]

In this respect, it is worth returning to Henri de Portal: his story has been simplified in its telling and re-telling. This is not to deny the vile persecution inflicted on his family in Languedoc or the dangers of his journey to England. The domination of 'escape' in Huguenot narratives, however, overshadows other factors, including longer term movement, in much the same way as the famine does in memory work concerning Irish migration. The pitiful arrival of young Henri in Southampton is treated as almost providential. Yet the fortuitousness of his embarkation in the port was hardly accidental. Southampton, as noted, had a well-established Huguenot church and many of its prominent members were established paper-makers who had settled there well before the Revocation.[109] It would seem almost certain that Gerard de Vaux, who apprenticed Henri, would have been instructed to do so by the de Portal family: de Vaux had been their near neighbours in France.[110]

A similar pattern can be observed with the Minet family. Isaac Minet had visited Dover *before* his escape there and had already established trading connections with the port. Aged fourteen, he was sent there by his father to learn English and his brothers were already settled in Kent by the time he arrived in 1686.[111] As Anne Kershen observes in relation to the long-term Huguenot settlement of Spitalfields, 'As the threat to religious freedom increased, some sixteenth-century French Calvinist merchants, with established trading connections and knowledge of England, transferred families and resources across the Channel.' She adds that 'Though some returned home in 1598, when the Edict of Nantes was pronounced, others remained, creating links in the chain and the nuclei of future communities.'[112] In emphasising the economics of Huguenot migration, Kershen suggests that Britain was attractive as a place of settlement because of its trading and manufacturing potential, alongside its (not undisputed) Protestant status in the late seventeenth century. Moreover, 'As stowaways or hidden passengers on board a ship crossing the Channel, the actual mechanics of escape were relatively easy.'[113]

Kershen's interpretation clearly rests uneasily alongside the testimony of the Huguenot refugees and the emphasis on persecution and the perils of the journey from France to England. As we have seen, in 1737 Isaac Minet rewrote his memoirs but again it was the immediate circumstances of why he and his family had to flee and the escape from Calais to Dover that dominated his account. It was a narrative whose meaning was presented in the form of a universal religious parable:

> it is a very terrible thing [which] makes people promiss [that] if god delivers them they will mend their wayes, & live more like true Christians than ever they did before, but [the] generallity of Christians, even [the] Reformed one are like [the] Israelites, noe sooner past [the] sea but they forgett their deliverance and goe a Stray.[114]

Isaac's memoirs, according to his descendant, William Minet, presented a 'picture of a past humble in its shortcomings, steadfast in its well-doing, of a life, in short, of piety and integrity'. Isaac, he added, was 'a character which may be taken as typical of the Huguenots who came out of France for the sake of their religion'.[115] That Isaac was a tough businessman whose wealthy family had deep trading connections to England *before* the Revocation was a past less easily instrumentalised. Instead, the tiny rowing boat on his coat of arms symbolising refugee status and modest origins provided an unthreatening and deserving model of routes to and roots in England.

As was the case with the memory of Jews leaving eastern Europe at the turn of the twentieth century, religious persecution of Huguenots has been emphasised and the economics of the movement downplayed to ensure sympathy and understanding. With the Huguenot escape memoir and later memory work, the perils of the journey have been especially to the fore to create the classic refugee narrative. This is not to go as far as some recent historiography that religious belief and persecution 'was less important in the Huguenot emigration than has usually been thought'.[116] Moreover, recognising the narrative strategy in which escape was highlighted does not mean diminishing the dangers of leaving France. As Kershen later acknowledges, London 'was at the end of a perilous and often unpleasant journey by sea and land'.[117] It is, however, to place the forced migration around 1685 in a longer time frame in which Huguenot movement had a more voluntary and economic aspect – a complexity that is becoming recognised, as noted in Chapter 2, in academic (if not popular) studies of Jewish and Irish migration. But simplified narratives of migrant upward mobility and integration as with those told of the Huguenots have had an impact beyond the historiographical.

This chapter has explored how the creation of a celebratory Huguenot success story was instrumentalised in the mid-nineteenth century positively to promote a model of self-help, industry and religious devotion and negatively in the form of anti-Catholicism. In the late twentieth and early twenty-first centuries, Huguenot journeys have been utilised *inclusively* to promote multiculturalism and to show the potential worth of contemporary migrants. It is now necessary to analyse how the Huguenots have been remembered as part of a *hostile* discourse towards more recent arrivals that continues today in the battleground over the politics of immigration and asylum entry. Those trying to enter Britain have to pass an informal test in which the mythologised example of the Huguenots has been used to 'prove' that later asylum seekers are neither genuine nor deserving. The beginnings of this process can be observed in William Cunningham's *Alien Immigrants to England* (1897), a pioneer study of the subject.[118]

Cunningham devoted a chapter to the Huguenots and his conclusion about their impact was unequivocal – it was 'not easy to exaggerate the importance of their direct contribution … and they have … left their mark on every department of English literature and science'.[119] Indeed, Cunningham was generally positive about how much 'we have gained from aliens' in the past. Yet Cunningham was wary of extending this analysis to the present. Even allowing for British insularity and reluctance to learn from others, he concluded that those aliens coming to Britain more recently were of a different nature. 'At all events', he concluded, 'we have not much to gain from imitating the institutions of the Polish Jews'.[120] Yet Cunningham, writing just before the aliens question became one of pressing national concern, was still cautious about the need for control. True, it was hard, he believed, to know what advantages were being brought by the East European Jews. Nevertheless, 'there ought to be hesitation on the part of the nation with a history like ours, in changing from welcoming aliens to refusing to admit them'.[121] Six years later, the balance in the immigration debate had shifted dramatically.

The report of the Royal Commission on Alien Immigration, arising out of pressure through political campaigning, especially in the East End of London, for controls, began with a deep historical overview. Much attention was given to Protestant refugees and a glowing and sweeping overstatement made of their influence:

> To the records of the trades introduced and maintained by the Alien Immigrant of the 16th Century must now be added those very many important and useful industries practised by the Huguenots in the 17th. The list so completed comprises most of the industrial trades in which we now excel.

Yet rather than simply a eulogy to these migrants, such praise was double-edged. Cunningham had queried what use the Russian Jews were to English life and the report of the Royal Commission raised the same question: 'That the immigrants in past times made us their debtors cannot be controverted ... [b]ut some will ask, can the Alien Immigrant of today claim to be our creditor, because our ancestors incurred a debt to the foreigners who sought asylum here?' Its answer to this and the further question of whether the 'Immigrants of today [were] the successors of those who benefited us?' was negative.[122]

While the path from the Royal Commission in 1903 to the passing of the Aliens Act in 1905 was not a straightforward one, the anti-alienists were generally successful in juxtaposing the 'desirable' Protestant refugees of the early modern period against the 'undesirable' Jewish newcomers from Eastern Europe.[123] Those that suggested that the aliens seeking entry could, if given the opportunity, follow the illustrious example of the Huguenots and other refugees were fighting a losing battle.[124] In the 1930s campaigners on behalf of refugees from Nazism were slightly more successful in arguing that if these Jews were allowed entry they could become the new Huguenots: 'The lesson of history as to the amazing benefits we have derived from immigrants cannot be disputed.'[125] In general, however, it has been the restrictionists who have won this battle over public history in Britain. As one twenty-first century commentator, Anthony Brown, argued for the Conservative think tank Civitas, when calling for strict controls against immigrants and asylum seekers:

> The fact is that the Huguenot, Jewish and East African Asian immigrations were all successful because they were limited immigrations in scale and duration of highly educated and skilled people whose progeny integrated well.

Like Cunningham, Browne argued that history did not necessarily repeat itself: 'They were one-off events that had a natural conclusion', concluding that 'The immigration now is completely different in degree and type'.[126] That the Huguenots, Jews and East African Asians all faced similar contemporary opposition is conveniently ignored. In the case of the Huguenots especially, there was enormous pressure for them to conform. Facing an ambivalent response, many re-emigrated and those remaining in Britain increasingly lost their distinctiveness.

By the late nineteenth century, most of what remained of the Huguenot presence in Britain was at the level of memory: essentially a pride in name and origins. In Southampton, the Walloon refugees had established their influence from 1567, one supplemented by French Huguenots in the following century. Centuries later their place of worship in Winkle Street was still known as the French church. Nevertheless, by the early eighteenth century, the services there were now Anglican and not Calvinist. The change came as a result of pressure from the owners of the chapel, Queen's College, Oxford, 'which threatened to refuse [the Huguenots] further use of it if they did not conform'.[127] Here was a model of integration but at the ultimate cost of assimilation. As has been suggested, 'The decision was not made without rupturing the unity of the French community in Southampton'.[128] Just a few yards away and part of the God's House complex were present, if only fleetingly, another religious minority – the Volga Germans. Also Protestants, they arrived at a very different moment – the last decades of the nineteenth century and on the fringes of the politicisation of the aliens question in Britain. The disparity between the responses to these two groups of Protestants – sixteenth/seventeenth century in one case and the cusp of the twentieth century in the other – reveal the shifting meanings associated with migrant journeys. The next chapter will explore what has been, in contrast to the Huguenots, a story subject to near total amnesia.

4

Volga Germans in the late nineteenth century: from refugees to foreign paupers

Background and arrival

On 13 December 1879 the *Southampton Times*' 'Shipping Intelligence' report-ed the arrival of the Royal Mail West India and Brazil Steam Packet Company's *Minho*. The ship had called at Buenos Aires, Rio de Janeiro, St Vincent, Lisbon and Vigo, bringing mail from all these ports. It also brought with it £6,650 in specie, all gold, a 'large cargo of general merchandise' and 'a full comple-ment of passengers'.[1] For a busy and fast expanding port in commercial Britain, there was nothing particularly unusual in the *Minho*'s disembarkation at Southampton.[2] Yet alongside this dockside report, the *Southampton Times* noted elsewhere an emergency meeting of the town's Board of Guardians. The Mayor of Southampton chaired this meeting prompted by the arrival of 'poor Russian refugees' who had been on board the *Minho*, now stranded in Southampton and for whom 'something must be done'.[3] In the weeks that fol-lowed, the nomenclature attached to these arrivals would change rapidly. It was a reflection of wider concerns about migrants in late Victorian Britain and beyond.

Initially (and rather patronisingly) those on board the *Minho* were de-scribed as 'poor Russians',[4] 'poor creatures',[5] and 'strangers in a strange land' who deserved protection from the unscrupulous.[6] Descriptions of them, however, became increasingly hostile: rather than helping them as deserving refugees, emphasis was now placed on how best and speediest to remove their unwanted presence from the locality. Furthermore, what had been initially a matter of local curiosity and charity would develop into a national and inter-national cause for concern, with some fearing it would become, at a time of increasing diplomatic tension across Europe, a matter of major embarrassment involving the governments of Britain, Russia and Germany. As one newspaper commented, 'This colony of destitute foreigners … have given no little trouble and anxiety to the authorities, both local and imperial'.[7]

That ninety-one individuals, comprising for the most part of just fifteen families, could lead to so much consternation reflects much wider global anxieties at work in the last decades of the nineteenth century. The story of the 'refugees' from the *Minho* on the one hand shows the complex nature of migration patterns and their global nature at this time. On the other, it reveals the ambivalence to such movements – especially to that of transmigrants. Chapter 3 emphasised that responses to the Huguenot refugees in the late seventeenth and eighteenth centuries were not always as welcoming as is now assumed at the level of popular memory. It has taken Richard Bean's challenging play, *England People Very Nice*, to counter the rose-tinted version of the reception they received: a seventeenth-century Bethnal Green barmaid confronting the East End presence of the Huguenots proclaims 'Fucking frogs! My grandfather didn't die in the English Civil War so's half of France could come over here'.[8] Two centuries later, the reception of these Russians was also complex, varied and fluid over time. Nevertheless, while their treatment reveals continuity, there was an important shift towards the negative. Through a micro-historical analysis of the experiences of the 'Russian' transmigrants, changing reactions in receiving societies will be highlighted, revealing the intricate relations between the local, the national and the global.

The complexity of migrant journeys has been emphasised throughout *The Battle of Britishness*. Even so, those on board the *Minho* were part of a particularly bizarre movement that confused many of the contemporaries confronting them, the label 'Russo-Turkish emigrants' being perhaps the most inaccurate, although one reflecting other concerns at an international level.[9] Subsequently the wider group of 'Russians' to which they belong have received only a meagre and relatively unsophisticated historiography – indeed, the wider memory work associated with them is limited and confused. Thus the file on their arrival and brief stay in Southampton in the local archives is a little misleadingly (though enticingly) labelled 'Brazilian refugees'.[10] In fact, all were born in St Marea Couparne on the Volga in the Samara province in Southern Russia where they worked the land, essentially in the form of wheat production.[11] They were descendants of a small colony of the so-called 'Volga Germans', part of the first wave of emigrants recruited by Catherine the Great in the 1760s in her attempt to help develop and modernise the Russian empire.[12] The background of these Germans was diverse. As Edith Frankel notes, they came

> from a wide range of German states – Baden, Wurttemberg, the Palatinate, West Prussia, Danzig – and even from German communities

in Poland and Galicia; and they belonged to different Christian denomi-
nations. While most were Lutherans, there were also colonists belonging
to the Catholic, Reformed and Mennonite Churches.

In terms of settlement, however, it was 'usual for a single, homogenous group
to form a colony'.[13] By the mid-nineteenth century, there were more than one
hundred 'mother-colonies' on the Volga, one-third of the total in Russia as a
whole. In 1861, the Volga Germans totalled roughly 200,000 – a population
that was growing rapidly.[14]

As with many minority groups such as the East European Jews, the reasons
behind the migratory movement of the 'Volga Germans' in the last quarter of
the nineteenth century were complicated and intricate. It is immensely difficult
and perhaps impossible to isolate particular factors, especially those relating
to economics and persecution. Nevertheless, as with the Jews and the Irish
and Huguenot migrants before them, the dominant memory work hinges on a
straightforward narrative structure. One of the major historians of the 'Volga
Germans', James Long, provides a lachrymose account of their situation in the
late Tsarist empire, presenting them as

> victims of forces beyond their control: natural elements, which made
> earning a living unpredictable and precarious; tsarist policies, which
> originally protected them, then neglected them, later discriminated
> against them, and ultimately alienated them; and virulent political
> nationalism, which made them pawns in the nationalist European rival-
> ries, leading to their persecution and exploitation as scapegoats.

In contrast to their image as clannish, and somewhat defensively, Long argues
that 'In fact, the Volga Germans were loyal, productive Russian subjects who
became deeply attached to their new homes and chosen motherland.'[15]

As will become apparent, none of the problems that Long highlights were
imaginary and nor does he invent the local sense of belonging developed by the
'Volga Germans'. Yet to place so much emphasis on their collective victimhood
not only denies them a greater element of human agency in the decisions they
made, it also makes it harder to understand the complexities (and sometimes
apparent contradictions) of their settlement and movement patterns in the
second half of the nineteenth century.[16] Moreover, the identities of the 'Volga
Germans' were multi-layered, fluid and dynamic enabling local patriotism to
combine with ethnic loyalty and, as the patterns of migration became ever
more diverse, linked to what had become a worldwide diasporic network.[17]

Struggling financially, and over-dependent on wheat, the decline of the
grain trade – a result of increasing foreign competition and falling yields – led
many younger 'Volga Germans' from the 1860s onwards to consider emigration, especially as high population growth had added to the pressure on

the land. In the 1870s another factor came into play – the threat of military service in the Russian army was looming. In 1874 the 'Russian government abrogated the Volga Germans' century-old exemption from military service'.[18] Rather than being aimed specifically at this minority, it was part of a wider campaign of 'Russification' in which some groups, especially the Jews, were largely deemed too alien and hounded with the goal of securing their emigration, whereas others, including the 'Volga Germans', were pressurised, often forcibly, to integrate further.[19] The latter were largely perceived as desirable in their economic utility and potential to become good Russians (although less so towards the end of the nineteenth century and beyond), but discouraged from expressing too much ethnic particularity. From the mid-1870s, with the growing mobilisation of reservists, some 4,000 'Volga Germans' went to Brazil to try their luck.[20] They were encouraged to do so during what has been described 'as the critical years in Brazil's colonization program'.[21]

As a result of a report from the Brazilian Minister of Agriculture, Commerce and Public Works, it was noted that 'Argentina and the United States were more successful than Brazil in attracting immigrants'. To remedy this problem, which was seen as crucial in developing the Brazilian economy, efforts were made to remove the barriers in the way of potential immigrants such as poor transportation, legal impediments, 'the creation of colonies far from markets on sterile, unprepared land' and the 'failure to make Brazil known in the countries from which the emigration which we need proceeds'. One group amongst others who were particularly singled out as desirable immigrants were the 'Volga Germans' and a scheme was implemented to 'seat 20,000 of these people on the plains of Parana'.[22] It has also been suggested that the encouragement of such emigrants was part of a desire to keep Brazil white and to 'counterbalance the huge, newly freed black population'.[23] The fact that less than 20 per cent of that total actually came to the province of Parana at a time when many other 'Volga Germans' went elsewhere suggests that it was not a particularly attractive option. It seems likely therefore that those who went were ill-informed of what awaited them. As Frederick Luebke notes, Parana was essentially 'still a frontier region as late as 1920, when its population had reached only 685,000'.[24]

The 'Volga Germans' on the *Minho* seem to have been stimulated by a mixture of economic uncertainty at home coupled with a naivety in believing tales from an agent who, in their own words, 'induced [us] to leave a good home, and to go to a better one … persuad[ing] us that a Fortune was to be made in Brazil'. This account was written at a point when these 'Volga Germans' were trying to defend their desire to return 'home', and thus there was a need to show themselves to be victims of those who were exploiting their goodwill. There are echoes here of the descendants of East European immigrants who claimed that their parents and grandparents had been duped into buying false tickets to America thus finding themselves unexpectedly in Britain. Nevertheless, those migrants from the *Minho* were not willing to represent themselves as mere tools of others: 'We made our mind up and started on our emigration tour on the 23rd of May, 1878, for Hamburg.'[25]

The lure of better prospects in the Americas went alongside a religious discourse that the 'Volga Germans' attached to their journey – both leaving from and returning to Russia. When the party, all Protestants (with the exception of one Catholic family), left Southampton they explained to their hosts in a letter of gratitude that 'We shall now return to our happy and dear, beloved fatherland and home, the good one we once left to go to a better one; but we soon found out that we made a mistake when we arrived in that Promised Land.'[26] In similar vein, when they eventually returned 'home', they praised the two men, George Lungley and Samuel Messerli, who had accompanied them on their epic journey: 'These Gentlemen brought Us to our own Dear Fatherland, like two good Shepherds, who bring their sheep from the Fields to their Home, and look after them with great care that none should be lost.' Beyond Lungley and Messerli they also praised the 'People of Southampton and all England who have done "Us" so much good and helped "Us" to the End. God our Lord will repay them both in body and soul thereafter.'[27] Indeed, there is a close parallel in their Biblical-inspired narration of their migrant journeys and those of their fellow Protestants, the Huguenots, centuries earlier.

As the British Minister in Rio put it, their 'short sojourn' in the Brazilian interior was a disaster.[28] The large majority of the 4,000 migrants who came to Parana in the 1870s were soon determined to leave, encouraged further by local hostility towards them which included anti-Protestant sentiment in what was an officially Catholic country.[29] Those on board the *Minho* had spent eighteen months in Ponta Grossa in the province of Parana, roughly one hundred and fifty miles into the interior of Brazil.[30] The 'Volga Germans' in Ponta Grossa – 2,440 out of the 3,809 migrants who settled in the province – were described in 1878 by the provincial president of Parana, Rodrigo Otavio, as 'extremely ignorant, fearful, lazy, envious, and, in spite of being extremely religious, lacking in a sense of true charity'. He went on to dismiss them as knowing 'only the culture of wheat; but having to plant corn and beans, they sowed the seeds and afterwards went over the ground with primitive plows, brought from Russia, which were drawn by three pairs of oxen. Confronted with the unsuccessful production they excused themselves and blamed the land. They harvested oranges by cutting down the trees.'[31] It is more than possible that this devastating and condescending critique was designed to ensure that it was the immigrants and not the Brazilian authorities who were to blame for the 'dismal failure' of the 'Volga Germans', especially as there was recent anxiety about the way in which 'our errors in relation to the emigrants [had been] exaggerated, and hateful calumnies raised against us'.[32] More sympathetically, if illustrating different forms of prejudice, a local newspaper noted on the migrants' departure from Southampton that 'Even the "heathen Chinee" is no match for South American emigration agents'.[33]

It is not certain where blame should be apportioned for the failure of this attempted re-settlement. The comparative success of other groups who settled in Parana at this time, especially the Poles and Ukrainians, suggests that Otavio's criticisms, while harsh, were not totally without foundation. Nevertheless, it is possible that as the tail end of a migratory movement, those on the *Minho* were unlucky and given land with less potential. What is clear is that this 'colonization venture', which was 'entered into on a comparatively large scale and with high hopes', very soon 'failed most miserably' in Brazil. It led many of the 'Volga Germans' to either seek return to Russia or to move onto Argentina, Uruguay and Paraguay where the land was slightly better suited to their expertise in wheat production.[34]

Those on the *Minho* had found that Ponta Grossa was not as promised:

> instead of the fertile lands which they were to be sent to, a barren tract of country was assigned to them, where what scanty crops they could grow were eaten up by ants, and thus they soon became impoverished.[35]

In the words of the migrants themselves, 'we made our mind up to return to Russia … as we could not get on at all in Brazil'.[36] They were some of the last to leave for Brazil and also the last to attempt to come back to Russia. But those receiving them in Southampton feared, in the words of a senior politician in the town, that 'this batch was only one of many hundreds that would be brought to this country from the Brazils if some means were not taken to prevent it'.[37] It should be noted that fear of future 'alien floods', rather than the reality of the situation, has often been the strongest card of the xenophobe. There is a particularly modern tone to the response of a local (Liberal supporting) newspaper in confronting what was in reality a group numbering fewer than one hundred people:

> Our laws are so beautifully designed to encourage the improvident among all classes that these people, we cannot doubt, soon found for themselves in a better position than they had occupied for very many months previously … [N]ot only are these people eating their heads off … but they fairly promise to become a considerable burden to this community.[38]

In fact, only a small number were left behind in Brazil by December 1879. Indeed, it was, indirectly, the antipathy towards the earlier return of these

Russian Germans from 1878 onwards across Europe that led those in the *Minho* to be stranded in the port of Southampton. Their journey 'home' reveals the full complexity and multi-layered nature of that term. It also exposes the importance of the 'local' in determining the movements of people and the growing fears associated with those in flux.[39]

The return journey

Initially the Russian government refused to allow those on the *Minho* the right to return. On 17 December 1879, the Russian Ambassador in London, M. Bartholomei, informed the Foreign Secretary, the Marquis of Salisbury, that as 'The Emigrants [have] decisively quitted the Russian subjection, the Imperial Government regrets not being able to authorize their admission in the confines of the Empire'.[40] He added that this statement 'ought to put an end to the useless and unjustifiable expectations of these Brazilian colonists'.[41] While this official response appears harsh, the exasperation of the Russian authorities was not simply the result of prejudice against this minority group. Because the government did not desire the 'Volga Germans' to leave, emigration was discouraged by making the granting of departure and the freedom to take capital out of Russia a one-way process – they had pledged not to return. Furthermore, some of those who had been allowed to return had done so at a financial and administrative cost to the Tsarist regime. Bartholomei in his first response to Salisbury on this issue stressed that those on board the *Minho* had left Russia on a voluntary but also on a conditional basis: 'in abandoning the Russian subjection they could not re-claim the protection of the Government, nor re-enter Russia'. There was no room for negotiation.[42] Nine days later, Bartholomei confirmed the Russian position: as the emigrants had 'definitively departed' the empire, they could not be allowed to return.[43]

Why then, over the next few weeks, was this decision slowly reversed? It seems that the *Minho* 'refugees' became very minor pawns in a diplomatic game at a time of Anglo-Russian tension, reflecting the late days of the Beaconsfield agenda in responding to the 'Eastern Question'. Eventually, pressure from the Foreign Office, and perhaps of equal if not greater importance, a promise by the British government to pay the expenses of the returnees, led to a promise to permit those on the *Minho* to come home.[44] In particular, the Local Government Board was sympathetic to the problems faced within Southampton where the Board of Guardians was being forced to support these destitute foreigners in the town. The local authorities in Southampton decided that it would be best if they paid the costs of returning those from the *Minho* to Russia. Additional funds were also provided so that the emigrants could re-establish themselves back 'home'. Such generosity was also designed as an incentive to the Russian authorities to reconsider the case.[45] The hope of those in Southampton was that this expense would, in due course, be reimbursed by central government: in the medium term, it would still be cheaper to pay their fare rather than look after them in Southampton.[46]

Much energy was thus spent diplomatically in both London and St Petersburg by the Foreign Office in persuading the Russian authorities to take back these particular 'Volga Germans'. Those on the *Minho* were doubly lucky that they were accompanied home by George Lungley of the Southampton Board of Guardians. Lungley, not unusually for those associated with the port and its increasing role in transmigrancy, had strong connections to the commercial world of mass migration: he had run a company for close to thirty years in Southampton for those emigrating to Australia.[47] It was his insider's knowledge that allowed the relatively smooth return of the *Minho* refugees. Even so, as he noted in his notes on the journey, 'I must say that in the thousands of emigrants that I have assisted to embark, I never found so difficult a task as was undertaken with these people'.[48]

When those on the *Minho* were first interviewed in Southampton through a translator, they claimed that they had been refused permission to land at Hamburg or at Antwerp and had thus obtained tickets from Rio to England.[49] This tallies with intelligence gained by Lungley from the British Ambassador in St Petersburg, Lord Dufferin. Dufferin informed Lungley that in 1878 eight hundred Russian Germans returning from Brazil were encamped in Antwerp and 'after great trouble … were conveyed to Russia at a cost of about £3000'. When another ship carrying a further two hundred such individuals arrived at Antwerp, they were refused permission to land 'but were transhipped outside the Harbour and sent on by sea to Russia'. The same story was repeated at Bremen. Dufferin was sure that the Royal Mail Company was aware of this earlier problem and knew that 'when the people landed at Southampton that the Minho would not be allowed to enter the Harbour of Antwerp'.[50]

At Hamburg itself, Lungley heard that 'Some time previously about 200 [Russian Germans from Brazil] had been received there and after great expense, the people at the [Emigration] Depot accompanied them to Russia'.[51] It is not clear what was meant by this 'Emigration Depot' in Hamburg as it predates the formal facilities in the port. In itself, this unrecorded 'depot' reveals how there is still a great deal to be learnt about emigration and transmigrancy patterns and procedures, even in places that have commemorated their past role in this neglected area of history.[52] The party from the *Minho* was to encounter difficulties at and around Hamburg, but through good fortune, persistence, and not a little anti-German prejudice on behalf of Lungley, their stay there was relatively brief.

Initially the local authorities in Hamburg were helpful, but their assistance, it soon became apparent, was dependent on Lungley allowing his charges to pass through the 'Emigration Depot'. He knew that this would lead to considerable delay and cost. As he later noted, 'knowing as I did that some of them had just passed out of Hospital at Southampton and on some slight pretense might have detained them for some days at great expense ... It was quite clear that arrangements had been made for them to stay in the Depot, [the authorities in Hamburg] not thinking for one moment that the people would pass through'.[53]

At Hamburg Lungley thus hurried his charges onto a night train east. One last attempt was made by the local police to stop the party but using his Foreign Office written assurances that the Russian authorities were willing to let the migrants return, they were allowed to proceed. The party, however, only got as far as Rheinbek where the train came to a halt.[54] Rheinbek was situated on the border between the city state of Hamburg and Prussia where the train was forced to stop. It played an increasing role from the 1880s onwards in the dumping of unwanted migrants, especially those returned from the United States. For the most part, Prussia grudgingly accepting these unwanted people.[55]

Lungley was astonished by what happened to his charges at Rheinbek: 'the carriage in which the people were located was detached from the train and a scene took place which I can scarcely describe. The people's baggage was thrown out of the baggage waggon without any enquiry ... and the train proceeded without us'. Lungley and his translator were bungled out of their carriages, sustaining minor injuries. In a wonderful evocation of English understatement when confronting the grim reality of immigration procedures, he later reported to the Southampton authorities that 'As may be imagined, I felt for a few minutes in rather an uncomfortable position'. Local officials arrived and Lungley was most affronted to be taken for a Russian. Lungley asked his interrogator 'whom he was' and in hearing the response, 'A German', stated that if 'you are a fair specimen, I think very little of you'. Utterly exasperated, Lungley still refused to let his charges return to Hamburg for the depot. When asked, however, what he intended doing with the people he responded 'I will make you a present of them ... I will give you them for nothing'.[56]

Faced with such stubbornness, not to mention Germanophobia by its mentor, the party was allowed to proceed, backed by fresh commitments from the British government that they would meet the costs of the journey back east. Already delayed by fog and ice, the party continued towards Russia, with only a short delay of three hours at the border as the identity of the ninety-one Russian Germans was confirmed. All in all, the journey back home from Southampton via London had taken close to two weeks. Lungley's detailed account of the journey gives little indication of the state of mind of his charges, focusing instead on the discomfort he faced, travelling in a separate and superior carriage.

On one level, the case of the *Minho* is relatively unusual in that it provides us with a (condensed) version of the journey from the migrants' perspective aimed at praising their temporary hosts and benefactors in Britain. On another level, the detailed narrative of their return journey, penned by Lungley, is more typical of the historical record in rendering them silent. All we know is that some attempt was made to help re-integrate them by the local authorities in Samara with blankets given to help them to cope with winter temperatures and a donation of £50 given by the Empress of Russia 'to assist them again establishing a home'. This welcome was a reflection of their relatively 'privileged' status, through British government intervention, compared to many of the returning 'Volga Germans'.[57]

Beyond the 'local'

What, then, can be gleaned from this story if one moves from the precise, if somewhat singular and unique story, to the general? First, it urges us to think 'locally', even when confronted with an overall narrative that is clearly global in its wider context and at a time of unprecedented international population movements. For Southampton, during the month the 'Volga Germans' were in the town, it was the major issue of the moment, especially as irritation grew with the delay in removing the arrivals and the cost of looking after them subsequently increased. When in late December 1879 the *Hampshire Advertiser* described the arrival of the 91 'Volga Germans' as amongst the 'most distressing events of the year' it would suggest that the newspaper had the misfortune and well-being of the *Minho* migrants in mind. By adding that 'we … reiterate the hope that the British Government will take these destitute aliens off our hands',[58] the direction of its concern becomes apparent.

Continuing with the importance of the 'local', while indulging in self-congratulation over the 'considerate treatment' that had been offered to the 'Volga Germans',[59] the reality was that in Southampton they were transformed from 'refugees' to 'immigrants' and then 'foreigners' in local discourse as the weeks passed,[60] and eventually dismissed as 'this useless and helpless colony'.[61] Indeed, one of the local, Liberal-supporting newspapers when hearing of their imminent removal noted, even 'with every feeling of consideration for the poor people themselves', that 'the inhabitants of Southampton will no doubt regard their departure as a "good riddance"'.[62] In addition, local officials were concerned that the example of those from the *Minho* might become a 'dangerous precedent' – one that could lead the town to be 'crushed with a burden of foreign pauperism' – a double danger to the Victorian charitable mind.[63] At times, the precision of what should, and should not, be provided for them extended into a farcically precise level. Serious debate was given to the exact nature of their Christmas dinner. In the end it was decided that they could not be provided with the same privileges of those in the workhouse which included roast beef. Instead they were given Irish stew but allowed, as were the inmates, plum pudding.[64]

The second point that can be highlighted concerning the significance of the *Minho* relates to late nineteenth-century attitudes towards migrants, refugees and concepts of asylum. In its small way, local responses to the 'Volga Germans' were a sign of a growing anti-alienism in Britain and the wider world, even if hostile responses were still contested. Beyond Southampton, reporting of their arrival reflected a debate that was beginning to gather momentum at a national level. The *Preston Guardian*, for example, presented the story in a positive framework, heading its news item 'An Asylum for Russo-German Emigrants'. If 'foreign pauperism' was a term that could agitate anger amongst contemporaries, British pride in providing 'asylum' prompted contrasting emotions. Focusing on the use of the former gaol which was quickly called into action to temporarily house the migrants, the *Preston Guardian* noted that 'The portion of the building set apart for their use has been comfortably warmed, and the men and women of the party have been busily engaged all day in cleaning the place and washing their clothes – the latter a work of especial necessity'.[65] Both the welcome given to and the desirability of the migrants was thus emphasised. In contrast, the *Pall Mall Gazette*, which was to play a leading part in the campaign for alien restriction in the early 1900s, presented the story problematically with the threat of worse to come:

> Some trouble is being caused to the Southampton poor-law authorities by the landing in the town of a number of Russo-German emigrants returning from Brazil. Eighty-two have arrived, and some hundreds are expected to follow. They are quite destitute, and the Russian Embassy declines to be responsible for them.[66]

That the 'Volga Germans' were of interest and concern outside the port of Southampton shows that migration, even of small numbers of people, was now deemed to be newsworthy. As noted in the close of the previous chapter, the anti-alien cause was still a long way from asserting itself as the dominant force before the turn of the twentieth century. Nevertheless, the *Minho* incident showed tendencies at a local and national level that were there to be exploited by restrictionists. In Southampton, for example, the presence of the 'Volga Germans' became an issue in which party politics between Liberals and Conservatives could be articulated most strongly. The issue, however, was not about whether they should be treated with more or less generosity – the focus was on the well-being of the town itself. Liberals accused the local Conservative council and MP of being slow and half-hearted in attempts to receive support from national government towards the upkeep of the migrants.[67] The Conservative-supporting *Hampshire Advertiser* responded that making political capital from the unfortunate problem 'might well puzzle any but the most ingenious and extreme members of a very bitter and unscrupulous party'.[68]

It is noticeable, however, that across the town's political divide, there was no disagreement about the need to move on – and move on promptly – what the same newspaper, predicting the language of the *fin de siecle*, labelled 'friendless aliens'.[69] If anything, and unlike the parliamentary debate in the mid-1900s, it was the Liberals who used the most hostile language against the migrants. It is also significant how quickly the migrants were perceived as being undesirable and undeserving. In Southampton, they were depicted as dirty, lazy, helpless and useless.[70] At a national level there were suggestions that the 'Volga Germans' might be shipped on to the British colonies but their reputation as unsuccessful migrants preceded them. The possibility, for example, of sending them to New Zealand was rejected by its agent-general in London and former Prime Minister, Sir Julius Vogel.[71]

Such anxieties about 'undesirable' aliens were to develop further and with a health panic in the early 1890s linked to the cholera and typhus epidemics in Hamburg and New York, it is no surprise that the ad hoc solution to dealing with those on board the *Minho* in what was an ancient and long abandoned building was replaced by a new and formal institution.[72] The Emigrants Home opened in 1893 and was supported by the local authorities, the major shipping companies and the American consul in the town.[73] From the 1890s onwards, Southampton became increasingly important as a place of transmigrancy, which, by the time of the First World War, was beginning to rival Liverpool in this respect. It was, of course, the war which was to largely destroy this lucrative trade. When the major shipping companies in 1922 opened Atlantic Park Hostel outside Southampton, one of the largest facilities in the world for transmigrants, it was to fail commercially and became a drain on them as they had to look after those left stranded by the new immigration quota laws of the American government.[74]

Returning to the late 1870s and early 1880s, the case of the *Minho* revealed how local authorities in Britain were largely unprepared for such an influx, in spite of the growth of migration through its ports. Thus when a deputation from the Southampton Board of Guardians asked the Local Government Board for advice, the best example that could be offered as a precedent was refugees who had arrived during the time of Lord Palmerston.[75] There is a certain irony in the national body advising the local body of this historical parallel as the one offered had an intimate connection to Southampton.

The administrative reference point was to Polish migrants and others who had taken part in the failed Hungarian Insurrection of 1848. They had served under the nationalist leader, Kossuth, and then fled to Turkey. After three years of detention there, they were sent by the Sultan to England where they were deposited in the ports of Liverpool and Southampton.[76] As these 'Polish' refugees (in fact, there were 270 Poles and 66 Hungarians who made up the party) were becoming a burden on the local state, encouragement was given for them to move on to America.[77] Some of the Poles and Hungarians, however, were hesitant to do so as they were anxious to return in better times to their homeland to fight for freedom, thus preferring to remain close to the continent: 'The advantage of coming to England was that the exiles could stay relatively close to their home countries and the scenes of revolutionary upheavals, which was ideal if one believed ... that the setbacks of 1849 were merely temporary and their period of exile would be short.'[78]

The dilemma of these refugees was expressed in a letter sent to the Home Secretary by a general in their ranks:

> Having taken part in the late Hungarian war, and, afterwards, been confined in the fort of Kutajah, we were compelled to leave Turkey and arrived at Southampton ... Being desirous of returning to our homes ... we came immediately to London, to accomplish our purpose. Here, we have been living upon the scanty resources which some of us had, and which are now exhausted.

They appealed for more funds to enable them to return to the continent as a longer stay in England 'will expose us ... to destitution'.[79] Such appeals were increasingly met with irritation at a local and national level. As with the 'Volga Germans' a few decades later, the Southampton municipal authorities were anxious at the mounting costs of looking after the refugees who were increasingly regarded as an undesirable nuisance, especially those who appeared rooted to England. Indeed, more Hungarians and Poles arrived throughout 1851, adding to concern in the town. The Home and Foreign Office were sympathetic and provided support and encouragement to the Poles and Hungarians to leave, mainly to America but in some cases to France.[80]

There were other reasons why these refugees caused the British government anxieties. These included earlier diplomatic wrangles involving the Poles – Austria wanted them to return through its territory so that they could be punished for their revolutionary activities. In addition, the presence of the refugees added further tension to relations between Russia and Britain – another parallel to the later story of the migrants from the *Minho*.[81] Yet that there was no collective memory within Southampton concerning the Poles/Hungarians less than three decades after their arrival reveals the marginality of migration in local culture and politics, mirroring wider trends at a national level. Evidence of antipathy towards the Poles, as well as support for them in their temporary sojourn, also reveals that anti-alienism had deep roots. As Bernard Porter notes in his study of refugees in mid-Victorian Britain, they 'were in a curious situation. Most of them were unloved by most Englishmen, who made them feel very little welcome, but tolerated their presence in deference to what was purported to be a great and selfless humanitarian principle: the doctrine of asylum'.[82]

That the Poles/Hungarians of 1851 and the 'Volga Germans' of 1879 were initially welcomed and then quickly moved on suggests that ambivalence was even stronger than Porter suggests and that the commitment to asylum was perhaps more tenuous *throughout* the Victorian era than has been generally accepted. Moreover, while Porter is technically correct to highlight that the British authorities from '1823 right through the nineteenth century did not expel a single refugee from Britain, or prohibit a single one of them from coming in',[83] this ignores the pressure put on those arriving to leave. Thus in August 1851, the Mayor of Southampton wrote to the government that if the Polish and Hungarian refugees his town was looking after refused to go to America or France, 'I have declined to give them further relief unless they were sick'. He added that through such pressure there was 'not one of them left here who is deserving any sympathy'.[84] Similarly, there was simply no question in late 1879 and early 1880 of the *Minho* refugees being allowed to stay in Britain. At best, and it was an option quickly dismissed, places in the colonies might be found for them.

In the decades that followed the arrival of the *Minho* emigrants, a local and national structure was put in place to deal with the 'alien', whether floating or permanent, especially the alleged medical threat which they posed. The 'Emigrant Home' in Southampton was in this respect a small local version of more impressive permanent facilities where migrants could be confined and inspected such as Ellis Island outside New York (1892) and by HAPAG (the Hamburg-American Line) in Hamburg also from 1892. It created traumatic and alienating processes that those such as Mary Antin and hundreds of thousands of other East Europeans would be forced to endure and 'pass' if their journeys 'west' were to continue. The closeness of the opening of these facilities and others in the early 1890s reveals the concern that was being manifested at a global level. It also exposes the international medical 'expertise' which was garnered to combat the migrant 'threat'.[85]

Before 1914, however, there was still resistance to such anti-alien anxieties. For example, the national and anti-alien *Standard* newspaper was overstating its case in 1906 when it claimed that in Southampton 'the town was heartily in sympathy with the [Aliens Act of 1905], for it had suffered badly at the hands of penniless foreigners, who frequently drift to the local workhouses or infirmary, and become a permanent charge on the rates'.[86] There was also a positive impact of transmigrancy on the town's economy and thus an overall increasingly positive response towards such movements. Local responses clearly mattered to those on the *Minho* and they made the difference between homeless destitution and their ultimate return to Russia. As Lungley concluded after his return to Southampton, without his efforts, they 'might have been [still] at Hamburg at the present time'.[87] More blatantly, local responses at the ports of Antwerp and Hamburg were part of a world to come – the concentration and medical inspection and rejection of immigrants, transmigrants and refugees.[88] If this was a growing phenomenon in the western world, it was one that had strong local variations and initiatives. On the one hand, it led to innovations that would often catch on elsewhere adding to their cumulative impact. On the other, in more liberal settings such anti-alienism was challenged and resisted.

The third significance of the *Minho* relates to the migrants themselves and their identities and ambitions. Their story appears, at first sight, unusual in that the 'refugees' on board were attempting to return 'home' and were therefore facing the increasing obstacles to free movement of peoples in reverse. Return migration has, until recently, been neglected both in academic study and popular memory. It was, however, an integral part of the process involving huge numbers of people travelling east to west and south to north in the period from the 1820s to 1914. Alongside step migration and transmigration, 'return' was part of a complex global movement facilitated by cheap and speedy transport and improved communications.[89] The case of the 'Volga Germans' has been especially subject to amnesia in the historiography of modern migration movements. And even the major historian of those 'Volga Germans' who left for the Americas expresses surprise that as well as moving on to Argentina some of those who went to Brazil 'even returned to Russia'.[90]

The *Minho* provides a case study that illustrates the dangers of generalising why people leave and shows the multi-layered meanings and complexity of constructing a place called 'home'. As has been noted, James Long in his study of the 'Volga Germans' in the second half of the nineteenth century reminds us that in spite of their sometimes precarious and unpredictable situation, the 'Volga Germans' developed a close attachment to the localities in which their (often distant) ancestors had settled within the Russian empire.[91] Economic, ecological and political tensions, and increasing intolerance at 'home' did not make the decision to leave an easy one. For many, including those on the *Minho*, disappointment in the place of emigration, the new but failed 'promised land', only intensified the sense of loss. The mean streets of New York and other fast expanding cities of America did not confront the immigrant with the immediate problems of survival as did the interior of Brazil. Nevertheless, hundreds of thousands of Europeans would return home or try their luck elsewhere in countries like Britain. The process of transmigrancy added further to the complexity of belonging and not belonging. It was big business, but also through its massive scale, an indication of the essential *mercurial* nature of migration – the harder one tries to pin it down, the more elusive and untrappable it becomes. Transmigrants act as a reminder, if one was ever needed, that migration is rarely if ever a simple matter of leaving one place and going to another.[92]

'Home', for perhaps the majority, was established, either temporarily or permanently, as somewhere in between. Thus after just a few weeks in Southampton those from the *Minho* felt confident to 'give three cheers for the Great Queen and the Royal Family of the good land of England'.[93] England, and especially the port of Southampton, if experienced only briefly and at a traumatic moment, was a place never to be forgotten. Fluidity is the key to understanding immigrants' experience from the nineteenth century onwards: their routes were often intricate, dangerous and lengthy and their roots laid down in many different locations. It should also be noted that some of the 'Volga Germans' did establish a sense of belonging in Brazil and became part of the rich 'cultural mosaic' of that nation. As one observer wrote as late as the 1960s: 'In the south of Brazil the journey of a few hours may easily carry one through areas representative of nineteenth-century European peasant communities of German, Polish, Italian, and Volga German types'.[94]

Were those on board the *Minho* refugees as first described by those receiving them in Southampton or simply immigrants/unwanted foreigners/ destitute aliens as they soon became known? Their motives for leaving were clearly partly economic as well as to a far lesser extent, millenarian. But it also reflected their marginality (in spite of their valued economic contribution) as a distinct ethnic group in the Russian empire and one which was vulnerable, especially with the fear of military conscription. The plight of the 'Volga Germans', because they *were* seen as ultimately assimilable, was not so desperate as the more extreme case of the unwanted Jews of the late Tsarist empire. Nevertheless, their future status and well-being was unclear as a result of what has been labelled the 'ambiguities of Russification'.[95]

James Long sees the treatment of the 'Volga Germans' as deteriorating rapidly in the last sixty years of Tsarist rule so that 'Increasingly, they became victims of circumstances and forces beyond their control'.[96] The initial refusal by the Russian authorities to accept the right of the Volga Germans to go back 'home' gives some indication of their uncertain position. As with so many groups already referred to in this study, including the best-known and most written about, the East European Jews, the division between refugees and immigrants, or as contemporary polemics would have it, between those deserving of asylum and those who were undesirable aliens, was in the eye of the beholder, or more basically, the local immigration or poor law official. The variability with which those on board the *Minho* were treated, even locally within a five-week period, illustrates the tensions of the time. It is thus not difficult to perceive what might lie ahead given the treatment of a group who might have been viewed positively as they were, in contemporary thinking, of 'Saxon' stock and Protestant faith.

The *Minho* was presented locally as ultimately a story with a happy ending with the immigrants returned safely home. In many respects – at least in the short term – it was, and while luck was on their side, those from the *Minho* played their part. Their letters expressing their gratitude to all concerned (bar, of course, the Brazilian authorities) in enabling their return 'home', but also their ambitions for a prosperous future back in the Russian empire, 'our own Dear Fatherland',[97] were set before those in high authority – not just in Southampton but also in London and St Petersburg. These 'Volga Germans' helped compose a portrait of their remarkable journey in which they clearly saw themselves as deserving of support. To them, they had been cruelly misled into emigration by the Brazilian authorities and agents. A closer reading provides other, less reassuring, narratives relating to the wider treatment of the 'Volga Germans' back from Brazil – ones that would emphasis their isolation and rejection in the ports of Europe and the 'new world' where they were neither perceived as refugees nor understood for their own specific historic background. Indeed, as they returned to the continent, Lord Dufferin remarked, showing both irritation about the problems they had caused, but also confusion as to who they actually were: 'Might not the Canadian Emigration Agent be glad to send these *Menonites* [my emphasis] to Canada?'.[98] In fact, the 'Mennonite villages in the Volga region were founded much later' than those who had been on board the *Minho*.[99]

Conclusion

This chapter will conclude by returning to the relationship between the 'local' and the 'global' at the level of memory. Given its importance in transmigrancy – in two months in 1904, for example, 8,000 East Europeans left the port – it is surprising that there is no official memorialisation of this trade in Southampton today.[100] The story of the 'Brazilian Volga Germans' has been totally forgotten despite (or even because) of their temporary home – God's

House, the former gaol and a fine medieval building, was for a long time the Archaeology Museum and the flagship of the heritage world in Southampton. Many people were involved in looking after those from the *Minho* who undoubtedly received kindness and genuine interest in their background as well as growing resentment from the less tolerant. In the local workhouse sadly one young girl from the ship died of consumption though happily a baby there was also safely delivered.[101] It is significant, however, that the complex of medieval buildings which was their former home *is* recalled with regard to the earlier, Protestant refugees of the sixteenth and seventeenth centuries. Encouraged to settle and generally welcomed, if on conditional terms, they are remembered positively and as an integral part of the town's history. The Huguenots, a history of the building emphasised, 'brought [with them] their industry, their skill, their genius, their love of liberty, their obedience to law'.[102]

This history of this remarkable site was written just fourteen years after the arrival of the 'Volga Germans' who were temporarily housed there. When its author, J. Aston Whitlock, noted that the building's history was 'one of progress' and usefulness including the 'welcoming of pilgrims',[103] it becomes apparent *why* there was no place for those from the *Minho*, migrants who had been dismissed by those in the town as 'a colony of paupers'.[104] Class undoubtedly played its role in the linked processes of memory and amnesia – Whitlock praised the Huguenots for their 'high-bred character'.[105] But the absence of reference to the 'Volga Germans' in his narrative, which closed by quoting the late Prince Consort on the need for harmony so that 'the old will live again in the new ... [enabling] the great traditions of the past [to] be happily, wisely and usefully combined with the highest aspirations of the present and the future', also reflected that attitudes to migration had changed over the centuries.[106] Like so many transmigrants of the time and beyond, the 'Volga Germans' were treated as 'people who do not fit' and thus were treated simply as 'matter out of place'.[107] Being a dissident Protestant in the late nineteenth century was simply no longer enough to ensure a welcome for those embarking on migrant journeys to and through Britain, especially with a new 'scientific' approach to distributing relief only to the 'deserving' poor. That the story of those on the *Minho* has been subsequently forgotten, especially in contrast to the Huguenots, reveals the ongoing tendencies in British culture, society and politics to deny both a tradition of intolerance, and a tradition of migration, in the nation's past. And those on the *Minho*, it should be noted finally, were simply ninety-one transmigrants out of the three million-plus who passed through Britain from the 1830s to 1914.[108] There are thousands more such neglected stories which remain to be rediscovered and retold.

The Nazi era

5

Constructing (another) ideal refugee journey: the *Kinder*

Introduction

Mollie Panter-Downes became for many Americans *the* voice of Britain during the Second World War.[1] She wrote for the *New Yorker* for half a century, a relationship which began in earnest with her powerful description of the *Kindertransport*. Set up by the British government and voluntary bodies in November 1938, this refugee movement eventually brought close to ten thousand children from Germany, Austria, Czechoslovakia and Poland, 90 per cent of whom were of Jewish origin. Panter-Downes went to Liverpool Street railway station in July 1939 to witness the arrival of one transport of children coming from Berlin.[2] When Panter-Downes died in 1997, the transformation of the *Kindertransport* into a celebrated event inside and outside Britain was yet to be completed. The lack of full awareness was reflected in her obituaries. One national newspaper dated Panter-Downes' article on the *Kinder* to 1937 and located the place of arrival to Victoria station,[3] while another vaguely stated that 'In the 1930s she sold the [*New Yorker*] … a piece about Jewish refugee children coming to England'.[4] References to her first report indicate that interest in the *Kindertransport* was beginning yet it was not fully formed. Just fourteen years later, another obituary, in this case of a refugee from Nazism, Arieh Handler, revealed that this process of rediscovery had now matured. Handler was born in Brno, then in the Austro-Hungarian empire, and brought up after the First World War in Germany. The obituary emphasised Handler's role in the '*famous* [my emphasis] kindertransport of German Jewish children to Britain'.[5] This chapter will explore the changing meanings associated with the *Kindertransport* and why in the twenty-first century it has become so prominent within heritage commemoration, even featuring in the BBC's revived heritage drama *Upstairs Downstairs* (2012).[6]

Like many of her later writings, Panter-Downes' account, 'Amid the Alien Corn', played with concepts of Englishness, especially in relation to class and ethnicity, in a self-aware, critical, but ultimately affirming manner. One of the people collecting the children from the station, a 'black-bearded gentleman', expressed frustration at the delays and bossy nature of the female organisers:

> 'Who are you, I'd like to know?' The official did not divulge, but said dip-lomatically that all they asked was fair play for everybody. 'Ugh!' snorted the minor prophet, unmoved by this jolly British public-school appeal.[7]

Throughout the article, the children, some 147 of whom arrived that day, are silent. Language and the strict formalities of the day created a barrier between the sensitive pen of Panter-Downes and the young refugees. Even so, she did her very best to present them positively, praising their calmness and tidy ap-pearance. They met, in short, a perfect middle-class vision of how children should look and behave. Nevertheless, the means of keeping track of the *Kinder* employed by the refugee organisers clearly disturbed the author. It was a theme she returned to throughout her article:

> Round their necks were numbered labels on which were written the names of these hundred and forty-seven little human parcels redirected by Hitler into a new life in a strange country. There was a baby in a red knitted cap in somebody's arms. She tried to eat her label, was thwarted, and began to roar.[8]

The guarantors of the children, noted Panter-Downes, were equally alienated by this form of bureaucratic identification: 'In every case the adult's first in-stinctive gesture seemed to be to take hold of the label round the child's neck, pull it off, and throw it on the ground.' Such a gesture worked: they felt 'better after that'.[9]

Panter-Downes' first experience at Liverpool Street station was meeting a reporter from the *Daily Express*. She told Panter-Downes: '"I've been sent along to meet three of these transports, and I don't care if I never see a refugee again"'. Her fellow journalist's lack of empathy clearly irritated the budding *New Yorker* writer. In spite of their different perspectives (the *Daily Express* was not noted for its sympathy towards refugees during the 1930s), their mutual presence at the station in summer 1939 emphasised that the arrival of the transports was still newsworthy, even six months after the scheme first came into opera-tion.[10] Even so, Nicholas Winton, who was a key figure in the organisation of the *Kindertransport* in Prague and London, had reflected a few months earlier that confronted with ongoing refugee crises, the 'average person … [is] too inured to such tragedies even to consider how they might be able to mitigate such suffering'.[11] In contrast, Panter-Downes was one of the few who managed to recognise fully the predicament of the children and that of the parents who had let them go: 'Everybody was very clean and neat, as though freshly dressed by mothers anxious for them to look their best'.[12]

Panter-Downes concluded by highlighting the ordinariness of the children. Her description escaped the pathos that overwhelmed (or was perhaps expected by) many of their contemporary observers. For example, one former *Kinder*, Helga Samuel, who came on one of the first transports arriving at Harwich by boat from Holland, recalled that

> Perhaps because I looked more lost and sad than the other children, I was picked out by a photographer … I began to cry so he put his arm round my shoulder and gave me a coin … Then he called over one of the helpers, and with her looking at the label round my neck he took our picture.[13]

Panter-Downes' calm approach was also aimed at informing her American audience of the children's potential. It was a necessary strategy for a nation whose Congress had been in the process of rejecting the chance of giving refuge to twenty thousand young refugees through the Wagner-Rogers Bill.[14] As she left, Panter-Downes recognised one of the children, a ten-year-old boy:

> I happened to have noticed him in the gymnasium. Otherwise, with the label off his neck, there was nothing to distinguish him from any other nice child who only wanted a chance to get going, to develop into a fine person to whom any country in the world might be proud.[15]

A refugee worker at Liverpool Street had explained to Panter-Downes that the children would not be settled in Britain permanently – homes might be found for them in America, Australia or 'wherever room can be found for them'.[16] The example of the individuals who had given so freely of time and money to look after the children was referred to throughout her *New Yorker* piece. Of the female refugee workers themselves, while there were waspish comments about their good looks and even finer clothing, Panter-Downes still recognised that some had 'given up their regular work so that they could devote all their time to the task of getting more children out of Germany'.[17] Yet her prose was delivered in an understated manner, with no emphasis on Britain as a whole offering asylum to the children. For all the power of Panter-Downes' sketch, the classic refugee narrative (stronger even than that attached to the Huguenots) which has subsequently developed about the *Kindertransport*, including the journey to Britain, was largely absent in her article. The smoothness and regularity of the transport's arrival is what strikes the reader, not its abnormality. Yet that it could be presented as a relatively mundane occurrence in a London station during the summer of 1939 and that Britain had recently let in relatively large numbers of refugees, even on a temporary basis and carefully selected, requires some explanation.

Early in 1852 the diplomatic wranglings between Britain and its continental rivals concerning the Poles and Hungarians referred to Chapter 4, as well as other 'dangerous' refugees, were still at a feverish level. The Foreign Secretary, Earl Granville, felt it necessary to confirm Britain's commitment to the concept of asylum and the 'general hospitality … extended by our institutions to all who choose to come to England'. Granville added that no exceptions could be made:

> It is obvious that this hospitality could not be so freely given, if it were not so widely extended. If a discretionary power of removing foreigners were vested in the Crown, appeals would be constantly made by the dominant party in foreign countries, for the expulsion of their political opponents who might have taken refuge in Great Britain.[18]

That commitment in practice had its limitations, as the treatment of refugees in the mid-nineteenth century through to the Volga Germans in 1879/80 was to expose. Nevertheless, the attachment to the principle of asylum proved an obstacle in the Conservative Party's campaign for the control of immigration in the 1900s. Eventually the Aliens Act that was passed contained a clause which exempted refugees from all other restrictions at the port of entry. Admission would be granted if aliens could prove that they were seeking admission 'solely to avoid prosecution or punishment on religious or political grounds, or for an offence of a political character, or persecution, involving danger of imprisonment or danger to life or limb, on account of religious belief'.[19]

From the perspective of the new Aliens Department of the Home Office, this legislation proved close to unworkable. The Aliens Act was, in the words of the Permanent Under-Secretary of State from 1908 to 1922, Sir Edward Troup, 'one of the worst ever passed'.[20] The Aliens Act was administered by the new Liberal government and at first there was a desire to implement its clauses as generously as possible. Immigration officials dealing with asylum seekers in the late twentieth and early twenty first centuries have operated on a basis of initial disbelief. In doing so, they have followed strict guidelines from the Home Office and Home Secretaries of different political hues. A century earlier, their predecessors were given the opposite instructions. In March 1906, members of Immigration Boards were told, notwithstanding the problems of getting 'corroborative evidence' from aliens, that 'the benefit of the doubt, where any doubt exists, may be given in favour of any immigrants who allege that they are flying from religious or political persecution from disturbed districts'.[21]

In the years before 1914 fears of alien subversion and criminality grew following incidents such as the 'Houndsditch Murders' and the 'Siege of Sidney Street' in 1910/11. Questions were increasingly asked whether it was right to give free entry to political refugees who were seen as a danger to the state and to law and order.[22] Such anxieties magnified after the First World War with the intensification of insular nationalism and the fear of revolution. Concomitantly, the commitment to asylum largely disappeared – the Aliens Restriction Act of 1919, for example, contained no 'asylum clause'. In 1929, the Labour Home Secretary, J.R. Clynes, told a Jewish delegation that the '"right of asylum" in so far as it exists or ever existed is not a right attaching to an alien, but is a right of the Sovereign State to admit a refugee if it thinks fit to do so'.[23] When Leon Trotsky in the same year applied to come to Britain his claim for asylum was rejected partly because it would 'create a precedent that may well become very awkward'.[24] In short, the universal commitment across politics proclaimed by Earl Granville in 1852 was now reversed. John Pedder, Home Office senior civil servant with regard to alien matters from the 1900s through to the early 1930s, was clear about refusing entry to Trotsky. Refugees had been allowed entry as a courtesy and no more: 'It is common to speak of the "*right* of asylum". There never has been any such *right*.'[25]

In the 1930s, Britain had no refugee policy as such, only aliens procedures which could be used more or less sympathetically for those seeking entry. For the British state, migrants from Eastern Europe were the least desirable, no matter what problems they were facing at home. And while Britain eventually allowed entry to some 80,000 refugees from Nazism before the outbreak of war, almost all these, including those on the *Kindertransport*, were on temporary visas. The hope and expectation was that they would move to other countries which were seen, in contrast to Britain, as places of permanent emigration.[26] It is true that in the debate in the House of Commons, in which the child refugee scheme was officially announced, there was a rediscovery of and pride in asylum.[27] Even so, the children were not given the status of refugees and there was no intention that they would stay indefinitely. Entry was, in the words of a Home Office overview of policy, strictly 'on condition that they would be emigrated when they reach 18'.[28] Indeed, one MP after making an impassioned plea that something must be done and places of refuge found, quickly qualified his position: 'I refer only to a temporary home. It would not be unwise if we were to allow 10,000 of these people to make their temporary home among us.'[29] If there was a historical parallel, it was to the Belgians in the First World War. Britain, according to the Home Secretary, Sir Samuel Hoare, had 'played an invaluable part in maintaining the life of the Belgian nation' by acting as host to 'many thousands of Belgian children'.[30] After the war the quarter of a million Belgian refugees, including the children, were quickly and unceremoniously returned home by the British state. Indeed, a Repatriation Committee was set up as early as 1917.[31]

On one level, therefore, the child refugees were privileged – they were allowed entry in contrast to most of their parents. Moreover, there was no question of fully extending the scheme to other countries. There *were* three exceptional transports from Poland. Significantly, however, they were funded from outside the Refugee Children's Movement.[32] It took the remarkable work of English individuals such as Doreen Warriner, Eleanor Rathbone, Trevor Chadwick and Nicholas Winton, and the Canadian, Beatrice Wellington, to expand its reach to Czechoslovakia.[33] Indeed, from this list it is apparent that within such pro-refugee circles 'women ... did the lion's share of the work'.[34] For these activists in Prague, there was an urgent desire to push London-based refugee organisations to acknowledge the 'seriousness of [the] situation'. There was, they wrote in December 1938, a 'Real danger expulsion necessitates equal treatment with German and Austrian children'.[35]

On another level, the *Kindertransport* was restrained within the confines of the existing aliens legislation – the children were not granted asylum but temporary refuge. It was a scheme with many flaws. First and foremost, the fundamental issue of whether it was right or necessary to separate the children from their parents remained largely unstated at the time and has rarely been confronted subsequently.[36] Second, in failing to asssess the suitability of guarantors, abuses – emotional, physical, sexual and economic – were inflicted on some children. For them, the *Kindertransport* left a traumatic legacy. In this respect, it must be emphasised that the organisers were working under extreme pressure and without proper resources. As Elaine Blond, one of the key figures within the Refugee Children's Movement recalled: 'In an ideal world we would have checked the characteristics and needs of each of the children and matched them with carefully compiled family profiles.' But as she adds, 'In an ideal world, refugee children would not have existed.' She admits that 'We made many mistakes'.[37] At best, it was a remarkable grassroots movement that brought out an altruistic zeal from thousands of ordinary people in Britain and provided love and security to many *Kinder*. Yet rather than present the scheme in its full complexity, a narrative has emerged, encouraged by many of the former children themselves and *Kindertransport* associations, that has become increasingly mythical and celebratory. Indeed, it has evolved into a fairy story of good (Britain) and evil (the perpetrators of the Holocaust) rather than a well-meaning if sometimes misguided human drama from the desperate years of the Nazi era. As the survivor Primo Levi noted, reflecting on his experiences in the *Shoah*, much of life takes place in the 'grey zone'.[38] The *Kindertransport* is no exception. But in the process of making this movement into a Manichaean morality tale, and again following the pattern of the Huguenots, descriptions of the refugee journey have played a central role.

Kinder narratives

Edith Milton (formerly Kahn from Karlsruhe, Germany) came to Britain in the summer of 1939 on a *Kindertransport*. With her elder sister, Ruth, Edith settled in Swansea and after the war they joined their mother who had managed to get to America. Her memoirs, *The Tiger in the Attic: Memories of the Kindertransport and Growing Up English* (2005), are a particularly rich and multi-layered account of the process of being a child refugee: the subtlety of this text reflects Milton's status as a professional writer.[39] Indeed, her reflexive style enables a deep insight into the construction of memory in what has been, if only recently, one of the most remembered journeys of any migrant group in the twentieth century, 'the century of the refugee'.[40]

Edith came to Britain aged seven and she has only opaque memories of boarding the train that was to take her out of Germany: 'I vaguely recall weeping adults, my mother presumably among them [her father was already dead by the time she left], although I do not remember her.' She does recall, however, that on the journey

> The guard came by now and then and made jokes, and the officer in uniform and with a swastika armband who collected our papers at the border looked upon me with what I took to be parental concern as he handed back my passport, which under my name – augmented by the Jewish 'Sarah' mandated by the Third Reich – had been stamped STATELESS.

In total contrast to what has become the dominant narrative of *Kindertransportee* journeys, Edith added that 'I remember feeling a shy affection for him, a sense of safety in traveling in this carriage under his care.' Edith had no memories of the subsequent boat trip to England, only being picked up as a 'refugee package' at Liverpool Street station.[41]

Edith's mundane and rather benign account of her journey is then contrasted just a few pages later with a reflection on the collective memory of the *Kindertransport*. In this second version, the author is happy to subsume her story and, in the process, to critique – and indeed to dismiss – her own earlier rendition of it:

> This is perhaps the time to confess that it took me more than forty years to understand that our transposition to England, mine and Ruth's, was a fragment of a larger and extraordinary history. The *Kindertransport* ...

has been the subject of a fair amount of recent literature and of several films. It could, in fact, be counted as a sort of miracle, and I am still amazed at my own bland passivity and ignorance about my escape, my total numbness.[42]

The notion of *escape* is one that has become central to describe the journeys of the *Kindertransportees* as it was within Huguenot autobiographical practice from the 1680s onwards. The major and semi-official history of the movement, published in 1990, is subtitled '10,000 children escape from Nazi Europe' and the word has been used regularly in recent testimonies. In an anthology of *Kinder* accounts gathered for the fiftieth anniversary of the movement in 1988, George Bendori, formerly of Stettin, succinctly constructs a 'classic' *Kinder* narrative. Indeed, it is notable that Bendori provides a *collective*, rather than an individual account, disclosing the same pressures to conform as is evident in the second and generic description of the journey in Edith Milton's memoir. First, it consists of parental sacrifice and painful separation: 'Our parents knew they would never see us again. We, the children, understood only that we would not see our families for a long time. We will never forget the heartbreak, the clinging together for the last time.' Second, Bendori progresses to the journey itself, one of danger, fear and uncertainty:

> Who can ever forget the feeling of having escaped it all even though we were only eleven years of age. Crossing the German-Dutch border the train could not move quickly enough for us as we feared a last-minute hitch. The final inspection of documents, the ruthless way of going through our meagre possessions carried out by stern SS men whose menacing looks left no doubt in our minds as to what they would have liked to do to us.

Third and finally, there is light and hope to counter the darkness of Nazism and persecution. Redemption came first in the form of Holland: 'And then the kind smiling Dutch ticket collectors who came into the compartment to ensure that nothing untoward would happen to us from then on. It was all behind us, we were free.' It was soon followed by the example of Britain: 'And then to Dovercourt [near the port of Harwich, Essex, where many of the *Kinder* arrived and were initially settled]. Bitterly cold in the winter of 1938–39 but still heavenly. The dedicated and kind staff who looked after us and did their utmost to make us forget what our little minds had absorbed.'[43]

It is revealing that there are tropes of the *Kinder* narrative that have remained constant and others that have changed over time. In 1999, a plaque was unveiled at the House of Commons 'In deep gratitude to the people and Parliament of the United Kingdom for saving the lives of 10,000 Jewish and other children who fled to this country from Nazi persecution on the

Kindertransport 1938–1939'.[44] From its earliest days, *saved* has been the description used to justify and then to celebrate the movement of refugee children to Britain. With its Christological connotations, the word emphasises the role played by the rescuers and tends to subsume the individuality of the rescued. The first history of the *Kindertransport*, given the cheerful and optimistic title, *The Great Adventure* (1944), highlighted 'Over 9,000 saved', and concluded that it was 'no small thing … to have given to [them] the opportunity to grow up in an atmosphere of decency and normality'.[45] The book of the award-winning Warner Brothers' film, *Into the Arms of Strangers* (2000), is subtitled, similar to the wording on the House of Commons' plaque, 'the British scheme that saved 10,000 children from the Nazi regime'.[46] Nevertheless, there are subtle discontinuities in the telling of the *Kindertransport* story that have equal significance.

George Bendori, for example, while using the term *saved*, adds a feature that was remarkably absent in contemporary discussions of the scheme when it was first proposed and then implemented in 1938: 'Only our unfortunate parents were left behind to face it all. Because of their foresight we were saved.'[47] From its origins, the *Kindertransport* was justified as protecting a precious remnant, almost as if the parents were already dead and the children orphaned. In *You and the Refugee* (1939), two leading campaigners, Norman Angell and Dorothy Buxton, noted how 'We see pictures of even tiny children at our ports, labelled like parcels, bundles of forlorn and helpless childhood, homeless, parentless, seeking refuge and sanctuary from the storm of cruelty and oppression which has swept their parents to penury, imprisonment, torture, death.'[48] Their book was an attempt to gain sympathy towards the refugees and to turn what Nicholas Winton called 'passive goodness' into 'active goodness'.[49] Angell and Buxton especially utilised the emotional intensity of the *Kinder* journey to elicit British empathy towards children of a different nationality and religion who were, they implied, now alone in the world.

More recently, awareness of the Holocaust has given these journeys even greater import which, rather than querying why the parents of the children – and other adults – were not considered for rescue, has confirmed their status as somehow doomed and beyond reach. Hannele Zurndorfer came on the *Kindertransport* from Dusseldorf. She lyrically reflects in her memoir on the significance of the journey: 'a train full of children, full of hope, leaving behind the broken hearts of mothers and fathers, empty homes and a future of "night and fog"'.[50] Before September 1939, at least, this later catastrophe was not inevitable. In Hannele's case, for example, her parents came very close to having the necessary paperwork and backing to leave for America via Britain.[51] As Louise London, the most authoritative historian of British immigration policy during the Nazi era, reminds us:

> We remember the touching photographs and newsreel footage of unac-
> companied Jewish children arriving on the Kindertransports. There are
> no such photographs of the Jewish parents left behind in Nazi Europe,
> and their fate has made a minimal impact.

London adds in relation to the construction of collective memory, 'The Jews excluded from entry to the United Kingdom are not part of the British experience, because Britain never saw them.'[52] It has taken the literary vision of William Chadwick, whose father was one of the key figures in organising the Czechoslavakian *Kindertransports*, to provide a memorial of sorts to 'All those who said goodbye at the airport and on the Prague station platforms but who were unable to follow.'[53]

The marginalisation of parents in early narratives of the *Kindertransport* is paralleled by the similar absence of the word 'escape' in relation to the journey. The poet, and former *Kindertransportee*, Karen Gershon, was the first to assemble a collection of accounts, *We Came as Children* (1966). It consists of the testimony of 234 *Kinder* but 'escape' appears only once and in relation to a parent and within the Second World War itself: 'After the fall of France, my father, who had been living in Paris at the time, escaped to England, landing at Plymouth.'[54] In contrast, another child in the volume related how 'at the frontier town of Aachen all Jews had to leave the train; all except myself were allowed to continue their journey'. He was searched bodily and his belongings were 'turned upside down', putting this special treatment down to his 'Aryan' looks. It was, as he emphasised, 'a harrowing and terrifying experience for a child', but rather than state that he then escaped, he simply wrote that 'Eventually I was allowed to leave.'[55]

For the vast majority of *Kinder*, leaving Germany, Austria and Czechoslovakia was relatively uneventful. It was still obviously dislocating and deeply distressing in the separation that it entailed. The journey was certainly not the carefree experience that those organising and reporting the movement in 1938 and 1939 wished to present. Thus in a BBC radio programme broadcast in February 1939, 'Children in Flight', featuring the children interviewing each other at the Dovercourt camp, Brigitte from Westphalia stated 'Oh we had a very good journey, but we must make it quite alone.'[56] Leslie Brent (formerly Lothar Baruch from Koslin) took part in the same programme and notes that 'We had been told to be positive in what we wrote down, and that certainly comes through in this broadcast.'[57] It would take another half century for an audience to be found for the testimony of those such as Hannele Zurndorfer and her description of the point of separation: 'the last clinging embrace: my face against the familiar tweed of my father's coat and the comforting feel of my mother's fur collar.'[58]

Not surprisingly, the refugee organisers highlighted the world ahead rather than that left behind in justifying the break between the two. They thus presented the process of leaving home as if it was to go to boarding school or summer camp. The first annual report of the Refugee Children's Movement, which was in many ways a self-vindicating instant history, quoted a volunteer helper on 'the excitement of their journey'. The report continued that in Germany 'When the children received the letter notifying them when to leave, they packed all their luggage and waited excitedly for the time to arrive.'[59] Nicholas Winton, reporting the first flight from Prague in January 1939 wrote in his diary that he 'did not see one of the kids crying. They were far too excited.'[60] Why then have we moved in memory work from the *Kindertransport* journey as an adventure to one in recent decades within which the concept of *escape* has become so central?

The identity of being a *Kinder* developed fully in the late 1980s at the time of the fiftieth anniversaries and reunions. It reflected a growing interest in and awareness of the Holocaust. For the first time, at least since their arrival in 1938/1939, the *Kinder* were subject to widespread public and media interest. Comparing the two major anthologies of *Kinder* testimony, published in 1966 and 1990 respectively, it is notable that there is far more variation in the former, *We Came as Children*, than in the latter, *We Came Alone*. There is a rawness of the testimony collected by Gershon at the time of the twenty-fifth anniversary of the movement lacking in the later volume. As a poet whose identity in relationship to place and belonging was complex and fluid,[61] Karen Gershon was not afraid to give voice to those who felt lost, lonely and rootless as well as to those who felt at home in Britain.

The heterogeneity of *We Came Alone* reflects not only the transitionary stage in which the former children were still establishing (or failing to establish) new lives for themselves, but also the absence of a collective identity that the later anniversary commemoration (and popular recognition of it) clearly imparted. Since 1988, and the major reunion, there has been a series of documentaries on the *Kindertransport*, plays, publication of memoirs, the unveiling of the House of Commons plaque in 1999 and, in 2003, the creation of a public space with a memorial at Liverpool Street station, the rail terminus where the children coming via the boat train at Harwich arrived in London.[62]

The memory of the *Kindertransport* has indeed become truly international – the major documentary of the movement, for example, was American-made. It reflects the fact that the British government only granted temporary permits to the children and many went on across the Atlantic, to Palestine/Israel and to other parts of the globe: the *Kinder* became a diaspora within a wider refugee movement. American interest also reflects a self-criticism about its refugee policies during the 1930s and especially the restrictionist rejection of the

Wagner-Rogers Bill in 1939.[63] Their different approaches to their past in this respect will be the major theme of the following chapter.

Britain, and its child refugee movement, becomes the shining example of help given and a contrast to restrictionism elsewhere, especially in America. Thus the American historian and archivist Vera Fast, in what is one of the most detailed and researched accounts of the *Kindertransport*, concludes that 'While the American Congress vetoed a bill to allow entry to unaccompanied Jewish children, Britain's parliament offered hospitality to as many as the refugee agencies could care for.' She adds that with regard to the Jewish refugee crisis in the 1930s, 'Doing the "morally right" thing had not been the response of the Western world in general. The refusal of Canada and the United States to accept any *Kinder* apart from those already on quota lists is a disgrace beyond apprehension.'[64] Fast goes further and gives her narrative, entitled 'Children's Exodus', a religious underpinning, but one based on the Hebrew Bible and not Christological interpretations of it. Not surprisingly, this self-affirming image of a safe refuge and as a place of redemption has been internalised within recent British memory work. The memorial statue is located in 'Hope Square' and dedicated to the *Kinder* 'who found hope and safety in Britain through the gateway of Liverpool Street Station'.[65]

When the memorial was unveiled in 2003, as one former *Kindertransportee* noted, by the next day it had 'become a functional part of the urban landscape of the station'.[66] In fact, the original sculpture by Flor Kent was replaced, amidst some controversy, in 2006. The new sculpture, by Frank Meisler, who himself arrived as a *Kindertransportee* at Liverpool Street station two days before the outbreak of war, consists of five children and their suitcases with a fragment of railway track. It is 'surrounded by 16 milestones, each bearing the name of a city from which the Kinder departed'.[67] Britain is thus the end of the line, but one that brought freedom and the rebuilding of lives. In Berlin, in contrast, the equivalent *Kinder* statue, also by Meisler, has railway tracks going in two directions – one towards Auschwitz – the fate of the parents – and the other towards Britain. To make sure there is no doubt left in the mind of the visitor, the Berlin memorial at Friedrichstrasse railway station is bluntly entitled *Trains to life – and trains to death*.[68] A similar juxtaposition occurs in the Imperial War Museum's permanent Holocaust Exhibition, although it is perhaps not consciously intended. The section on refugee policy during the 1930s, within which the display 'Ten Thousand Children Reach Safety in Britain' is prominent, is followed by one of the most chilling items presented in the exhibition as a whole – a dissecting table from a Nazi euthanasia centre for children regarded as mentally or physically unfit.[69]

Inevitably, the trauma of the Holocaust has made its mark on post-war Jewish identities whether at an individual or collective level. Susan Soyinka's mother came to England in 1938 as a young refugee from Vienna and was one of the few members of her family to survive the Nazi era. Soyinka has written a powerful account of the evacuation of the Jews' Free School (including some *Kindertransportees*) to Mousehole, Cornwall, entitled *From East End to Land's End*. As she emphasises:

> What is particularly poignant about this story for me is that at the very time these children were travelling south-west to love and safety in Cornwall, my own Aunt Sonya [her mother's sister] – born like several of the evacuees in 1927 – together with thousands of other Jewish children, travelled on a train going in exactly the opposite direction from Drancy, Paris to Auschwitz in Poland where a very different fate awaited them.[70]

Such clear bifurcation between 'here' and 'there' – that is between places of destruction and places of safety – is understandable in the shadow of the *Shoah*. It reflects the desire to make sense of a world gone mad and to find a form of redemption, even if this means utterly demonising the continent of Europe and romanticising Britain and other countries of refuge. The tension between critical and mythical engagements of the past, between history and memory is nowhere more exposed than when confronting the destruction process, especially when recalled within remnants of families who were devasted by its enormity. Towards the end of his remarkable evocation of the truly diasporic Ephrussi clan, Edmund de Waal is overwhelmed by the cataclysm of the war years and the impact it had on his continental Jewish forebears: 'I can't make people and places things fit together any more. These stories unravel me.'[71]

Even so, the family archaeology carried out by de Waal is meticulous and there are no simplistic meanings attached to geography. His great-grandfather found refuge in Britain: 'On 1st March 1939 Viktor receives his visa, "Good for a single journey", from British passport control in Prague.' Six years later, he died, aged 84: '"Born Odessa. Died Tunbridge Wells" reads his death certificate.' Yet as Edmund de Waal adds, the heart of his life story was elsewhere. Viktor 'Lived ... in Vienna, the centre of Europe.'[72] But the popular instrumentalisation of Holocaust journeys – and especially those involving railways – requires both the collapsing of chronology (1930s/Second World War) and the Manichaean division of Europe (places of destruction/places of rescue). It also necessitates the simplification that there were no other possibilities of rescue for the Jews of the continent beyond exceptional schemes such as the *Kindertransport* or that it was somehow naturally ordained that the parents of the children should be excluded. As a 25-year old, Norbert Wollhelm helped organise roughly twenty transports that left Berlin. His testimony collected for the Warner Brothers' documentary on the *Kindertransport* emphasises the dual function of Friedrichstrasse with regard to Jews during the Nazi era. Unlike Meisler, however, Wollhelm is insistent on more precise dating: 'It was my duty to see them off … I did not realize, and I could never realize, that only a year and a half later, from the same railway station, trains would go in the other direction to Hitler's slaughterhouses.'[73]

The concept of 'escape' becomes crucial to the narrating of this story and the melding of all *Kinder* journeys into one. Many former *Kindertransportees* who left by train report the relief felt when they crossed over the border into Holland. Such fears were not without foundation. The child removed from the train at Aachen whose testimony appeared in *We Came as Children* has already been mentioned. On a larger scale, Mollie Panter-Downes was told in a matter-of-fact way by a refugee worker at Liverpool Street that of the transport of 147 children, twelve 'were taken off the train at the frontier by the Nazis, nobody seems to know why. They just got on the train and took the children off.'[74] Yet most such pre-war journeys were largely incident-free (contrasting with the last *Kindertransport* which left Holland in May 1940 on board a steam freighter, the SS *Bodegraven*, that was attacked first by German planes and then by a local defence unit on the Cornish coast).[75] Vera Fast has emphasised the variation in experience of the 'Exodus and Arrival', noting that occasionally 'a parent would act as chaperone. Ruth Michaelis's mother took her and her brother "all the way to their first foster family … in Kent, and then she went back to Germany". David Lewinski's mother accompanied him to the Dutch border.'[76] Like Norbert Wollheim, Arieh Handler was a young Jewish adult who helped with the children's transports within the Third Reich. Handler had come to Britain as a refugee in 1937 but such work on the *Kindertransport* necessitated frequent returns to Germany. Only, however, with hindsight, he recalled, was it 'frightening … I didn't allow it to be so at the time.'[77]

But to accept that many *Kinder* journeys had been untraumatic (in contrast to the initial separation from family) fails to meet the heroic expectations of a definitive refugee narrative. Leslie Brent, for example, 'cannot remember too many details' of leaving Berlin, but he has the *aide-memoire* of a recently rediscovered photograph taken after the crossing of the border by a Dutch journalist. His facial expression, as Brent notes, 'is distinctly wistful.'[78] Similarly, Hannele Zurndorfer recalled

> Of the journey I remember very little. There were children sitting beside us and opposite us; a blur of faces. But it was a strange journey: no larking or fooling about, as is usual on excursions where a lot of children are together. We were all subdued and thoughtful, wondering where we should end up and how it would all be.[79]

The mixture of sadness, confusion, tiredness, excitement and worry that made up the normal *Kinder* journey are perhaps too complex a set of emotions to be portrayed at a popular level. Walter Kammerling from Vienna recalls leaving the station there: 'I was just 15 and somewhat dazed and hardly appreciated the enormity of the situation. I certainly did not realise that it was the last time I would see my parents and Ruthi [his seventeen-year-old sister]'.[80] The state of contemplation and dazedness, however, struggles to conform to popular expectations. Instead, the narrative that *is* now dominant is summarised in one newspaper report on a *Kinder* reunion: 'Rail evacuees retrace their Shoah escape. Dozens of Holocaust survivors … retraced the journey that saved their lives 70 years ago'.[81]

In late 1938, a reporter from the (normally anti-alien) *Evening Standard* noted that 'Full of excitement at visiting a strange land the children showed little effect of their long journey and rough crossing, or indeed of the modern tragedy in which they have been involved.'[82] On the surface, Mollie Panter-Downes also 'saw no signs that these children had ended a long journey and had possibly looked their last on what they had been brought up to believe was their Fatherland'. Yet she was willing to probe further and was told by a refugee worker that they 'crumple up later when they're going to bed'.[83] The sense of loss at the time was real. It is, however, only hindsight brought with later knowledge of the devastation inflicted by the Holocaust that provides the journey with its life or death intensity, or in the title of one memoir, *A Chance in Six Million*.[84] The tendency to link all Irish famine journeys to 'coffin ships' or to repeat the story of Huguenot escape hidden in a wine barrel has been noted in previous chapters. The equivalent within the *Kindertransport* is to claim that individuals were on the last children's transport before war broke out, even though this was in reality only the experience of a minority.[85] Again, this is not to understate the increasing seriousness of the situation – on 1 September 1939 a transport arrived at Harwich, having got through the closed Dutch-German border, but there were others that tragically never materialised because of the outbreak of war.[86] As Elaine Blond recalled, 'the saddest sight of all [at the Refugees Children Movement] was the piles of unanswered, even unopened, letters stacked in the office for weeks after the declaration of war. They stayed there until we knew, absolutely, that nothing could be done.'[87]

Moreover, the focus on the train and ferry transports and the danger of being taken off has obscured the fact that at least 10 per cent of the *Kinder* arrived direct from Hamburg by ship, often on famous liners such as the *Manhattan*, to the port of Southampton.[88] One was Marianne Elsley, originally from Rostock and whose family had moved to Berlin. As was the case with Edith Milton, Leslie Brent and many others, she states that 'My memory of those times is pretty detailed and accurate, but for some reason the journey to

England is a great blur in my mind.'[89] After four hours on a train she arrived in Hamburg where the *Manhattan* was 'lying huge and comfortable' in the harbour:

> Life suddenly changed. Here was warmth, luxury, a nice cabin for four, friendly officials in uniform, huge dining-rooms, long corridors with mirrors, carpeted stairs and all sorts of unexpected signs of civilisation, which I had not expected on a ship. [90]

Child refugees such as Marianne would not therefore have experienced Liverpool Street station – the main Southampton to London rail terminus is Waterloo. Her comments on reaching the station and England in general have a wider significance: they challenge the simplistic narrative of *Kinder* arrival that has become dominant. 'On our side we still felt hemmed in. Freedom cannot be accepted in a few hours. We had had a tiring journey, although everything had been made easy as possible for us.'[91]

A slightly smaller percentage of *Kinder* flew to Croydon airport, mainly from Prague, and there were other ports of arrival, including Dover.[92] Liverpool Street station has become the fixed point of arrival, however, in recent constructions of the *Kindertransport*, acting as a place where railways and railway lines are integral to escape and freedom and not oppression and ultimate annihilation. As one of her advocates in the dispute over the sculptures suggested, Flor Kent 'conceived the idea of a memorial to the Kindertransport as a tribute to the nation … She publicly linked Liverpool Street Station to one of the greatest acts of British benevolence' and the children's arrival there is evocatively portrayed in the BBC's *Upstairs Downstairs* (2012), the station swathed in mist and the scene accompanied by the stirring singing of 'Jerusalem'.[93] In the same redemptive mode, in autumn 2009 more than twenty former *Kinder* joined Sir Nicholas Winton to re-visit their rail journeys from Prague some seventy years earlier. They eventually arrived at Liverpool Street having been met by dignitaries along the way, and tellingly subject to much international media interest throughout.[94] As William Chadwick notes, mythology has taken over the story of Nicholas Winton and the *Kindertransports*. A statue of Winton has been erected in Wilson railway station in Prague even though 'Sir Nicholas probably never set foot on [its] platforms … and the child he holds was not one of his children'.[95]

Memory battles

To complete the *Kinder* narrative, emphasis is placed on the gratitude to Britain and how the generosity of its parliament and people has been repaid by the remarkable contribution of the former child refugees to the artistic, cultural and commercial life of the nation. The 'minor miracle' of the children's transports brought to Britain's shores the future film director, Karel Reisz, and members of the Amadeus Quartet who would 'enrich the musical life of Britain and the wider world'.[96] Not surprisingly, there has been no place in the 'official' *Kinder* memory for Norbert Rondel, 'sometime wrestler and car dealer', who came to Britain on the scheme from Berlin and who had 'an unusual variety of scrapes with the law'. An intimidating and violent figure, his contributions to British society included imprisonment for grevious bodily harm and acting as the 'hard man' for the notorious landlord, Peter Rachman.[97]

It is hard to imagine that any one of the five child figures represented in Meisler's London and Berlin sculptures would later emerge as future Norbert Rondels – lacking individuality, Meisler's stylised girls and boys, largely looking upwards, exude optimism and straightforwardness. Similarly, while Flor Kent's earlier statue of a female *kind* is far more subdued, it is inconceivable that this sad and utterly innocent girl would ever become part of London's underworld life of organised crime. Yet the subsequent achievements and contributions of the former *Kinder* need to be placed in the perspective of what was their intended future. Aside from their re-emigration at eighteen, the official position from the Home Office was that 'no encouragement [must be] given to them to qualify for the professions or for "black-coated" occupations'.[98]

Another former *Kinder* who defies narrative expectations is Gustav Metzger, founder of the auto-destructive art movement in the 1950s. It has been suggested that he could be regarded as

> the Kindertransport's greatest failure: instead of building a constructive life for himself in postwar Britain, he invented a destructive life – or a destructive art. His art is a refusal to forget, to assimilate, to move on. His anger at the world is almost that of an alienated child.[99]

Metzger has not featured in any commemorative work on the *Kindertransport* yet in many ways he is a figure whose approach reveals so much about the inner dynamics of this movement. As has been suggested, Metzger's work is 'about memory and the merging of the present and the past, death and life, life and art'.[100] Born in Nuremberg of Polish Jewish parents who died in the Holocaust, critic Norman Rosenthal suggests that Metzger carries 'with him that agonised sense of guilt that is the lot of all survivors' and, it might be added, many of other former child refugees from Nazism. Yet the neglect of Metzger in *Kindertransport* memory work and representation is not accidental. Rather than redemption, his life work has been 'largely spent drawing precise attention to the endless potential of mass destruction, military and environmental … constantly inventing strategies to look directly at horrors both potential and real that have come to haunt [the twentieth] century and [beyond]'.[101]

Frank Meisler's sculpture at Liverpool Street station is perhaps as far removed from Metzger's auto-destructive art movement as is possible to imagine. To Metzger, 'Auto-destructive paintings, sculptures and constructions have a life time varying from a few moments to twenty years'.[102] Such approaches have been made manifest in German counter-monuments to the Holocaust.[103] In contrast, Meisler's figures are there to last forever. There is a wider significance of Meisler's work in relation to *The Battle of Britishness*: 'Hope Square' in Liverpool Street station is the only major memorial in a public space to the refugee presence in Britain. There are, in contrast, several devoted to *emigrants* leaving the country, for example in Liverpool, Portsmouth, Larne (Northern Ireland), and Helmsdale (Scotland) as well as exhibitions on this theme, as at the National Maritime Museum in Falmouth, Cornwall and the National Museum of Scotland (Edinburgh).[104] Even transmigrants have received recent recognition within local heritage. In Kingston upon Hull, through the energy of historian Nicholas Evans and a receptive city council, efforts have been made at the end of the twentieth century and into the new millennium to mark the arrival of 'Over 2.2 million transmigrants [who] passed through [the port from the 1830s through to 1914] en route to a new life in the US, Canada, South Africa and Australia'.[105] In this context, the absence of refugee commemoration is striking.

The *Kinder* have therefore gained a privileged place in collective memory in a country in which, until very recently if at all, most refugee and migrant journeys have largely been forgotten in spite of the fact that they have been and continue to be part of the everyday reality of modern Britain. Playwright Clare Bayley has noted the tension between this absence/presence in relation to contemporary asylum seekers and their attempts to reach Britain through desperate means, such as hiding on freight containers ferried across the English Channel and at the mercy of 'people smugglers'. Bayley finds 'the stories of migrants and refugees incredibly compelling. Our lives are so sanitised, yet, in the midst of them, all this is going on.' As she astutely observes, and mirroring Lubaina Himid's reflections on slavery and British memory, 'It's so close to us and so invisible.'[106]

Even within the Nazi era, the mythologised, aggregated and now celebrated *Kindertransport* contrasts with the memory of other journeys relating to victims of fascism, including the Basque refugee children of the Spanish Civil War. Close to 4,000 arrived in Southampton from Bilbao in May 1937 on the *Habana*, providing a precedent at an administrative level for the *Kindertransport*. There were those at the time who thought the idea to bring the Spanish children to Britain was a disaster in the making. The secretary of the Save the Children Movement, Mr Golden, argued that the journey from Bilbao was too long and the dislocation was too great a risk for the children.

Golden told the Home Office that 'he would sooner see them die in their own land than rot slowly in exile where they deteriorate physically, morally and mentally'. Rather than being redemptive, taking the children away from their parents and all that was familiar to them would lead to the 'creation of Refugees with all the dire consequences associated with a state of Refugeedom'.[107]

It was left to the *Daily Worker*, newspaper of the Communist Party of Great Britain, to invest a more positive meaning into the journey of the *Habana*. Desperate for an uplifting story after the victories of the Nationalists, it described how 'A ship of tragedy left Bilbao', arriving several days later in England as 'a ship of hope'.[108] Its portrait of its passengers as constituting 'The happiest boat surely in the world today' did not reflect the emotional state of the children. Nor did it recognise the collective nausea they experienced in a ship carrying four times its normal load of passengers and experiencing rough seas on its journey.[109] As a British doctor on board prosaically noted, 'four thousand wretchedly seasick children crowded into an old boat whose very latrines are apt to regurgitate in sympathy, are not a pretty sight'.[110]

Subsequently, lacking the more dramatic narrative of the Holocaust, the story of these Basque children has been obscure in comparison to the *Kindertransport*. At an individual level, as one of the former refugees, Oscar, recalls, 'England forgot about us'. After a series of dead-end jobs, he returned to Spain in 1948 to better himself:

> When you are in a place, and the landscape for you is very small and you don't see how you can do anything there, because there you are considered a refugee, or because the people don't realise that you had to do something else, you have to take a risk.[111]

Collectively, also, the 'story of the Basque children has been ignored by most historians of the period'. But as Jim Fyrth in his study of the Spanish aid movement in Britain during the 1930s reminds us, 'it was an epic of the British people's history. It affected almost every part of the country, and changed many people's lives [leaving] lasting links [with] the Basque lands … Those involved have never forgotten.'[112] Only recently have efforts been made to commemorate these earlier child refugees at a local level and it is still the case that nationally these journeys of the Basque children remain neglected.[113] Yet it is not only the Basque refugees during the 1930s who have been subject to amnesia. There are other Jewish journeys of forced migration in this decade which, in contrast to the *Kindertransport*, have been either marginalised or have been too challenging to be remembered. One of these, in Chapter 6, the partner chapter of Part III, is that of the *St Louis*, which, unlike the *Kindertransport*, has become notorious in North America but is largely unknown in Britain.

To conclude: *Kindertransport* memory has parallels to that over Britain and slavery in which abolitionism and abolitionists are remembered and the intensive activity in the slave trade is conveniently forgotten. The *Kindertransport* itself involved exclusion (of adults) but this is an inconvenient detail in subsequent and idealised memory work. There is thus a bitter, but unintended, irony that Frank Meisler's sculpture of the *Kinder* at Liverpool Street station was initially entitled 'Statue of Liberty'.[114] Meisler's parents were deported first from Danzig to the Warsaw ghetto and subsequently murdered in the Holocaust.[115] In reality, the Statue of Liberty, emblematic of America as home to the persecuted and oppressed, neighbours Ellis Island, symbolic now of racist restrictionism in the age of mass migration. It is, however, hard to conceive that such connections were intended in Meisler's naming of his tribute to Britain or to tell from his memorial that the country never intended to provide permanent refuge to these children. Memory of the *Kindertransport* has been instrumentalised to show how generosity is integral to British character. But as Louise London has passionately argued in response to claims that Britain 'has a proud tradition of taking in refugees over many centuries', that even 'if it isn't proud, even if it doesn't fit the political message, this country also has a history of not taking in refugees'.[116] This ambiguity was excruciatingly realised by the Kammerling family in Austria. It is thus fitting to close this chapter with the testimony of its youngest member, Walter:

> My 17 and 18 year old sisters were too old to go [on the *Kindertransport* with him] as the age limit was 16. My eldest sister, Erika, could leave on a domestic permit, being over 18, but Ruthi did not qualify for a domestic permit nor the *Kindertransport*. She went with my parents to Theresienstadt … [117]

6

The *St Louis* and after: refugee journeys without end?

Introduction

It has been noted that in the attempt to define Britishness – whether at the level of high politics or popular discussion – belief in fair play, decency and tolerance spanning history has been central. Tolerance especially is identified as a 'core British value'. To some, Britain's past treatment of refugees was a manifestation of such 'innate' tolerance. Chapter 1 analysed the 2006 Mass-Observation directive on national identity. It will be helpful to return briefly to this archive with specific reference to the granting of asylum. One Observer quoted with pride two former refugees who many decades later still 'raved over what a wonderful country had been to and for them'.[1] While recognising a parallel tendency towards insularity ('the English play cricket and play the game. Continentals do not ... '), another Observer, a retired charity worker from Sussex, was quick to qualify

> we do have a proud record of welcoming refugees to our shores, from the Huguenots, through to those fleeing from Russia at the beginning of the last century, to Jews escaping from the Nazi hordes in the 1930s to the plight of the Kenyan Asians in March 1968.[2]

Similarly, six years earlier, in another Mass-Observation survey, 'Coming to Britain', which probed attitudes to newcomers past and present, the dominant note was that Britain had a very positive record in the past:

> One thinks particularly of the sizeable population of Jews seeking refuge from the pogroms in Eastern Europe in the late nineteenth century and the Jews seeking refuge from Hitler in the last century ... After such

[movements] I do not think Britain can ever be accused of failing to offer a home to those in need.[3]

Indeed, there was resentment of a particular prompt in the directive provided by Mass-Observation's organisers: 'one MP during a recent debate in the House of Commons shouted that if Anne Frank had sought asylum in Britain, she would have been turned away'. Revealingly, rather than interpret this polemical intervention as a way of exploring attitudes to those trying to find refuge *now*, some Observers believed this was an attack on the country's refugee policy during the Nazi era:

> The truth is that a great many people did find asylum in Britain at that time and I knew some of them. If the MP had bothered to read the story of the Frank family he would have known that Otto Frank was offered the opportunity to flee to Britain or America by friends and relations who had already found refuge. He turned it down because he had business interests in Holland.[4]

There was one alternative voice within the 195 responses to the 2000 directive. The Observer was uneasy about his hostility towards present-day asylum seekers in the light of the past:

> one cannot help recall the plight of the European Jewish refugees before the Second World War, and how they were spurned in large numbers by both Europe and the USA. Their fate was awful and one has to ask how many more would have been saved if the UK and US were less restrictive.[5]

Even though this Observer ultimately did not change his contemporary attitudes, reassuring himself that asylum seekers now were simply economic migrants in disguise, his comments show that there was at least some awareness that British generosity towards Jewish refugees from Nazism was not all positive. Yet it remains, as Louise London has pointed out, that there is a 'gulf that exists between the memory and history of that record'.[6] Indeed, there is often shock expressed when evidence of negative past attitudes is exposed on this topic. In another Mass-Observation survey from 2006 – 'History Matters – or does it?' – a journalist from Cheltenham noted, when reading an anthology of the organisation's previous work from the 1940s, that he was 'struck how many of the same themes came up – especially in attitudes to refugees from Germany which were very similar to "asylum seekers" today'.[7]

The historiography and popular memory work on refugee policy during the Nazi era is thus marked by the binaries of accusation versus defensiveness, and by self-criticism versus self-congratulation. The case study of the *St Louis*, however, will illustrate the complexity of British immigration procedures

during the 1930s and the problems that emerge if they are crudely categorised as either inherently generous or utterly mean-spirited. Told briefly, the
German cruise ship, part of the Nazi-controlled Hamburg–America line, left
Hamburg in May 1939 carrying more than 900 Jewish refugees on board for
Cuba. Arriving at the port of Havana, the Cuban authorities rejected all but a
score of those that it had initially offered landing passes to. The *St Louis* was
forced to return to Europe. Ultimately 287 were to be allowed temporary entrance to Britain, or roughly 30 per cent of the total. Nevertheless, in Britain it
has not proved to be such a 'usable past' as the *Kindertransport*, a paradox that
will be explored and explained further in this chapter.

As emphasised in the sister chapter to this section, the *Kindertransport* has
been remembered as an act of *saving* Jews during the Holocaust, regardless of
the fact that it occurred before the war and the implementation of the 'Final
Solution'. One figure in particular, Nicholas Winton, the British businessman
who was involved in the rescue of Czech Jewish children, has become known
as 'Britain's Schindler'.[8] As William Chadwick perceptively notes in explaining the Winton phenomenon, 'We crave Heroes (and prefer to ignore Brecht's
counter comment, "Pity the country that needs heroes!") and almost always we
prefer to focus our wonderment and our adulation on a single figure.'[9]

In contrast, the *St Louis* is now represented as the 'Voyage of the Damned',[10]
or one of 'men, women and children floating across the Atlantic toward certain
doom'.[11] Indeed, it has 'become a symbol of the world's abandonment of Jewish
refugees from Nazi Germany'.[12] The ship's journey has been given even wider
significance. In promoting a fictionalised story of the *St Louis*, Holocaust survivor and Nobel Prize winner, Elie Wiesel, claims that it provides 'an excellent
introduction for young readers wishing to understand contemporary history
and its traumatic and moral challenges'.[13]

Ironically, in relation to such reflections on the *St Louis*, the first attempt
to create a narrative of its journey, *Bound for Nowhere*, a short film sponsored
by the American Jewish Joint Distribution Committee and released in August
1939, presented the story as one of rescue and the well-being of its passengers who were now safely deposited in Belgium, Holland, France and Britain.
They were 'never again to return to the land they were forced to leave'. The
film concluded on an uplifting note, praising the 'noble examples' of the receiving countries and the importance of Jewish philanthropy in the rescue of
the refugees. With our knowledge now of what was to happen in the next six
years there was a touching naivety about its final statement: 'Goodbye *St Louis*,
goodbye to a terrible past.'[14] These words, however, emphasise the importance
of precise chronology. No one then, not even the leading Nazi antisemitic
ideologues, could yet have imagined and envisaged what was to happen to
European Jewry. Within weeks, the fragility of this safety as related in *Bound*

for Nowhere was exposed. Yet in the post-war re-telling of the ship's journey in 1939, the messiness and inherent ambivalence of contemporary perspectives and responses – made up of elements of pessimism and optimism, hospitality and exclusion – have been distorted and smoothed over by hindsight. The starting point has become the death camps and killing fields of the *Shoah*.

In his last speech, Auschwitz survivor Rabbi Hugo Gryn used the *St Louis* as a morality tale in which the 'only decent person in this whole story is the German captain of the ship. He tries to do whatever he can. He negotiates with the United States, with Columbia, with Chile, with Paraguay, with Argentina – but nothing comes of it.' The ship was then forced to return to Europe where the majority were taken in by Holland, France and Belgium and the rest by Britain. Yet rather than focus on those who ended up in Cuba and Britain, attention has been devoted to the six hundred-plus who remained on the continent. It is why to Hugo Gryn and others such as his fellow Auschwitz survivor, Elie Wiesel, the story of the *St Louis* imparts such an important and universal warning:

> How you are with the one to whom you owe nothing, that is a grave test and not only as an index of our tragic past. I always think that the real offenders at the half way mark of the century were the bystanders, all those people who let things happen because it didn't affect them directly.[15]

It is worth contrasting the indifference of the 'free world' to the *St Louis* as located by Hugo Gryn, to Frank Meisler's pleasure that his memorial to the *Kindertransport* would be located at a busy railway station: 'The people who saved us were for the most part anonymous. They had the capacity to reach out to Jewish children and overcome intolerance … perhaps the same goes for today's commuters.'[16] In telling the story of the Holocaust – an event now where there is little place in its narration for ambiguity – the bystander can either be a selfless force for good, or, alternatively, an aider and abetter of genocide.

In mythic representations of the *St Louis*, those dumped on the continent become lost in the 'night and fog' of the Holocaust and the possibility that some of those may have survived confuses the clarity of the storyline. It was, argued Arthur Morse in what was the first popular rediscovery of the episode, 'impossible to know how many' were murdered 'in the German gas chambers.'[17] Such vagueness enabled morally well-meaning – but ultimately misleading – statements such as 'Other than the 288 that came to Britain and the 22 who were allowed to land in Cuba, none of the others survived. None of them.'[18] In fact, through painstaking research, researchers at the United States Holocaust Memorial Museum have concluded that 365 of the 620 who were allowed in by France, Belgium and Holland in 1939 survived the war.[19]

Naga is a young Eritrean refugee in a squatter camp in Calais. He is desperate to be granted asylum in the UK. He 'came to Calais via Sudan, Libya and Italy [and] has already been deported from Britain once' having tried to enter as a stowaway. Life, he says, 'is like a wave. You go, come back, go, come back, this is the way of life.'[20] The *St Louis* was a luxury cruise ship, and although conditions deteriorated returning to Europe, they cannot be compared to the filth, misery and perils of Naga's journey. Yet on one level the fluidity and uncertainty of contemporary asylum seekers and their lack of status in a world of bureaucratic restrictionism is not totally removed from the experiences of those on board the *St Louis*. Some of those in Holland, France and Belgium were able to make it to America as late as the first years of the war. These included Liane Reif-Lehrer who journeyed with her mother and brother from France to Spain to Portugal and finally from Lisbon to Newark in November 1941.[21] Again, the 'neat' refugee narrative of home–persecution–flight–resettlement, or, alternatively, of the anti-refugee sequence of persecution–flight–rejection–return–death is rarely conformed to either in the case of the *St Louis* or of obscure asylum seekers such as Naga. The reality is far more complicated and untidy given the many layers of state control that typify the modern world.

After rejection by Cuba, Captain Gustav Schroeder of the *St Louis* deliberately sailed his ship past the coast of Florida, hoping but failing to shame the American government into action – the Roosevelt administration denied permission for him to land his passengers there.[22] Canada similarly refused.[23] It is for this reason that the dominant story of the *St Louis* has been one of 'refuge denied',[24] with the authors of the major books, film and documentaries being North American.[25] The story also has received prominence at the United States Holocaust Memorial Museum, which opened in 1993, where passenger lists, tickets, and telegrams from the passengers are used 'dramatizing American indifference'.[26] In response to such telegrams, according to the Museum's first official guide, 'the White House maintained its silence on refugee issues'. It concludes, 'Only the 288 passengers who disembarked in England were safe. Of the rest, only a few survived the Holocaust.[27] At the equivalent national permanent Holocaust exhibition at the Imperial War Museum (2000), the entry of refugees is dealt with largely through the story of the *Kindertransport* and thus far more positively.[28] There is brief mention of the *St Louis* but even then the emphasis is on *American* restrictionism in contrast to the response from Western European states: 'On 3 June 1939 the US State Department refused entry to refugees on the ship St Louis … Neither Cuba nor the US would take them in. After extensive press coverage, Britain, France, the Netherlands and Belgium agreed to divide the refugees between them.'[29] What is rarely mentioned is that those on board the *St Louis* were not treated by contemporaries as simply refugees. Instead, they were transmigrants who would be taken in at best on a temporary basis.

On 11 June 1939 the British government received a now much-quoted telegram from the 'Passenger Committee' of the ship:

> 907 PASSENGERS ON S.S. 'ST LOUIS' HALF WOMEN AND CHILDREN REFUSED LANDING IN CUBA IN SPITE OF PERMITS AND NOW ON RETURN VOYAGE TO HAMBURG BEG TO BE SAVED BY BEING GRANTED ASYLUM IN ENGLAND OR AT LEAST DISEMBARKATION AT SOUTHAMPTON AS RETURN TO HAMBURG IMPOSSIBLE AND ACTS OF DESPERATION WOULD BE UNAVOIDABLE.[30]

The British government was anxious to avoid the *St Louis* arriving at a port in England as it would then be harder to remove them: 'It would be easier to reject such individuals while they were on German soil than to refuse them admission to this country and enforce them to return to Germany.'[31] More sympathetically, but with the same emphasis on their temporariness, Sir Alexander Maxwell, Permanent Undersecretary at the Home Office, later described the refugees on the *St Louis*, and others stranded in Britain because of the war, as being of the '"bird of passage" type'.[32]

The hope of British officials and politicians was that the ship would return to Hamburg and then, through individual selection, they would be able to ascertain 'whether [the refugees] were of a desirable or undesirable class'. What they feared if the ship arrived direct was that it would be 'something of the nature of a general jail delivery at the instance of the Gestapo'.[33] In fact, the selection was made in Antwerp where the ship was finally allowed to dock. There is little doubt that the British authorities deliberately chose refugees with close relatives in Britain or who had visas to America and could thus leave once their quota number had been reached.[34] They were also encouraged to take some passengers from the *St Louis* by the promise of payment towards their maintenance made by the American Jewish Joint Distribution Committee. In the House of Commons, it was emphasised by Sir Osbert Peake, Under-Secretary of State for the Home Office, that the 'special arrangements … cannot be regarded as a precedent for the reception of refugees'. It was the 'special circumstance which would justify us making an exception in this case'.[35]

Peake and others were wary of giving encouragement to the Nazis that might lead to a repetition of this episode – indeed, the *St Louis* was only one of many such 'refugee' ships travelling the oceans in the year before war. The others, however, have been largely forgotten. In late 1938/early 1939, for example, the German Hapag-Lloyd *Cordillera* travelled to Guatemala via Dover with 300 Jewish refugees on board alongside its normal cruise passengers. Like the *St*

Louis a few months later, they were also refused permission to land. Unlike those on the now infamous ship, the refugees on the *Cordillera* were subject to antisemitic abuse from the crew. As Nicholas Evans concludes,

> Ocean liners may have been at sea thousands of miles away from the heart of European prejudice, but they were in their own way conduits for prejudice and symbols of fascism as much as they were the very means of escape.[36]

Indeed, the story of the refugees from the *Cordillera* was only rescued from total obscurity because it was observed by the literary couple Osbert Sitwell and Beverley Nichols who were on the same ship. It was a chance encounter that has been rediscovered by the latter's biographer.[37]

British officials were also worried about providing ammunition to the vocal anti-alien press in Britain. The *Daily Express*, as we have seen with regard to the *Kindertransport*, was one of the most virulent in its antipathy towards the refugees in the mainstream media.[38] Indeed, the *Daily Express* had maintained an anti-alien stance since its formation during the 1900s. It echoed Peake's comments with regard to the *St Louis* that the example must not be repeated: there was 'no room for any more refugees in this country … If we give refugees a home in this country they become a burden and a grievance.'[39]

Those allowed into Britain docked at Southampton on 21 June 1939 on board another Hamburg–America ship, the *Rhakotis*, where they had been transferred at Antwerp alongside those destined for France. Their arrival was not a major occasion, partly as the day after the King and Queen were due in Southampton following a royal tour to Canada. When the refugees came into the port the 'town [was] forging on with preparations for one of the most memorable days in its centuries-long history'.[40] Nevertheless, if the royal arrival led to 'Unforgettable Scenes',[41] the *St Louis* refugees did not pass by totally unnoticed. The Jewish refugee organisations in Britain, however, were anxious not to cause any alarm in the light of what they feared was rising anti-alienism. A spokesman told the local newspaper that 'This party of refugees consists of good, middle-class German Jews, and includes a large number of persons of skilled professions. Some of them are very distinguished.' Their temporary status was also emphasised.[42] The *Times* gave their arrival a mere two inches and again gave space to British Jewish organisations, especially their insistence that those on the *Rhakotis* would not 'constitute any real addition to the number of refugees who would have been permitted temporary residence.'[43]

It was very different for the ex-*St Louis* passengers in Southampton: for them the moment of disembarkation had a special meaning. The journey from Antwerp had been uncomfortable 'crammed into a cargo ship, sleeping on bunk beds in the hold and sharing two toilets', as the fifteen-year-old, Jewish refugee, Gisela Knepel (later Feldman) recalled: 'What a contrast to the liner – but we didn't care. We felt safe.'[44] The local newspaper quoted one of those stepping foot on dry land from the *Rhakotis*. 'Speaking in broken English', the refugee emotionally proclaimed that 'We saw the shores of Cuba, and of Holland, Belgium and France – but all from the deck of a ship. Now we are really landing at last.'[45] Another 'knelt down and kissed the earth'.[46] Like the *Kinder* who had been arriving in the port since late 1938, those on the *Rhakotis* were soon whisked off by train to Waterloo. Yet if Southampton is remembered by the refugees it was because the bunting and decorations they first encountered were mistakenly believed to be for them, and not for the King and Queen.[47] For the *Kinder*, entry to Britain has been given a more lasting significance. Lotte Bray, for example, a seventeen-year-old from Halle, left Germany 'in typical fashion, a thorough search by a woman who stole my watch and a small signet ring'. In contrast

> The journey was uneventful and as we landed at Southampton we saw our first British bobby and – wonders of wonders – he smiled at us. I think it was then I made up my mind that I would never leave England if it was at all possible – a country where a policeman actually smiled must be a good place to settle.[48]

The refugees on board the *St Louis* were anxious to stress that half their number were made up of women and children, thereby highlighting innocence and justification in claiming asylum.[49] But the reality was that this was a relatively large group with a sizeable number of male adults. Thus the refugee organisations and the British government were both at pains to downplay the significance of the arrival of the 287 on board the *Rhakotis*. Most of the men were then sent to the temporary Kitchener refugee camp near Sandwich, Kent, one of many neglected sites of transmigrancy in British heritage and history.[50]

As emphasised previously, the *Kinder*, too, were on temporary permits, but it was a scheme that was much heralded at the time, and, if largely forgotten for decades after the war, has proved a highly successful story since its rediscovery in the late 1980s. In North America, the *St Louis* has a major place in memory work as a lost opportunity of rescue. In Britain, the ambiguity associated with the terms on which those on board were allowed entry is too great for it to be collectively remembered with any sense of triumph or moral superiority. Gisela Feldman's parents were of Polish origin and the family was particularly vulnerable in Nazi Germany. Her father was one of those deported in October 1938 and was still out of the country when her mother decided to leave on the *St Louis* with her two daughters. They were three of the 288 who arrived on the *Rhakotis* on 21 June 1939. Gisela's passport was stamped by the local Immigration Officer and highlights the everyday reality of alien immigration procedures:

LEAVE TO LAND GRANTED AT SOUTHAMPTON THIS DAY ON
CONDITION THAT THE HOLDER WILL EMIGRATE FROM THE
UNITED KINGDOM AND WILL NOT TAKE ANY EMPLOYMENT
OR ENGAGE IN ANY BUSINESS, PROFESSION OR OCCUPATION
IN THE UNITED KINGDOM.[51]

Both Gisela and her mother managed to subvert these restrictions by taking up work as domestic servants, the most common occupation for refugee women in Britain during the 1930s.[52]

Anton Haas (later Tony Hare), born in Moravia during the First World War, also came to Britain on the *Rhakotis* following the same route as Gisela Feldman. His parents found a place for him on the *St Louis* and through bribery and persistence in a matter of weeks he assembled the necessary paperwork to obtain an exit permit. Yet in spite of finding safety and re-building his life in Britain, he cannot find much place for celebrating the nation's role during the epic journey of the *St Louis*. In his autobiography, *Spanning the Century: The Story of an Ordinary Man in Extraordinary Circumstances* (2002), while Hare accepts that he was lucky in having escaped and was pleased 'to find myself in Britain rather than Cuba', he 'found the attitude of the British government both very degrading and unjust'. As a Czech citizen, he was dismayed at the role of Chamberlain in imposing the Munich agreement and as a Zionist over Britain's Palestine policy. He was also angered about the conditions imposed on his entry by the British state. Haas had 'a guarantee from a British citizen that I would not be a burden to the British taxpayer, a guarantee which was in addition backed by the Joint American Jewish Aid Committee'. Even so,

> When my only possession, namely my £100 for which my father had paid £300 to the Nazis, was impounded by the British government to be returned to me when I left the country or became a British citizen, I really lost my faith in justice meted out by government.[53]

The marginal, semi-legal and temporary status of the Feldmans and Tony Hare on arrival in Britain is thus not the basis of a heroic, usable past. It is significant, therefore, that the story of the *St Louis* has been re-told only once in a major British cultural form – and by a writer who has taken great delight in subverting standard historical narratives.[54]

Representation

Julian Barnes's *A History of the World in 10 ½ Chapters* was published in 1989 and further established the author as was one of the major British literary talents of the post-war era. 'History' is a theme that runs through much of

Barnes's work, but it is in a playful, postmodern form. Fact and fiction are melded and chronology subverted. Barnes recognises that historians construct their pasts and thus make up stories, an approach that he relishes in much of his writing. The voyage of the *St Louis* forms one of 'Three Simple Stories', or Chapter 7 of his book, the other two relating to the *Titanic* and to Jonah and the whale.[55]

In the Parenthesis to *A History of the World*, Barnes states that 'We make up a story to cover the facts we don't know or can't accept; we keep a few true facts and spin a new story round them.'[56] Yet in his treatment of the *St Louis*, the third of his 'simple stories', the bulk of Barnes's chapter at a superficial level is a straightforward narrative which appears to draw heavily on the early accounts by Morse (1968) and especially Thomas and Morgan-Witts (1974). At another level, the book's recurring theme of Noah's Ark reappears in his re-telling of the story. In the refugee memoirs of Huguenot Dumont de Bostaquet, the biblical Flood was utilised to make sense of the cataclysmic world of the *dragonnades*. Within a religious discourse, the Ark is God's form of rescue for the virtuous.[57] But in the secular world of Julian Barnes, and as with an earlier chapter in *A History of the World*, the Ark does not necessarily protect its passengers, just as Turner's *Slavers* reverses the biblical myth.

Thomas and Morgan-Witts end their account of the 'voyage' in Southampton: 'After precisely forty days and forty nights of wandering on the high seas, the last passengers from the *St Louis* had found their Promised Land.'[58] Barnes closes similarly, emphasising the number '40', subverting the redemptive biblical allusion (melding together the story of Noah in Genesis and the departure from Egypt in Exodus) of his journalist-historian predecessors: 'On Wednesday, 21st June the British contingent from the *St Louis* docked at Southampton. They were able to reflect that their wanderings at sea had lasted precisely forty days and forty nights.' He adds that for the others on the *St Louis*, 'Their chances rose or fell depending upon the country to which they had been alloted'.[59]

Randomness and the absence of any divine purpose clearly appeal to Barnes. He also relishes the vicious irony that the refugees on the *St Louis* were formally booked on the Hamburg–America Line as 'tourists, travelling for pleasure'. These words 'were an evasion … as was the purpose of their voyage'.[60] Throughout his *A History of the World* Barnes returns to the theme of boats and vessels that are meant to bring pleasure and protection yet end by being the source of death and destruction, most notoriously with *Titanic*. The story of the *St Louis* is utilised to show the chaos and dislocation of the modern world, a relatively early example of a major British writer engaging with the Holocaust to provide a critique of modernity. As has been suggested of Barnes's book, 'What is brutal, frightening, and degrading about the history of the world is not the stories that link events together …, but the events themselves, those moments in time, moments in space, where human ignorance, stupidity, violence, and hate are laid bare.'[61]

Contemporary descriptions of the *St Louis* describe it as a 'storm tossed ship',[62] one which was 'roaming the high seas'.[63] In subsequent histories, documentaries and films, the emphasis has been on the 'voyage' of the *St Louis*. Barnes also uses the word 'voyage', but with his juxtaposition of its status as a cruise ship and the reality that its passengers were rejected Jewish refugees, he subverts with irony its more positive meanings: 'After a voyage of 10,000 miles, the *St Louis* docked at Antwerp, 300 miles from its port of departure.'[64] Both length of trip and its nautical nature would seem to justify the use of the word 'voyage', but the word also implies an element of choice and freedom which fails to reflect the acute dilemmas faced by German Jewry in 1939. The fact that uncertain landing passes to Cuba were purchased shows the desperation of those on board. The importance of terminology and the loaded nature of key words to describe migration has been explored in Chapter 2. 'Voyage', for example, would be regarded as inappropriate to describe the 'Middle Passage' and its totally involuntary nature. The utter lack of choice was bitterly satirised in black British artist, Keith Piper's *Go West Young Man* (1987): 'I first heard that joke as they loaded us into the hold of the ship ... 400 years ago'. This work features the 1789 'Description' of the *Brookes*.

Early in his story of the *St Louis* passengers, Barnes wonders whether 'Perhaps their escape from Germany felt as miraculous as that of Jonah from the whale'.[65] The reader knows that this is not to be the case and that money will be the key factor of how they will be received. 'How much are refugees?', he asks, and responds that in the 'world of entry permits and panic it is always a seller's market'.[66] It is important to restore agency to refugees and not to present them merely as passive victims. Too often, as anthropologist Liisa Malkki argues, there is the 'expectation of a certain kind of *helplessness* as a refugee characteristic'.[67] To refer to the Jews' 'voyage' on the *St Louis*, however, overempowers their choice and understates their desperation, as Barnes's aphorism on the economics of the crisis coolly exposes. It is significant in this respect that Tony Hare, as one of the refugees on board, in his memoir remembers one of the films devoted to the ship as *The Journey of the Damned* rather than its correct title, the *Voyage of the Damned*.[68]

Here, then, is a story that would be hard to reconstruct with Britain in the guise as hero or villain. It appeals to Barnes for the same reasons that it could not become part of the 'heritage industry', a development that Barnes himself has parodied violently in *England, England* (1998).[69] The *St Louis* episode (Barnes's brief intervention aside) has failed so far to become part of British collective memory. Thus when the story *was* presented to the public in 1996 it was on Channel 4, the minority television station and tellingly as 'Secret

History' and by an (Iranian exile) Canadian director.[70] Yet embracing the convoluted and troubled journeys of the refugee passengers on board the *St Louis* and the ambiguity of responses they reflect is not impossible. Indeed, it has been reflected in some recent memory work in both America and Britain. The remaining section of this chapter will explore approaches to the *St Louis* that have emerged in recent years. Sometimes subtle and sophisticated, sometimes simplistic, they reveal the ongoing battles over the meanings of the ship and why it is still deemed relevant in a new century and a very different world. In particular, these debates will be related to the intricate and ambivalent nature of immigration procedures during the Nazi era.

The popularisation of the Holocaust in the late twentieth century, linked to its Americanisation, has led to a simplification of the three principal 'actors' – perpetrators, victims and bystanders – to explain its scale and ferocity. As explored in Chapter 5, complexities of geography have been rendered comprehensible by presenting the places of destruction as limited in number, 'other' and evil rather than being part of the everyday world in thousands of locations. Journeys would thus be to the world of destruction and, more rarely, to deliverance and freedom. The *St Louis* in summer 1939 defies such expectations and generalisations. Its *German* captain was sympathetic to his passengers and it was partly his actions in sailing close to America that brought so much attention to the ship. The return to Europe was, in reality, neither to absolute safety nor certain death. Yet to work as either an indictment of past indifference or as a future warning, its storyline has been made more dramatic and unambiguous. Hence, since the rediscovery of the *St Louis* from the 1960s, there has been a common assumption that all or most those distributed to France, Holland and Belgium were murdered during the Holocaust. Such conjecture continued into the 1990s when interest in the ship's journey intensified. Thus in the United States Holocaust Memorial Museum it was asserted that only a tiny number of those sent from Antwerp to France, Holland and Belgium were alive at the end of the Second World War. The Imperial War Museum's permanent Holocaust Exhibition (2000) also states that 'most … did not survive the war'.[71] More blatantly, an education pack produced in the early 2000s by the Holocaust Memorial Day Trust in Britain specifically states that 'Of those 936 refugees who returned to Europe, only 350 survived the war years.'[72] The real number of deaths has been reliably estimated as 254, an appalling figure, but representing just over one-quarter of the total passengers and 40 per cent of those who were taken in by the three continental countries.[73]

The recent work sponsored by the United States Holocaust Memorial Museum tracing what happened to those sent to France, Holland and Belgium has stripped away some of the mystification relating to the journey of the *St Louis*. In confronting this new research, Holocaust historian, Deborah Lipstadt, has been particularly open and reflexive. She traced her early knowledge and interest in the subject to reading Arthur Morse's *While Six Million Died*, repeating this pioneer if sensationalist historian of Allied responses that it was impossible to know how many were 'caught up in the jaws of the Nazi murder machine'. Lipstadt now acknowledges that this is now 'simply wrong'. Likewise, Lipstadt has changed her perspective on contemporary responses to the refugees on the ship:

> When I began to teach about the Holocaust in general and America's response in particular, I always cited the saga of the *St Louis* as an example of America's coldheartedness. Later, as I developed a more nuanced understanding of the period, I understood the constraints faced by American officials ...

In particular, Lipstadt highlights that there were 'many other ships crossing the Atlantic at the same time ... and there were many people on the lists waiting for permission to enter the United States whose quota numbers were ahead of those on the *St Louis*'.[74]

To explain is not necessarily to condone. But Lipstadt is still convinced – because of the *St Louis*'s brief closeness to the shores of Florida and the 'lights of Miami' – that 'Certainly some exception to the rule could have been made'.[75] It remains essential, as Michael Marrus has warned, in Holocaust research, especially in relation to free world and Allied responses, to 'give contemporaries a fair hearing'. Only recently has this occurred in relation to refugee policy during the Nazi era.[76] If there was an early tendency in such work to condemn, as typified by Morse at a more popular level, then there is a growing trend towards apologetica, as reflected in the analysis of William Rubinstein's *The Myth of Rescue* (1997). Subtitled 'Why the democracies could not have saved more Jews from the Nazis', Rubinstein has used the *St Louis* as a 'perfect example of the ahistorical treatment of these events'. Rubinstein suggests that with the arrival of the ship in Antwerp and the dispersal of the refugees, 'One would have thought that ... justice was done by the Western world for these wretched Jews'.[77] Instead, Rubinstein quotes Michael Berenbaum, then of the United States Holocaust Memorial Museum that this was a classic case of 'man's inhumanity to man' as these Jews would soon largely become victims of the Holocaust.[78]

Politics and procedures

Rubinstein is right to point out the misuse of hindsight in critiquing democratic responses. Nevertheless, by failing to mention the absolute refusal of

Canada and the USA to take the *St Louis* refugees he ignores what is an important case study in understanding the responses and reactions of these North American countries. Yet beyond such polemical approaches – both offensive and defensive – to the journey of the *St Louis*, more precise questions have been raised in the twenty-first century about the nature of immigration policies both at the time and subsequently.

In her thorough investigation of British immigration procedures during the Nazi era, Louise London concludes in *Whitehall and the Jews* (2000) that 'selection and exclusion' were central. Rather than being another polemical intervention in an emotional field, London's analysis is based on extensive research into the archives of the British state and refugee bodies. Justifying her statement that processes were designed 'to keep out large numbers of European Jews', London provides statistics that make her point clearly. She contrasts 'the estimated 500,000 to 600,000 family and individual case files in the archives of Britain's main Jewish organisation dealing with refugees and the number of Jewish refugees actually admitted, which totalled about 80,000'.[79]

Taking the period from 1933 to 1939 as a whole, in many ways the *St Louis* was untypical – it was late in the pre-war refugee crisis, the numbers on board the ship were very high and the amount of media attention was unprecedented. Even so, its journey in May/June 1939 has become emblematic, especially in North America, of both the increasingly desperate Jewish search for refuge and the liberal democratic response to that need. The *St Louis* provides potential on the one hand for hard questions to be asked, but also, on the other, for its atypical nature and now mythical status to be exploited for polemical affect. Both contrasting tendencies are apparent in recent pedagogic interventions with regard to the ship.

In the British case, reflecting the work of Louise London, secondary schoolchildren have been asked to consider 'Why do you think the government wanted to pre-select the refugees allowed into Britain? Do you think this was fair?'[80] In America, the prize-winning fictional version of the *St Louis*, Kim Ablon Whitney's *The Other Half of Life* (2009), is accompanied by 'questions for discussion'. One of these, following the approach of Arthur Morse, focuses only on negative responses to the refugees on the ship, adding to its ahistorical treatment by assuming their subsequent murder:

> Why do the officials in so many countries refuse sanctuary for the Jews aboard the MS *St Francis* [the fictional version of the *St Louis*]? Would the officials have refused if they had known they were sending the passengers to their death?[81]

One model of enquiry opens up questions, the other closes them off. The American educational example is more emotionally satisfying with its absolute certainties. The more searching (if less influential) approach coming from Britain, however, provides a way into the ambivalence that was at the heart of immigration procedures within most liberal democracies. It helps tease out why some Jewish refugees and not others were allowed entry during the 1930s. Most such journeys out of the Third Reich were far more mundane than those on the *St Louis* and, before November 1938, were less clearly about 'refuge'. It made immigration officials at ports of entry rather than figures such as President Roosevelt the 'kings' of decision-making.[82] The remaining part of this chapter will explore how these procedures were experienced at a grass-roots level. It will illustrate the less sensational aspects of day-to-day policy but also the strains and anxieties inflicted on those seeking entry.

Lilli Palmer became a film star adored on both sides of the Atlantic, admired for her beauty and talent. In mid-1930s Britain, however, she was just one of many aliens trying to find work as an actress in the struggling film industry. In spite of backing from the emigre director, Alexander Korda, her problem was paperwork. Jewish in origin, she left the Third Reich and lived a life on the margins flitting between France, Switzerland and Britain. In Basel, she considered her options, rejecting the option of Switzerland: 'No film industry, and the theatres overflowing with German refugees. There was nothing for it: back to England.' Yet such a decision was not without its problems. 'During the Channel crossing I braced myself for the impending battle with the immigration authorities, rehearsing various opening gambits and fitting answers to possible traps ... and to scan the officer's face carefully in order to guess my best mode of attack'.[83]

Arriving at Dover, she 'knew at once that I had no chance at all ... Silence would be my best weapon.' Palmer then recites her immigration record as read from an immigration officer's perspective through her 'grey alien's registration card':

> 'Entered on a visitor's visa – applied for labour permit – permit refused. Second application granted ... ' He broke off and looked at me accusingly. I looked back without a word. Another officer joined him and together they peered at the offending document while the first man proceeded, raising his voice: 'Applied again for a labour permit – permit refused – alien requested to leave the UK.'

Her request for a visa was refused and her documents returned. Asking what she should do, the officials told her to 'Go back'. Palmer responded 'Where to? Do you want me to swim the Channel?' The response to this suggestion and the ultimate decision of these immigration officers in many ways provides a summary of British procedures in the 1930s: 'Look here, Miss ... , we're not here to solve your problems. We're here to see that aliens don't give any trouble.' Nevertheless, they relented slightly. On being told that she was going to watch a film she had recently made, the officials told her that 'We're going to let you have a visitor's visa for two weeks, non extendable', warning Palmer that 'it's no good you asking for no labour permit [and with that they] banged down the rubber stamp on my passport, making me a present of two weeks' life in England'.[84]

Palmer was lucky that she was in these two weeks taken under the wing of Gaumant-British who offered her a long-term contract and applied successfully to the Home Office stating that she would be a 'valuable asset to the British film industry'. But what Palmer did not 'know was that Gaumount-British, cunning and cautious, applied for only three month's extension at a time. They told me that the Home Office would not grant a longer one, and I had to resign myself to shaking in my shoes every time the three months were up.'[85] Emeric Pressburger, like Korda, another refugee film impresario, had similar experiences of British immigration control procedures but he remembered them less whimsically than Palmer. 'England', he recalled, was 'a very, very difficult country for foreigners to come to'. The reality as a German Jew was that he wanted to have permanence and was faced with the problem that he could not 'go anywhere else'. And in the same manner to Palmer, he had rehearsed his answer to the port officials:

> And you know to the question, 'How long do you intend to stay here?' you mustn't say, 'I intend to stay forever' ... You want to be correct in everything but you are forced to lie straight away so you answer, 'Six months', and then you extend the six months.

Pressburger concludes with comments that go against the grain of the dominant narrative of British refugee policy during the Nazi era: 'I believe that anyone that comes to the country under the same circumstances that I did cannot love the Immigration Officers.'[86]

If this was true of figures as talented as Palmer and Pressburger, the problems facing ordinary 'aliens' in trying to enter Britain can be imagined. While the dominant image of British officialdom in relation to the *Kindertransport* has been the 'smiling policeman', as remembered by Lotte Bray and featuring in the title and cover of the organisation's major history,[87] there are some who have alternative recollections. Marianne Elsley's ship journey on the *Manhattan* from Hamburg to Southampton has been explored in the previous chapter. Still on the ship in the English dock, she recalls several hours after its arrival and prior to disembarkation that 'an immigration officer had come aboard, and we filed past him with our papers. He had been efficient and friendly, but we were so used to hostile officials that we were frightened, and feared for some hitch, some irregularity that might have prevented our landing.'[88]

There *were* those turned away by British officials. Another young Jewish actress, Hanne Nussbaum, was rejected at Dover and had to return to Paris. Her friends urged her to try again but she was resistant: 'I kept saying: "No. England refused me and France took me in"'. Eventually, her friends prevailed and she was allowed in.[89] Another person who was initially denied entry was the father of future Conservative Party leader, Michael Howard as noted briefly in Chapter 3. In 1937 Bernat Hecht, a Romanian and therefore of the 'wrong type' of Jew within the mindset of British officialdom, was, like Hanne Nussbaum, initially 'refused leave to land' in Dover. He did not possess a Ministry of Labour work permit and 'was unable to give a period for his stay'.[90] Hecht returned to Ostend on the *Prince Leopold* ferry and then was successful in gaining temporary entry through the support of an East End politician, J.H. Hall. The local MP wrote on behalf of a synagogue which wanted to employ Hecht as a temporary cantor for the High Holy Days.[91] As with Palmer and Pressburger, Hecht managed to extend his alien labour permit, contrasting with his father who was in the country without any paperwork at all for close to two decades.[92]

The problems Bernat Hecht faced in gaining entry to Britain and the illegality of his father have been exploited by opponents of Michael Howard. The irony of Howard's anti-immigrant stance was even greater because of an accident of geography. Howard was MP for Folkestone, Kent, which along with Dover, where his father had been initially refused entry, was, as explored earlier in this study, the focus of a moral panic about asylum seekers in the late 1990s and early twenty-first century.[93] Howard's family story emerged in 2005 before the General Election in which immigration was to be a key issue. At the time, one commentator, Paul Gilfeather, gleefully related how 'Michael Howard has gone to extraordinary lengths to keep this skeleton [relating to his grandfather] locked in the Hecht family cupboard.' Yet while Gilfeather noted that Howard had now admitted that his grandfather was an illegal immigrant, there was 'No mention of his dad [and] his heroic trip to the UK by boat, packing only determination – and a dream of a better life'. The truth, according to Gilfeather, was that 'his own father was the kind of person Mr Howard claims is bleeding us dry and should be turned back at our borders'.[94]

The reality is that Bernat Hecht's journey from Belgium to Britain on the *Prince Leopold* was not 'heroic'. At the point of this controversy, novelist and journalist Jonathan Freedland had recently completed his own family memoir of settlement in Britain. Within it he had gently queried the *Fiddler on the Roof*-style escaping the pogroms narrative of his grandfather's departure from Russia. With regard to Bernat Hecht, Freedland astutely observed that 'of all the immigrant stories one can tell, the attempt by Jews to escape Hitler's Europe in the 1930s is the one most likely to win the British people's understanding.[95] 'Recognition' is perhaps the more appropriate word than 'understanding', because in the popular imagination the focus is still on danger, heroism and escape, and not on the tedious paperwork and officialdom which determined whether aliens would be allowed entry, on what terms and for how long. Edmund de Waal's study of his family has briefly featured in the previous chapter. He notes that for those stuck in Austria after the *Anschluss*, they become part of the increasingly desperate mass:

> People are becoming the shadow of their documents. They are waiting for their papers to be validated, waiting for letters of support from overseas, waiting for promises of a position. People who are already out of the country are begged for favours, for money, for evidence of kinship, for chimerical ventures, for anything written on any headed paper at all.[96]

Some of his relatives, well-connected from a famous banking and trading family were lucky. Many others were not. The focus on the *St Louis* – and the intensive attention it received at the time from politicians and media alike – can make or obscure such connections to more mundane everyday decisions by bureaucrats that impacted on Jewish and other aliens during the 1930s.

The world of immigration entry facing Bernat Hecht and others in the devil's decade was thus not utterly removed from that of the young Eritrean, Naga, mentioned briefly earlier in this chapter. Refugees and asylum seekers, then and now, have been rejected in Dover by officialdom though Naga's journey to Britain, as with so many contemporary asylum seekers, was truly horrific and dangerous.[97] Before the summer of 1938, when the government imposed visas in order to select more carefully those to whom it would allow entry, the Home Office relied 'upon a muscular prohibition of leave to land at the ports'.[98] As Sir Samuel Hoare warned the Board of Deputies of British Jews reviewing five years of entry policy since the Nazi rise to power, it was

> necessary for the Home Office to discriminate very carefully as to the type of refugee who could be admitted to this country. If a flood of the wrong type of immigrants were allowed in there might be serious danger of anti-semitic feeling being aroused in this country.[99]

The concern of both the government *and* British Jewish organisations was that 'it was very difficult to get rid of a refugee … once he had entered and spent a few months in this country'.[100] Even so, refugees from Nazism were occasionally deported under the terms of the Aliens Restriction Act of 1919. 'In the summer of 1939 five Jewish stowaways off a ship from Antwerp were prosecuted, remanded in custody, recommended for deportation and deported.'[101] In this context, the *St Louis* refugees who had also come from the port of Antwerp to England had exceptional status in the eyes of British officialdom.

Some have raised the question of whether parallels can be drawn between the *St Louis* with those refugees today escaping by ship and refused entry.[102] The dreadful journeys of the latter, most notoriously in Australia and Oceania with the *Palapa* and *Tampa* in 2001 and, in December 2010, a boat so obscure it had no name which disintegrated at Christmas Island, will be explored in the concluding chapter of this study. Such linkages may seem simplistic given the totally different worlds and experiences of such sea journeys in 1939 and in the early twenty-first century. Tony Hare recalls catching a taxi in Hamburg to board the *St Louis*. 'At this moment I felt hardly like a poor refugee fleeing from his country'.[103] Yet the connection that can be made is that refugee migration is rarely straightforward. As Hare adds with learnt British understatement, even when embarking on the luxury liner 'another part of me was well aware that the situation was rather grim and my prospects for the future were anything but easy'.[104] In the words of Deborah Dwork and Robert Jan Van Pelt, 'The refugees' escape around the world defies traditional plotlines. Unlike other histories that start and end at conventionally established dates, this history has many starting points, even more end dates, and actors scattered across the globe'.[105] The comments of Dwork and Van Pelt relate to refugees from Nazism but, it will be argued here, they have a much wider resonance with regard to other victims of forced migration.

This case study of the *St Louis* will close by emphasising that even for the refugees on board who were sent to Britain, their journey did not always end there. Some *did* manage to go to their favoured destination, America. But those that remained in Britain at the start of the war were immediately transformed from transmigrants to enemy aliens. Some were interned and subject to deportation. Refugee journeys, both metaphorically and on an everyday level, never truly end – and certainly not for the 27,000 who were interned in Britain. Of these, several thousand were deported, including 400 'boys' from the *Kindertransport*.[106]

Eugen Spier was a German Jew who had come to Britain as an entrepreneur before the Nazi rise to power. Despite (or even because) of his friendship with Churchill, he was, much to his frustration and anger, one of the first to be interned and sent first to a camp in Lingfield, Surrey, and then to Canada. 'How on earth the Government conceived the idea of sending some of these [refugees] to Canada and Australia is beyond my comprehension'.[107] In 1941, Spier was sent back across the Atlantic and interned in the Isle of Man. Later that year he was released and made his way back to London where 'Suddenly my eyes caught sight of a poster put up by the Ministry of Information reading: "Is your journey really necessary?"'.[108] The farcical nature of Spier's transatlantic adventures did not match the tragedy of the *St Louis* (although many refugees were to drown when the *Arandora Star* taking other 'enemy aliens' to Canada was sunk by a German torpedo). But there were direct linkages – for example, 'Dr Fritz Kassel of Frankenstein, Germany, spent five years in an internment camp in Victoria, Australia, while Hans Kutner landed at a camp near Montreal.' Both had been on the *St Louis* as had Selmar and Elsa Biener from Magdeburg who were interned on the Isle of Man.[109]

Internment and deportation was a huge disappointment to those who were looking to start a new life and contribute positively to the war effort. It reversed refugee expectations of deliverance and progress. As Walter Igersheimer, a young German Jewish adult, recorded bitterly on arriving at a hastily assembled internment centre in Canada:

> So this is our new camp. This is the promised land! We sit down at the edge of one of the pits. Water drips down on us from the leaky roof. We can smell the toilets ... which have backed up with shit. Nobody feels like speaking. Our illusions, beliefs, and hope have been shattered.

The mood of his group was not improved by the instant greeting of crude antisemitism from their guards.[110]

Neither the *St Louis* nor the *Kindertransport* stories were typical of refugee journeys during the 1930s. Most of those who came to Britain during this decade came through procedures that were rarely newsworthy and were not subject to such contemporary celebration or condemnation (or, for that matter, subsequent memory work). It remains, as Louise London estimates, that perhaps as little as one-fifth of those applying to Britain were allowed entry.[111] Yet extraordinary or not, the journeys of the *St Louis* and the *Kindertransport* reveal the tensions that emerged during the 1930s and the Second World War when the forcibly displaced were placed within and between the socio-legal categories of 'alien', 'refugee' and transmigrant. It is, for example, important to remember that some of those who came to Britain on the *Kindertransport* did so on paperwork forged by refugee workers to get round Home Office procedures. Such 'illegality' is associated with contemporary asylum seekers and not with a refugee movement that is now idealised. The reality is more complex.[112]

The overall result was that some Jews from the Third Reich were to be allowed temporary entrance to Britain through a variety of collective schemes as well as individual applications in what were often messy and ongoing journeys. The numbers were relatively small in the context of the many who had applied to seek refuge, but large compared to those allowed entry to Britain from 1918 to 1933. Some concept of 'refugeedom' had thus been re-established during the Nazi era but it was still queried by those who viewed these forced migrants to Britain as undesirable and illegal aliens. Such battles at a popular and state level did not disappear. During the Second World War thousands of refugees were interned as 'enemy aliens' and immediately after it Holocaust survivors were turned away from Britain itself and especially Mandate Palestine as the *President Warfield/Exodus 1947* episode graphically and emotionally illustrated – those on board the ship accused Britain of ignoring the plight of European Jewry during the Second World War. Now the 'naval might' of Britain was being turned against women and child survivors but during 'the years of the rivers of blood no ships were available to help and rescue Jews'.[113] Yet while the journeys of *Exodus 1947* have become ever more obscure in British culture (in contrast to the ship's fame/infamy in Israel and America), the arrival in June 1948 of its near chronological neighbour, the *Empire Windrush*, is increasingly remembered and celebrated. Part IV will explore the memory work (including the silences that have emerged) associated with the movement of new Commonwealth and other black migrants and the desire to create less exclusive and – within limits – more pluralistic versions of British history.

IV

Colonial and postcolonial journeys

7

The *Empire Windrush*: the making of an iconic British journey

Journeys of betterment

In 1955 Donald Hinds came from Jamaica to work for London Transport. Alongside his work on the buses, Hinds was a regular contributor to the *West Indian Gazette*. The newspaper was formed in 1958 by the Trinidadian, Claudia Jones, and its content reflected a growing and culturally dynamic West Indian intellectual milieu in Britain. Its content explored domestic problems, including racist violence and discrimination, faced on an everyday level by West Indian migrants. In addition, the *West Indian Gazette* also revealed a strong international cross-fertilising of ideas within the 'black Atlantic'.[1] Hinds published his *Journey to an Illusion: the West Indian in Britain* in 1966. It was the first sustained non-fiction account of this movement written by an individual of such migrant origin. A mixture of interviews, astute observation and autobiography, Hinds's narrative is powerful and it makes for grim reading with the testimony emphasising rejection and the struggle to find a place called home. As its title implies, the book destroys the 'myth of the "Mother Country"'. The story is one of disappointment as the long-ingrained 'Englishness' of the migrants – reflecting centuries of presence in the Caribbean – is rejected by Britain's white population when confronting the perceived 'otherness' of the West Indians.[2]

Yet for all the focus on the positive virtues and values associated with Britain as the centre of a multi-racial Commonwealth, Hinds was anxious not to romanticise the reasons why West Indians had emigrated after the war. He emphasised the reality of economics over idealism: 'Migration has always been the salvation of the West Indies'. After the war, however, both America and the Latin American republics were essentially closed: 'It seemed that there was nothing to do but to turn to Britain.' Yet there was a difference – rather than simply another country, 'Their passports described them as British subjects: citizens of the United Kingdom and Colonies'. They were legally entitled to stay and as Hinds noted, by 1960, of the 100,000-plus West Indians who had come to Britain, 'only about thirteen thousand had returned home'.[3]

Hinds left the port of Kingston in August 1955 on board the SS *Auriga* which eventually took 1,300 other West Indian migrants, the large majority of them being Jamaicans, to Britain. They arrived in Plymouth eighteen days later.[4] In many ways, the journey of the SS *Auriga*, which, alongside its sister ship, the SS *Castel Verde*, regularly sailed from Jamaica to the south/south-western coastal ports of England – especially Southampton and Plymouth – was typical of much post-war West Indian migratory movement which began in earnest in the mid-1950s.[5] But rather than the *Auriga*, the *Castel Verde* or other such ships, it is the *Empire Windrush* which has become symbolic of not just West Indian but, to an extent, all post-1945 'New Commonwealth' journeys to Britain. It marked, in the words of its most prominent recent chroniclers, Mike and Trevor Phillips, 'the irresistible rise of multi-racial Britain'.[6] Indeed, it has been portrayed as fundamentally changing national identity as a whole. According to an educational guide produced by the BBC to accompany its '*Windrush* Season', which commemorated the fiftieth anniversary of the ship's arrival, it represented 'a pivotal point in modern British history. The whole notion of what it means to be British was thrown into chaos, Britain was never to be the same again.'[7]

It is true that Hinds's early account *does* include brief mention of the *Empire Windrush* through the use of personal testimony. His narrative gives the ship, if only in passing, a special status in the story of Caribbean migration to and black presence in Britain. *Journey to an Illusion* provides a clearly delineated chronology of British black history with the Second World War acting as a clear dividing line:

> Though British cities such as Cardiff, Liverpool and London's dockland area have had black people living in them for centuries, West Indian migration to Britain after the war had no connexion with these people. It was the munition workers and the demobbed members of the forces who served as the frontiersmen.[8]

Those in the RAF especially played a key role in Hinds's account which in-fluenced much subsequent historical and sociological writing on the subject. Returning to the West Indies after the excitement and relative freedom of Britain during the war, these men were frustrated by the lack of opportunities offered to them and thus the prospect of return was enticing. According to an ex-RAF man interviewed by Hinds, 'That was the time that the S.S. *Empire Windrush* became a household word in the West Indies as ex-servicemen and their relatives trekked north. After a while people started writing to us, asking us to meet their relations and see that they received some sort of accommodation.'[9]

These two sentences were, however, the only mention of the ship in Hinds's account, reflecting that it had been partly forgotten by the 1950s. 'The "Windrush" Story' did feature in an overview of West Indian migration to Britain, *They Seek a Living*, written by travel writer, Joyce Egginton and published in 1957.[10] It is significant, however, that Egginton's analysis, which alternated between the patronising (referring to the West Indians as child-like) and the progressive (she had no objections to black–white sexual relationships), began by *reclaiming* the ship's connection to Caribbean migrant journeys:

> [T]he *Empire Windrush* [was] an old Nazi strength-through-joy cruiser [the *Monte Rosa*] which had been captured by Britain during the war. Six years later [after its arrival in Tilbury], in March 1954, it was to become really famous when it foundered off the Algerian coast and, because of the courage of 1,500 aboard, all but four of her crew were saved.

It was necessary for Egginton to remind her readers that the '*Windrush's* journey to the West Indies and back in the first half of 1948 was also epic, although no one visualised the consequences at the time'.[11] In spite of Egginton's efforts, the *Empire Windrush's* status was still somewhat obscure from the late 1950s through to the 1970s before it was rediscovered and celebrated in the last decade of the twentieth century. Indeed, even the fortieth anniversary celebrations in 1988 were relatively muted, reflecting perhaps a wider context in which the Conservative government under Margaret Thatcher emphasised (and legislated for) a mono-cultural national identity rather than celebrating diversity of origins.[12] But the arrival of the *Empire Windrush* was still marginal, including within British black consciousness and historiography. Studies of the black community and its history in Britain published from the early 1960s, for example, mention it in passing or not at all.[13] Even the pathbreaking 1998 television series on the *Windrush* was promoted to the BBC by its production company on the basis that it was exposing hidden history: 'Of all the epic tales still to be told of British life in the twentieth century, one of the most compelling is the day [of its arrival nearly] 50 years ago'.[14]

In 1968, the *Sunday Times* colour magazine *did* run a major feature on the *Empire Windrush*, referring to its arrival twenty years earlier as an 'historic moment'. This article, written at a time of intense racial tension following Enoch Powell's inflammatory speeches, was noteworthy, as was the case with Egginton eleven years earlier, for the *rediscovery* of the *Empire Windrush* and its Caribbean passengers. Major elements of the later myth of the *Empire Windrush* were present in this article, including its Biblical title, 'Voyage to the

Promised Land' and the claim that it brought 'the first of the Commonwealth immigrants to arrive in Britain'. Significantly, however, it did not prompt other memory work in relation to its journey.[15]

At a more popular level, the changing meanings attached to the *Empire Windrush* are revealed by comparing knowledge of the ship in the 1980s with twenty years later. In a survey of immigration history aimed at a mass readership, James Walvin's *Passage to Britain* (1984) does not even mention the *Empire Windrush*.[16] Similarly, in his autobiography published a year later, Jamaican-born musician, Leslie Thompson, who had lived in England since the 1920s, had only confused memories of what he names the *Emperor Windrush*.[17] In contrast, Robert Winder's *Bloody Foreigners: The Story of Immigration to Britain* (2004), the wider significance of which has been explored at various stages of this study, devotes a lengthy section to the ship. Indeed, it is by the far the longest on a particular migrant journey in his wide-ranging and extensive narrative.[18] And it was no surprise in 2006 that when the Department for Culture, Media and Sport launched its 'Icons – a portrait of England' project – one of the attempts to create a plurally defined national identity by 'New Labour', the *Empire Windrush* was one of a 'dozen quintessentially English characters, objects and places'. It was chosen alongside the Spitfire, 'cups of tea' and *Alice in Wonderland*. By then, the mythology of the *Windrush* was well-established: it was *the* 'ship that brought the first Caribbean migrants to Britain'.[19]

That the *Empire Windrush* has become core to narratives of British history is revealed in three bestselling, popular accounts of the nation's chronological evolution. In 2008, 2009 and 2011 the ship's journey featured respectively in television historian, Hugh Williams' *Fifty Things You Need to Know about British History*;[20] newspaper editor, Stephen Pollard's *Ten Days that Changed the Nation*;[21] and broadcaster and travel writer, Stuart Maconie's *Hope & Glory: The Days that Made Britain*.[22] Moreover, in all three cases, the *Windrush* received especial attention in publicity for the books and was singled out in their covers. Its arrival 'changed the make-up of the country' and was paired with the journeys of Sir Francis Drake on the one hand and 'Bobby Moore raising the Jules Rimet trophy' on the other.[23] All three tend to ignore past black migration to the 'motherland': those on board the ship, according to Williams, 'were Britain's first Caribbean immigrants'.[24]

It will be argued, against Hinds's chronological structure (and those suggested by the Icons project and the three popular histories just glossed), that the *Empire Windrush* was both part of a longer migratory pattern of black people to Britain *and*, in its way, untypical of movements before and after its arrival in Tilbury Docks in June 1948. Yet to make its arrival with its 492 (official) West Indian passengers privileged in the world of heritage, it has been necessary to 'tidy' elements of its journey in order to make all those coming from the 'New

Commonwealth' after the Second World War part of the 'Windrush generation'. It has been suggested that reference to its arrival 'is now so ubiquitous' that similar to Captain Cook's landing at Botany Bay, 'the spatial event is replaced by a historical stage'.[25] In the process, the *Empire Windrush* has been given an even greater significance than was the case in 1948, exceptional though it was then treated. As Mike and Trevor Phillips acknowledge in what has become the standard history of its now famous journey: 'In hindsight, the moment of arrival captured by the *Windrush* has become a symbol for all those occasions when we, or any of the other black people who have become part of the British nation, stepped off our separate gangplanks.' The triumphalist tone of their narrative is made even more explicit in the subtitle of their chronicle of the *Windrush*: 'The Irresistible Rise of Multi-Racial Britain'.[26] And as was the case with *Exodus 1947*, so important is the mythology of the *Windrush* that the particularity of its journey has become close to irrelevant. Thus a well-meaning chronology of modern music suggests that

> When the Empire Windrush docked at Southampton, a new Britain was born. On board was the first wave of West Indian guest workers, answering a British government advertisement for cheap transport to the mother country to fill the post-war labour shortage.[27]

Inaccurate in all its details, this narrative still works by meeting twenty-first century expectations of the ship's significance: 'The seeds of multicultural Britain were duly sewn.'[28]

Popularly perceived as coming direct from Jamaica to England, the *Windrush*'s route was, in reality, far from straightforward. The ship had come from Australia, and after Jamaica it visited Mexico, Cuba, and Bermuda.[29] Moreover, it had a far more varied set of passengers than is often assumed. Indeed, there was a flow of passengers *before* it reached England, reflecting the opportunistic commercial underpinnings of its journey and the complexity and intensity of global migration after the Second World War. It was thus picking up migrants wherever they could be located: the ship had 'left England with a group of Polish refugees bound for Latin America, and on the return voyage there would be some vacant space on the troopdeck'.[30] On the way back it dropped off Polish migrants in Mexico and men from the Gloucester regiment in Bermuda.[31] Arthur Curling was a Jamaican on board the *Empire Windrush*. Interviewed in 1998, he reflected that 'There were 500 of us on that ship. Nothing would have been said if we had been 500 white Hungarians or Poles or French'.[32] In fact, there were sixty Polish women, war refugees, whose remarkable journeys had taken them from 'Siberia, via India, Australia, New Zealand and Africa to Mexico'.[33] Furthermore, while often described as carrying only Jamaicans (and more precisely Jamaican men), more than 20 per cent of its black passengers were from other Caribbean islands.[34] It also included RAF men returning from leave, perhaps a score of women in addition to the Poles and one child, the thirteen-year-old Vince Reid. Yet it remains that most contemporary reporting of and responses to the *Empire Windrush* focused on the adult male black West Indians, generalised as Jamaicans, reflecting the racialised discourse affecting their reception.[35] As Matthew Mead notes in his close reading of the key archive record, 'the uncomplicated route of the Windrush from Kingston to London, with its homogenised carriage of Jamaicans, represents too simple a story'.[36]

Further confusing the picture, but linking the ship to wider migratory patterns of the immediate post-war years, it contained a score of stowaways. Sam King has become one of the most famous passengers and inside chroniclers of the *Empire Windrush*. Having served in the RAF, he returned to Britain on the ship and subsequently achieved prominence as the first black mayor of Southwark as well as in the black church movement. His autobiography was published at the height of the *Empire Windrush* celebrations in 1998 reflecting the growing approbation and respect given to those connected to the ship. King's account adds to the growing myth of the *Empire Windrush*, highlighting its historical significance. His reference point, as has been the case with other descriptions of migrant journeys analysed in this study, was the Pilgrim Fathers: 'We dubbed ourselves the pioneers of the second *Mayflower*.' Nevertheless, his narrative adds much detail to the ship's journey and he stresses that 'Mention must also be made of the additional unlicensed, unauthorised "barracudas" who surfaced later in the voyage.' These stowaways were looked after well, he claimed (perhaps thereby understating some of the tension between the West Indians on board), by the other passengers:

> All along, we were mindful of the 'barracudas' who had to lie low and could not make use of the opportunity to touch land ... It was decided that clothes should be lent. Fortunately, there were officially twenty women passengers, so the lone female stowaway was put in their care. Meals were smuggled out to them or unused meal tickets passed on.[37]

The presence of these 'barracudas' was also documented by the British government. Official papers noted less sympathetically than King that 'A number of stowaways succeeded in getting on board and mingling with the men, and although no definite figures are available it appears that they number in the region of 20. A few of them have already been prosecuted and fined and imprisoned at Gravesend.' In this particular case, the black stowaways were only a small percentage of the total passengers, but they were still an irritation to the civil servants who were anxious to monitor the exact numbers on the *Empire Windrush*.[38]

War narratives

All in all, its rather tortuous journey from Kingston to the Kent port of Tilbury took close to four weeks. Those West Indians on board had a variety of backgrounds. Although the majority had been to Britain in the war either in the RAF or as munitions workers,[39] others had never seen the country but were able to respond to the adverts in the Jamaican *Daily Gleaner* for the chance to take part in its exceptional journey. They paid the (not unsubstantial) sum of £28 10s for the privilege, and reflecting the frustration at life chances in the Caribbean, most of the spaces were taken up quickly.[40] But it tends to be the ex-servicemen – roughly 120 out of the 492 – who have been the focus of attention – a narrative is thereby created in which those who had bravely and loyally fought for the 'mother country' were then coldly rejected by it after the war's conclusion. It is a storyline that dominates the prize-winning novel, *Small Island* (2004), by second-generation British Caribbean writer, Andrea Levy whose father and uncle travelled on the *Windrush*.[41] Levy confirms that she was 'motivated by ignorance [in British society] about the involvement of West Indian servicemen' during the Second World War and that 'The ignorance was mine as well'.[42]

One of Levy's main characters, Gilbert Joseph, had been an RAF driver in Britain during the war, returning on the *Empire Windrush*. Gilbert fights a futile battle with another returning (white) veteran, Mr Bligh, to persuade him that the West Indians have a right to be in post-war London:

> Listen to me, man, we both just finish fighting a war – a bloody war – for the better world we wan' see. And on the same side – you and me. We both look on other men to see enemy. You and me, fighting for empire, fighting for peace. But still, after all that we suffer together, you wan' tell me I am worthless and you are not.

But Gilbert's eloquent claim for equality of sacrifice and purpose and for a share in being part of the dominant national narrative is beyond Mr Bligh. Bligh represents in the novel what would become the Powellite tendency in post-war Britain.

Powell in his infamous 'Rivers of Blood' speech delivered in Birmingham in April 1968, made reference to a 'respectable street in Wolverhampton', his constituency. Eight years previously

> a house was sold to a Negro. Now only one white (a woman old-age pensioner) lives here. This is her story. She lost her husband and both her sons in the war. So she turned her seven-roomed house, her only asset, into a boarding-house.

Powell added that she 'worked hard and did well, paid off her mortgage and began to put something by for old age'. This tale of thrift and self-help, however, is abruptly disrupted: 'the immigrants moved in', her tenants left and the 'quiet street became a place of noise and confusion'. The invasion is relentless and attempts are made to remove her by intimidation: 'She is becoming afraid to go out. Windows are broken. She finds excretia pushed through her letter-box.'[43] This war widow was never identified (nor the street that met Powell's description of immigrant take-over). In fact, the story was being replicated in different parts of the country, fitting the characteristics of an 'urban folk legend'. It was part of a moral panic in which Powell's provocative speeches found popular support and made life uncomfortable for all non-white minorities in Britain.[44]

Communication between Gilbert and Bligh through their rival versions of the national story are rendered literally impossible. Levy makes this explicit through Bligh who responds to Gilbert: 'I'm sorry … but I just can't understand a single word that you're saying.' Bligh wishes to remove Gilbert and his wife, Hortense, from his house, just as Powell would advocate through schemes of voluntary repatriation and the National Front in compulsory form: 'now I'm back we intend to live respectably again. It's what I fought a war for.'[45] As with *Exodus 1947*, memories of the Second World War had become a battleground of contested places, identities and ideologies.

Gilbert's story reflected the disappointing reality for many of those on board the ship. Levy's powerful, moving and historically informed narrative is part of a reaction to counter a common imagery that, as Mike and Trevor Phillips suggest, appears in 'many contemporary histories [where those on the *Empire Windrush*] turn up as a sort of sudden infestation whose numbers account for various social problems'.[46] That the Phillips brothers were not imagining this pathological treatment of post-war black migration to Britain is confirmed in the brief treatment it receives in the late Roy Porter's *London: A Social History* (1996).

Porter was an innovative and sensitive historian whose work deconstructing concepts of madness was especially pathbreaking. It is thus worth quoting Porter at length *not* as an act of muckraking but because his account illustrates the failure of most mainstream (including progressive) historians to treat the black presence in Britain other than as essentially problematic. The depressing cycle of black immigration, racism, controls and then second-generation rioting, is typical of how the profession (usually briefly), confronts the subject:

> Britain's imperial chickens came home to roost with the flaring of racial tensions from the 1950s, associated with New Commonwealth

immigration ... . The great majority of immigrants initially settled in London, and a few areas – Brixton, Notting Hill, Camden Town and Southall – bore the brunt. London's first race riot erupted in Notting Hill in late August 1958 ... . Racial tensions simmered through the 1960s and 1970s, associated with poverty, unemployment, rotten housing and a growing bush war between blacks and the police. In 1981 rioting, burning and looting resulted in an orgy of damage in Brixton.[47]

Against such representations, the desire to show that those on the *Empire Windrush* and subsequent ships were part of a new and affirmative development in black migration to Britain – one linked intimately and positively to the Second World War – is made understandable. In the BBC's televised version of *Small Island*, for example, there is a redemptive ending with the black family shown as rooted, respectable and prosperous in twenty-first century Britain, able to acknowledge and celebrate its mixed heritage.[48] But a variety of problems emerge from such an approach to correct negative readings of the recent black British experience, several of which will be outlined here and continued in the next chapter. First, continuities have been lost sight of or downplayed. Second, the *untypical* nature of the *Empire Windrush* in the context of the immediate post-war years has been ignored. Third (and the focus of Chapter 8, the sister chapter in Part IV), the diversity of non-white movement to Britain – both before and after 1948 – has been hidden by the focus on *West Indian* migration.

The *Windrush* in Black British history

Turning to the first difficulty: historians of the *Empire Windrush* have not, it is true, totally ignored the previous black presence in Britain. Tony Sewell, in *Keep on Moving: The Windrush Legacy* (1998), states in his introduction that 'It must be noted that there were Africans in Britain from Roman Times. We can trace a long history of black settlement in Britain before and after slavery.'[49] Similarly, the Phillips brothers acknowledge that 'there had been groups of black people living in Britain long before ... Slavery and the vagaries of imperial adventure deposited substantial numbers in various parts of the country. By the time the *Windrush* arrived there were already black communities who could trace their ancestry back a couple of centuries.'[50] Nevertheless, for Sewell, 'the great wave of post-war migration from the Caribbean to the UK can be said to have begun with the fateful voyage of the Windrush. The history of the black diaspora in Britain begins here.'[51] And, for the Phillips brothers, 'on 22 June 1948 the *Windrush* sailed through a gateway in history, on the other side of which was the end of Empire and a wholesale reassessment of what it meant to be British'.[52] While they recognise that the *Empire Windrush* was a 'real boat ... carrying real passengers', it has become more than this – a 'vital, necessary link between our nationality and the historical accident from which it springs, and, for us, the outline of the arrival and its consequences is also a journey which sketches out the shape of our identities'.[53]

If, for the Phillips brothers, the *Windrush* had a universal importance and relevance, for others it possessed an even greater significance for the black British communities. The celebrations in 1998 thus provided a key moment to instrumentalise history in a positive direction. Jamaican-born artist and sculptor George Fowokan Kelly wrote impassionately that

> The history of those who arrived on the SS Empire Windrush and fought to lay down the foundation of our community, is our history. We must record their deeds for our children, for they should not have to live without a history. They are born into a society in whose history they are not mentioned, where they play no part except as victims of the slave trade.

He added that with the younger generation of black people in Britain, 'Nothing they learn about England makes them feel they are regarded, as belonging to it.' History, argued Kelly, 'teaches a people about their destiny, it teaches that those with no sense of the their own history are without a sense of direction for the future'.[54] Similarly, at a grassroots level, there were projects in 1998 such as the 'Descendants of the Windrush [schools] project' aimed at those whose parents and grandparents came to this country from the Caribbean: 'This is an important "right of passage" – it teaches about self and helps children to feel proud to be part of this society'.[55] More polemically, radical poet Abdul Malik in his 'Poet of the Tides', demanded that

> Black Britain will reverberate regenerate
> reciprocate reactivate
> lost faith
> from 1998
> the 50th Anniversary
> of West Indian vitality.[56]

Not unreasonably, those who have laboured long and hard to reveal the traces (and sometimes large-scale nature) of Afro-Caribbean and Asian settlement in Britain before the *Empire Windrush* were unimpressed by the idea that the ship was *the* starting point for black migration to the 'mother country', acting as *the* 'mother ship'.[57] In September 1998, Hakim Adi, editor of the Black and Asian Studies Association (BASA), noted that

> The last few months have witnessed a number of events to mark the fiftieth anniversary of the *Empire Windrush*. It is not the intention here to question the historical significance of this event, although it is to be lamented that many inaccurate claims about its importance have been made. What is more unfortunate is that more has not been made of an opportunity to promote the wider history of African, Caribbean and Asian people in Britain.

As a consequence, Hakim Adi concluded, 'much of the work which has been undertaken over the last few years to document the pre-1948 history has largely been ignored throughout the *Windrush* celebrations.'[58]

Indeed, the only element of the fiftieth anniversary events given coverage by BASA was a speech given by the actor, musician, lawyer and activist, Cy Grant, on 22 June 1998 in which the former Guyanese RAF Flight-Lieutenant was anxious to place the *Empire Windrush* in a wider context. It was a broader vision enabled, perhaps, in part because Grant did not come back to England, as has been erroneously suggested, on this subsequently famous ship.[59] Cy Grant argued that it was important 'not to see this event purely within a Caribbean context. It is of relevance to all minorities in all countries, as well as the peoples of the third world.' Of equal importance, he emphasised, was the need not to 'forget that black people were here long before Windrush. Our presence goes back to Roman times, as soldiers. From the 16th to the 19th centuries black people were here as seamen, servants, artisans, society pets and dandies, as well as musicians.' Furthermore, referring to the early modern era, Grant noted that there 'had been calls to send Africans back to Africa, where they belonged; Queen Elizabeth I led the way'. In this respect, Grant was anxious to draw the connection between deep and recent British history: 'When you think of it, the experience of the Windrush generation was not much different from what it was then. And that is why this [*Windrush*] season is so important – to acknowledge our history. Our histories are inextricably bound together.'[60] Grant's historical overview and final statement raises the further question: which histories and which connections should be made to the *Empire Windrush*?

Historians and black activists were not the only ones to place the arrival of such ships in the post-war era in the context of earlier black settlement. In the hands of British officialdom such pre-history was more precise and far less positive. This chapter began with Donald Hinds's account, including his brief mention of earlier black settlements in the ports of Britain, especially Liverpool, Cardiff and London. It was these historic linkages, too, that civil servants in Whitehall made with regard to the *Empire Windrush*. But they did so to problematise rather than to normalise the arrival of the ship and its black passengers.

In October 1948, the Colonial Office provided the 'Working Party on the Employment in the United Kingdom of Surplus Colonial Labour' with a historical overview of the 'problem'. It dated the presence of black people only to the First World War – the earlier history, which will be confronted in the following chapter, was not acknowledged. It was also confined geographically in the bureaucratic imagination to the 'sea-port towns' of Liverpool, London, Cardiff, North and South Shields and Hull, doing so in order of size. Before the Second World War it believed that including their 'English wives', these communities totalled some '15,000 persons'.[61] The tone in this official summary in describing the places where these 'Colonials' were based was disparaging: 'In all of the sea-port towns … the colonial communities live in the most depressed and sordid part of the town. In Liverpool and Cardiff in particular their districts are no more nor less than "coloured ghettoes".' Relationships between the white and black populations in these towns were also perceived as problematic and the riots of 1919 were emphasised especially in this official report. There had been progress, it was acknowledged, but this was not the case with Liverpool.[62] Indeed, the fear of the Colonial Office was that those on the *Empire Windrush* would make their way to these existing communities and that Liverpool particularly was an undesirable location for them to go – it was suffering heavy unemployment and shortage of accommodation.

Overall the Colonial Office was happy that the 800 West Indians who had come to Britain from December 1947 to October 1948 – principally on board the *Empire Windrush*, *Almanzora* and *Orbita* – had been reasonably well settled with regard to jobs and housing. Its concern was that they should be distributed widely across Britain to avoid a concentration of black people: to the Colonial Office, past examples of 'ghettoisation' in the port communities were regarded as dangerous and subversive. 'It should be stressed', the overview concluded, 'that those who are unemployed are mostly in Liverpool and Cardiff, and that their presence there aggravates an existing unemployment problem of colonials'.[63] A slightly later report from the Colonial Office also pointed to the tensions that had arisen with marriages involving 'Colonials' and local women and how the resulting 'family units … became a social problem'. It, too, concluded that 'We have no doubt that the most undesirable thing that can happen is that large numbers of new coloured workers should be forced or encouraged to go into these areas.'[64]

In the 'official mind', therefore, although there were differences between and within the major various departments involved – the Colonial Office, Home Office and Ministry of Labour – those that came on the *Empire Windrush* and other such ships in 1948 were perceived as part of a longer black movement to Britain. The pioneer historian of the black experience in Britain, Peter Fryer, in his classic study, *Staying Power* (1984), was a journalist for the *Daily Worker* who reported the arrival of the *Empire Windrush*. It prompted his later work which, as noted in the Introduction, lovingly researched the black presence in Britain from the Roman era onwards.[65] But unlike later historians inspired by Fryer, this presence was perceived by politicians and civil servants as dating only to 1914; it was linked therefore to influxes resulting from the First World War. Rather than stable and rooted, the black presence was viewed as transitory. Furthermore, it was in need of constant monitoring and control by the government, with a concerted effort to remove its presence altogether.

In its perverse way, officialdom thus saw those on the *Empire Windrush* and other black migrants in 1948 as part of a continuum. In contrast to the recent dominant narrative of the ship's wider significance, they did not, therefore, regard their arrival as a starting point of something fundamentally new. Of equal significance, officials regarded those on the *Empire Windrush* as being part of a self-contained movement. In this respect, their analysis was not without strong foundation. It brings us to explore the second problematic identified with recent *Windrush* commemorations – that in many ways those on board were idiosyncratic within the pattern of immediate post-war black migration to Britain.

The *Windrush* and national identity

There is a neat irony in the choosing of the arrival of the *Empire Windrush* as 'quintessentially English' in the 2006 'Icon' project. On the day the ship arrived a group of ten MPs wrote to Prime Minister, Clement Attlee, worried that it 'may encourage other British subjects to imitate their example and this country may become an open reception centre for immigrants'. Their concern was that those on the *Empire Windrush* had not been 'selected in respect to health, education, training, character, customs and above all, regardless of whether assimilation is possible or not'. To these MPs, the future well-being of the nation was at stake:

> The British people fortunately enjoy a profound unity without uniformity in their way of life, and we are blest by the absence of a colour racial problem. An influx of coloured people domiciled here is likely to impair the harmony, strength and cohesion of our public and social life and to cause discord and unhappiness among all concerned.

They thus called for action – legislation if needed – to stop such movements 'in the political, social, economic and fiscal interest of *our* [my emphasis] people'.[66]

The Home Office was less concerned than these MPs about the arrival of the *Empire Windrush*. Civil servants drafted a reassuring response for Attlee to send to the backbenchers, emphasising especially that a matter of principle was at stake. It was a 'traditional element in United Kingdom policy that British subjects, of whatever colour and whether of Dominion or Colonial origin, are freely admissable to the United Kingdom'. Moreover, with so many foreign workers in Britain, it would be hard to exclude a particular group on what would obviously be racial grounds: to do so, the Colonial Secretary warned, 'would give rise to a fierce reaction in the Colonies themselves'.[67]

On a more pragmatic level, the Home Office was not convinced, contrary to the view expressed by these MPs and some newspapers, that there were many more from the Colonies 'awaiting an opportunity of a passage'. The draft argued that

> The grounds for this fear are not clear. There was a peculiar combination of circumstances in the case of the Jamaican party which are not likely to be repeated. In the first place, the passages at a particularly favourable cost were available on a troop ship, and in the second place, some two-thirds of the men arrived were ex-servicemen who had money in their pockets from their gratuities. Even so, not all the cheap troop-deck passages were taken up.

The letter concluded that the evidence suggested that 'the episode is a comparatively isolated one'.[68] Similar reassurances were given in the House of Commons by the Colonial Secretary, Arthur Creech Jones, before the *Empire Windrush* arrived: 'It is very unlikely that a similar event to this will occur again in the West Indies.'[69]

In most respects, the government's analysis was correct – the numbers on the following ships were much smaller – 180 on the *Orbita* in October 1948, just 39 on the *Reina del Pacifo* three months later and 253 on the *Georgic* in summer 1949.[70] Aside from those who had been in Britain during the war, the country was not an attractive proposition to those seeking to migrate. Indeed, it was only the closing down of the American option through the McCarren-Walter Immigration Act of 1952 (which limited West Indian migration to one hundred a year) that made larger numbers consider Britain. Eric Hudson came to Britain in 1944 joining the RAF. His post-war pattern of migration reveals the difficulties experienced and flexibility required to find a country that offered the best opportunities. Eric remained in Britain after the war but

> decided to go back to his native Jamaica in 1948, took a brief look at it, tried England again in 1949, departing once again from England to resettle in the United States but after two years he ran up against 'The McLaren [*sic*] Act' which forced him to return to the UK.

Even then it took a long time for Eric Hudson to find a position which reflected his talents. Eventually, however, he found success as a youth and community worker in Leicester.[71]

Hudson, therefore, was going in the opposite direction to the migrants on the *Empire Windrush*. It was the relatively isolated and exceptional nature of this ship that meant special care was taken over the arrival and settlement of its passengers. Well before the ship left Kingston, the Ministry of Labour, Ministry of Health, Home Office and Colonial Office were cooperating to ensure that no 'awkward incidents' should arise.[72] Once it became clear that there was a sizeable group of West Indians on board, temporary accommodation (a deep shelter in Clapham) was found and the Ministry of Labour did its best to find employment for these privileged black migrants across the country.[73] Indeed, the publicity its journey had already attracted ensured that the arrival of the *Empire Windrush* in Tilbury would achieve additional media attention, including what has subsequently become iconic Pathe newsreel footage. The arrival became a set piece in diplomacy with a carefully prepared speech from I.G. Cummings of the Colonial Office broadcast to the West Indians on board.

'First of all', stated Cummings, he wanted to 'welcome you to Great Britain and express the hope that you will all achieve the objects which have brought you here'. Cummings then provided practical advice on housing and employment, especially aimed at those who had not been in the country before. Cummings' address was partly motivated by the desire to control as far as possible what was, as he acknowledged, a voluntary movement of individuals. It was also a genuine attempt at showing empathy, as with his closing statement: 'All that remains for me to say is that I wish you the very best of luck.'[74] There was a particularly acute ambivalence in the case of Cummings. As the Phillips brothers note, his address had a 'tone of patronising kindliness', reflecting his 'iron neutrality as … a senior Civil Servant'. But as a man of mixed heritage – his father was from Sierra Leone – he later revealed that he was 'desperately anxious about the migrants' prospects'.[75]

Those on board reciprocated the welcome, most famously in the case of the Trinadadian calypso singer, Lord Kitchener (Aldwyn Roberts), and his specially written song, 'London is the Place for Me'. According to his romanticised testimony given to the Phillips brothers, 'when the boat had about four days to land in England, I get this kind of wonderful feeling that I'm going to land on the mother country, the soil of the mother country'. As he sang:

> You can go to France or America, India, Asia or Africa.
> But you must come back, to London city.

Ironically, Lord Kitchener had strongly considered going to America before the opportunity arose to come to England on the *Empire Windrush* and he was to return to Trinidad in 1963.[76] It is significant, however, that in the Pathe newsreel commentary, Lord Kitchener, described as the West Indians' 'spokesman', is featured and this verse was especially emphasised. Kitchener, according to the newsreel commentary, was giving 'their [collective] thanks to Britain'.[77]

Three years later, Lord Kitchener recorded the song for the first time, adding final lines which 'by being transparently false ... exposes the irony of the preceding verses':

> I cannot complain of the time I have spent.
> I mean my life in London is really magnificent;
> I have every comfort and every sport
> And my residence is at Hampton Court.
> So, London, that's the place for me.[78]

In the Pathe newsreel, Aldwyn Roberts looks uncomfortable. He is forced into a contrived performance of loyalty in which his lyrics focus only on England.[79] It contrasts with his general post-war oeuvre as a 'postcolonial anti-Columbus', including his re-working of 'London is the Place for Me'. Taking Kitchener's work as a whole, 'the journey into exile aboard the *Empire Windrush* ended with a re-imagining of home as a place somewhere *en route* between Africa, the Americas and Europe'.[80] In addition, Kitchener and other calypso performers provided 'sharp satirical commentatories on the character of contemporary political life and the absurdities of racism within it'.[81] But rather than placing the *Windrush* within what Paul Gilroy has termed 'the Black Atlantic',[82] the tendency beyond Lord Kitchener has been to domesticate and confine it to a specifically British landscape. Thus 'Windrush Square', in the heart of Brixton, opened in 2010, 'symbolis[ing] the beginnings of modern British multiculturalism'. And far from being imposed from above, its nomenclature was the 'popular choice' of local residents, businesses and organisations.[83]

Windrush mythologies and silences

Returning to June 1948, neither Cummings nor Lord Kitchener were fabricating their welcome and anticipation of arrival respectively. Even so, there was a strong element of ritualised performance about their discourse marking the arrival of the *Empire Windrush*. At a public level both hid their private ambiguity about Britain. Indeed, several months later, Lord Kitchener recorded 'Sweet Jamaica' which contains the line 'Many West Indians are sorry now/They left their country and don't know how'.[84] The journey of the *Empire Windrush*, like that of the SS *St Louis* and *Exodus 1947*, was thus mythologised as it was taking place. In relation to immediate post-war immigration patterns and control procedures, it was exceptional and not that significant. On the level of rhetoric, while it would take another forty or fifty years for the *Empire Windrush* to be rediscovered, much was already established in June 1948 *before* it arrived. After it had left Kingston, in newspapers and in parliament, there was discussion about its progress. The details of where it came from – the London *Evening News* referred to Barbados – and where it was arriving at – the sympathetic anti-racist MP, Tom Driberg, mentioned Southampton – were fuzzy, but the very fact that it was subject to such interest indicates that a wider significance was given to the ship.[85]

It was also the case that the care and attention to detail in dealing with the *Windrush*'s arrival was very much an exception in terms of New Commonwealth migration to Britain, including those from the West Indies. For example, an earlier ship carrying a smaller number of Jamaicans, the *Almanzora, did* dock in Southampton in December 1947

> completely unheralded ... The state did not succour them with handouts or cheap accommodation; they spent the weeks after disembarking trying to stave off the coldest winter of the [twentieth] century by ... loitering for as long as possible in the warmth of the Underground and Lyons Corner Houses.[86]

In fact, the presence of roughly two hundred black West Indians on the *Almanzora* (out of 1,000 passengers) caused a local stir, but only in respect of the '31 coloured men stowaway[s]'. Yet while it was noted 'stowing away in ships appeared to be getting an organised business, not only in Southampton, but in other ports as well', there was no national panic about the black arrivals on the *Almanzora*.[87] Indeed, locally there was a 'happy sequel' as the youngest stowaway, Jubert Bygrave, aged just sixteen, was exempted the normal 28 days imprisonment and instead was found clothes, accommodation and work in Southampton. It was thus presented as a story encapsulating 'the real spirit of Christmas'.[88] The reality was, however, that the other stowaways and the rest of the black passengers on the *Almanzora* were left to fend for themselves: Alan Wilmot, who had served in the Royal Navy and RAF remembers that 'It wasn't like the Windrush: there was no publicity for us. It was a case of every man for himself. I never knew what it was like to be broke, hungry or homeless until I came to this country. I couldn't even afford a cigarette.'[89]

The arrival of the *Almanzora* in December 1947 has subsequently been largely forgotten with regards to post-war Caribbean migration to Britain, including within the port of Southampton. Such amnesia occurred in spite of it being the immediate precursor to the *Windrush*. The story can even be taken earlier, to March 1947 when the *Ormonde* 'arrived in Liverpool with around 100 Jamaican migrants'.[90] It is perhaps no accident that there is a lacuna concerning the *Almanzora* and *Ormonde* coming into Southampton and Liverpool respectively in 1947. It reflects the London-centric bias of much British migratory history and memory. In reality, however, non-metropolitan ports and places of entry have been of equal and indeed greater numerical significance.

While in some respects the growing recognition of the *Empire Windrush* has stimulated greater awareness of the depths and variety of black history in Britain, it has also led to discomfort for those whose family stories do not quite fit into its overarching narrative. Charlotte Williams was born in North Wales with a Guyanese father and a white Welsh mother. Her father, Denis, an artist, came to Britain *before* the *Windrush* on a British Council scholarship aboard the *Marine Merlin*. The later celebration of the *Empire Windrush* provided, on one level, a much needed sense of identity to Charlotte Williams with her mixed heritage. But it has also produced a form of exclusion as her life story does not connect easily into *Windrush* mythology, including its male-centredness. Charlotte states that she does not have 'a boat or any mass movement to reference [myself]; there's no single port of exit or entry, no date or event that at once serves to bind [my story] together'.[91] Indeed, female experiences of migration and settlement have been marginalised as a result of the focus on the *Windrush*. On the ship itself, little is heard of the score of Caribbean women such as Maisie Simpson described in 1968 as 'a tough and merry woman of 54' who was a hairdresser in Kingston before emigrating on the *Windrush*. She 'always wanted to see the mother country' and put up with slights and the operations of an informal colour bar, remarking cryptically that 'I came to drink the milk, not count the cows'.[92] One of the stowaways was Averill Wauchope, a Kingston dressmaker, whose fare was paid by the other passengers when she was discovered on board. She featured briefly in Joyce Egginton's narrative of the *Windrush*.[93] Yet overall Simpson's is a very rare female black migrant voice.[94] Indeed, Egginton concluded that, 'Wauchope excepted, it was a young man's invasion'.[95] It is a gender imbalance that postcolonial writers such as Caryl Phillips in *The Final Passage* (1985) and Andrea Levy in *Small Island* have tried to correct through their respective characters Leila and Hortense in their novelistic treatments of Caribbean settlement in Britain.[96] As Phillips has emphasised in relation to the televised version of *The Final Passage* (Channel 4, 1996), it was essential to focus on Leila:

> The story of migrants in the twentieth century is of family tension, crisis, split. It's about the hopes and dreams you bring with you … People grow up very fast, they change very quickly, and often it's the woman who is left literally and metaphorically holding the baby.[97]

Phillips' and Levy's literary representations of migrant women have been supplemented by heritage work such as that carried out by the Brighton and Hove

Black History group and its pioneer exhibition on Caribbean nurses who came to Britain in the 1950s and 1960s. For many it was their first journey away from home: one nurse remembered that 'she cried all the way to the UK'. It was an extremely brave undertaking for young women who came to the country not knowing anyone and finding themselves often isolated because of their origins.[98] Another local oral history project, based in Chapeltown, Leeds, *When Our Ship Comes In: Black Women Talk* (1992), was set up to 'honour and acknowledge the presence, resistance and survival of the older Caribbean women' in Britain who have been neglected in relation to their menfolk.[99] It included psychiatric nurse Jean White who despite discrimination and casual racism built up a career over a quarter of a century at St James' Hospital. After twelve years she was 'given my blue uniform to be in charge. When I put it on I felt, at last, I'm here.'[100]

Jannett Creese was another Caribbean nurse who came to Britain, arriving from St Vincent in the Windward Islands during 1959. Like Jean White she progressed through the nursing ranks, using 'staying power' to overcome prejudices from patients and the medical world alike and eventually settling in Stockport in the north-west of England. Her life story was published by Stockport Library Community Services in order to show the importance of the black presence in the town. If there is a desire within her narrative to celebrate a neglected aspect of Stockport's history, Jannett is equally at pains to correct the imbalance inherent within a *Windrush*-centric (and thereby Jamaican-biased) history of post-war Caribbean migration to Britain:

> I spent five days in Trinidad waiting for the ship that would take me to England. This boat was the Ascania, and not the Empire Windrush that had sailed from Jamaica eleven years before with the first wave of economic immigrants.

She is still apologetic about challenging the 'myth' of the *Windrush*, so untouchable as it has recently become. Even so, in her autobiography Jannett ultimately affirms the importance of *other* Caribbean migrant journeys from the 1950s onwards:

> I guess one could say that is ignorant and unforgivable, but I never knew the history of the Windrush until a year before the celebrations of the fiftieth anniversary. I put it down to not knowing many Jamaicans of that era, and there were so many ships that no one spoke about the Ascania, the T.D. Venezuela, the Sorrento and the Irpania.[101]

It has also been forgotten that those that came on the same ship from the Caribbean to England were in the minority during the 1950s – many journeyed via the continent of Europe, or what Joyce Egginton referred to as 'the hard way'. Italian shipping companies were cheaper but their route was 'by sea to Genoa, by train from Genoa to Calais, then cross-Channel steamer to Dover' which was both tiring and disorientating.[102]

Conclusion

The construction of the *Windrush* myth since the late twentieth century has led to both inclusion and exclusion. With regards to the former, in February 2010, the same point at which 'Windrush Square' was officially re-named in Brixton, there was a call from Patrick Vernon of the Afiya Trust for the institution of a public holiday – 'Windrush Day' – to 'celebrate the contributions of black, Asian and other minority communities to Britain over the last sixty years'.[103] Here, the arrival of the ship in June 1948 is imagined as the basis for an open, multicultural society, one that acknowledges the role of newcomers in building Britain and accepts the diversity of the nation's past and present.

Indeed, the stress placed on contribution is the key to understanding the ease with which the *Windrush* story has become so easily integrated into post-war British heritage. Boris Johnson, as Mayor of London, opening the newly improved Windrush Square, emphasised that:

> It is fitting the name … remains almost 62 years after the First West Indian immigrants arrived on the Empire Windrush, many choosing to make London their home. *The positive contribution that this community has made not only to Brixton, but the whole of London and the UK is unmistakable* [my emphasis].[104]

Stuart Maconie provides his own emphasis on where the impact of this offering from the *Windrush* generation is felt most clearly: 'With all due respect to all the future mayors and magistrates aboard, nothing that they bring to these shores will be of more significance than music. In Lord Kitchener's first jaunty song are the seeds and echoes of all the black music to come'.[105] Maconie, who began his journalistic career on *New Musical Express* and still writes about pop music and presents it on the radio, provides a list extending backwards and forwards from June 1948:

> From Cleo Laine to Dizee Rascal, from Croydon's Samuel Coleridge-Taylor in the sphere of classical music to the jazz pianist Julian Joseph, from Joan Armatrading to Tinie Tempah, the Specials and Steel Pulse to the Real Thing and the Sugababes, the *Windrush* would make waves across the airwaves and change the way Britain sounded for ever.[106]

There is, however, a need for caution in such emphasis on the famous and culturally talented who made their mark in Britain. Closer chronologically to the arrival of the *Windrush* and thus operating in a different world from its later celebration, Joyce Egginton quoted a survey in 1955 that highlighted that while 13 per cent of West Indians had clerical posts before migrating, only 5 per cent were engaged in white-collar jobs in England. Conversely, 14 per cent were labourers in England whereas 'only three percent had done that type of work in the West Indies'.[107] Similarly, the sociologist, Ruth Glass, with data that extended up to 1958, concluded that 'In London, 60 per cent of the men and 66 per cent of the women had semi-skilled and unskilled manual jobs. In the West Indies, in their previous occupations, only 21 per cent of the men and 23 per cent of the women ... had been in these rather low categories'.[108] Any rounded study of the *Windrush* generation has therefore to acknowledge what Egginton labelled 'The Disenchanted' – those that returned or moved on elsewhere unable to deal with the harsh realities of being a black migrant in post-war Britain.[109]

Yet if nothing else, the inclusion of the *Empire Windrush* as an 'icon' of Englishness allows acceptance of inward migration to be part of the nation's history, albeit limited to the post-1945 era. Even then, for some, tolerance of the older generation of West Indians, such as those who arrived on the *Windrush*, is regarded as exceptional. To them it confirms a hierarchy of migrant acceptability. It rests alongside opposition to groups who have been deemed to be less assimilable either through race or religion: in short, it reflects the more exclusive reading of *Windrush* mythology.

Responding to the Mass-Observation directive in summer 2006 on 'Core British Values', a retired lorry driver from Basildon, Essex, noted that 'As soon as I saw Gordon Brown's proposal I wondered how long it would be before the Moslems started jumping up and down perceiving yet another anti[-]Moslem slight.' In contrast 'it seems ... the West Indians, the "Windrush generation" have become as English as the rest of us'. Even so, he added, 'Many of the second generation are hankering for the West Indies and its life style.' He then used the (alleged) personal testimony of one of the older generation to make his point and to reveal the pressures placed on minorities to conform to a cliched version of national identity:

> My friend Hughie came on the Windrush, [and] when I asked him about the Notting Hill Carnival he said 'I don't have anything to do with that wog rubbish, I go down the pub for a proper English Sunday with a couple of pints and a game of darts. Then spend the Bank Holiday watching cricket.'[110]

Similar tendencies can be located within Stephen Pollard's *Ten Days that Changed the Nation*. In what is a book of extremes, a positive reading of 22 June 1948 is provided: 'The *Empire Windrush* immigrants were more than symbolic. Their presence changed Britain, and for the better.'[111] But eight chapters later, and Pollard's readers are presented with another date – 14 February 1989 and Ayatollah Khomeini's fatwa demanding the execution of Salman Rushdie. What then follows is a diatribe against Muslims, including those in Britain, and especially their leadership. Faced with cultural or state loyalty on behalf of British Muslims, there is no room for ambiguity, argues Pollard, a former leader writer for the *Daily Express*: 'there ought to be no dilemma, no debate and no choice.'[112]

More subtly, the dichotomy between integrating *Windrushers* and separatist Muslims is drawn by Stuart Maconie. Maconie's confrontation with ethnic and migrant difference has been explored in the first chapter of this study. In *Hope & Glory* he returns again to the themes of national identity and belonging. In Handsworth, Birmingham, Maconie revels in its diversity – especially when entering a public library and discovering its kindergarten space: 'There were Brummies and Barbadians and Bahrainis, a polyglot uproar of fun, a kaleidoscopic selection of hats, hairstyles and knitwear.'[113] Indeed, Maconie's *Windrush* chapter as a whole demolishes the premise on which Enoch Powell's vision of a nation about to self-destruct was based. Instead, a tradition of migrant settlement in the deep British past is emphasised by Maconie with the conclusion

> However yours came they came from somehow and from somewhere. Because the only thing native to these islands are the Skiddaw slates and the Borrowdale volcanics, the limestone dales and the chalk downs. The only thing that is British about the island is the island's rock itself.[114]

Handsworth Library represents to Maconie the glory of multiple past roots enabling the vitality of twenty-first century Britain. There is, however, 'one wrong note sounded here' which spoils its otherwise 'messy, magnanimous free-for-all of tolerance and good humour' – a request for entrants to the 'Young Muslim Writer Award of the Year'. To Maconie, the competition brought with it 'a baggage of "faith" and fatwa, antiquated ritual and life-denying rules'.[115] Maconie's sense of Englishness is porous and he rejects Powell's racial determinism when the Conservative politician defined the nation through his 'Rivers of Blood' speech. Food, music and dress and other forms of popular culture are there to be reinvented. But to Maconie, difference as manifest through Muslim faith and religion is more troubling and potentially divisive. In contrast, Maconie takes pride in the 'really neat tale' that the former Nazi ship, the *Monte Rosa*, was 'renamed *Empire Windrush* in 1947 after the sweet and gentle and very English river that runs through Bourton-on-the-Water and other dreamy Cotswolds villages'.[116]Maconie's pluralistic notion of national identity has its limits, but it is not one stretched by the story of the *Windrush*.

Cultural critic, Lola Young, has suggested that 'whenever those scenes from the 1948 Pathe newsreel were shown, they were loaded with meaning, burdened with representational weight, laden with ambivalence'.[117] Few, however, have wished to embrace this ambiguity and complexity, instead using the *Windrush* for more simplistic and often overtly political purposes. In the future, much will depend on how carefully the ship's arrival is contextualised and how far the atypical nature of its journey in 1948 is acknowledged. So far, a narrow reading of the *Windrush* has promoted the distortions already noted. These include the neglect of women as against male migrants and more generally the experiences of those who came some years later in even greater numbers on a variety of ships and from all the West Indian islands. It has also led to a triumphalist story line with the emphasis on contribution and successful integration. Such memory work has enabled criticism of other migrant groups who are accused of separatism and subversion.

Furthermore, in existing historiography and memory work, the emphasis on the *Windrush* has especially led to the marginalisation of African life stories as well as consideration of those coming from the Indian subcontinent. Partly as a result of this geographic focus, pre-*Windrush* black settlement in Britain has been relegated in importance or totally ignored. There is no space in popular narratives, for example, for Ernest Marke, who came to Britain as a young stowaway in the First World War from Sierre Leone. He lived amongst the black (and especially West African) communities of Liverpool, Cardiff, Manchester and London in the inter-war period and beyond. His autobiography, initially published in 1975, makes no reference to the *Empire Windrush*. Marke's autobiography, outlining a career inside and outside the law, provides a very different storyline to that now provided for those Caribbean migrants who arrived in June 1948.[118]

In his maverick and polemical 'new right' dismissal of black British history, Roy Kerridge makes one valid point against what he calls 'Windrush History' – its potential to create, as Jannett Creese's memoir hints, a 'Jamaico-centric' narrative:

> So persuasive is Windrush history that two students of my acquaintance, asked to write of their family experience on 'coming to Britain', guiltily described Jamaican parents on the 'Empire Windrush'. In fact, both students had African fathers and English mothers.[119]

It is to such black migrants, and their less celebrated and largely forgotten journeys to Britain, that this study will now turn.

8

Stowaways and others: racism and alternative journeys into Britishness

Early Black British history

In an 'Anthology of Writing about Black Britain', originally entitled *Empire Windrush*, its editor, Onyekachi Wambu, argued that the 'landing of the SS *Empire Windrush* at Tilbury Docks on June 21, 1948 [*sic*] began a process that has steadily and radically transformed Britain. The *Empire Windrush* was the first ship bringing home the people of Empire as settlers.' Wambu, like other *Windrush* commemorators, acknowledges that 'They had, of course, come in the past from Africa, the Caribbean, Hong Kong, and the Indian subcontinent as students, sailors, artists, political activists, and slaves.' But Wambu goes further in identifying those on the *Windrush* as exceptional: 'this time they were coming as free men and women, seeking work.'[1] It has been suggested that with the '1998 Windrush anniversary celebrations ... one could almost sense a new historical myth being formed; the notion that there had been no black people in England before 1948'.[2] Wambu modifies this distortion but creates his own by ignoring the fact that (aside from learning), the earlier black presence in Britain almost totally revolved around the need to find work – whether in the civil or military realm. His chronology also distorts the reality that immediately before, during and after the arrival of the *Empire Windrush*, a larger number of black people were coming to Britain. They came through very different types of migrant journeys, as this chapter will explore.

In the draft prepared for the Prime Minister aimed at reassuring the worried backbenchers about the significance of the *Empire Windrush*, it was acknowledged 'that there has been a steady trickle of coloured Colonials reaching here as stowaways who have been a considerable nuisance'.[3] Those on board the *Empire Windrush*, it was agreed by all the government departments involved, should be treated 'as distinct from stowaways and unemployed seamen such as comprise the 2000 persons at Liverpool'.[4] In February 1948 a policy was formulated 'to prevent colonial stowaways from landing in the UK'. This 'problem' was intensifying and the civil servants involved felt 'more convinced than ever that sooner or later more action must be taken to keep out the undesirable elements of our colonial population'. Nevertheless, it was important that 'This should not … be read as suggesting that the Empire Windrush passengers are undesirable.'[5] Indeed, it was the more casual and less controllable movement typified as 'stowaways' that exercised the minds of civil servants and politicians when dealing with black migration up to the early 1950s.

In 1950 and 1951, the Labour Cabinet considered the possibility of introducing immigration controls based on colour. Formal measures were rejected but throughout all the discussions the need for stricter procedures to limit the number of stowaways was accepted. There was, within the category of 'coloured colonials', a clear hierarchy of undesirability/desirability:

> Since 1945 certain new developments have occurred which have result-
> ed in an increase of at least 5,000 persons almost all of whom are West
> Africans and West Indians. Among these new immigrants the trouble-
> some elements are (1) Stowaways (2) Seafarers and to a lesser degree (3)
> fare paying immigrant workers.

The stowaways were the largest group, consisting of at least 1,600 and still growing in number. According to government statistics, roughly two-thirds of the stowaways came from West Africa and about one-quarter from the West Indies.[6] It was recognised that, with regard to immigration control, 'Any solution depending on an apparent or concealed colour test would be so invidious as to make it impossible of adoption'. Nevertheless, there was favour in support of informal measures that would in fact (though never publicly acknowledged) be 'confined to coloured persons', especially stowaways, 'whose continued presence here is obviously objectionable'.[7] In practice, the government began to crack down on the use of British Travel Certificates as proof of identity. These certificates were initially intended for travel within West Africa, enabling 'men to travel from British territories to neighbouring French territories'. They were not intended for travel abroad but the Colonial Office was aware that, since the war, West African stowaways coming to Britain had been 'using these Certificates for the purpose of establishing their nationality'.[8] With a more disbelieving approach to such documentation, in the first nine months of 1950 alone, one hundred colonial stowaways were turned away.[9]

The racing tipster, Prince Monolulu, claimed to be a 'descendant of Ethiopian kings'.[10] His real name was Peter Mackay and he was born in British Guiana, coming to England in the early 1900s.[11] A well-known figure in society as a whole, many of Monolulu's circle were West Africans. It included Ernest Marke and others from the Caribbean who were pretending to be Africans. They were former seamen who had struggled to get work after 1918. These men made their living in inter-war Britain on the margins of society, as 'crocusers' (quack doctors) and tipsters, trading on their perceived exoticism and magical powers.[12] It was for his closeness to 'real' and 'imaginary' Africans that Monolulu had a deep awareness, in spite of his fame (he appeared in films and on the radio), of the treatment of obscure black stowaways after the Second World War. In his autobiography, published in 1950, Monolulu wrote with anger about the 'Colour Bar' in Britain and especially in relation to discrimination at the port of entry: 'If a black man comes to this country as a stowaway he is promptly sent back to his own country. A white stowaway stays and is given work.'[13]

Such procedures were not new. In the 1920s, through racist measures such as the Special Restriction (Coloured Alien Seamen) Order (1925), it was, as Neil Evans has shown, almost impossible in the eyes of the local authorities – especially the police – in places such as Cardiff to be both black and British.[14] Even the possession of a British passport was not enough to escape the designation of 'alien'.[15] As one particular manifestation of such racialised and exclusive constructions of Britishness, during the 1930s the Home Office became concerned about the increasing number of *Lascar* seamen who were settling in Britain.

In the view of the Home Office, the problem was the result of the loose issue of Certificates of Nationality and Identity to British Indian seamen. As Rozina Visram has emphasised, the India Office objected to these seamen being subject to the 1925 Aliens Order and used these certificates to counter its discriminatory impact. She concludes that 'Such a stand by the India Office is significant and runs counter to the accepted notions of a monolithic racist state.'[16] Nevertheless, the Home Office continued its campaign against such Indian sailors, especially when the number entering Britain was increasing during the late 1920s and early 1930s. The case of Abdullah Karim was used by the authorities as an example of the problems that had emerged and how these might be avoided in the future. Little is known of Abdullah Karim other than the material collected in police files. He was born in Karachi but had, when he applied for a Certificate of Nationality, no proof of his identity.[17] According to the Lincolnshire Constabulary, before his arrival in the United Kingdom he had been 'working in the capacity as a sailor on ships between India, England, and America, for the past ten years'.[18] The Chief Constable of Lincolnshire summarised the problem bluntly in a letter to the High Commissioner for India: Karim was a 'coloured seamen who claims to be a British subject'.[19]

In the words of Special Branch, Karim had 'deserted ships on three known occasions, the last time being on the 2nd of May 1937, when he deserted the S.S. "City of Canterbury" at Glasgow'.[20] Evidence from the Glasgow police indicated that he had first 'deserted' in May 1931 from the *City of Baghdad* and had then settled in the city, finding employment in Chinese boarding houses. He had moved to Liverpool and then Blackpool.[21] At the time of his application for a Certificate of Nationality Karim was employed by a conjuror, 'Prince Bahram Khan', at Thompson's Amusement Park, Skegness, and calling himself (in an act of reverse colonial discourse) 'Tarzan'.[22] The Home Office was concerned that an order to return to ship under the Merchant Shipping Act could only be made within six months of the date of desertion and that *Lascar* seamen were abusing that clause and settling in ever greater numbers. In this particular case, the police caught up with Karim in time and he was 'repatriated' on board the SS *City of Baroda* on 27 October 1937.[23] Only later was it discovered through the High Commissioner for India that Abdullah Karim did indeed possess British nationality.[24] Such legal niceties were of little concern to the authorities – their aim was to stop the settlement of *Lascars* in Britain by their 'desertion' and subsequent 'disappearance'.[25]

Abdullah Karim/'Tarzan' was not alone amongst the *Lascars* in finding an occupation as an 'exotic' performer in seaside resorts such as Blackpool and Skegness.[26] More common, however, was work as pedlars which became an increasingly common sight in Britain during the 1930s. The testimony of one of these men who came to England in 1938 was recorded during the 1980s by the Bradford Heritage Recording Unit. It reveals the commonality of this experience as well as the day to day struggle to survive:

> It was a village experience, go out and earn some money. In the village there was no other job besides helping your parents on the farm, so I thought of going abroad ... In those days there were not many jobs even for English people, never mind the foreigners. They used to peddle around with clothes, handerchiefs, shirts, socks, this and that ... When I landed over here I had £20 in my pocket, after one year I had the same money so you can estimate what sort of life we were leading.[27]

In spite, however, of their increasing familiarity and utility in town and countryside, at the level of popular representation these pedlars were viewed as slippery and dangerous. In 1939 the first BBC television documentary on ethnic diversity in Britain was broadcast, exploring 'London's East End, introducing Cockney and Jew, Lascar and Chinaman, and others of its inhabitants'.[28] It briefly featured Sar Wan Singh, a former Lascar seaman who had worked as a pedlar in the East End of London for the past three years. Based on the research of Mass-Observation, and written and presented by its leader, Tom Harrisson, the commentary for the programme was purely negative in its portrayal of the Indian presence in what was the most diverse area of London: 'All the time now Lascars are coming ashore and settling. They are presenting a new racial problem for the East End.' As with Abdullah Karim in the Home Office files, Singh is rendered largely speechless and placeless in the documentary, even though when he was interviewed previously it became apparent that he had brought his wife and family to the East End. By 1939, Sar Wan Singh had established strong roots there. This part of his testimony, however, was edited out of the broadcast. Similarly, William Goldman's powerful memoir of growing up poor in the East End, published in 1940, could find no voice or empathy for the Indian pedlars whom he experienced in the public baths. They were simply 'mystifying' to the otherwise universalistically minded and socialist Goldman: 'You never heard them … You saw them enter the bath as uncompromisingly dark Asiatics, but if you happened to be about when one of them was leaving, he struck you as having much more of an affinity with the yellow races.'[29] It would be another half century before oral history projects such as that of the Bradford Heritage Recording Unit would recover the life stories and humanity of such individuals.[30]

At the start of the Second World War, it has been estimated that there were anywhere between five and over eight thousand Indians and other Asians in Britain. It was, as Visram notes, 'not a monolithic group. A sprinkling of women, wives and children was represented in this diversity. The picture of their lives that emerges is complex and varied, and belies the traditional notions of the process of migration and settlement.'[31] It included those of both working-class and professional background who, by 1939, had created a complex institutional structure, including the long-lasting Indian Workers' Association (formed in 1937 by pedlars in Coventry) reflecting its 'plural identities'. It was a 'resourceful and vibrant community, engaged in a variety of professions and careers' which made 'notable contributions to British life'.[32]

The Home Office, however, could only see this population as a nuisance, and it seems certain that the issue of Lascar 'desertion' was exaggerated by the authorities, reflecting their desire to keep out the 'alien' coloured population. But by problematising *Lascar* seamen, whether through legal measures or in Harrisson's television programme and Goldman's classic working-class autobiography, within the cultural realm, their energy and bravery was lost sight of both at the time and in subsequent memory work. It took the pathbreaking oral history of Caroline Adams in her *Across Seven Seas and Thirteen Rivers* (1987) to rescue from oblivion the 'life stories of pioneer Sylhetti settlers in Britain'. As Adams summarised, their migrant journeys were complex: 'For some, there would be sudden death by torpedo; for others, a few voyages and a return to the village, some would spend a lifetime at sea, and others were to be the *Londonis*, the pioneers of a mass migration.'[33]

Amongst those interviewed by Adams as one of the early *Londonis* was Syed Rasul who graphically described his first alienating experiences on board a Merchant Navy vessel:

> They took me down, inside the ship, such a strange place. I was fright-
> ened, because I had never seen anything like that before. Then the sea
> started to go ... *oh my God!* ... for six or seven days I didn't have any cup
> of tea or food or anything. Still I had to work. I swore to God, when I get
> back I am never going to leave my home and family again.

Yet showing the resilience, staying power and communal strength of so many migrants who ended up in Britain, Rasul persisted:

> The other men looked after me, they said, 'Don't worry, after a few days
> the sea will go smooth.' It was true, I was alright when I got used to it.[34]

Caroline Adams through her work amongst these early settlers in the East End – by the time her book was published there were roughly 35,000 Bengalis in the area and over a quarter of a million Bangladeshis in Britain as a whole – had the vision, as did the Bradford Heritage Recording Unit, to rescue the testimonies of those that came before 1945. She realised that these elders might often be seen in the wider community simply as 'anonymous "Asians"'. In contrast, she pointed out that for 'every white-bearded elderly Bangladeshi gentleman strolling with dignity to the mosque, or beleaguered by racist attacks in a de-crepid council flat, there is a life history'. There was to be discovered 'a tale of magic and mystery in Assam, adventure in the North Atlantic, romance in the Blitz, or simply the unfolding of a long life and all its lessons'.[35] Adams was doing a rare thing and working against the dominant archive record. She was giving voice to those who the British state and its media, or dominant sections of it, would have restricted entry, re-classified as 'alien' and banished from its soil.

The attempt in the early 1950s to stop the 'illegal' movement of West Africans, and to a lesser extent, West Indians, was thus far from new: it reflected an ongoing desire to stop the permanant settlement in Britain of 'coloured' migrants whose journeys were deemed irregular. By the later 1940s the attention had largely shifted away from the *Lascars* to those originating from either the Caribbean or Africa. West African stowaways especially were now perceived as a menace by the British state in the years immediately following the end of the Second World War. A racial hierarchy was established with the assumption that 'the British West Indian seemed a finer type physically than the West African'.[36] Such movement of Africans was criminalised and pathologised – it was hard to monitor and there was the additional fear that they added to racial problems in the old dockland communities such as Liverpool which suffered renewed racial violence in the late summer of 1948.[37] Unless loopholes could be found to immediately deport the stowaways, the most that could be done was to imprison them for up to twenty-eight days (if successfully prosecuted) and to impose a small fine. Thereafter, however, they were 'able to remain'.[38]

David Oluwale and the politics of stowaways

Little has been written about this sizeable movement of 'illegal' black migrants to Britain who fail to meet the narrative expectations that have (increasingly) been met by those on board the *Empire Windrush* – the journeys of stowaways and others were, by nature, piecemeal. Moreover, those embarking on them were beyond the law and doubly outsiders. Unlike many on the *Windrush*, they had no immediate link to Britain or to its war effort. Ultimately, whatever the hardships, the story of those on the *Empire Windrush* has been constructed as one of hard won victory – 'climbing up the rough side of the mountain', in the religiously inspired words of Sam King's autobiography.[39] It was a battle against adversity, but one that was eventually successful, leading to an intensified sense of national belonging. For many years the testimonies of those on board were neglected yet, in a new context – that of constructing a comfortable multiculturalism – the myth of the *Windrush* is now firmly established. But to rescue the experiences of the obcure stowaways and others who came to Britain after 1945 from West Africa has been even more challenging to the nation's self-image of a decent and welcoming 'island'. It is a problem reinforced by the nature of surviving historical evidence.

In the records held by the National Archives, 'coloured stowaways' are presented in three ways. First, they appear as lists of statistics according to port of arrival and place of origin. For example, a table amalgamating the figures for 1946, 1947 and 1948 records that for the port of Liverpool the total was 336. It included 61 from Sierra Leone, 42 from the Gold Coast, 52 from Gambia, 54 from Jamaica and the largest number, 102, from Nigeria.[40] Second, there are case studies of individuals such as that relating to Godwin Sachale who had arrived at the Surrey docks on the Norwegian vessel, *Lido* in February 1950. The eighteen-year-old, born in Effra, West Africa, claimed British nationality, but this was not accepted by the port authorities in London 'there being no documentary evidence of such nationality'. He was returned to Dakar and a warning was sent there not to issue him with a British Travel Certificate in case he attempted to re-enter the country. The Chief Inspector at the Port of London added in a damning summary that Sachale 'was without means and appeared to be a poor type of native'.[41] Third, there are police and regional newspaper reports on the arrest and prosecution of the stowaways focusing on the local administrative problems they had caused.[42] Taken together, these sources provided the 'evidence' from which civil servants concluded that 'the average stowaway is ill-suited for absorption into the economic and social life of this country', his presence creating 'difficult social problems'.[43] In these surviving documents, the stowaways are represented as an undifferentiated mass. Their voices are seldom heard and, when they are, it is in the form of procedural interrogation and through the prism of suspicion and disbelief.

In the papers of sociologist, Michael Banton, now housed at Black Cultural Archives in London, there is a small file labelled 'Stowaways 1950'. It includes some letters, most written by West Africans. Amongst them is a remarkable letter from Amos Olalekau, a twenty-year-old from Abeokuta, Nigeria. Olalekau was serving a short sentence in Winchester prison having been unable to prove his nationality when arriving on a ship landing at Southampton. As was the case with Godwin Sachale, Olalekau was facing deportation on his release. Emphasising that he was a 'British Subject surely', he made clear that 'if you send me back, I am coming back again … until my people tye me with rope, and if they tye me I must cut and come back to Europe again'.[44] On the surface, this letter and the others in this collection *do* provide the West African stowaways with an authentic and contemporary voice. But, following the work of Gayatri Chakravorty Spivak, we need to ask whether the 'subaltern' can really 'speak', or if he/she is still silenced by colonial discourse.[45]

Assuming that these letters are genuine (some were clearly copied by civil servants), they were given to Banton as part of his pioneer research into black life in post-war Britain, published as *The Coloured Quarter: Negro Immigrants in an English City* (1955). Banton received assistance from government departments, especially the Colonial Office, and it was presumably through these contacts that he received the stowaway letters.[46] The details within them conform to the problem as perceived by officialdom – they include reference to crime, (sexual) disease, naive expectations of Britain with its streets paved with gold, and, as with Olalekau, the determination to return to the 'mother country'. His letter of protest closes with the statement 'Don't think if you send me back to Lagos I will not come back. I am comming back because I still under Union Jack.'[47]

Banton reproduced some of these letters in *The Coloured Quarter*.[48] Overall, however, the voice of the African is rarely heard in his groundbreaking study – the first sociological/anthropological treatment of black British life that was not written under the direct intellectual influence of race science. As with the civil service and judicial files, statistics and the perspectives of (white) authority figures dominate his account. Even so, there is the sign of a more progressive world to come, and Banton, early in his study, noted that some of the West Africans

> became assiduous students at evening classes run by the local authorities; a number have done very well for themselves. In recent years nearly all the stowaways have been ambitious young literates. The view held by some persons in official positions that the stowaways are the 'dregs' of their own countries cannot be upheld.[49]

Ultimately, however, the 'official' view prevailed in *The Coloured Quarter* and Banton concluded that the problems faced by the West Africans were 'of the immigrants' own making … Many of the stowaways were delinquents in their own countries and have only continued in the sort of behaviour to which they were accustomed.'[50]

Spivak concludes her study of *sati*, or widow self-sacrifice, in eighteenth-century India, that – taking into account the surviving archive and the nature of colonial power relations – 'The subaltern cannot speak.'[51] In the case of African stowaways in the late 1940s and early 1950s, we do not need to conclude so pessimistically: Olalekau's letter, and his plea to be part of England, represents a form of migrant resistance. Yet whether in Colonial Office files or in the more humane narrative provided by a young white sociologist/anthropologist, these letters were used by contemporaries to problematise the presence of the black stowaways. Only now and only partially, can the stowaway perspective be restored to the historical analysis.

Banton's research focused on the classic area of migrant settlement, the East End of London. African stowaways were, however, arriving in all British ports in the immediate post-war era. Indeed, Olalekau taunted the recipient of his letter by stating that if he came back after being deported 'It may be [I] am not going to land at Southampton, I may land at Glasgow, or Liverpool, or London etc.'[52] One place he did not mention, but could easily have done so, was Hull. In the summer of 1950, the government's Inter-Departmental Committee on Coloured People in the UK received a report on this port. It started with stowaways and outlined what it saw as a major and growing problem:

> In the last twelve months, 83 stowaways were landed at Hull. 30, being non-British, were shipped back to their port of departure. Of 53 British Nationals, and Colonials, 45 were prosecuted and spent 28 days in gaol. On discharge, some found their way back to Hull. The majority of these were unemployable, being undisciplined, not amenable to instruction and tribal in background.

It concluded that there was a 'strong feeling [locally] that stowaways of British nationality should be deported.'[53] In Hull, between 1946 and 1948, a total of 175 stowaways were found, the largest number (70), as was the case with Liverpool, coming from Nigeria.[54] One of these individuals, through his catastrophic experiences in England ending in his appalling death, has subsequently become notorious.

David Oluwale arrived at Hull on 3 September 1949 on the *Temple Bar*. The ship, travelling from Lagos, was carrying ground nuts and initially nine stowaways. Six were 'turned off the ship before it set sail. Oluwale was one of the lucky three who evaded detection.'[55] The nineteen-year-old Oluwale had left to make a better life for himself, struggling in Lagos as an apprentice tailor. As was the case in the West Indies, there were few oppportunities in West Africa following the dislocation of the Second World War. Sentenced to the obligatory twenty-eight days, the Hull magistrate said that the three stowaways would have been 'better off staying at home digging up groundnuts'.[56] David Oluwale was sent to prison in Leeds and spent much of the next twenty years in that city. The first four were relatively uneventful and it seems from the testimony of other African migrants that knew him that Oluwale established a reasonably happy life for himself, if unable to fulfil his early aspirations. He was, according to Kester Aspden, who has rescued David Oluwale's life and death from obscurity, 'popular and easygoing, a lively conversationalist who loved his Saturday nights at the Mecca ballroom.'[57]

In 1953, Oluwale's life was to transform into a vicious circle of violence, mistreatment and incarceration, one that only ended with his tragic death in May 1969. A first bruising encounter with the police led to a recurring pattern of imprisonment, followed by lengthy stays in Victorian-origin mental institutions where he was subjected to electric shock treatment and, on release, a life as a tramp where he was subject to physical and psychological bullying by the local 'law enforcers'. It culminated in his death in the hands of two policemen when he drowned in the River Aire having earlier been beaten. Oluwale, as Aspden notes (following Mary Douglas), was regarded as mere dirt – 'matter out of place' – by the police and they did their best to remove his 'soiling' presence.[58]

Only limited justice was achieved when eighteen months later the two police officers were given minor custodial sentences but they were not prosecuted for murder or even manslaughter. At the time, the case achieved national publicity and was part of a growing anger in the Afro-Caribbean community against police brutality. Locally the case provided the opportunity of taunting the constabulary on the terraces of Leeds United:

> The River Aire is chilly and deep – Ol-u-wa-le
> Never trust the Leeds police – Ol-u-wa-a-le.[59]

To the novelist, Caryl Phillips, born in St Kitts but brought up in Leeds, the story of David Oluwale has particular resonance. His *Foreigners: Three English*

Lives (2007), includes that of the Nigerian stowaway.[60] It has been suggested that 'The graffiti on a Leeds wall that reverberates through the story – "Remember Oluwale" – will prove impossible to disregard.'[61] Certainly, there is a growing movement to carry out this belated act of remembrance. In fact, Oluwale was never subject to total amnesia. In 1972 Jeremy Sandford wrote a radio play on his life, *Smiling David* which was published two years later, although it focused more on his homelessness than the racism he experienced.[62] Jamaican-born Linton Kwesi Johnson also devoted a poem to him, 'Night of the Head' in his rebellious and impassioned *Dread Beat and Blood* (1975) collection:

> Such a victim of terror as he was,
> Oluwale on the last onslaught,
> just broke into pieces and died.[63]

Thereafter, his story largely disappeared for three decades. As Aspden comments, 'Whereas the name Stephen Lawrence [the black teenager murdered in 1993] is seared into the public memory, the Oluwale case has been largely forgotten outside the city of Leeds and the ranks of those tuned in to the history of English racism.'[64]

In the latter part of the first decade of the twenty-first century, however, Olawale has been rediscovered. In 2007 alone Aspden's remarkable work of historical detection – *The Hounding of David Oluwale* – and Phillips' literary version of his life in England were published. In 2009, Oladipo Agboluaje's powerful stage adaptation of Aspden's book toured the UK to critical acclaim.[65] There is an ongoing appeal, led by academic Max Farrar of Leeds Metropolitan University, to create a permanent memorial to David Oluwale in the city of his death, one intended to 'help the city reconcile itself with the past and move forward'. While recognising the progress made, the memorial appeal has the objective of acknowledging 'how much further we have to go before we have a city where equal rights and justice prevail for everyone, whatever their colour and social status'.[66]

Kester Aspden notes that 'Few of Oluwale's words have been recorded for posterity' and even these come in the form of evidence given to the court – there is a parallel here to the material on stowaways and to the story of Abdullah Karim held in the National Archives.[67] Aspden's narrative touches upon the personality of David Oluwale through such evidence and from the testimony of his fellow African and other black migrants who knew him in better days or worse. His work, however, is aimed at getting to the truth of what happened to him, rather than being a 'probing of Oluwale's life or his personality'.[68] In partial contrast, Phillips melds court material with fiction to present a hauntingly sad portrait of Oluwale's life in Britain, setting it alongside that of Francis Barber, the Jamaican former slave who became servant of Samuel Johnson, and

Randolph Turpin, Britain's first black world champion boxer. Whereas Aspden is clear that he does not 'pretend to identify' with Oluwale, Phillips uses the stowaway to explore the nature of Englishness and the black experience in the country's deep and recent past.[69] The novelist's ambivalent place in this construct is what makes this work so disturbing and moving. Agboluaje also uses fiction in order 'to rediscover David, to recuperate him as a person'. His objective, following Farrar, was to 'exhume David in order to give him a befitting memorial'.[70]

Before this treatment of the Nigerian migrant draws to a close, two questions remain to be answered relating to the memory work associated with David Oluwale. First, why is that such intensified efforts are being made, forty years after his death, to remember him? To Agboluaje and others, there is clearly a need to achieve a sense of justice – historic and for the future if not realistically now in a court of law. With regards to the latter, the playwright asks: 'Can a story like David's happen again?' He responds pessimistically: the 'statistics of deaths in police custody make chilling reading'.[71] Aspden likewise states at the start that 'My story of David Oluwale has a public context – I believe that it says something about Britain, then and now'.[72] He has added elsewhere that while the police service has accepted the need to confront institutional racism following the Stephen Lawrence murder, some 'high-profile successes have disguised some unacceptable realities. There have been hundreds of suspicious deaths in custody since the records began in 1970, and black people are over-represented in the roll call'.[73] By focusing on official injustice in the past, current abuse, including that of rough sleepers, can also be brought into the spotlight.

There is also, in the re-visiting of this tragedy, a desire to root David Oluwale, to find finally for him a place called home. Phillips' melancholic *Foreigners* establishes, in spite of their 'otherness', the Englishness of these three troubled black lives, all blighted by racism and misfortune. He concludes his evocative work by visiting the cemetery where David Oluwale is buried:

> Soon there will be no more burials in this place. Everybody can rest peacefully. You have achieved a summit, David. Climbed to the top of a hill, and from here you can look down. You are still in Leeds. Forever in Leeds.[74]

Farrar, in his desire for a physical memorial for Oluwale, has similar desires to honour his presence in the city as well as to recognise the police racism and intolerance of the homeless that David experienced so horrifically.

The second question is to ponder what future place David Oluwale will have in the future construction of national memory. In spite of the efforts of Sandford, Farrar, Johnson, Phillips, Aspden and Agboluaje, memory work of this Nigerian stowaway is still in its infancy and relatively marginal. In many ways his story is a brutal counter-narrative to the *Empire Windrush*: the 'coloured stowaways' were unambiguously regarded by the British state as undesirable, dangerous and criminalised from the start. No effort was made to welcome them – on the contrary all attempts were made to discourage their journeys to Britain and to punish them, as far as was legally possible, including by deportation. In 1948, when considering what occupations could be found for those on the *Empire Windrush*, a government official quipped that they could be sent to Africa to pick groundnuts. His humorous, if tasteless, aside was not taken at all seriously in the Ministry of Labour which was responsible for the placement of these men.[75] The Hull magistrate who suggested the same solution to David Oluwale and his fellow two stowaways was not joking.

Ultimately, the stories of those on board the *Empire Windrush*, however harsh, can be (and have been) presented with a redemptive ending. Slowly, they have become part of the narrative of the Second World War, still crucial to the formation and reformation of national identity in Britain. In 2008, for example, as noted, the Imperial War Museum hosted an extended exhibition 'From War to Windrush' . The visitor was encouraged to

> Discover the stories of some of the thousands of West Indian men and women who served in the British forces and Merchant Navy during the First and Second World Wars. 60 years after the MV *Empire Windrush*, explore how their wartime experiences helped shape Britain's modern West Indian populations.[76]

The *Windrushers* are now beginning to become part of the nation's story – they, and their descendants are here to stay. In February 2009, in what was perceived as a landmark moment in British television, the popular BBC 'soap opera', *EastEnders*, had its first all black episode, focusing on the story of the West Indian character, Patrick Trueman, who arrived in London during the 1950s.[77] It became, as black journalist, Hannah Pool suggested, 'more like a history lesson' than light entertainment: 'Last night we had the Notting Hill riots, steel pans, carnival, Martin Luther King and Rosa Parks.' As Pool added, reflecting the ease with which the ship has become a comfortable part of everyday multicultural heritage in Britain, 'I half expected Patrick to mention how he walked off Windrush with his brother Trevor McDonald and how thrilled he is his grandson Lewis Hamilton is doing so well.'[78]

In the Imperial War Museum, Britain's official repository of war memories, such an act of *Windrush* inclusion has now taken place (albeit temporarily), adding to that which has already occurred with the Holocaust and the survivors who rebuilt their lives in Britain. As noted in the previous chapter, 'Windrush Square' has been created in Brixton symbolising 'the beginnings of modern British multicultural society'.[79] Such celebration and inclusion has led the British National Party's leader, Nick Griffin, articulating the politics of cultural despair, to view 1948 as the year 'when Britain's prelapsarian idyll ended'.[80] Griffin's views are not totally isolated and perhaps find some resonance within the right wing of mainstream British nationalism as articulated by the journalist and writer Roy Kerridge.[81] It remains, however, taking British society and culture as a whole, that the *Empire Windrush* has become part of everyday history. No such incorporation or sense of closure is possible in the case of David Oluwale. Oladipo Agboluaje's play ends with David talking to his mother, exhausted by and excluded from what he thought was his 'mother country':

> You must believe me when I say I tried my best. I really tried. But I've had enough, *Maam'mi* … I did my best. In fact I'm fed up with this country. *Ilu yitisu mi* [I've had it with this country]. I want to go home … I want to go home. I want to go home … [82]

Other African journeys

The remaining case studies of this chapter, all featuring other Nigerian migrant journeys, provide different (but in many ways equally depressing) stories of the treatment of first-generation settlers in Britain. These three family life stories come from the years following both the First and Second World Wars. Yet there is also another, more hopeful, narrative that succeeds them. In all the examples to be detailed below, the (male) Nigerian migrant was returned to Africa, forcibly in at least two of the cases. What is also evident, however, is the 'staying power' and remarkable contribution of their children in Britain. For them, there is an engagement with their fathers' histories, especially relating to the reasons behind their movement into and out of the country. As with David Oluwale, the obscure African migrant has been partially recovered from the 'enormous condescension of history'.[83]

The first story relates to the father of one of the most successful and internationally acclaimed singers in the post-war era, Shirley Bassey. Often dubbed in her early career as the 'Girl from Tiger Bay',[84] Bassey was indeed born in the Butetown dock area of Cardiff in 1937, despite popular belief to the contrary.[85] Her father, Henry, came from the port of Calabar in Nigeria and her mother, Eliza, from north Yorkshire.[86] Butetown was (in)famous the world over, the moniker 'Tiger Bay' reflecting from the mid-nineteenth century onwards its role as a '"sailortown" *par excellence*, providing the seamen ashore with a number of recreational diversions, some of which were illegal'.[87] Alongside and linked to its reputation for danger and crime, was the idea of 'Tiger Bay', imagined either through fear or fascination, as the world in miniature – either representing the delights of a cosmopolitan melting pot or the nightmare of miscegenation. The local newspaper gave voice to this ambivalence and popular anthropology through a poem published in 1902:

> Here all dominions, races and opinions
> Have many precious specimens on view,
> Maltese and Arab, German, Jew, and Carrib –
> The meek Hibernian and the mad Hindoo ... [88]

The emphasis on the exotic and the sensational, and especially the vice associated with Bute Street, distorts the fact that a settled black community, or more accurately, communities had evolved in Tiger Bay by 1914 from its initially transient populations. The testimony of Harriet Vincent relating to her family history reveals how permanent structures and stable relationships came into being. Vincent's father was of West Indian origin and he worked as a cook and a steward at sea. He came to live in Cardiff – first as a confectioner and baker, and then as the owner of a boarding house with his (white) locally born wife. In the pre-First World War neighbourhood of Tiger Bay, Mr Vincent 'was its natural organiser', present at funerals and offering advice to all. Moreover, 'the Vincents, as a respectable mixed marriage in a racially mixed community, were among those who especially helped to hold it together'.[89] His daughter rememberd that, according to Mr Vincent, 'You had to respect everybody ... If you give respect you can command it.'[90] Unfortunately, outside Tiger Bay that view was not widely held and indeed such mixed relationships and even more so the children emerging from them were seen as particularly threatening: 'outbreaks of racial tension [such as the 1919 riots] were peculiarly threatening to their own personal lives'.[91]

In Liverpool an even older and larger black community was to be found. There were also many sailors of West African origin in this port city, including many of the ethnic group Kru from Liberia known for their seafaring traditions and ability who worked on the Elder Dempster line based in Liverpool.[92] Smaller in number were those of Nigerian origin, including Thomas Bassey who settled in Liverpool before the First World War. Also from Calabar, but not related to Henry, he was well-educated and, like Harriet Vincent's father in Tiger Bay, an informal community leader. 'Immaculately dressed with bowler hat and brolly', his son recalls that 'He always wanted to be self-sufficient ... He always taught us to be independent and proud.'[93] By 1914, the black community of Liverpool had grown to roughly 3,000 people.[94]

These port communities and others such as those in the East End of London, Glasgow, North and South Shields, Hull and Southampton housed the majority of Britain's black population before 1914. There were other in-dividuals scattered around the country, including Joseph Bruce from British Guiana, the son of slaves. He settled in Fulham, married a Scottish woman, Edith, in 1912 and worked initially as a labourer. Their daughter, Esther, was born later that year and was the only black child in her school. Her father toler-ated no racism on her behalf and although relatively isolated, Esther recalls the pride with which 'my dad spoke about famous Black people living in England in those days, such as the composer, Samuel Coleridge-Taylor'.[95] Another was Harold Moody, a Jamaican doctor who came to London during the 1900s, founding the integrationist League of Coloured Peoples in 1931.[96]

With the use of black seamen in the First World War and as workers and soldiers in the conflict and demobilisation after it, the non-white population in Britain increased markedly. In Cardiff it grew from roughly 700 to 3,000 by 1919 and in Liverpool it expanded to around 5,000.[97] In an increasingly hostile world with the growth of nationalism, xenophobia and racism, the port com-munities of Liverpool 1 and Tiger Bay offered mutual protection, although it soon emerged, not safety from attack and invasion with the brutal and murder-ous 1919 race riots.[98] It was to Tiger Bay and its large and expanding Nigerian seafaring population that Henry Bassey would naturally gravitate in 1919.

Henry Bassey joined the Merchant Navy, being discharged after the war. That this was a common path for such young men is shown in the Board of Trade records where his details, summarised on an index card (Fireman, iden-tity number 350580, born Calabar, British West Africa, nationality British, father British) are to be found alongside four others of that surname.[99] Until he was imprisoned in 1938, Henry Bassey lived in or close by Tiger Bay, still working as a seamen. The biographer of his daughter provides a summary of a typical journey Henry made, this one in July 1926 when he signed on as a fireman and trimmer on the *Treverack* alongside other West Africans:

> Two and a half weeks after setting sail they arrived in Philadelphia and spent five days on shore … Four weeks later they were in the old slave-trading hub of Rio de Janeiro where they spent a week … Another week's sailing and Bassey was in the river port of Rosario de Santa Fe [Argentina] … And after that a full month spent sailing across the Atlantic, before reaching his final destination, Amsterdam, on 10 November.[100]

At this point Henry Bassey had formed a relationship with Eliza in Cardiff and their first child was born in 1926. They were married the following year and by the time Shirley was born in 1937 the couple had already six children to-gether. Henry was popular in the district for his love of music and for throwing house parties for its sailor population.[101] But just thirteen months after Shirley was born, Henry Bassey was arrested for sexual offences against minors. The deeply disturbing details of the case suggest that the crimes occurred between 1932 and 1937 involving two girls, one of whom was nine years old at the time of the first rape. He was found guilty at the Glamorganshire Winter Assize in Cardiff of all charges of carnal knowledge and indecent assault, recommended for deportation and refused leave to appeal.[102]

The evidence is both harrowing and compelling. Nevertheless, the refusal to allow an appeal is troubling only in respect of the strong connection in the popular imagination at this time between black people and sexual transgression. Like most racial representations, it was classically bifurcated and profoundly ambivalent. Black women have been imagined as sexually desirable and exotic. Thus in her early career Shirley Bassey was 'the Sexy singer from Cardiff's Tiger Bay' with a 'voice like soup laced with whisky' and a 'fur-topped, skin-tight dress'.[103] Conversely, her father and his contemporary black sailors were viewed as a sexual menace to white women, one of the major triggers of the 1919 race riots in Cardiff.[104] The *Sunday Express*, for example, while not excusing the violence in the port, noted that it was 'naturally offensive to us that coloured men should consort with even the lowest of white women'.[105] Indeed, most of the Africans who were deported by courts in the inter-war period were for sex-related offences, including a fifty-year-old, Samuel McAuley, found guilty of procuring and brothel keeping by a Manchester court in 1934. Two years later he was deported back to Sierra Leone but he 'Committed suicide shortly after the vessel sailed'. McAuley, as Sierra Leonean, would have been legally a British subject but it is revealing that in the deportation ledgers of the Home Office his nationality is described simply as 'Coloured'.[106]

Henry Bassey appears in the same ledger as McAuley. The singer's father was due to serve a five year sentence in prison before 'deportation to West Africa'.[107] Intriguingly, in the subsequent ledger, in which the deportation order was implemented in 1943, Henry Bassey (who also appears with an Africanised name of Okun Apanuso) has his nationality categorised under the label 'Others', which included stateless Poles, Armenians, Indians, Palestinians, Syrians and Javanese.[108] As a Nigerian, Henry Bassey was British, and his Merchant Navy papers confirm that nationality. While the city-state of Calabar had a distinct history, by 1914 it was integrated into the new colonial nation of Nigeria run by a central administration in Lagos by a British governor general.[109] It was not his place of origin but the nature of his offences and his colour that literally rendered him legally (or illegally) 'other' to the British authorities. The (more reassuring) narrative provided in Muriel Burgess' 1998 biography of Shirley Bassey – while inaccurate in much of its detail – still hints at a wider truth about the precarious position of the black seafaring population in inter-war Britain:

Henry Bassey jumped ship in the Twenties and went to live in Bute Street. As with many of the defecting sailors, he had no legal documents and lived permanently in the shadow of possible deportation should anything go wrong ... Henry Bassey never bothered to legalise his position and that was one of the reasons he was deported back to Nigeria.[110]

With the shame attached to the crime, Eliza, possibly with the support of the local council, moved her family including the young Shirley Bassey, to the (largely) white, working-class community of Splott.[111] It was a brave or foolhardy move given their vulnerability and potential isolation as a 'mixed race' family in this adjoining district to Butetown. The poet and doctor, Dannie Abse, recalls of his immigrant Jewish childhood in Cardiff that he was not allowed to go beyond Splott, being told by his mother to avoid the docks: 'People get knifed in Tiger Bay'.[112] Shirley Bassey herself developed a difficult relationship with the neighbourhood of her birth. In his family memoir/history, *The Tiger Bay Story* (1993), Neil Sinclair notes that while the 'international star ... has contributed to [its] fame ... throughout the world ... [u]nfortunately her relationship with the community itself is quite sour'.[113] As early as 1956 it was correctly predicted that with a 'contract to sing in Las Vegas [and] another for Hollywood, Tiger Bay will not see much more of her now'.[114] Yet Sinclair concludes that Shirley Bassey is 'still part of what made Tiger Bay. And she has a right to live in Europe in self-exile in her own self-made glory!'[115]

There was thus no place for the itinerant black Nigerian sailor, Henry Bassey, in Britain before 1945. In spite, however, of the horrors of his crime and the banishment of his family, the influence of the Tiger Bay musical culture he promoted lived on through his daughter. As Sinclair adds, if somewhat romantically, 'Such a talent as hers is the result of the West African heritage of Tiger Bay where Calabar, Kru, Igbo, Soso and Yoruba seamen met Celtic and Anglo-Saxon brides'.[116] The second and third case studies of individuals with white/Nigerian parents are less famous and traumatic, but they equally show the problems of facing a racially exclusive Britishness, this time in the years immediately following the Second World War.

Seamen were not the only transient West African population that were part of British society before the Second World War. An elite group of students was also present. They were educated in British universities and these scholars soon created their own formalised infrastructure. The earliest was, as the pioneer historian of immigration in Britain, Colin Holmes, notes, 'the Union for Students of African Descent, the origins of which stretched back to 1917, and the Gold Coast Students' Association'. He adds that the 'most significant step forward in student organisation, however, came on 7 August 1925 with the foundation by a Nigerian law student, Ladipo Solanke, of the West African Students' Union (WASU)'.[117] Alongside the League of Coloured Peoples led by Harold Moody, WASU was to provide the most sustained intellectual leadership of Britain's black communities. It was to promote a far more radical Pan-Africanist and anti-imperialist ideology than Moody's organisation.[118]

In contrast to the treatment of black sailor communities in the ports of Britain, the government in the inter-war period was concerned that African students should be well treated. In 1931, the Colonial Office supported the idea of creating a club for African students in London. The chairman of the Africa Club, Sir Percy Nunn, stated that

> The project was of importance not only for humanitarian reasons but in the interests of our own country. The treatment which natives of Africa received in London frequently caused them to go back to Africa embittered in their feelings towards Great Britain and the Empire.[119]

After 1945 the number of West African, and especially Nigerian students coming to Britain increased – as did Colonial Office concern both about their numbers and monitoring their progress. As early as August 1945 one civil servant commented that 'We are simply swamped out at the moment. The latest batch of West Coast students are arriving this weekend – over 30 strong. We only had two days notice of the fact that some of them had departed from Lagos.'[120] In 1946, it was decided to appoint liaison officers for the West African students to ensure that they were suitable for courses and integrated successfully. Major H.B. Shepherd was appointed to look after the Nigerian students and he was appalled by the reception they had received: 'There is no use denying that there is colour prejudice in the British Isles and that that prejudice operates at its worst against West Africans.' Shepherd added 'But nothing is ever done to counteract that prejudice except an occasional statement in the House of Commons to an empty House and an occasional letter in the Times.'[121] By 1953, the number of such West African students in Britain had exceeded 2,500.[122] The final two family narratives to be studied here included Nigerian fathers who came to study in post-war Britain. Their treatment confirms the analysis of Major Shepherd who remained a largely isolated voice in government circles.

In 1965, the Institute of Race Relations, founded in 1958, produced a set of essays by African, Asian and West Indian students entitled *Disappointed Guests*. Based on an essay competition held two years earlier, there were seventy-three entries, with just five written by women. By far the largest number were from Nigerian students making up roughly one-third of the total.[123] Ten were published, including that of Chikwenda Nwariaku who was born in Nigeria in 1929 and who studied civil engineering at University of Durham and Imperial College, London.[124]

Dissecting what he called the 'paternal posture', Nwariaku outlined the slow process of disillusionment about Britishness which began at home in his Methodist-run school in Nigeria. He then outlined the petty and not so petty discrimination in housing and other aspects of everyday life he and other Africans faced in England. Highlighting the patronising attitude he often experienced, including within the National Union of Students, Nwariaku saw this manifest in the workplace especially. In Andrea Levy's *Small Island* the fiercely proud Hortense is humiliated in her attempt to become a teacher in England, the qualifications she had gained in Jamaica cruelly dismissed.[125] Similarly, away from fiction, Nwariaku queried whether it was necessary that 'a Nigerian, trained in nursing in Nigeria by … sister tutors sent from this country, should be required to repeat three years of nursing training in Britain?'.[126] What the author referred as the 'most emotive aspect of colour discrimination' in Britain was, however, 'deliberately omitted from this examination': 'the question of so-called mixed marriages'.[127] Even so, he could not resist commenting it was 'within the sexual context that colour discrimination assumes its most ugly visage'.[128]

Having returned to Nigeria, the ex-student wrote in anger, but also despair, that

> Those who hate and condemn this natural association between two human beings are blinded by their belief that the Negro is different and also inferior, and the sole basis for judgement is skin colour. This particular aspect is not limited to any class and its emotional root reduces the chances of rational cure.[129]

The experiences of Phil Frampton's parents in Birmingham just five years after the war's end correlate closely to the pattern outlined by Nwariaku.

The Golly in the Cupboard (2004) is Frampton's searing autobiographical exploration of his own background, utilising his own memories, the records of the children's charity, Barnado's, and historical reconstruction.[130] Frampton is now a successful writer and community worker. He has also led a remarkable campaign as chair of the Care Leavers' Association to ensure the release of personal files of individuals who were adopted, fostered or put into care.[131] His father, Isaac Ene, was a engineer from Nigeria who was studying at Aston Mining College (now Aston University) in Birmingham. Frampton's mother Mavis was a newly qualified school teacher and the two met, probably in 1950, at the city's International Students' Club.[132] In the words of a Barnado's official report in 1953, reflecting both the racial and sexual mores of the early post-war era, 'misconduct took place'.[133] In 1953, Phillip Frampton was born, described with remarkable anthropological certainty by Bernardo's as 'half-caste with black hair, sun-tanned appearance, Nigerian features'.[134] The problematic nature of his racial origin was made coldly explicit in another official report in 1953. Under the section 'Any other physical defects or maladies', the form was filled in 'Half-caste'.[135] Mavis's mother was horrified by her daughter's 'mixed race' relationship and it seems that under her pressure, Isaac was returned in disgrace to Lagos in December 1952 by the Colonial Office.[136] While correspondence continued between Mavis and Isaac, the latter never saw his son and soon after Phillip's birth he was abandoned to be brought up in a series of children's and foster homes, suffering racism, abuse and neglect throughout his childhood. As his mother was told by Barnardo's in 1955, 'I fear a Nigerian half caste is almost impossible to find adopters for'.[137]

In 1999, after a long struggle, Phil Frampton was allowed access to his Barnardo's files, and amongst the 733 pages were fragments of details about his father who came from a prominent Nigerian family. There were several trails to be followed but the search was elusive. Nevertheless, Frampton was 'reassured to discover in the files that the man he had thought irresponsible for all these years was forced to leave the country'. Before knowing that Isaac had no choice whether to stay in Britain or not, Frampton states that, assuming Isaac had simply abandoned Mavis, 'I'd had a low sense of his personal integrity'. The former orphanage boy's narrative has by no means a simple, redemptive ending. Nevertheless, the information in the Barnardo's file 'made me feel better about [Isaac]'.[138]

If Phil Frampton has made a remarkable contribution to British society, against all the expectations of the children's charity that put him into care, the same can be said equally (if not more so) of the poet and writer, Jackie Kay. Kay's background is not dissimilar to that of Frampton – even if it was separated by close to a decade and the (slow) emergence of more racially tolerant attitudes in Britain. Her father (Jonathan), too, was a Nigerian student, studying agriculture at Aberdeen University in the early 1960s. Jackie's mother, Elizabeth, was from the Scottish Highlands and training to be a nurse. They met in an Aberdeen dance hall and Jackie was born in 1961. The couple stayed together briefly before Jonathan returned to Nigeria. Jackie was given up for adoption. As one of her aunties told her later, 'The climate wasn't right. You see back in the sixties, people just didn't have babies with black men. Well, no up here at any rate.'[139]

Unlike Phil Frampton, Jackie found a secure home and was adopted by a Socialist couple in Edinburgh, the second 'coloured' child they had taken into their family. Her birth father remained a romantic 'African' mystery throughout her youth but, unlike Phil Frampton, she was able to find him, her half-brother and other Nigerian blood relatives as well as her birth mother. *Red Dust Road* (2010) is Kay's 'autobiographical journey' to discover her roots. Earlier in her life, Jackie Kay was confronted by the blatant racism of the 'person who shouts

Wog and Nigger' and the more subtle exclusion of being asked in her home city of where she came, implying 'that I didn't belong in Scotland'.[140] In that atmosphere if 'somebody asked me if I wanted to visit Nigeria ... I took offence at that'.[141]

It took a more pluralistic world and involvement in black pride organisations to shift her perspective and to accept her multiple roots and complex parentage. In Nigeria, her uncle gave her pods from a *Moringa oleifera* tree. Returning to her home in Manchester in 2009 Jackie Kay planted these pods and imagined 'a magical moringa, years and years away from now; its roots have happily absorbed and transported water and minerals from the dark, moist soil to the rest of the splendid tree'.[142] Indeed, Kay's diverse heritage and the story of her Nigerian father and Highlands mother have provided inspiration for her prize-winning and much loved work, utilising old Scots and African vernacular. As with Frampton's exploration of his past, her poetry and prose do not provide an easy, redemptive ending. There is, ultimately, a sense of irretrievable loss. In visiting Nigeria, 'the home of the ancestors', Kay cannot penetrate her father's story: 'you wouldn't reveal the name of your village, your sons or your daughter'. Unable to re-create his migrant journey she must 'years before you are actually dead/bury you right here in my head'.[143] Born a little earlier than Jackie Kay, Pauline Black had a similar background. Her father was a Nigerian engineering student, Gordon Adenle, and her mother from a poor (Jewish) East End background. Pauline was adopted and only with the death of her foster mother did she seek out her birth father. Sadly, he died a year before the search and he remains to her a mystery, 'Almost like a fantasy figure'.[144] As with Jackie Kay, her father and his past remains elusive: 'It's almost as if he comes to visit, just to remind me that I am his. But the feeling is fleeting and soon gone. Perhaps it doesn't really happen at all?'[145]

Conclusion

As has been noted, David Oluwale had his nationality labelled as 'Wog' by the Leeds police. Elsewhere in this chapter other Africans and Asians from specific British colonies were classified simply as 'coloured', 'other' and a 'racial problem', and their children dismissed as 'half-caste'. The social and cultural contribution of Shirley Bassey, Jackie Kay and Phil Frampton, therefore, is all the more remarkable given the pathological approach to those of West African and South East Asian origin who were deemed so problematic by the British state and society and culture as a whole. It was a negative response that also extended to the women who formed relations with these men, and one that was present in academic work on the black communiites of post-war Britain. As

Chris Waters has noted, in the 1950s and 1960s, 'While race relations writers repudiated the popular stereotypes of Black male sexuality that gave rise to such ideas, they continued to represent white women in inter-racial marriages as "unstable" deviants from socially sanctioned norms.'[146]

David Oluwale, too, may have had wanted to create a successful life and establish a family in Britain but he was never allowed to fulfil his ambitions. In the imaginative writings of Caryl Phillips, his hopes when leaving Lagos are combined with the reality of his life in Britain:

> Back home, a long time ago before this nightmare descended upon your young shoulders. Back home, where you spoke of your life in the future tense. Back home, this girl with fine manners and good breeding might have been your wife. You studied hard at your school under the guidance of Christian missionaries. You worked with a burning desire to escape to your future as soon as possible.[147]

In the early twenty-first century, there is now a well-established Nigerian population in Britain exceeding two hundred thousand, its ethnic and political diversity reflecting that of the country from which it originated.[148] Poverty remains a problem but there is also a middle-class and highly educated British Nigerian emerging.[149] The award-winning British rapper, Tinie Tempah – part of Stuart Maconie's list of black musical heroes following the *Windrush* featured in the previous chapter – is of second-generation Nigerian origin. His parents, Rosemary and Patrick Okogwu 'came over to the UK in their 20s from Nigeria' and settled in a council estate in south London. Tinie relates their family narrative which encapsulates that of many aspiring Nigerian migrants in Britain since the 1970s: 'I watched my parents go from having very basic jobs to educating themselves, to buying a house [in the leafy suburbs]. They set a really good bar for what they wanted their kids to achieve.'[150]

And if David Oluwale had no choice but to come to Britain as a ship stowaway in the late 1940s, later Nigerian migrants were able to make the journey in a far more comfortable and legal manner by aeroplane, even if their initial experiences were still a struggle. Buchi Emecheta arrived in Liverpool from Lagos in 1962, not yet eighteen years old and already the mother of two babies: 'I came to England in a plush first-class suite with a nurse for the children.' Her first impressions were not positive: 'England gave me a cold welcome … It felt like walking into the inside of a grave. I could see nothing but masses of grey, filth, and more grey, yet something was telling me that it was too late now.'[151]Emerecheta persisted and slowly built a reputation for herself as an outstanding author writing for both an adult and a younger audience. Like Jackie Kay was to do a little later, Buchi Emecheta melded her experiences and family history in Nigeria and Britain to inform her fiction and autobiographical writing.

In a different artistic form, Pauline Black was at the heart of the '2-Tone' British music scene in the late 1970s as lead singer of 'The Selector'. She changed her surname from 'Vickers' to 'Black' in order to reflect her pride in her father's African origins. Her more assertive identity was also expressed musically. In its origins, the '2-Tone' movement was fiercely anti-racist in its politics (although this was not always appreciated by some of its fans) and musically reflected a fusion between Jamaican reggae, ska and rocksteady and British 'new wave' and punk. Pauline, inspired by the black power movement in America and rejecting the politics of deference, thus declined the path offered by

> divas of all divas, Shirley Bassey. Much to my mother's horror, I nick-
> named Ms Bassey 'Burly Chassis'. I loathed her stentorian singing style,
> her revealing sequined gowns and her cheesy perma-grin. She was not
> the role model I craved even if she was a homegrown talent and came
> from Tiger Bay. As far as I was concerned, [she] belonged to another
> age, an age of 'knowing your place'.[152]

She concludes her autobiographical 'journey so far' not redemptively, but by acknowledging that 'the more I have learned about my families' histories and where I fit into the puzzle that I had been trying to solve from the age of four, the more real I have become'. There is, she accepts, no 'neat ending to my story'. But through her varied career as singer, actress and broadcaster, she has come to terms with her diverse roots. Pauline now embraces her mixed-race origins which proved so difficult when she was growing up in a white household and in a white area: 'My father's colour envelops me and that is unconditional love of a kind. Indeed, one almost might say black by design.'[153]

That at least the stories of those of an earlier generation of African settlers who were so brutally rejected can now be considered – if not fully re-told – also reflects that some progress has been made. Jackie Kay's father was from the Igboo tribe in Nigeria and Amaudo is its village of peace. The 'Road to Amaudo', she writes, is a 'winding and long red dust road … . at time impassable'. Kay adds 'but pass people do, men and women and children', concluding 'kaudo di, kandu di [let there be peace, let there be light]'.[154] But with reassurance available in the form of the 'myth of the *Windrush*', it will take a major shift in self-reflexivity before David Oluwale's journey and those of other marginal migrants – with their ultimate note of rejection and humiliation – are recognised as being part of the *mainstream* of British history and heritage. Only then will it be possible for what Kay describes as 'lost time' to be confronted.[155] So far, there are still limits in acknowledging the scale of misery that

Britain inflicted on its 'colonial' populations within the island stories it tells of itself.

Conclusions

9

Britishness and the nature of migrant journeys

Means and meanings of transport

> And there are so many stories to tell, too many, such an excess of inter-twined lives events miracles places rumours, so dense a commingling of the improbable and the mundane! (Salman Rushdie, *Midnight's Children*)[1]

This study began by following the critical intervention of bell hooks – rejecting the neutrality of the term 'travel' and instead embracing the more intensive and multi-layered notion of 'the journey'. The *migrant* journey, as has become apparent throughout *The Battle of Britishness*, often involved tension between the physical and the psychological; the actual movement of people that oc-curred and its wider symbolism and refraction through memory work. As Kathy Burrell notes, even migration specialists within academia 'have been slow to acknowledge the significance of physical time-spaces of migration journeys'. Burrell focuses on the 600,000 Poles who between 2004 and 2009 came under the UK's Worker Registration Scheme. She highlights how flying together with cheap airlines such as Ryanair 'exposes the migrants to each other in ways that other forms of travel, such as the car, simply do not'. Indeed, Burrell suggests it represents a new, if safer version of travelling steerage in the long nineteenth century.[2] Whether these emotional (and uncomfortable, though brief) journeys from Eastern Europe will be remembered in the future by these individuals and their descendants remains to be seen. Interviewing the Polish migrants close to the time of their departure has made it clear to Burrell 'that rather than being a means to an end, the journeys migrants make *are* their migration projects. All of the tensions and emotions of migration are there embedded in the materiality of travelling; not at either the end of the migration experience, but there at the heart of it.'[3]

For many previous migrant groups, however, for whom no immediate testimony was taken, amnesia of the specifics of the journey has been the norm. In its place, collective group mythology has become a substitute for individual or family memories. In George Lamming's classic novel charting West Indian migration to Britain after the war, *The Emigrants* (1954), the author notes how the particular vessel they were on (and one significantly never named), was hardly noticed by those on board – its purpose was purely functional:

> During the past three or four days the passengers had spent their time anticipating the novelty of ports the ship would call at [it was travelling from Venezuela to Trinidad to England], recalling what they had seen and questioning the decisions they had made … The ship itself was simply the vehicle that had taken them from one experience to another. They had found no time to look at it.[4]

Caryl Phillips came to England from St Kitts with his parents in the late 1950s. In 1997 he re-visited the journey on board a banana boat. Phillips' account of his 'voyage from the Caribbean' was accompanied by a picture of the *Empire Windrush* landing in England.[5] The illustration prompted a response from an ex-national serviceman, Brian Breton, who had been on board the ship on its penultimate journey in 1954:

> What on earth – or, indeed, on sea – has [the] picture of the troopship Empire Windrush to do with the story … of West Indian migrants … Caryl Phillips, whose first novel The Final Passage was prompted by his migration as a baby from St Kitts, came to this country in 1958. That was four years after the Empire Windrush sank in the Mediterranean …

Rather than a pedantic correction, Breton's intervention was to highlight another (tragic) aspect to the ship's history. As noted in Chapter 7, on its last journey the engine room blew up leading to the loss of four lives.[6] Yet in the competing narratives of the ship's longer nautical career it is now only its history relating to West Indian migration to Britain that is remembered. There is thus a reversal of the situation in 1957 when Joyce Egginton wrote the first overview of West Indian presence in post-war Britain and rescued its history as a *migrant* ship.[7] Its previous and disturbing life as the *Monte Rosa* during the war will be glossed shortly.

Such was its symbolic importance, the journey of *Exodus 1947* and others ships carrying 'illegal' Jewish immigrants were labelled the new *Mayflower* by Zionist leaders. Chaim Weizmann, soon to become Israel's first President, told the Anglo-American Committee set up in 1946 to determine the future of

Palestine, that for those on such ships, it was worth the difficulties and dangers on board: 'after their escape from the jaws of death, these people are ready to accept and endure, because this leaky boat on which this boy or girl travels is their *Mayflower*.'[8] Similar attempts have been made with regard to the *Empire Windrush*. Sam King, its most eloquent and frequently quoted migrant passenger, described it as a 'little Mayflower … Immigration to this country really started with that boat.'[9] This particular metaphor, however, has been criticised by black critic Tony Sewell for the dominant and racist history that it evokes: 'Some have compared [its arrival] to the Mayflower landing in America but the imagery breaks down once you think about the way the black Americans arrived at those shores.'[10]

In 1984, the centennial of the Statue of Liberty was celebrated in America. Interviewed six years later by the oral historian Studs Terkel, Maggie Holmes, a black American domestic worker, responded: 'I got damned mad because it was sickening to me. That was not made for me. We didn't come through Ellis Island. Do you understand what I'm saying? What are you celebrating? You came here in chains in the bottom of the ships and half-dead and beaten.'[11] Brian Klug glosses her statement:

> What she is saying … is that black Americans with African ancestry were not in the same boat – not metaphorically and not literally – as the tired, poor and huddled masses that emigrated to the New World yearning to be free. (The first ship bringing Negro slaves to America reached Jamestown in 1619, one year before the Mayflower docked at Plymouth Rock.)[12]

Holmes's anger, like that of Keith Piper's *Go West Young Man*, reflects the power politics of memory work: what is remembered/forgotten and by whom? In this particular case, the trauma of the 'Middle Passage' – a 'living and wrenching aspect of the history of the peoples of the African diaspora, an inescapable part of their present impossible to erase or exorcise'[13] – was so great that all such journeys by ship have become tainted within the world of those of such slave origin. That the 'Middle Passage' remains less central in 'mainstream' history and heritage causes ongoing anguish.

Jan Carew has noted that it is not only in George Lamming's work that the West Indian migrants 'are barely aware of the ocean's existence' – it is a feature also of Austin Clarke's novel, *Survivors of the Crossing* (1965). In Clarke's *The Meeting Point* (1967), 'the emigrants have moved to air travel and are more at ease'. Carrew concludes that 'Perhaps we all carry deep in our unconscious minds the traumatic memory of the ancestral crossing in the Columbian and slave era.'[14] In contrast, Caryl Phillips asked his mother what she did on the ship taking her from St Kitts to England: 'She took her time answering, and then she said that she worked out how to get to the lifeboats with me in her arms and with her eyes closed … I asked about the rest of her time crossing the Atlantic. She looked blankly at me.'[15] *The Battle of Britishness* so far has emphasised especially the role of ships in migrant journeys – real and metaphorical – a focus that reflects its chronological coverage and will be continued in this concluding chapter. In this respect it is deeply significant that in memories of water-based migratory journeys, there is a distinct division between, on the one hand, the Jewish world (and of other groups with refugee histories) or those whose movement was more voluntary, and, on the other, those in the African diaspora.

To Jews, the ship/boat/vessel can be evoked a means of escape to freedom, most blatantly in the form of Noah's Ark (a story, as noted in Chapter 6, subverted by Julian Barnes in his *A History of the World in 10½ Chapters*), or, in its miniature form, Moses' basket. It is a symbolism taken further within Christian iconography in which 'the ship is … a symbol of the church' and linked to the saving of lost souls.[16] Jonah did not avoid God's wrath by fleeing from Nineveh to Jaffa and taking a ship bound for Tarshish, but to him it represented a man-made solution to avoid his responsibilities and the whale itself acted as a vessel to save him from certain death. This study has explored counter examples such as the problematic journey of the *St Louis*. In an earlier age, some Jews supposedly granted safe passage in the English expulsion of 1290 were 'shipwrecked murdered and robbed' as the final act of humiliation and antisemitic brutality.[17] Nevertheless, the *expectation* in Jewish tradition is that ships might provide the means to find safety away from oppression. It is no accident that the Danish example of the 700 little fishing boats which rescued the Jews by taking them across to Sweden in October 1943 has dominated the representation of the *saving* of Jews during the Second World War in Holocaust memorialisation – whether in Denmark itself, Sweden, Israel or America.[18]

The ship/boat is now firmly linked to rescue even though there were those during the Holocaust who were deported across sea. Laura Varon was one of the few survivors from the Jews of Rhodes. In July 1944 almost all of the Jews off the island were rounded up; close to two thousand were loaded onto three cargo ships bound for Piraeus before the train journey to Auschwitz. Varon described how 'Nearly seven hundred people were crowded into a ship designed to carry cargo and a crew of six'. A further one hundred Jews were picked up of the island of Kos adding to the misery on board.[19] The sea journey took six days in which there were deaths through exhaustion, heat and disease and the risk of attack – those on a boat from Crete perished when it was sunk after bombardment. For Varon and the others, the sea journey marked 'the transition … from one life to the other'.[20] Indeed, in other testimony from Rhodes's survivors, the description of sea and train deportations meld into one.[21]

Such appalling experiences could have been shared by many other Jews. Early in the war, a scheme to deport all Jews to the island of Madagascar was considered by leading Nazis. It was rejected at the end of 1940 as being too risky in terms of available shipping. Hitler was reported as stating that 'He would provide the entire German navy for that purpose, except that he would not subject it to the risk of attack.'[22] Returning to the pre-history of the *Empire Windrush* as the *Monte Rosa*, she was used briefly during the war, alongside the *Donau* and the *Gotenland*, to transport Jews from Norway to their eventual destination of Auschwitz. Some 760 Jews were deported from Norway by ship and only 25 survived. The *Monte Rosa* took 21 Jewish deportees on 20 November 1942 and a further 27 six days later.[23]

Overall, however, sea transportation was marginal in the history of the Holocaust – the Norwegian deportations, for example, only occurred due to *local* initiatives and the chance availability of shipping over which Adolph Eichmann, the key administrator of the 'Final Solution', had no direct control.[24] Instead, railways proved to be the transport answer to implementing the 'Final Solution'. Subsequently, within a variety of memory works, the train has become symbolic of the destruction process, even though the specifics of deportation journeys have been neglected. As Simone Gigliotti suggests, 'The Holocaust train resonates in testimonies, literature, and visual culture as the vehicle to a fatal destination, rather than mobile residence to a life-threatening compression that both prepared deportees for, and disconnected them, from the camp world.'[25]

The use of railways in the *Kindertransport* is now presented as the poignant exception of escape that proves the rule of destruction during the Nazi era. David Gurion, who was soon to become the first Prime Minister of Israel, was anxious that the vessels taking 'illegal' Jewish immigrants to Palestine should not be 'large ships, but small boats, 200 passengers in each! And many such boats!'[26] This was for practical reasons – it would be hard for the British navy to intercept them all – but it may also have been for reasons of propaganda, partly aimed at winning over world opinion and evoking, to some at least, the memory of the Danish acts of rescue. To the other 'classic' group of refugees, the Huguenots, ships were similarly remembered as the (dangerous) means of escape, although persecution as galley slaves meant that there was a greater ambiguity towards journeys by water.

In the case of the Vietnamese, desperation meant that the journey of escape could be constructed as the only positive choice to be made: 'Making the decision to escape is like going to war. You do it because you think it's necessary, but you never want to do it twice.'[27] In 1980, shortly after arrival in England having survived a month in a small boat carrying 393 refugees floating towards Hong Kong, To Minh Dieu wrote in a reception camp:

What have we got left? An old sailing boat, our only transport to combat the ocean. Our fear for our life was not all that great because we had a great hope of survival: let's go to another part of the world, the world of FREEDOM where we will be welcomed with love.[28]

The Vietnamese description of England as 'paradise', which echoed that of young Holocaust survivors who were sent to the Lake District at the end of the Second World War, reflected more the horror of past experiences. It does not do justice to the mixed reception given to them in the receiving country as well as their later obscurity and marginality in society as a whole.[29]

In the case of the Vietnamese refugees, reflection on the terror of persecution and the traumatic journey took its physical and psychological toll beyond the initial desire to express gratitude to those who had granted them asylum.[30] Outside the Vietnamese community itself, however, their stories, like those of the child survivors before them, remain largely forgotten. The *Tu Do* (meaning freedom), a small fishing boat which travelled 6,000 kilometres to Australia with 38 Vietnamese refugees on board, is now displayed at the Australian National Maritime Museum, Sydney.[31] There is not yet an equivalent space or prominence given to these incredibly dangerous and brave journeys in a parallel heritage site in Britain. The local initiative 'From Auschwitz to Ambleside' recording the experiences in the Lake District of child survivors of the Holocaust some sixty years after the event suggests that the inclusion of these Vietnamese refugee narratives in the future is not impossible.[32] So far, however, Vietnamese boat people lack a suitable framework within which to be incorporated into a wider British 'island story' to mirror the way in which the Holocaust (or parts of its history) has been absorbed since the late twentieth century.

Ships also provided certain migrant groups with the means to profit from international trade. Writing of medieval England, Patricia Skinner highlights how 'Jewish merchants were itinerant, and must have been crossing the Channel regularly, especially from southern enclaves such as London, Winchester and Canterbury, or the burgeoning East Anglian trade centres.' She adds a note of caution, however – the absence of records does not allow any assessment of the pitfalls of such business journeying.[33] On a more spectacular level, the 'port Jews' of early modern Europe developed global trade networks, including an involvement in the burgeoning world of slavery and colonialism as was the case with some Huguenot entrepreneurs. Nevertheless, these wealthy Jews of Sephardi origin could be marginal figures even if they had converted to Christianity – *conversos* were subject to the whims of the Inquisition. Jessica Roitman has typified their experiences as a double journeying. They embarked on remarkable journeys that were both physical between the world's continents and ones of contested and evolving identity – from Judaism to Christianity (and sometimes the reverse with the possibilities of religious toleration emerging in Holland, England and the 'new world').[34]

For Jews (and Huguenots), the journey by ship could thus provide the means of either making a living or, for both groups and others such as the Vietnamese of making an escape, even if such efforts were often thwarted and if sometimes watery vessels could be part of punishment, persecution and danger. Referring to ancient Palestine, Nadav Kashtan concludes that 'Practical and symbolic aspects of seafaring in the sources ... illustrate the ambivalent attitude of Jews to the sea'.[35] There is, however, little such ambiguity for those within the African diaspora. It has been far harder to view the ship in positive light and many of the representations of the post-war West Indian journeys to Britain are saturated with the memory of slavery. In Donald Hinds's account, the connection is blatant:

> Towards the end of the journey the ship stank. The stairs smelt of vomit and urine, and each day reminded us of the horrors our forbears must have suffered during that terrible Middle Passage; but this leg of the journey of the slavers was the best of the three. It was the one of great profit, the sea routes which gave Europe the financial resources to be great.[36]

Similar images were evoked in literary form in Sam Selvon's *Moses Ascending* (1975), a satire on the evolution of post-war black Britain from first to second generation. The main character is surprised when the police make mass arrests following a black nationalist gathering in Trafalgar Square:

> There were no protests from any of the passengers [in the Black Maria] saying that they was innocent and shouldn't be here, nobody struggling to get out like me ... Like we was in the hold of a slave ship. I remember them stories I used to read, how the innocent starboy get condemned to the galleys.[37]

From a very different political and social perspective, V.S. Naipaul's *The Middle Passage* (1962), a travelogue of a journey from Britain to the West Indies to South America, never escapes the spectre of slavery and its utter destructiveness. His ship 'would go from St Kitts to Grenada to Trinidad to Barbados: one journey answering another: the climax and futility of the West Indian adventure. For nothing was created in the British West Indies ... '[38] Even contemporary discussions of the *Empire Windrush* have been linked to the Middle Passage: 'merely to read the House of Commons debate ... is to be made to appreciate how British political leadership, including Labour, managed to see it not as a free movement of voluntary labour but as a sort of slave transportation engineered by evil agencies somewhere in the Caribbean'.[39] References to slavery even appear in nurse Jannett Creese's gentle autobiographical account of her journey from the Windward Islands eventually to Stockport. The *Ascancia*, *Venezuela*, *Sorrento* and *Irpinia* all 'brought immigrants to Britain, and also took people back to the West Indies. The thought "human cargo" does spring to mind!'[40]

There is little in Caribbean testimony to match the description of Baldev Singh who travelled from India to Britain by ship in 1958 as an eleven-year-old with his mother and five other relatives: 'It was the first time I'd ever been on a boat – fantastic! We thought it was a different world. It took us 20 days to come across – 20 days of luxury. We used to see things we'd never seen before – the sea and the size o' the boat!'[41] The parents of comedian, Sanjeev Bhaskar, came at a similar time. Of Sikh origin also, they were part of the huge, bloody and still neglected movement of people during the partition of India:

> They were born under the British Raj and in 1947 they, along with 15 million people were uprooted. They came from the part of the Punjab now in Pakistan, and moved to the bit now in India. They settled not far from Delhi, and then my father came here as an economic migrant.

As he adds, 'For that generation, having been uprooted by partition, coming here was less of an upheaval than you might imagine.'[42]

Taking away white Asians, it was estimated that in 1951 there were just over 30,000 Indians and 5,000 Pakistanis in Britain with the figure rising to over 80,000 and 25,000 respectively just ten years later. In the five years after 1961 it more than doubled again in spite of the racially discriminatory Commonwealth Immigrants Act (1962). This post-war South East Asian migration was highly concentrated in origin: 'When one considers the size of the two countries it is surprising that emigration has been confined to the Punjab and Gujarat and to half a dozen areas in the two wings of Pakistan.'[43] It also reflected chain migration from the same villages/regions and increasing family reunification. The majority of Sikh and Hindu immigrants had been uprooted during the partition and followed similar journeys to the family of Sanjeev Bhaskar. High mobility from the Punjab also reflected the fact that this region especially had traditionally high levels of migration *before* partition.[44]

For Muslim migrants, especially Pakistanis, the 'myth of return' was particularly strong in the early years of settlement in Britain in what was an almost exclusively male movement.[45] As one Bradford Muslim recalled: 'Initially when people came to the UK, they were very much a sort of migrant worker. That was their mental attitude: that we would work, find a pot of gold and then disappear, but events overtook everything.'[46] Life and work was hard, often working night shifts in the cotton and wool mills of northern England. Making a fortune in Britain was near impossible and eventually a decision was made to bring families to the place of settlement. For the younger generation, the journey itself, increasingly by aeroplane, could be an exciting adventure:

> All I can remember is my mum saying that we're going somewhere to join your dad, and, obviously, she must have mentioned England ... I didn't realise it was going to be such a long distance, but my mum did explain something about an aeroplane ... so I was quite thrilled ... at the thought of flying in a, we call them flying birds, you know ... I kept looking out of the window and I just saw little specks and my mum said they were villages. It looked like a jigsaw and it was amazing ... [47]

At the same time, and similarly without traumatic memories of the journey itself, more than a million and a half British migrants left for Australia between 1945 and 1970. James Hammerton and Alistair Thomson describe the four-week ship journey as a 'liminal period' enabling the migrants to adjust to the idea of a new life: 'the no-man's-land of the boat was, essentially, a secure temporary home' whereas 'flying to Australia was a rather unsatisfactory rite of passage'.[48] In this particular case, Michel Foucault's concept of heterotopia manifested in the ship as a 'piece of floating space' which enables 'the greatest reservoir of imagination' is at least partially realised.[49] In contrast, it has taken what is essentially a second-generation writer, Caryl Phillips, to imagine the Caribbean journey to Britain as being the 'Final Passage' and even then the memory of slavery and colonialism is never far away and permanent settlement in the 'mother country' far from certain.[50]

Escape

There is, however, one important element in common within the autobiograph-ical practice of the Jewish and black diasporas, and of other groups who have been persecuted – the need to portray the background to the journey and/or the journey itself (even to freedom) as traumatic. In the case of the Huguenots, the example of the young Henri de Portal and his escape from France hidden in a barrel typified popular representations of such migrant journeys, even though many such Protestant refugees were able to leave more freely, building on earlier trade and other connections to England.[51] Bud Flanagan stated in his autobiography that the 'little town of Radom [where his parents came from] was famous for two things: its chairmaking and its pogroms'.[52] In fact, there were no such pogroms at the time when his parents left, certainly not before the 1880s.[53] Yet the narrative of persecution and escape is now integral to the story of Jews leaving Tsarist Russia. Thus according to that source of popular folk memory and often unreliable history, Wikipedia, Flanagan's parents 'Wolf and YettaWeintrop were Polish Jews who fled to London in the mid 1870s as a result of Eastern European pogroms.'[54]

The *Kindertransport* has become perhaps the classic portrayal of refugee *escape* to Britain in recent years. The danger of the journey itself has been overstated, with the shadow of the Holocaust shaping autobiographical and biographical accounts of this movement and ultimately bringing the children's refugee movement within the remit of the *Shoah*. Frequently, references are made to the lateness of leaving, as in the obituaries (2009 and 2010 respectively) of artists Harry Weinberger and Susan Einzig. In both cases the last months of peace are truncated for dramatic effect: 'He was lucky to have got out on the last kindertransport leaving Czechoslavakia, on 20 July 1939',[55] and 'In the spring of 1939, Einzig found herself on one of the last Kindertransport trains to reach Britain before the outbreak of war.'[56] In the latter case bare details of the murder of close relatives in the Holocaust follows immediately. Ironically, those children who *did* survive the 'Final Solution' during the war and came to Britain immediately after were told to keep quiet about their experiences. But the need to conform to such expectations of 'escape' to Britain has even informed narratives of the *Empire Windrush*, especially through the testimony of Sam King.

King's autobiographical contributions have been consistent in emphasising how there was a concerted effort to turn back the *Windrush*: 'As we got closer to England there was great apprehension on the boat because we knew the authorities did not want us to land'.[57] King believed that the HMS *Sheffield* was close by to deal with any disturbances resulting from such action being taken against those on board the *Windrush*.[58] His story has been elaborated by Vince Reid, the youngest West Indian on board:

> people were saying that there's a British warship that was shadowing the *Windrush*, and there was talk that they might blow us out of the water, that they might sink the ship. Because there was some people didn't want black people coming to England. And there was this fear that they might very well sink the [ship], so there was an element of danger.[59]

As part of this desire to highlight the antipathy against its passengers, Sam King has quoted the Colonial Secretary, Creech Jones, as stating that while he could not stop the arrival of the West Indians, 'There's nothing to worry about because they won't last one winter in England.' That Creech Jones never made that public statement is not the point here. The significance is that this imaginary official utterance has been much cited; it is utilised to highlight the achievements of the *Windrushers* in making successful lives in Britain *in spite* of this hostile reception. As King wrote in 1988, 'It gives me some satisfaction to repeat [Creech Jones'] words 40 winters later': indeed, *Forty Winters On* was the title of the first *Windrush* anthology.[60] Moreover, King, and his fellow chroniclers of the *Windrush*, Mike and Trevor Phillips, have increasingly utilised the term 'survivors' to describe the remaining West Indian passengers from this ship, implying almost that they had overcome some natural or man-made disaster and more specifically within common usage, evoking the memory of the Holocaust.[61]

Critiquing the use of 'survivor' is in no way to belittle either the discrimination and prejudice faced by these West Indians or their resilience in making Britain a place called home, despite the opposition they faced. Many did return to the Caribbean, including Arthur Robinson who spent twenty-four years in the RAF. Robinson went back to Kingston in the 1960s, stating at the time of the twentieth anniversary of the *Windrush*'s arrival 'It was always in my mind to [go home]; the trend toward prejudice seemed to be worsening'.[62] It took enormous staying power to put up with decades of abuse and discrimination. Migrant groups coming in to British society have to emphasise that they are hard-working, deserving and loyal; the word 'survivor' is one that naturally evokes sympathy. In this respect, the discourse of the 'genuine' refugee who has escaped danger has a greater potential appeal to public empathy than that of the casual immigrant 'on the make'. Achievements later can be constructed as part of an inspiring 'rags to riches' story, as with the case of Henri de Portal, rather than an opportunist foreigner who has gained at the expense of the 'native'. And the desire to portray suffering en route is part of the process of proving authenticity and desirability.

In his classic evocation of East European Jews in America, *World of Our Fathers* (1976), Irving Howe asked 'Was the Atlantic crossing really as dreadful as memoirists and legend have made it out to be?' Howe had no doubt that the 'imagery of the journey as ordeal was deeply imprinted in the Jewish folk mind'. He concluded that the suffering was real and persistent although descriptions have 'contributed to rhetorical exaggeration'.[63] In reality, experiences differed – not all Jewish migrants at the turn of the twentieth century, for example, travelled steerage, even if the majority did. The importance in terms of the remembered journey is that there is an expectation that it was hard and disorientating – again, this helps, as with the 'escape' of his parents recreated by Bud Flanagan, to emphasise that they were refugees and *not* immigrants.[64] 'Escape' is also a term used to describe Irish famine journeys even though it was not generally the poorest who managed to leave.

Such expectation of the journey's misery is most intense with regards to slavery. Not surprisingly, the horror of the 'Middle Passage' was emphasised by abolitionists and has been a constant feature of the representation of slavery thereafter. A controversy emerged when it was suggested by Vincent Carretta that Olaudah Equiano, whose autobiography was first published in 1789, was not, as he claimed, born in Africa but in South Carolina.[65] The reason Equiano made this claim was crucial, Carretta argues, because the abolitionists at this stage were aiming to end the slave trade and not slavery – 'if he had said he was born in South Carolina he would have been much less useful'.[66] Equiano's fellow abolitionists 'were calling for precisely the kind of account of Africa and the Middle Passage that he supplied. Because only a native African would have experienced the Middle Passage, the abolitionist movement needed an African, not an African-American, voice'.[67] Again, the point here is not to join the debate of whether Carretta is right or not, but to highlight that the heated debate reflects the anxiety of many that Equiano's description of a slave journey from Africa be authentic.[68]

Rather than an intriguing case study of the multi-layered nature of autobiographical practice and the complexity of Equiano's writing, there is anger that the suggestion could be made that the first account written in English by an African of the slave journey was in any way constructed. Abolitionists on both sides of the Atlantic, and those re-remembering slavery thereafter, need the internal gaze provided by Equiano's description of the ship's 'cargo' to prove the vileness of the 'Middle Passage'. Indeed, it is the immediacy and accessibility of his account that has made his text so important across the centuries. There is the initial cruel destruction of innocence when Equiano was taken under the decks of the nameless slave ship:

> there I received such a salutation in my nostrils as I had never experienced in my life: so that, with the loathsomeness of the stench, and crying together, I became so sick and low that I was not able to eat … I now wished for the last friend, death, to relieve me …

It was shortly followed in Equiano's testimony by a more general observation designed to appeal to the humanitarian instincts of his readers: 'The shrieks of the women, and the groans of the dying, rendered the whole a scene of horror almost inconceivable'.[69] Here, Equiano, as with other contemporary texts on the 'Middle Passage', was attempting a form of closure, emphasising the extremity of the suffering, but also suggesting the limits of description. It predicts the testimony (or counter-testimony) of Holocaust survivor, Elie Wiesel: 'Auschwitz is something else, always something else … The truth of Auschwitz remains hidden in its ashes'.[70]

The Promised Land

In contrast to the pain of the journey itself, migrant destinations are often perceived and represented as the 'Promised Land'. This was true of the narratives constructed by the Huguenots and then the Volga Germans in the late seventeenth and nineteenth centuries respectively, reflecting their strict religious devotion, but it has also been articulated in a secular form as with the *Empire Windrush*. With regards to the last mentioned, Tony Sewell argues that 'It is the image of the ship, and the idea of an Exodus and journey to a promised land, that has been at the heart of the African experience since slavery', a process that continues through the initial migrants and now their children and grandchildren. For the new generation, Sewell sees the challenge as building 'a promised land where they can respect their ancestral backgrounds as well as take their rightful place as key players in the building of a new Britain'.[71]

Britain's own mythology as a place of tolerance, fair play and decency fits neatly into the discourse of a 'promised land'. Growing up in Lagos, Buchi Emecheta recalls that

> Whenever my father pronounced the words 'United Kingdom', it sounded so heavy, so reverential. It was so deep, so mysterious, that my father always voiced it in hushed tones wearing an expression as respectful as if it were God's Holiest of Holies.[72]

The ship has a key role in the construction of this self-image. It becomes a real and symbolic transporter of people between 'there' and 'here' – that is from persecution and exploitation to freedom and acceptance. It was, for example, exploited by Cunard after 1933. When the *Queen Mary* was launched in 1934 the British shipping company presented its vessels and their tolerance – and indeed encouragement – of Jewish passengers as 'a strike for racial justice'. An implicit comparison was being made by Cunard to its competitors in Nazi Germany, now controlled by the Nazi state under the amalgamated Hapag-Lloyd line. Included within this Aryanised fleet was the luxury liner, the *St Louis*, soon to become notorious.[73] During this decade, British Jews, insecure of their own status, were happy to subscribe to such national mythology.

In 1938 the SS *Alba*, a ship carrying coal from Wales to Italy, sank near St Ives, Cornwall. Five of its multi-national crew lost their lives, a nautical disaster immortalised by naive painter, Alfred Wallis. Amongst the dead was a Hungarian Jewish mess-room boy, George Kovacs. Kovacs was buried in Plymouth which possessed the nearest functioning Jewish cemetery and community. At his funeral the Reverend Wolfson paid tribute to the

> spirit of heroism and self-sacrifice which all those concerned with the wreck willingly showered upon the unfortunates, and through their efforts helped to strengthen the bonds of sympathy, linking man to man, no matter to what race or creed he belongs.[74]

It has been noted that, given the international context, it is 'easy to see why the [local] rabbi took this chance … to draw an implicit contrast between Cornish rescuers and German anti-Semites'.[75]

In contrast, after the Second World War with the *Exodus* affair and what became a battle consisting of 'Immigrant Ships versus the British Navy',[76] silence has ensued within national memory. Likewise, it is the role of the Navy in the suppression of the slave trade that has been remembered and *not* (until recently) that in enabling it to prosper by its protection of British-owned ships journeying through the 'Middle Passage'. By such partial memory work and by processes of amnesia the ship is maintained as a British icon reflecting all that is positive about the nation.

At the level of popular culture, Yinka Shonibare's 'Nelson's Ship in a Bottle', a temporary installation on Trafalgar Square's fourth plinth (2010/11) at least begins to explore the ambiguities associated with the British navy. A 1/30th replica of Nelson's flagship,[77] the sculpture, according to the artist, 'considers the relationship between the birth of the British Empire, made possible in part by Nelson's victory at the Battle of Trafalgar, and multi-culturalism in Britain today'.[78] Shonibare was born in London to Nigerian parents of 'wealthy, middle-class background', part of the economically mobile community referred to in the previous chapter. The family moved back to Lagos when he was three in the mid-1960s and then he returned to England and a public school education. His sculpture is playful and intended to be both celebratory of London's diversity and energy *and* critical of the damage inflicted by imperialism. With similar ambiguity, it highlights the linkages of geography and exchange of goods powered by the British Empire. Ultimately, the ambivalence of Shonibare's *Victory* is rooted in a deep understanding of British and other colonial histories. He wants those experiencing his sculpture to recognise 'interdependence'. It is, for him, 'a metaphor for city life'.[79]

Similar twoness was present in grassroots responses to the 2007 bicentenary commemorations of the ending of the slave trade. Marcus Wood has explored representations of the *Brookes* slave ship imagery in these events, concluding with a parade past the Houses of Parliament organised by the local initiative, YAA Carnival Village. At the centre was a woman with a huge boat worn as a carnival headdress:

> When I asked her what it meant she explained that it was both the *Brookes* and the *Windrush*, it was both sadness and a commitment to the triumphant survival of the descendants of slaves, and their arrival in Britain after the independence of the ex-slave colonies. The little black boat hanging over the side of her sculpture is both a literal lifeboat, and the *Brookes*, carried on, and carrying on, from the Caribbean into Britain.

As Wood concludes, 'What a joyful reinvention of a very bleak image, what a complicated metaphor, what imagination.'[80]

Yet as Wood also acknowledges in relation to the 2007 commemorations, such interventions were exceptional: 'if you stand back and look at the bigger map of popular cultural responses to Atlantic slavery, I have serious doubts about the extent to which in Britain we have gone beyond, or desire to go beyond, the original myths in which the emancipation movement of 1807 was enshrined'. The slaves are still symbolically imprisoned, disempowered and faceless. Nationally, emphasis continues to be placed on the role of the British abolitionists and the subsequent role of the navy in suppressing the slave trade, as exemplified in the Royal Naval Museum, Portsmouth, and its semi-permanent exhibition, *Chasing Freedom*.[81]

Control

The ship in particular has the redemptive appeal at a popular level in offering the end of persecution and an escape to better places, special or otherwise, or freedom from enslavement (as with Steven Spielberg's 2007 evocation of slavery and abolition, *Amistad*).[82] But a counter-narrative also exists that de-monises migrants in transit and advocates the stopping of such journeys to justify and implement restrictive immigration procedures. As emphasised throughout this book the history and memory of migrant journeys is about the politics of power. In the 1840s and 1850s, for example, we have seen how those campaigning for the rights of Irish migrants used the death and misery of the 'famine ships' to make their case. The image of the 'coffin ship' therafter was exploited by Irish nationalists in the Republican cause. Indeed, the recon-struction of 'famine ships' from the late twentieth century onwards (perhaps a development that is unique amongst the heritage of migrant vessels) reflects the desire to show the oppression that the Irish migrants were facing and their ability, as with the *Jeanie Johnston*, to determine their own fate. In a different manner and context, Mary Antin also attempted to instrumentalise positively the migrant journey in *The Promised Land*. She universalised the experiences of Jews leaving Tsarist oppression in order to show the worth of immigrants at a time of growing xenophobia and restrictionism. Conversely, politicians and others have blamed the migrants themselves for the conditions they endured en route to new lands. They have suggested the filth and disease that came with the journey showed the migrants' fundamental unsuitability to become part of the nation – rather than the exploitation endured to get there.

In 1892, when the early campaigners for the ending of free entry into Britain were concerned to keep the issue in the public mind, an edited collection, *The*

Destitute Alien in Great Britain, was collated by Arnold White. White, a political journalist, protectionist and social Darwinian, became one of the most vociferous and enduring anti-alienists in Britain. In his volume the migrant journey to Britain was bifurcated with the Huguenots contrasted with the East European Jews. That of the former conformed to the classic refugee image – authentic in the cause of flight, innocent of all crimes, unthreatening and thus utterly deserving of asylum:

> Persons of gentle birth, pregnant women, old men, children and invalids, many who had never seen the sea before, braved its perils, and entrusted themselves in open boats in their eagerness to escape. They fled in French, English and Dutch merchant vessels, hidden under bales of good, heaps of coals, and in empty casks.[83]

Once given asylum, the Huguenots would contribute generously and loyally to the British nation. The latter, at the London docks, were presented by the Reverend G.S. Reaney in the collection as a 'mass of alien, dirty, miserable immigrants' pouring out 'from the decks of some continental ship'. They were brought over, almost conspiratorially, 'to crowd into the very cities, streets, workshops and houses from which the [British] emigrants [had] just steamed away'.[84] The moral answer, argued Reaney and the others in White's collection, was to put a stop immediately to this undesirable movement before it was too late.

At a higher political level, William Evans Gordon MP, the leading force on the Royal Commission on Alien Immigration (1902/03), tried to make similar capital from the alleged condition of the Jewish steerage passengers on the ships carrying them to Britain. He repeatedly asked a port examining officer, a Mr Thomas Hawkey, if he had observed 'anything peculiar as to their want of cleanliness or their condition more generally?' Hawkey, however, did not provide the answer expected from such leading questions, responding 'I think they are clean'.[85]

The new popular press from the 1890s onwards reinforced the anti-alien message of White, Reaney, and Evans Gordon and also played on the metaphor of the ship in its relentless campaign against the entry of East European Jews. In January 1903, for example, the *Daily Express* carried a full-page feature entitled 'Alien Undesirables'. Maps of Europe and London revealed a military-style takeover with ships reflecting the numerical threat. The text confirmed this illusion: 'The alien is invading London and the country generally, not in single spies, but in battalions.' The immigrants, according to this newspaper, were without any sense of human worth or dignity: 'On board ship the alien is not a particularly clean or happy-looking object'.[86] Just over a year earlier, a cartoon in the same newspaper presented a long line of aliens disembarking from a ship with baggages labelled 'microbes' and 'dynamite'. In language that predicted that of the tabloid press and its attacks on 'benefit scrounging' asylum seekers a century later, the *Daily Express* queried whether 'In view of the fact that so much undesirable riff-raff and the pauper sediment of other countries are sifting on to our shores, isn't it about time for John Bull to stop giving them the welcome hand?'[87]

Such restrictionism, informed by an underlying racism and paranoia, continued through the twentieth century and beyond. In 1976, Roy Faiers, founder and editor of the best-selling heritage magazine, *This England*, raged at the new form of (black) migrant entry, through aeroplane, but maintaining the watery invasion metaphor: 'Regrettably, the know-alls have opened the flood gates until our cities throb with trouble.' Faiers continued that 'England is *our* home. Heathrow is our front door. We are entitled to open it or shut it to whomsoever we like.'[88] At the time of the 2009 European Union elections in Britain, Nick Griffin, leader of the extreme right-wing British National Party was asked whether he had indeed made a 'call to sink boats containing African migrants'. Griffin did not deny the charge but clarified 'What I said was that what needs to be done as an example is to sink a couple of boats near the shores of Libya. Throw them lifebelts so they can paddle back so they understand they will never get to Europe.'[89] While Griffin's fantasies might be rejected as the racist rantings of a neo-nazi, the interception and maltreatment of migrants, especially those from the developing world, have been features of many western nations' policies in the last decades of the twentieth century and now into the new millennium. Indeed, in 2011, following the 'Arab Spring' revolutions, 14,000 people fled Libya on boats in the first five months of the year. Up to 1,200 of these drowned in unseaworthy vessels, facing hostile responses from potential European places of refuge.[90]

In August 2001, the *Palapa*, a small fishing boat with 348 people, mainly Afghan refugees, was drifting dangerously on its way from Indonesia to Christmas Island, territory owned by Australia. On the verge of sinking, the passengers were picked up by a Norwegian tanker, the *Tampa*. There then followed eight days of wrangling in which the Australian government attempted to force other countries to take the refugees. Meanwhile, 'through bouts of food poisoning and diarrhoea, with near revolts and times of raging and despair, the asylum-seekers from the *Palapa* remained on the *Tampa's* deck'. Eventually, they were sent to the small republic of Naura in the Pacific Ocean before 'processing' through Australian immigration procedures. Strict controls were then introduced by the Australian government – boatloads of 'illegal people' would subsequently be intercepted at sea and returned to the port of departure. Such actions, as Caroline Moorehead notes, had their precedent in British Palestinian policies of the late Mandate period. She adds that between

September and November 2001, 'thirteen Indonesian boats filled with asylum-seekers tried and failed to reach Australia. Four were intercepted and sent back. One sank.' The remaining eight were unseaworthy and their 'human cargo transported to Nauru or Manus Island.'[91] The new procedures cost Australian $500 million to implement but 'Punishment and deterrence had paid off. Only three boats arrived in the next three years.'[92] Such restrictionism reflected a continuation of a 'whites only' post-war Australian immigration policy in which those of the right 'race' and religion were welcomed and others reject-ed.[93] These incidents were tragically repeated in December 2010 when up to one hundred asylum seekers were wrecked off the rocks of the Australian ter-ritory of Christmas Island. More than a quarter of them drowned.[94] Australia is not alone in such matters – the concept of 'Fortress Europe' and the asylum policies of the European Union are designed also to keep out the world's un-wanted. The idea of 'processing' asylum seekers outside the prosperous West is also gaining ever wider acceptance.

Memory

Just as is the case with the commemoration of slavery, it is crucial to restore agency to migrants against the dominant negative imagery of the media and hostility of politicians and public. In this respect, it is worth returning to the Atlantic Park Hostel during the 1920s referred to briefly in Chapter 4. The ref-ugees there, largely Jewish Ukrainians fleeing civil war, pogroms and famine, were left stranded in this huge transmigrant camp outside Southampton due to the racist restrictionism of the western world. Their response to their mis-fortune was not passive – they organised hunger strikes and protests, including a parade that matched that of the YAA Carnival Village in 2007 for wit and sophistication. The refugees presented Atlantic Park as a ship with them as a League of Nations of passengers, evoking especially Chaplin's *The Immigrant* (1917) and the hardships, pathos and hopefulness of the transatlantic journey. The carnival float of the Atlantic Park migrants provided both a parody of eth-nicity as well as an attack on the racial essentialism that excluded them from potential receiving countries, especially America.[95]

As has been illustrated throughout *The Battle of Britishness*, the myth of a tolerant and decent society that protects the needy and vulnerable has enabled Britain to remember *some* migrant journeys. Others, however, such as those linked to the transmigrants of Atlantic Park or the Volga Germans have been subject to near total amnesia. Some are too troubling to be remembered within Britain itself but are recalled elsewhere as in Ireland and the Irish diaspora relating to famine journeys and *Exodus 1947* in Israel and the Jewish diaspora.

In contrast, there has been, for example, the increasing celebration of the *Kindertransport* as reflected in the creation of 'Hope Square' in Liverpool Street Station. The tendency towards the celebratory has also prompted the active forgetting of other journeys in which migrants were curtailed or re-routed or, alternatively, were kept out of the public gaze, as was the case with the small number of refugee Jews allowed temporary entry from the *St Louis* in 1939. Remembering British efforts to deny refugees their chosen destination might evoke unsavoury contemporary associations such as to the *Palapa/Tampa* and other notorious incidents on the sea. It is significant, in this respect, that the lack of knowledge of *Exodus 1947* prompts the chronicler of the *Palapa/Tampa* to mis-date British Palestinian policy in turning away 'illegal' Jewish ships to the 1930s and not to the immediate post-Second World War era.[96]

Other, less dramatic migrant journeys have also run counter to national self-affirming narratives, including those of the African and West Indian stowaways after 1945. The tragic story of David Oluwale simply does not square with the image of the British nation on so many different levels – he was treated as dirt, 'matter out of place' and until recently, such discarding has occurred also in national and local memory work. And Amon Saba Saakana's *Blues Dance* (1985), a novel graphically portraying the problems faced by young black Britons at a time of violent social unrest, presents a different reading of Liverpool Street Station than 'Hope Square'. At first Saakana's principal character, the young Afro-Caribbean Michael Blumenthal, provides a benign reading of the British past that would confirm the sentiments of the later memorial:

> He had been to this station once or twice before, and it always brought to his mind the pictures he had seen of old England ... He had found something romantic and intimate about these pictures. It was as though there was a hidden humanity, a hidden love that once sparked in the heart of this cold, alienated and racist country ...

There is, however, no redemption, not even in the past: 'if that was so, why were there slaves? The soul-heart was always stink and corrupted, he finally concluded.'[97]

Even migrant journeys to Britain that *do* 'fit' have required modification. There is little attention, for example, given to contemporary rejection and hostility towards now idealised refugee movements such as the Huguenots and those from Nazism, or recognition that many of them moved on across the Atlantic seeking better opportunities and a warmer welcome. At a more fundamental level, there is still limited acceptance of the magnitude and variety of migrant journeys to Britain. Some of the case studies in this book are rescued from oblivion and their recovery here gives an indication of the richness of this neglected tradition in British history. Other case studies have focused on those that either at the time or subsequently have become (in)famous. It is worth dwelling very briefly on ship journeys of great repute where the migrant aspect has been downplayed or forgotten.

Rarely is it recognised, for example, that the *Titanic* was designed as an *immigrant* ship and that most of its passengers were migrants from Europe and beyond travelling steerage.[98] If not on such a spectacular and disastrous level, many of the famous British luxury liners of the 1930s, including the *Queen Mary*, carried Jewish refugees alongside the rich and famous. It took the poetic vision of Louis Macneice to recognise their plight on such ships and record it for posterity. In spring 1939 Macneice visited America on board the *Queen Mary*, remembering in his autobiography that it was 'packed with refugees, mainly Jews from Central Europe who covered their basic sorrow with volubality, fuss; only for a moment or two when they stopped troubling the water could you see the wreckage on the floor of their mind'.[99] His encounter with 'These disinterred from Europe', the 'friendless', prompted his poem *Refugees* (September 1940):

> Gangways – the handclasp of the land. The resurrected,
> The brisk or resigned Lazaruses, who want
> Another chance, go trooping ashore. But chances
> Are dubious. Fate is stingy, recalcitrant.[100]

The marginality of migration in British memory, heritage and history has led to such transatlantic journeys being remembered as being merely for pleasure rather than incorporating, for some, the chance to find refuge and better opportunities. And if such famous ships have had their migrant experience removed from their histories, there is even greater obscurity of the millions of journeys made by ordinary people coming to Britain over many centuries. These include the eight million plus Irish from the 1800s to 1921 who went to Britain, America, Canada, Australia and many other destinations, as explored in Chapter 2. Two and a half million alone fled in the decade from the mid-1840s during the height of the famine.[101] As David Fitzpatrick notes in his collection of personal accounts of Irish migration to Australia, 'The letters in this book tell us little of the experience of the voyage. Diaries and diary-letters of sea voyages constitute a distinctive genre for middle-class passengers in the nineteenth century, but they are rarely found among the surviving correspondence of poorer Irish emigrants.'[102] Even more invisible were the three million-plus European transmigrants who passed through Britain from the mid-nineteenth century through to the start of the First World War.[103] Indeed, for many migrants, the physical journey was complex and involved many different stages, including return 'home'. The case of the Volga Germans on the *Minho* in 1879 is unusual in that there is the historic record to reconstitute their journeys even if their own voices are rarely prominent or unmediated in the surviving archive.

This study has explored the relationship between the physical journey and its symbolic importance. The significance of the latter has often distorted the specifics of the former, with the importance of nomenclature to the fore: just as the *Mayflower* became the name of all boats carrying the 'Pilgrim Fathers' to America, so *Exodus 1947* has become all ships with Jewish illegal immigrants to Palestine and the *Empire Windrush* all West Indians (and even other new Commonwealth) migrants to Britain. Indeed, as noted the last two mentioned have been dubbed the 'new' *Mayflowers* in an attempt to foster historic import. In terms of identity formation and the communication through 'ritual performance' in constructing collective memory, the symbolism and metonymic naming politics of the migrant journey is crucial. But, returning to the work of Paul Gilroy and his use of the ship as metaphor in the 'black Atlantic', there is a need also to consider the specific detail of the where and when of such journeys.

Gilroy emphasises that 'ships were the living means by which the points within [the Black] Atlantic world were joined. They were mobile elements that stood for the shifting spaces between the fixed places that they connected.' He adds that 'Accordingly they need to be thought of as cultural and political units rather than abstract embodiments of the triangular trade.'[104] Recently the importance of going beyond the general and the faceless has been recognised in memorialisation of slavery in Britain. Thus in Lancaster, the fourth largest British slave port, the slavery memorial includes a list of Lancaster slave ships, the number of slaves they transported and the name of their captains, thereby bringing closer to home the town's close relationship to the trade.[105] Similar attempts have been made since the 1990s in museum exhibitions, renaming and heritage trails in Liverpool and Bristol to connect the everyday of the 'local' with the dynamics of the 'triangular trade'. Such interventions have helped remember particular individuals such as Pero, slave of Caribbean slave owner, John Pinney. Peto, brought back to Bristol from Nevis by Pinney, is now commemorated by a footbridge in the city.[106] By such memory work it is not just migrant and minority groups which can be connected to neglected or suppressed pasts – processes that are often controversial and contested. And as this book has illustrated, the battle of Britishness, of who belongs and whose history is dominant, is particularly acute when confronting past roles in racism and genocide (even as bystanders), as well as in the slave trade and colonialism.

There is also, returning to the work of Kathy Burrell on the importance of the journey in the wider migrant experience and subsequent identity construction, the need to recognise its inherent danger and discomfort. The catastrophic losses on slave ships and Irish coffin ships are relatively well known, or at least so within the surviving diasporas of these groups. But the death rate more generally for migrants until the second half of the nineteenth century remains to be acknowledged. In the eighteenth century, for example, German migrant mortality rates across the Atlantic were as high as 20 per cent.[107] Moreover, the *Titanic* was not the only ship that sank in the late nineteenth and early twentieth centuries carrying immigrants and refugees – as noted the *Norge* eight years earlier in 1904 was lost leaving 635 drowned.[108]

More recently, undocumented migrants and asylum seekers have taken terrible risks, often at the hands of people-smugglers, to enter the developed world, including Britain. The fifty-eight Chinese migrants who were found dead in Dover in June 2000 were perhaps simply the most infamous (but still largely nameless) examples of such desperate journeys. Danish artist, Nikolaj Larsen, is one of the few to give voice to these foolhardy migrants. In the catalogue entry to his *Promised Land* three-screen film installation at the Folkestone Triennial, Larsen reproduces the SMSs sent to him by Hasan, an Iranian exile, from his makeshift home next to the port of Calais:

> i am very tired of being here
> i try very time but i cant come to england
> 2 time i go to eurotunnel
> one time it was very near to success but securite
> take me.[109]

Unlike his friends, Hasan was unwilling to risk swimming to one of the ferries bound for Dover and boarding as a stowaway, unsure of his ability to survive in the freezing water.[110] The dangers of such 'illegal' journeys are indeed immense and evoke those of an earlier epoch. A painting by a 'Vietnamese child-trafficking victim showing how he entered Britain' in the back of a lorry evokes – with its faceless and contorted figures – those of the slave ship *Brookes*.[111] The narratives of sexual, physical and work exploitation faced by such migrants in the western world also provoke similar and not altogether inappropriate analogies to the 'Middle Passage'. And as noted in the introduction, the process of flying has not ended all the discomfort, danger and humiliation of migrant journeys.

The *endings* of migrant journeys have also developed a symbolic and political importance all of its own. This book began with a study of Dover and it will return to this emblematic place in its conclusion. Coming back to England on a 'banana boat', Caryl Phillips was looking forward to seeing the town's famous white cliffs, having never seen them other than in pictures. To him, they had a deep significance and one that reflected the different memories evoked by place and a sense of belonging:

Their much revered place in British history is generally connected to the Second World War, but for the West Indian emigrants of the fifties and sixties [they] signified the end of a long arduous journey across the Atlantic which had brought them from one world and placed them in the heart of another.

To those such as his parents 'They travelled in the hope that the mother country would remain true to her promise that she would protect the children of her empire.' Such hopes were soon quashed, but to Phillips, the sight of the cliffs has a different meaning: he was 'happy to be home. As I look at the white cliffs of Dover I realize that I do not feel the same sense of nervous anticipation that almost forty years ago characterized my parents' arrival'. Phillips has *travelled* (his word) towards Britain 'with a sense of knowledge and propriety, irrespective of what others, including my fellow passengers, might think'. The new arrivant, he concludes, unlike those a generation earlier, was the 'ship ... not me'.[112]

The shifting meaning of this iconic fortress site in England reflects the dynamics of memory work and representation. They were evoked powerfully in Jamaican reggae star Jimmy Cliff's *Many Rivers to Cross* (1969):

Wandering I am lost
As I travel along the white cliffs of Dover.

Cliff's song concludes that 'I merely survive because of my will'.[113] There is a long distance travelled from the alienation and struggle of Phillips' parents arrival in England, and the angst portrayed in Cliff's lyrics, to the (relative) ease of topographical ownership typified by Caryl's later travel writing. But there are still silences in memory work and heritage representation – nowhere is it acknowledged publicly, for example, that as one of the Cinque Ports, Dover was a place of expulsion for the Jews in 1290.[114] There is a small plaque, unveiled in 2005, to the 'Memory of 58 Young People from China who died near here on 18th June 2000', but it is hardly part of the mainstream heritage world of Dover and its 'White Cliffs' experience'.[115] At the same time and place as this tragedy, there was a 'vociferous animal rights campaign' against the live export of animals through Dover. As a local pro-asylum activist and port worker, Geoff Lear, recalled at the time of the memorial's unveiling: 'I was increasingly struck by the contrast in society's behaviour: cruelty to sheep – a huge, continuing protest; deaths of 58 young people – silence'.[116] These awful endings to journeys in 1290 and 2000 were no doubt *not* in the minds of those designing the new British passport in 2010. It features the White Cliffs alongside village greens and stately homes in an attempt to construct a benign evocation of Englishness.[117] Yet perhaps the exclusionary (as well as the welcoming traditions) of Dover is not that inappropriate a symbol in a state document that has been used both to allow in and bar migrants – both past and present.

Recognition of the refusal to allow in some migrants and the struggles faced by many who were requires a degree of self-criticism rarely found within the nation state. The sanitised and ahistorical 'myth of the *Windrush*' transformed in the twenty-first century into an icon of Britishness, reveals the silences that emerge with celebratory heritage and its concomitant lack of self-reflexivity. In 1968, however, the difficulties faced by the Caribbean *Windrush* passengers *were* emphasised by the *Sunday Times* feature on its twentieth anniversary. The article acknowledged that half had returned home or moved on to North America. Sam King in far less celebratory mode than would typify his later contributions to *Windrush* mythology stated that while he had put up with much, 'I wouldn't consider bringing my parents to a country where an Enoch Powell or Duncan Sandys might cause them to be thought of as less than they are.' Yet while King was willing to consider that his children could 'go to Canada or America like my brothers and sisters' if Britain did not take advantage of their skills, another *Windrush* veteran, Euston Christian, was more optimistic for the chances of the second generation, anticipating the perspective of Caryl Phillips:

> My daughters have all been born, bred and schooled in England. I think the only difference between the people on the Windrush and our children is this: we came asking for our rights and they are going to demand them as black Englishmen.[118]

Similarly, Buchi Emecheta recalls how in 1968 Enoch Powell's 'Rivers of Blood' speech gave her a 'sinking feeling': she had to reassure her young daughter that she would not be sent 'home' to Africa.[119] A little later, and more established, Emecheta considered moving to north London. She viewed a house in Crouch End owned by a Trinidadian with a passion for parrots. One bird had been named after the notorious Conservative politician and the landlord had taught it to say 'I am Enoch Powell and will die slowly and then slowly roast in hell'.[120] Emecheta appreciated the gesture. United in resistance, these black migrants from Africa and the Caribbean were determined to stay in England as were their children. As Buchi Emecheta's son told his sister after the Powellite onslaught, 'You're home, silly … Africa is home for mother and father, not ours.'[121]

The Battle of Britishness has shown, however, that journeys can also be constructed as *less* welcoming over time. In 1939, on the eve of the Second World War, the *St Louis* was presented by the American Jewish Joint Distribution Committee as a success story: its passengers embarking in Antwerp were 'never again to return to the land they were forced to leave'.[122] Seventy years later, a party of survivors from this ship in Florida found President Roosevelt guilty. Roosevelt was complicit 'by acts of omission in crimes of genocide' in his refusal to allow the refugees entry to America.[123] The mock trial, according to Gisela Feldman, who later settled in Manchester and was one of the 'jurists', would 'show the world how little people cared about those passengers'.[124]

Concluding thoughts

The fluidity of memory and representation and their constant contestation reflects the importance of power and the changing status of migrants in wider society. There is much at stake and Patrick Geary reminds us that 'All memory, whether "individual", "collective", or "historical", is memory *for* something, and this political (in a broad sense) purpose cannot be ignored.'[125] Historical geographer, Doreen Massey, observes that 'The identity of places is very much bound up with the *histories* which are told of them, *how* those histories are told, and which memory turns out to be dominant.'[126] Thus some narratives that were marginal or totally neglected have, more recently, become part of the mainstream. In his writing more generally, especially *Foreigners*, Caryl Phillips has established a bond, however problematic, between the black presence and English history. This connection is made even stronger in the work of Fred D'Aguiar. In the poem *Sweet Thames* (1992) written for BBC2 television, Sukhdev Sandhu notes that D'Aguiar's aim is to 'reclaim the river for those who would use it as a symbol of a nation being deluged by unwanted immigrants', or to 'filter out … the pollution of xenophobic invective'.[127] The poem/film begins with Lord Kitchener's calypso disembarking from the *Empire Windrush*, moving back in time to Olaudah Equiano, and then forward again to Harry Surju, a black nurse attempting to bring his wife, Sheila, to England from Mauritius in the face of Home Office objections. Their experiences and contributions across time are juxtaposed against those that have used river images to counter immigration, such as Enoch Powell and Margaret Thatcher.[128]

There is the confidence in the work of Phillips and D'Aguiar to suggest that it is Powell and Thatcher who are, in fact, the pollutants of Englishness (as exemplified in the ventriloquism of Emecheta's parrot) and not the migrant newcomers whose roots are often deep in national/local history – if not always in collective memory. In Stuart Maconie's *Hope & Glory* (2011), Powell is regarded as being out of time even in 1968 when 'the Beatles were singing "All You Need is Love" … and *Hair* was wowing them in the theatres'. Maconie adds that

Forty-odd years on from Powell's stentorian demagoguery … no one has the whip hand in a kaleidoscopic, chaotic but essentially peaceful

> Britain and Enoch stands revealed as not so much Virgil looking at the
> Tiber but Canute standing helpless before the tide.[129]

Phillips was just a baby when he arrived from St Kitts in 1958 and D'Aguiar was born in London in 1960. Their writings reflect a more self-confident second-generation perspective as does Andrea Levy whose *Small Island* fictionalises the '*Windrush* generation' utilising detailed historical and popular work on the topic. The success of Levy's novel, and its serialisation by the BBC in 2009, suggests a welcoming of the *stories* of post-war black migration if not necessarily an acceptance of the migrants and their descendants themselves.[130] Contemporary racism is far from ignored in such work, and there is no denial of the dislocation caused by migration. Ultimately, however, Britain, and even, more specifically, England, can be a 'place called home'. At its most brutal, the first generation was denied any such possibility of belonging, callously in the case of David Oluwale whose nationality, according to Leeds police officers, was simply 'wog'.[131]

Yet in between the self-assurance of Phillips in his later writings on Englishness, and the racist rejection typified by the experiences of Oluwale and other stowaways, lies the ambivalence in and unease with trying to become part of the nation that typifies most of those who have embarked on migrant journeys to Britain. This book has emphasised twoness – welcoming and rejection, and fame and obscurity – in the making and re-making of Britishness. Across these binaries, however, are constant ambiguities and questioning of certainties. It has allowed obscure stories to be rediscovered and new forms of identity to be accepted as part of the island story – even if simultaneously others are regarded as beyond the pale. With such lack of clarity a sense of belonging fully to the nation can be highly prized yet ultimately elusive. It will be fitting, therefore, to end this study on a note of exquisitely painful ambivalence by revisiting *The Settler's Cookbook* of Yasmin Alibhai-Brown. Britain, by the end of her journey through food, is 'My country – now irreversibly my country'. Alibhai-Brown's is equally a political as much as a personal response – especially to those such as Norman Tebbit who as late as September 2000 (and thus nearly thirty years since she arrived in Britain as a refugee from Uganda), queried the worth of her British passport.[132] In 2007, expectantly, she heard Gordon Brown give his first speech as Prime Minister to the Labour party annual conference:

> He used the word *Britishness* about seventy-eight times … His patriotic whacks gave me a headache, though, and I took to my bed, forlorn once again. What the future holds seems as uncertain as ever. Perhaps I should keep a bag half packed. Just in case.[133]

Notes

Notes to Introduction

1 Patrick Manning, *Migration in World History* (New York: Routledge, 2005), p. 1.
2 Jan Lucassen, Leo Lucassen and Patrick Manning (eds), *Migration History in World History: Multidisciplinary Approaches* (Leden: Brill, 2010).
3 Manning, *Migration in World History*, p.xiii.
4 *Ibid.*, p. 143.
5 *Ibid.*, p. 2.
6 Bryan Cheyette, *Constructions of 'the Jew' in English Literature and Society: Racial Representations, 1875–1945* (Cambridge: Cambridge University Press, 1993), pp. 5–6.
7 Homi Bhabha, 'Introduction', in Homi Bhabha (ed.), *Nation and Narration* (London: Routledge, 1990), p. 3.
8 Cheyette, *Constructions of 'the Jew'*, p. 6.
9 Peter Fryer, *Staying Power: The History of Black People in Britain* (London: Pluto, 1984), p. xi.
10 See, for example, Peter Mandler, *The English National Character: The History of an Idea from Edmund Burke to Tony Blair* (London: Yale University Press, 2006), p. 4; Patrick Wright, *On Living in an Old Country: The National Past in Contemporary Britain* (London: Verso, 1985), *passim*. More specific, but less satisfactory, is Mark Connelly, *We Can Take It! Britain and the Memory of the Second World War* (London: Pearson, 2004).
11 Colin Holmes, *John Bull's Island: Immigration and British Society, 1871–1971* (Basingstoke: Macmillan, 1988).
12 Fryer, *Staying Power*.
13 Rozina Visram, *Asians in Britain: 400 Years of History* (London: Pluto, 2002).
14 Robert Winder, *Bloody Foreigners: The Story of Immigration to Britain* (London: Little, Brown, 2004).

239

15 James Walvin, *Passage to Britain: Immigration in British History and Politics* (Harmondsworth: Penguin, 1984).

16 Panikos Panayi, *An Immigration History of Britain: Multicultural Racism since 1800* (Harlow: Longman, 2010).

17 Anne Kershen, *Strangers, Aliens and Asians: Huguenots, Jews and Bangladeshis in Spitalfields, 1660–2000* (London: Routledge, 2005).

18 John Solomos, *Race and Racism in Britain* (Basingstoke: Macmillan, 2003).

19 Lloyd Gartner, *The Jewish Immigrant in England, 1870–1914* (London: George Allen & Unwin, 1960).

20 Bill Williams, *The Making of Manchester Jewry, 1740–1875* (Manchester: Manchester University Press, 1976).

21 See my review article, 'New Narratives, Old Exclusions? British Historiography and Minority Studies', *Immigrants & Minorities* vol. 24 no. 3 (2006), 347–51. An exception is provided in Paul Ward, *Britishness Since 1870* (London: Routledge, 2004) which does incorporate some of the new work on immigrant and minority history.

22 See, for example, Paul Gilroy, *Between Camps: Nations, Cultures and the Allure of Race* (London: Allen Lane, 2000), which provide important linkages and Bryan Cheyette's forthcoming work on Jews and postcolonialism, which is eagerly anticipated.

23 See Raphael Samuel and Paul Thompson (eds), *The Myths We Live By* (London: Routledge, 1990) and Paul Thompson, *Oral History: The Voice of the Past* (third edition, Oxford: Oxford University Press, 2000).

24 Examples include 'memory boxes' prepared for children about to lose their parents to AIDS in Africa. See Gideon Mendel, 'Memories are made of this', *Guardian*, 29 November 2006. For a variety of 'top down' and 'bottom up' forms of memory work in dealing with traumatic history, see the essays in Erica Lehrer, Cynthia Milton and Monica Patterson (eds), *Curating Difficult Knowledge: Violent Pasts in Public Places* (Basingstoke: Palgrave Macmillan, 2011).

25 Jeffrey Olick and Joyce Robbins, 'Social Memory Studies: From "Collective Memory" to the Historical Sociology of Mnemonic Practices', *Annual Review of Sociology* vol. 24 (1998), p. 133.

26 Jonathan Boyarin, *Storm from Paradise: The Politics of Jewish Memory* (Minneapolis: University of Minnesota Press, 1992), p. 4.

27 See the comments of Kathy Burrell, 'Going Steerage on Ryanair: Cultures of Migrant Air Travel between Poland and the UK', *Journal of Transport Geography* vol. 19 (2011), pp. 1023, 1027, 1029.

28 T.W.E. Roche, *The Key in the Lock: Immigration Control in England from 1066 to the Present Day* (London: John Murray, 1969), p. 4.

29 Jack Shenker, 'Nato units left 61 migrants to die of hunger and thirst', *Guardian*, 9 May 2011.

30 Burrell, 'Going Steerage on Ryan Air', pp. 1023–30.

31 Huma Querishi, 'Brides and prejudice', *Guardian*, 13 May 2011. The *Guardian*, through its then social services correspondent, Melanie Phillips, initially exposed this procedure in February 1969. See Alan Travis, 'Extent of 70s "virginity tests"

revealed', *Guardian*, 9 May 2011 based on research carried out by the Australian academics, Marinella Marmo and Evan Smith.

32 Salman Rushdie, *The Satanic Verses* (Dover, Delaware: The Consortium, 1992 [1988]), p. 4.
33 'Man who died on deportation flight was "heavily restrained"', *Guardian*, 15 October 2010.
34 Les Back, 'Falling from the sky', *Patterns of Prejudice* vol. 37 no. 2 ((2003), p. 344.
35 Rushdie, *The Satanic Verses*, pp. 157–9.
36 Back, 'Falling from the sky', p. 348.

Notes to Chapter 1

1 Peter Unwin, *The Narrow Sea: Barrier, Bridge and Gateway to the World – the History of the English Channel* (London: Review, 2004 [2003]).
2 *Ibid.*, pp. 3–4.
3 *Ibid.*, p. 4.
4 Panikos Panayi, *The Enemy in Our Midst: Germans in Britain during the First World War* (Oxford: Berg, 1991).
5 R.M. Morris, supplementary history of the Home Office Immigration & Nationality Department, 1963 in National Archives (NA) HO 367/2. This history updated that written by Mr Eagleston during the Second World War in NA HO 213/1772.
6 Refugee Council Newsletter Online, 21 April 2011, accessed 22 April 2011.
7 Home Office, *Life in the United Kingdom: A Journey to Citizenship* (London: HMSO, 2004), p. 15.
8 Home Office, *Fairer, Faster and Firmer: A Modern Approach to Immigration and Asylum* (London: HMSO, 1998), p. 35.
9 Morris, 1963 in NA HO 367/2.
10 Colin Holmes, *A Tolerant Country? Immigrants, Refugees and Minorities in Britain* (London: Faber and Faber, 1991), p. 3.
11 Bill Williams, *Jews and Other Foreigners: Manchester and the Rescue of the Victims of European Fascism, 1933–40* (Manchester: Manchester University Press, 2011) provides a fine example in this respect.
12 Home Office, *Life in the United Kingdom*, p. 43.
13 Winterton speech reproduced in Norbert Kampe (ed.), *Jewish Immigrants of the Nazi Period in the USA* vol. 4, part 2 (New York: K.G. Saur, 1992), p. 338.
14 *Hansard* (HC) vol. 565 col. 83 (21 February 1957).
15 Panayi, *An Immigration History of Britain*, p. 11, significantly in a chapter entitled 'A Country of Immigration?'.
16 Home Office, *Life in the United Kingdom*, chapter 2.
17 J.A. Williamson, 'England and the Sea', in Ernest Barker (ed.), *The Character of England* (Oxford: Clarendon Press, 1947), p. 506.
18 Ernest Barker, 'An Attempt at Perspective', in Barker (ed.), *The Character of England*, p. 552.

19 John Pennington, 'The British Heritage' in Pennington (ed.), *The British Heritage* (London: Odhams Press, 1948), p. 7.

20 Ernest Barker, 'An Attempt at Perspective', in Barker (ed.), *The Character of England*, p. 552.

21 Ernest Barker, *National Character and the Factors in Its Formation* (London: Methuen, 1927), p. 47.

22 Arthur Bryant, *The National Character* (London: Longmans, Green & Co, 1934), p. 6.

23 Arthur Mee, *The King's England: Kent, the Gateway of England and its Great Possessions* (London: Hodder and Stoughton, 1936), p. 1.

24 *Ibid.*, p. 144.

25 *Ibid.*, p. 145.

26 Jonathan Coad, *Dover Castle* (London: Batsford/English Heritage, 1995), p. 41.

27 H.J. Mackinder, *Britain and the British Seas* (London: William Heineman, 1902), p. 15.

28 'Don't Believe the Hype', *iNexile: The Refugee Council Magazine* (February 1999), pp. 12–13.

29 Mary Douglas, *Purity and Danger: An Analysis of the Concepts of Pollution and Taboo* (London: Routledge, 1996 [1966]), p. 41.

30 Tony Kushner, *Remembering Refugees: Then and Now* (Manchester: Manchester University Press, 2006), Chapter 5.

31 Steve Cohen, *Deportation is Freedom! The Orwellian World of Immigration Controls* (London: Jessica Kingsley Publishers, 2006), pp. 54–5.

32 Maggie Morgan, 'Port Under Siege After Gipsy Bands Head West to Good Life', *Daily Express*, 21 October 1997; *Independent*, 20 October 1998.

33 Winder, *Bloody Foreigners*, p. 61.

34 *Ibid.*

35 'Strangers at Dover: The Huguenots', permanent exhibition and 'The Huguenots' in 'Invaders and Settlers', temporary exhibition, September 2010 to September 2011, in Dover Museum, visited 8 July 2011.

36 Vesna Maric, *Bluebird: A Memoir* (London: Granta, 2009), p. 54.

37 *Ibid.*, p. 54.

38 *Ibid.*, p. 28.

39 Oliver Burkeman, 'The frontline', in Sam Wollaston, Ian Katz and Rick Williams (eds), *Welcome to Britain* (London: The Guardian, 2001), pp. 36–9.

40 Victor Sebestyen, 'A Tidal wave of displaced people', *Evening Standard*, 27 June 2000 quoted by Julia Neuberger, *The Moral State We're In: A Manifesto for a 21st Century Society* (London:HarperCollins, 2005), pp. 304–5. For the mixed response to these deaths, see Mass-Observation Archive: 'Coming to Britain', summer 2000 directive.

41 See the grim details through the 'Roll call of deaths of asylum seekers and undocumented migrants', from 1989 to the present, through the Institute of Race Relations fact files at www.irr.org.uk, accessed 2 July 2011.

42 Figures given by John Morrison in *iNexile*, August 2000.

43 *Guardian*, 17 February 2003. *In This World* won the Golden Bear award at the Berlin

Film Festival in 2003.

44 Philip French, 'Passage to Kilburn', *Observer*, 30 March 2003.

45 BBC Radio 4, 'Britain by the Backdoor', 2001; Myles Harris, *Tomorrow is Another Country: What is Wrong with UK's Asylum Policy* (London: Civitas, 2003), pp. 2–3.

46 *Economist* 'Where Do You Stand?', posters on immigration, viewed Euston tube station, 13 July 2011 and accessed through *Economist* website, 15 July 2011.

47 Winder, *Bloody Foreigners*, p. xii.

48 Unwin, *The Narrow Sea*, p. 308.

49 *Ibid.*

50 See Dallal Stevens, *UK Asylum Law and Policy: Historical and Contemporary Perspectives* (London: Sweet & Maxwell, 2004), Chapter 5 which covers legislation from 1999 to 2002.

51 Eitan Bar-Yosef and Nadia Valman, 'Introduction', in idem (eds), *'The Jew' in Late-Victorian and Edwardian Culture: Between the East End and East Africa* (Basingstoke: Palgrave Macmillan, 2009), p. 14.

52 Krishan Kumar, *The Making of English National Identity* (Cambridge: Cambridge University Press, 2003), p. 251.

53 Home Office, *Community Cohesion: A Report of the Independent Review Team Chaired by Ted Cantle* (London: Home Office, 2001), p. 9.

54 *Ibid., passim.*

55 Gordon Brown, 'The future of Britishness', Fabian Society lecture, 14 January 2006.

56 John Denham, 'Promoting Community Cohesion', speech to the Industrial Society and Runnymede Trust, 18 March 2002.

57 Home Office, *Community Cohesion*, p. 20.

58 Derek McGhee, 'The Paths to Citizenship: a Critical Examination of Immigration Policy in Britain since 2001', *Patterns of Prejudice* vol. 43 no. 1 (2009), pp. 40–64, p. 43 for the Brown 2008 speech.

59 David Cameron speech, 5 February 2011 available at www.number10.gov/news/speeches-and-transcripts/2011/02/pms-speech-at- … , accessed 11 February 2011.

60 Paul Gilroy, *'There Ain't No Black in the Union Jack': The Cultural Politics of Race and Nation* (London: Hutchinson, 1987).

61 Speech given in Eastbourne, 16 November 1968 in Bill Smithies and Peter Fiddick (eds), *Enoch Powell on Immigration* (London: Sphere Books, 1969), p. 77.

62 John Solomos, *Race and Racism in Britain* (2nd editition, Basingstoke: Macmillan, 1993), pp. 228–9.

63 Paul Gilroy, 'Melancholia or conviviality: The politics of belonging in Britain', in Sally Davison and Jonathan Rutherford (eds), *Race, Identity and Belonging* (London: Lawrence and Wishart, 2008), p. 54.

64 Bob Rowthorn, 'Migration Limits', *Prospect* no. 83 (February 2003), pp. 24, 26, 27.

65 David Goodhart, 'Too diverse?', *Prospect* no. 95 (February 2004), p. 30.

66 *Ibid.*, p. 36.

67 Gordon Brown, speech to the Fabian Society, 14 January 2006. See *Guardian*, 14 January 2006 and analysis in the introduction.

68 *Observer*, 15 January 2006.

69 Gordon Brown contribution to round table, 'Britain Rediscovered', *Prospect* no. 109 (April 2005), p. 20.
70 Tristram Hunt, 'History lessons we should learn', *Observer*, 15 January 2006.
71 Goodhart, 'Too diverse?', p. 37.
72 Goodhart, 'Foreword: Britain Rediscovered', *Prospect* no. 109 (April 2005), p. 3.
73 Goodhart, 'Too diverse?', p. 34.
74 *Ibid.*
75 John Denham, Smith Institute lecture, 2 March 2010, www.smith-institute.org.uk/past, accessed 28 September 2010.
76 Goodhart, 'Too diverse?', p. 37.
77 *Ibid.*, p. 36.
78 Gary Younge, 'Bitter white whine', *Guardian*, 26 February 2004.
79 British Council speech, 7 July 2004, http://politics.guardian.co.uk/labour/story/0.9061,12556550,00.html, accessed 9 July 2004.
80 Peter Mandler, *The English National Character: The History of an Idea from Edmund Burke to Tony Blair* (New York: Yale University Press, 2006), pp. 7–8.
81 For 'New Right' usage of this speech but distancing itself from 'fake and sentimental patriotism' see Roger Scruton, *England : An Elegy* (London: Chatto&Windus, 2000), pp. 211–12.
82 Brown, British Council speech, 7 July 2004.
83 Speech available at www.fabians.org.uk/events/speeches/the-future-of-britishness, accessed 20 September 2010.
84 Gordon Brown, British Council speech, 7 July 2004.
85 *Ibid.*
86 Gordon Brown, 'The Future of Britishness'.
87 Speech to the IPPR quoted in David Conway, *A Nation of Immigrants? A Brief Demographic History of Britain* (London: Civitas, 2007), p. 1.
88 See 'A Moving Story: Is there a case for a major museum of migration in the UK?' (discussion paper, Migration Museum Working Group, IPPR, July 2009).
89 *Ibid.*, pp. 5–6.
90 *Ibid.*, p. 95. See also Anthony Browne, *Do We Need Mass Immigration?* (London: Civitas, 2002).
91 Harris, *Tomorrow is Another Country*, pp. 17,47.
92 *Ibid.*, p. 48.
93 In 2009 the British National Party was in legal trouble for limiting its members to the 'indigenous British' and 'closely related and ethnically assimable or assimilated aboriginal members of the European race'.
94 Billy Bragg, *The Progressive Patriot: A Search for Belonging* (London: Black Swan, 2006).
95 *Ibid.*, p. 242.
96 *Ibid.*, pp. 12–13.
97 *Ibid.*, p. 14.
98 *Ibid.*, pp. 15–16.
99 *Ibid.*, pp. 27, 29.

100 *Ibid.*, pp. 113–14.
101 *Ibid.*
102 Roy Strong, *Visions of England* (London: Bodley Head, 2011), p. 6.
103 Denham, 2 March 2010 Smith Institute speech.
104 *Ibid.*
105 Stuart Maconie, *Adventures on the High Teas: In Search of Middle England* (London: Ebury Press, 2009), pp. 338–43.
106 *Ibid.*, pp. 220, 222–3.
107 *Ibid.*, pp. 224–5.
108 Stuart Maconie, *Hope & Glory: The Days that Made Britain* (London: Ebury Press, 2011), pp. 159, 171.
109 Gordon Brown, British Council speech, 7 July 2004. See Scruton, *England: an elegy*, p. 67.
110 Scruton in *Prospect* no. 109 (April 2005), p. 21.
111 *Ibid.*, p. 8.
112 Tony Blair, *A Journey* (London: Hutchinson, 2010), p. 524.
113 *Ibid.*, pp. 204–5.
114 Matthew Taylor, 'Millions paid in compensation to detained migrants', *Guardian*, 27 September 2010.
115 Gilroy, 'Melancholia or conviviality', p. 53.
116 Tariq Modood, *Not Easy Being British: Colour, Culture and Citizenship* (Stoke: Trentham Books, 1992).
117 Robin Richardson, 'Preface', in Modood, *Not Easy*, p.xi.
118 Bhikhu Parekh (ed.), *The Future of Multi-Ethnic Britain* (London: Profile, 2000).
119 Tariq Modood, 'A defence of multiculturalism' in Davison and Rutherford (eds), *Race, Identity and Belonging*, p. 84.
120 Yasmin Alibhai-Brown, *Who Do We Think We Are? Imagining the New Britain* (London: Penguin, 2001 [2000]), p.xviii.
121 *Ibid.*, pp. xviii–xix and Yasmin Alibhai-Brown, *After Multiculturalism* (London: Foreign Policy Centre, 2000), p. 58.
122 Tariq Modood, *Multiculturalism: A Civic Idea* (Cambridge: Polity Press, 2007), p. 10.
123 Tariq Modood, *Still Not Easy Being British: Struggles for a Multicultural Citizenship* (Stoke: Trentham Books, 2010), p. 105.
124 *Ibid.*, p. 1 and *passim*.
125 Gordon Brown, Fabian Society speech, 14 January 2006.
126 Mass-Observation Archive, University of Sussex: Directive Summer 2006, Part 2 (hereafter M-O A: DR Summer 2006).
127 See Dorothy Sheridan, Brian Street and David Bloome, *Writing Ourselves: Mass-Observation and Literacy Practices* (Creskill, NJ: Hampton Press, 2000).
128 M-O A: DR E2977, Summer 2006.
129 M-O A: DR M3190, Summer 2006.
130 M-O A: DR O3082, Summer 2006.
131 M-O A: DR H1703, Summer 2006.

132 M-O A: DR R1468, Summer 2006.

133 M-O A: DR R470, Summer 2006.

134 M-O A: DR W3731, Summer 2006.

135 M-O A: DR B1475, Summer 2006.

136 M-O A: DR B3227, Summer 2006.

137 M-O A: DR W1382, Summer 2006.

138 M-O A: DR L2606, Summer 2006.

139 M-O A: DR B3568, Summer 2006.

140 M-O A: DR C3167, Summer 2006.

141 M-O A: DR 3817, Summer 2006.

142 On Jews, food and the East End, see Tony Kushner, 'Jew and Non-Jew in the East End of London: Towards an Anthropology of "Everyday" Relations', in Geoffrey Alderman and Colin Holmes (eds), *Outsiders & Outcasts: Essays in Honour of William J. Fishman* (London: Duckworth, 1993), p. 44. More generally, see Panikos Panayi, *Spicing Up Britain: The Multicultural History of British Food* (London: Reaktion Books, 2008).

143 'Kids believe curry is Brit native dish', *Daily Mirror*, 18 April 2009.

144 On Bevin in this period, see Donald Bloxham and Tony Kushner, *The Holocaust: Critical Historical Approaches* (Manchester: Manchester University Press, 2005), pp. 193–4.

145 Robert Colls, *Identity of England* (Oxford: Oxford University Press, 2002), p. 130.

146 Paul Langford, *Englishness Identified: Manners and Character 1650–1850* (Oxford: Oxford University Press, 2000), p. 70.

147 Reproduced in George Mikes, *How to be a Brit* (Harmondsworth: Penguin, 1986), p. 54.

148 The essay was first published in part in the literary journal, *Horizon*, in December 1940. It is reproduced in full in Sonia Orwell and Ian Angus (eds), *The Collected Essays, Journalism and Letters of George Orwell* vol. II *My Country Right or Left 1940–1943* (Harmondsworth: Penguin, 1984), pp. 74–134 (p. 75).

149 Kumar, *The Making of English National Identity*, pp. 226–7.

150 Orwell and Angus (eds), *The Collected Essays*, p. 75.

151 Ekow Eshun, *Black Gold of the Sun: Searching for Home in England and Africa* (London: Hamish Hamilton, 2005), p. 49.

152 Pauline Black, *Black By Design: A 2-Tone Memoir* (London: Serpent's Tail, 2011), p. 60.

153 M-O A: DR B3019, Summer 2006.

154 M-O A: DR D3501, Summer 2006.

155 M-O A: DR W3731, Summer 2006.

156 Melissa Kite, 'Want to be a citizen? First learn to queue', *Sunday Telegraph*, 14 February 2010.

157 See, for example, *Daily Express*, 20 February 2010.

158 See comments of Mark Taylor of Barking and Dagenham Council in which he stated migrants played a relatively small part of the housing shortage in his borough, quoted in Anjana Ahuja, 'Is Britain full?', *The Times*, 16 February 2010.

159 Hadley Freeman, 'It takes more than learning to queue to make a person truly British', *Guardian*, 17 February 2010.
160 M-O A: DR M3712, Summer 2006.

Notes to Chapter 2

1 Yasmin Alibhai-Brown, *The Settler's Cookbook: A Memoir of Love, Migration and Food* (London: Portobello Books, 2008), p. 1.
2 Anne Kershen, 'Introduction', in Anne Kershen (ed.), *London: The Promised Land? The Migrant Experience in a Capital City* (Aldershot: Avebury, 1997), p. 1.
3 David Jonisz, 'Living Memory of the Jewish Community' collection, British Library Sound Archive, C410/177; 'The Orphans Who Survived the Concentration Camps', BBC 1, 5 April 2010.
4 Michael Perlmutter, 'The Bonds of Windermere', *Journal of the '45 Aid Society* no. 18 (December 1994), p. 8.
5 Lawrence Langer, *Admitting the Holocaust: Collected Essays* (New York: Oxford University Press, 1995), p. 46.
6 'Eyewitness', 10 September 1947, BBC Home Service. BBC Written Archives, Caversham. I am grateful to James Jordan for this reference.
7 Peter Gray, *The Irish Famine* (London: Thames and Hudson, 1995), p. 97.
8 Frank Neal, *Black '47: Britain and the Famine Irish* (Basingstoke: Macmillan, 1998), Chapter 3.
9 La Thann Xuan, 'Story of a Refugee', *New Homeland*, January 1980, produced by BCAR Reception Centre, Thorney Island, Refugee Council archives, EV/QU S9.1.
10 See *BCAR Annual Report 1978/1979* (London: BCAR, 1979), p. 5.
11 Bryan Cartridge, 'Note for the Record: Vietnamese Refugees', 14 June 1979 and resettlememt figures for Vietnamese refugees, 1 May 1979, in National Archives, PREM 19/129.
12 Simone Gigliotti, *The Train Journey: Transit, Captivity, and Witnessing in the Holocaust* (New York: Berghahn Books, 2009), p. 18.
13 James Hathaway, 'Forced Migration Studies: Could We Agree Just to "Date"?', *Journal of Refugee Studies* vol. 20 no. 2 (2007), p. 354.
14 Stephen Castles, 'Towards a Sociology of Forced Migration and Social Transformation', *Sociology* vol. 37 no. 1 (2003), p. 30.
15 *Ibid.*, p. 24.
16 *Ibid.*, p. 21.
17 Raphael Samuel and Paul Thompson, 'Introduction' in Samuel and Thompson (eds), *The Myths We Live By* (London: Routledge, 1990), pp. 18–19.
18 Jonathan Boyarin, *Storm from Paradise: The Politics of Jewish Memory* (Minneapolis: University of Minnesota Press, 1992), p. 3.
19 Charlotte Erickson, 'Jewish People in the Atlantic Migration, 1850–1914' in Aubrey Newman and Stephen Massil (eds), *Patterns of Migration, 1850–1914* (London: Jewish Historical Society of England, 1996), p. 1; Patrick Fitzgerald and Brian

Lambkin, *Migration in Irish History, 1607–2007* (Basingstoke: Palgrave Macmillan, 2008), p. 8.

20 Erickson, 'Jewish People', p. 3.

21 For a perceptive overview of the series, see Jerome De Groot, *Consuming History: Historians and Heritage in Contemporary Popular Culture* (London: Routledge, 2009), Chapter 4.

22 See Gemma Romain, '*Who Do You Think You Are?* Journeys and Jewish Identity in the Televisual Narrative of David Baddiel', in James Jordan, Tony Kushner and Sarah Pearce (eds), *Jewish Journeys: From Philo to Hip Hop* (London: Vallentine Mitchell, 2010), pp. 332–48.

23 David Cesarani, 'The Myth of Origin: Ethnic Memory and the Experience of Migration', in Newman and Massil (eds), *Patterns of Migration 1850–1914*, pp. 250–2.

24 Bud Flanagan, *My Crazy Life* (London: Four Square Books, 1962 [1961]), pp. 13–14.

25 Samuel Chotzinoff, *A Lost Paradise: Early Reminiscences* (London: Hamish Hamilton, 1956), p. 42.

26 *Ibid.*, pp. 43–4.

27 Nick Harris, *Dublin's Little Jerusalem* (Dublin: A. & A. Farmer, 2002), p. 1.

28 Cesarani, 'The Myth of Origins', p. 250.

29 Lloyd Gartner, 'Notes on the Statistics of Jewish Immigration to England, 1870–1914', *Jewish Social Studies* vol. 22 no. 2 (1960), pp. 97–102.

30 Wolf Benninson, interviewed by Bill Williams, Manchester Jewish Museum, oral history interviews, J24.

31 Miriam Field, interviewed by Bill Williams, Manchester Jewish Museum tapes, oral history interviews, J84.

32 Chotzinoff, *A Lost Paradise*, p. 55.

33 *Who Do You Think You Are?*, BBC 1, 23 February 2009 and Zoe Wanamaker, interview by Simon Round, *Jewish Chronicle*, 26 June 2009.

34 *Who Do You Think You Are?*, BBC 1, 23 February 2009.

35 Chotzinoff, *A Lost Paradise*, pp. 58–9.

36 Lew Grade, *Still Dancing: My Story* (Glasgow: Fontana/Collins, 1987), p. 21.

37 *Jewish Chronicle*, 19 April 1912.

38 Per Kristian Sebak, *Titanic's Predecessor: The S/S Norge Disaster of 1904* (Laksevaag: Seaward Publishing, 2004).

39 Chotzinoff, *A Lost Paradise*, p. 41.

40 See the ten interviews listed under the category 'Immigrant Journey' in the computer index to the tapes, compiled by Rickie Burman, and available at the Manchester Jewish Museum, with a copy at the Parkes Library, University of Southampton.

41 Sidney Epstein, Manchester Jewish Museum, oral history interviews, J81.

42 Grade, *Still Dancing*, p. 21.

43 Interviewed in 'Interface: The Russian-Polish Pogroms of the Late 19th Century: An Introductory Exhibition', Redbridge Jewish Community Centre, November 1986, text in Tower Hamlets Local History Library, 430/430.

44 Oscar Handlin, 'Foreword', in Mary Antin, *The Promised Land: The Autobiography of a Russian Immigrant* (Princeton, NJ: Princeton University Press, 1969 [1912]), p.v, xi. All direct quotes will be taken from this edition.

45 *Ibid.*, p. xii.

46 Werner Sollors, 'Introduction' in Antin, *The Promised Land* (New York: Penguin, 1997), p. xxix.

47 Antin, *The Promised Land*, p. 91.

48 Steven Belluscio, *To be Suddenly White: Literary Realism and Racial Passing* (Columbia: University of Missouri Press, 2006), p. 186.

49 Antin, *The Promised Land*, p. 36.

50 Barbara Sicherman, *Well-Read Lives: How Books Inspired a Generation of American Women* (Chapel Hill, NC: University of North Carolina Press, 2010), p. 210.

51 Antin, *The Promised Land*, p. xix.

52 Sollors, 'Introduction', p. xvii.

53 Antin, *The Promised Land*, p. 177.

54 Antin, *The Promised Land*, p. 178.

55 Betty Bergland, 'Rereading Photographs and Narratives in Ethnic Autobiography: Memory and Subjectivity in Mary Antin's *The Promised Land*', in Amritjit Singh, Joseph Skerrett and Robert Hogan (eds), *Memory, Narrative and Identity: New Essays in Ethnic American Literatures* (Boston, MA: Northeastern University Press, 1994), p. 66.

56 Mary Antin, *From Plotzk to Boston* (Boston: W.B. Clarke, 1899).

57 Israel Zangwill, 'Foreword', Antin, *From Plotzk to Boston*, p. 8.

58 *Ibid.*, p. 80.

59 Antin, *The Promised Land*, pp. 178–9.

60 Antin to Ellery Sedgwick, 30 July 1911 in Evelyn Salz (ed.), *Selected Letters of Mary Antin* (Syracuse, NY: Syracuse University Press, 2000), p. 55.

61 Antin, *The Promised Land*, p.xxi.

62 See Roger Daniels, *Coming to America: A History of Immigration and Ethnicity in American Life* (New York: HarperPerennial, 1991), Chapter 10 'The Triumph of Nativism'.

63 Molly Crumpton Winter, *American Narratives: Multiethnic Writing in the Age of Realism* (Baton Rouge, LA: Louisiana State University Press, 2007), p. 38.

64 Antin, *The Promised Land*, p. xxi.

65 *Ibid.*, p. xxi.

66 *Ibid.*, pp. 226–8.

67 *Ibid.*, p. 364.

68 Sicherman, *Well-Read Lives*, p. 209.

69 *Ibid.*, p. 198.

70 Rose Cohen, *Out of the Shadow: A Russian Jewish Girlhood on the Lower East Side* (Ithaca, NY: Cornell University Press, 1995 [1918]).

71 Harris, *Dublin's Little Jerusalem*, p.ix.

72 Grade, *Still Dancing*, p. 23.

73 See census entry for the Weintrop (or Weintrob) family for 12 Hanbury Street,

Spitalfields, 1891, accessed at the National Archives, 18 July 2009.

74 Bernard Gainer, *The Alien Invasion: The Origins of the Aliens Act of 1905* (London: Heinemann, 1972).

75 David Feldman, 'The Importance of being English: Jewish Immigration and the Decay of Liberal England', in David Feldman and Gareth Stedman Jones (eds), *Metropolis – London: Histories and Representations since 1800* (London: Routledge, 1989).

76 Howard Jacobson, *Roots Schmoots: Journeys Among Jews* (London: Penguin, 1993), p. 2.

77 Even so, and while covering a broad chronology, Kerby Miller's classic *Emigrants and Exiles: Ireland and the Irish Exodus to North America* (New York: Oxford University Press, 1985) is based on 'over 5,000 emigrants' letters and memoirs' (p. 4).

78 Peter Gray, 'Memory and the commemoration of the Great Irish Famine', in Peter Gray and Kendrick Oliver (eds), *The Memory of Catastrophe* (Manchester: Manchester University Press, 2004), p. 49.

79 Thomas Flanagan, 'Critical Introduction: Rebellion and Style: John Mitchel and the Jail Journal', in John Mitchel, *Jail Journal* (Dublin: University Press of Ireland, 1982), p. vii.

80 For a subtle analysis of Mitchel's key writings in the 1850s and the famine see Christopher Morash, *Writing the Irish Famine* (Oxford: Oxford University Press, 1995), Chapter 3.

81 See Edward Laxton, *The Famine Ships: The Irish Exodus to America 1846–1851* (London: Bloomsbury, 1997), pp. 102–3.

82 Diary entry, 12 September 1849 in Mitchel, *Jail Journal*, p. 170.

83 Morash, *Writing the Irish Famine*, p. 61.

84 Flanagan, 'Critical Introduction', p. ix.

85 Diary entry 1 June 1848, in Mitchel, *Jail Journal*, p. 15.

86 Diary entry, 26 April 1949 in Mitchel, *Jail Journal*, p. 242.

87 Diary entry, 20 July 1849 in Mitchel, *Jail Journal*, pp. 153–4.

88 Diary entry, 16 January 1849 in Mitchel, *Jail Journal*, p. 87.

89 Stephen de Vere, letter, 30 November 1847 in Parliamentary Papers 1847/48 (415) 'First Report from the Select Committee of the House of Lords on Colonization from Ireland', p. 45. The letter was originally written to Lord Monteagle in the Colonial Office. See National Archives CO 384/79 for the letter and correspondence relating to it.

90 'First Report of the Select Committee', questioning of T.F. Elliot, p. 44.

91 Oliver MacDonagh, 'The regulation of emigrant traffic from the United Kingdom', *Irish Historical Studies* vol. 9 no. 34 (1954), p. 169.

92 Vere Foster, *Work and Wages, or, the Penny Emigrant's Guide* (London: W.F. Cash, 1855 [fifth edition]), p. 1.

93 The letter and diary was initially sent to his cousin, Lord Hobart, at the Colonial Office. See National Archives CO 384/88. It was then published in House of Commons papers, 1851 (198) XL.433.

94 *Ibid.*

95 Vere Foster to the Colonial Office, 6 November 1851 in National Archives CO 384/88.

96 Robert Whyte, *The Ocean Plague: A Voyage to Quebec in an Irish Emigrant Vessel* (Boston: Coolidge and Wiley, 1848), p. 3.

97 *Ibid.*, p. 2.

98 In a speech on St Patrick's Day in 1848, Thomas D'Arcy McGee referred to the famine ships as 'sailing coffins' and they soon became known as 'coffin ships'. See Fitzgerald and Lambkin, *Migration in Irish History*, p. 173.

99 Whyte, *The Ocean Plague*, diary entry 4 June 1847, p. xx.

100 *Ibid.*

101 Diary entry, 15 June 1847, p. 30.

102 Marcus Rediker, *The Slave Ship: A Human History* (New York: Penguin, 2007), p. 38.

103 Whyte, *The Ocean Plague*, diary entry 28 July 1847.

104 *Ibid.*, p. 12, 13, 109–10.

105 William Smith, *An Emigrant's Narrative, or a Voice from the Steerage* (New York: William Smith, 1850), p. 8.

106 *Ibid.*, pp. 12, 24.

107 *Ibid.*, p. 27.

108 *Ibid.*, p. 28.

109 *Ibid.*, p. 34.

110 John Denvir, *The Irish in Britain from the Earliest Times to the Fall and Death of Parnell* (London: Kegan, Paul, Trench and Trubner, 1892), p. 120.

111 Jim Rees, *A Farewell to Famine* (Arklow: Arklow Enterprise Centre, 1994), p. 11.

112 See, for example, 'The Depopulation of Ireland', *The Illustrated London News*, 10 May 1851.

113 Graham Davis, 'The Historiography of the Irish Famine', in Patrick O'Sullivan (ed.), *The Irish World Wide: History, Heritage, Identity* vol. 6 *The Meaning of the Famine* (Leicester: Leicester University Press, 1997), p. 36.

114 National Archives, HO 45/2428, 'Riot on Board Irish Passenger Vessel'. See also *Londonderry Journal*, 6 December 1848.

115 Neil, *Black '47*, p. 74.

116 Davis, 'The Historiography of the Irish Famine', p. 17.

117 *Ibid.*, p. 21.

118 *Ibid.*, p. 25.

119 Miller, *Emigrants and Exiles*, p. 293.

120 Brenda Collins, 'The Origins of Irish Immigration to Scotland in the Nineteenth and Twentieth Centuries' in Tom Devine (ed.), *Irish Immigrants and Scottish Society in the Nineteenth and Twentieth Centuries* (Edinburgh: John Donald, 1991), p. 9.

121 James Mangan, *Gerald Keegan's Famine Diary: Journey to a New World* (Dublin: Wolfhound Press, 1991).

122 Jason King, 'Famine Diaries? Narratives about Emigration from Ireland to Lower Canada and Quebec, 1832–1853' (unpublished M.A. thesis, McGill University, Canada, 1994), Chapters 1 and 2; Jim Jackson, 'Famine Diary: The Making of a Best

Sellar', *Irish Review* vol. 11 no. 1 (November 1991), pp. 1–8.

123 See, for example, Laxton, *The Famine Ships*, pp. 57–8.

124 Gray, *The Irish Famine*, p. 107.

125 MacDonagh, 'The regulation of the emigrant traffic', p. 169.

126 'The *Jeanie Johnston*: The Story of a Proud Irish Emigrant Ship' (Blennerville: The Jeanie Johnston Company, no date). The replica ship has its permanent home in Dublin but sails across the world. On a tour of the ship, the guide emphasised that its story went from a 'sad story' – that is the famine – to a happy one, that of the settlement and success of the Irish in America. Tony Kushner, site visit, Dublin, 20 November 2010.

127 See Fitzgerald and Lambkin, *Migration in Irish History*, p. 165 for comment that 'replica ships of this period, such as the *Jeanie Johnston*, are assumed erroneously to be "coffin ships"'.

128 Miller, *Emigrants and Exiles*, pp. 3, 6.

129 Cathal Poirteir (ed.), *Famine Echoes* (Dublin: Gill & Macmillan, 1995), pp. 246, 252.

130 Miller, *Emigrants and Exiles*, *passim*.

131 Bergland, 'Rereading Photographs and Narratives', p. 55.

132 Colin Holmes, *John Bull's Island: Immigration and British Society, 1871–1971* (Basingstoke: Macmillan, 1988), p. 21.

133 James Fergusson to Robert Giffen, Board of Trade, 13 March 1891 in National Archives, CAB 37/30/31.

134 Report on Immigration, April 1892, in National Archives, FO 37/31/8.

135 See Robert Colls, *Identity of England* (Oxford: Oxford University Press, 2002), p. 239.

136 H.J. Mackinder, *Britain and the British Seas* (London: William Heinemann, 1902), p. 178.

137 *Ibid.*, p. 181.

138 *Ibid.*, p. 191.

139 *Ibid.*, p. 358.

140 See Ken Lunn and Ann Day, 'Britain as Island: National Identity and the Sea', in Helen Brocklehurst and Robert Phillips (eds), *History, Nationhood and the Question of Britain* (Basingstoke: Palgrave Macmillan, 2004), pp. 129–33.

141 See, for example, Geoffrey Green, *The Royal Navy and Anglo-Jewry 1740–1820* (London: Geoffrey Green, 1989); Marika Sherwood, 'Black Seamen in the Royal Navy', *Black and Asian Studies Association Newsletter* no. 13 (October 1997), pp. 13–36.

142 Marika Sherwood, 'And Again: More on the Royal Navy', *Black and Asian Studies Association Newsletter* no. 39 (April 2004), p. 22.

143 Marcus Wood, *Blind Memory: Visual representations of slavery in England and America 1780–1865* (Manchester: Manchester University Press, 2000), p. 17.

144 Alan Rice, 'Exploring Inside the Invisible: An Interview with Lubaina Himid', *Wasafiri* no. 40 (Winter 2003), pp. 23, 24.

145 *Ibid.*, p. 24.

146 'Dicky Sam', *Liverpool and Slavery: An Historical Account of the Liverpool-African Slave Trade* (Liverpool: Bowker & Son, 1884), p. 4.

147 See, however, Ramsay Muir, *A History of Liverpool* (London: University of Liverpool Press, 1907), Chapter 12, 'The Slave Trade, 1709–1807'.

148 Fritz Spiegl, 'Foreword', in 'Dicky Sam', *Liverpool and Slavery* (Liverpool: Scouse Press Centenary Reprint, 1994), p.ii.

149 Paul Gilroy, *The Black Atlantic: Modernity and Double Consciousness* (London: Verso, 1993), p. 4.

150 Wood, *Blind Memory*, pp. 14, 17.

151 'Dicky Sam', *Liverpool and Slavery*, p. 31.

152 Wood, *Blind Memory*, pp. 19,33.

153 See English Heritage, 'Sites of Memory: The Slave Trade and Abolition' (English Heritage leaflet, no date) for some examples.

154 Fred D'Aguiar, 'At the Grave of the Unknown African', in Fred D'Aguiar, *British Subjects* (Newcastle: Bloodaxe Books, 1993), pp. 21–3.

155 *Ibid.*, pp. 26–7, 36.

156 John Oldfield, *'Chords of Freedom'. Commemoration, ritual and British transatlantic slavery* (Manchester: Manchester University Press, 2007), p. 2.

157 Author site visit, 13 August 2009.

158 Wood, *Blind Memory*, pp. 23–4.

159 See Ian Baucom, *Spectors of the Atlantic: Finance Capital, Slavery, and the Philosophy of History* (Durham, NC: Duke University Press, 2005).

160 Wood, *Blind Slavery*, pp. 45, 55.

161 Oldfield, *'Chords of Freedom'*, p. 102.

162 John Oldfield, 'Introduction: imagining transatlantic slavery and abolition', *Patterns of Prejudice* vol. 41 nos 3–4 (2007), p. 239.

163 National Archives, HO 215/211, report of Military Liason Office, 13 March 1941.

164 Broadcast translation in NA FO 371/61822 E7699.

165 Thus in the world of heritage, the popular drama series, 'Garrow's Law', which constructs the legal world of late eighteenth-century England, had an episode devoted to a court case closely modelled on the notorious case of the *Zong*. BBC1, 14 November 2010.

166 bell hooks, 'Representing Whiteness', in Lawrence Grossberg, Cary Nelson and Paula Treichler (eds), *Cultural Studies* (New York: Routledge, 1992), p. 343.

167 James Clifford, 'Traveling Cultures', in James Clifford, *Travel and Translation in the Late Twentieth Century* (Cambridge, MA: Harvard University Press, 1997) p. 39.

168 hooks, 'Representing Whiteness', p. 343.

169 Jeremy Leigh, *Jewish Journeys* (London: Haus Publishing, 2006), cover and pp. 68–9.

170 Shabnam Grewal, Jackie Kay, Liliane Landor, Gail Lewis and Pratibha Parmar (eds), *Charting the Journey: Writings by Black and Third World Women* (London: Sheba Feminist Publishers, 1988), p. 2.

171 Ziauddin Sardar, *Balti Britain: A Provocative Journey Through Asian Britain* (London: Granta, 2009 [2008]), p. 7.

172 Sukdev Sandhu, *London Calling: How Black and Asian Writers Imagined a City* (London: HarperCollins, 2003), p. 295.

173 Raphael Samuel, *Island Stories: Unravelling Britain* (London: Verso, 1998), pp. 16–17.

174 James Young, *The Texture of Memory: Holocaust Memorials and Meaning* (New Haven, CT: Yale University Press, 1993), pp. x–xi.

175 Rediker, *The Slave Ship*, p. 10.

176 Samuel, *Island Stories*, pp. 16–7.

177 *Ibid., passim.*

Notes to Chapter 3

1 Albert Vajda, *Remade in England: From Her Majesty's Alien to Her Majesty's British Subject* (Edinburgh: Polygon Books, 1981), pp. 9, 11.

2 On the reception camps for the Hungarian refugees, see National Archives, HO 352/141–9.

3 Vajda, *Remade in England*, pp. 13, 18.

4 *Ibid.*, pp. 13, 18.

5 Mr K. Paice to Sir A. Hutchinson, 6 November 1956, National Archives HO 352/141.

6 Tony Kushner and Katharine Knox, *Refugees in an Age of Genocide: Global, National and Local Perspectives during the Twentieth Century* (London: Frank Cass, 1999), Chapter 8.

7 Nushin Arbabzadah (ed.), *From Outside In: Refugees and British Society* (London: Arcadia Books, 2007), p. 18.

8 *News Chronicle*, 9 November 1956.

9 Kushner and Knox, *Refugees in an Age of Genocide*, p. 248.

10 The short film was made possible by a grant from the British Film Institute Experimental Film Fund and was shown at the National Film Theatre as part of the 'Free Cinema 6' series in March 1959. It is available on DVD as part of the British Film Institute, *Free Cinema* (BFI, no date).

11 See Tony Kushner, *Remembering Refugees: Then and Now* (Manchester University Press, 2006), pp. 63–70.

12 *Ibid.*

13 Home Office, *Fairer, Faster and Firmer. A Modern Approach to Immigration and Asylum* (London: HMSO, 1998), p. 35.

14 On Victor Hugo, see the section 'Prominent Refugees – Refugees Who Have Made a Difference' on the UNHCR website, www.unhcr.org/pages/49c3646c74-page7. html, accessed 14 July 2009.

15 Hannah Arendt, 'We Refugees', in Jerome Kohn and Ron Feldman (eds), *The Jewish Writings: Hannah Arendt* (New York: Schocken Books, 2007), p. 264, originally published in *Menorah Journal*, January 1943.

16 Noel Currer-Briggs and Royston Gambier, *Huguenot Ancestry* (Chichester:

Phillimore, 1985), p. x.

17 Ruth Whelan, 'Writing the Self: Huguenot Autobiography and the Process of Assimilation', in Randolph Vigne and Charles Littleton (eds), *From Strangers to Citizens: The Integration of Immigrant Communities in Britain, Ireland and Colonial America, 1550–1750* (Brighton: Sussex University Press, 2001), p. 463.

18 *Ibid.*

19 Linda Colley, 'Britishness and Otherness: An Argument', *Journal of British Studies* vol. 31 (October 1992), p. 320.

20 Preface to John [Jean] Migault, *A Narrative of the Sufferings of A French Protestant Family at the Period of the Revocation of the Edict of Nantes* (London: John Butterworth, 1824), p. xiii.

21 Patrick Wright, *On Living in an Old Country: the National Past in Contemporary Britain* (London: Verso, 1985).

22 Bernard Cottret, *The Huguenots in England: Immigration and Settlement c. 1550–1700* (Cambridge: Cambridge University Press, 1991), p. 191.

23 Graham Macklin, '"A quite natural and moderate defensive feeling?" The 1945 Hampstead "anti-alien" petition', *Patterns of Prejudice* vol. 37 no. 3 (2003), pp. 277–300.

24 Ed Miliband speech, Labour Party conference, 28 September 2010, www.bbc.co.uk/news/uk-politics-1142611?print=true, accessed 30 September 2010.

25 Michael Howard, advertisement on immigration in *Sunday Telegraph*, 23 January 2005.

26 Michael Howard, speech at Conservative Party annual conference, 5 October 2004, http://politics.guardian.co.uk/conservatives2004/story/0,15018,1320222,00.html, accessed 18 November 2004.

27 Refugee Council press release, 28 September 2010, www.refugeecouncil.org.uk/news/archive/press/2010/september/280910_pressr, accessed 1 October 2010.

28 Tony Blair, *A Journey* (London: Hutchinson, 2010), pp. 204–5.

29 See National Archives, Ho 405/20669 for the irregularities in the information by Michael Howard's father, Bernat Hecht. More generally, see Michael Crick, *In Search of Michael Howard* (London: Simon & Schuster, 2005), Chapter 1.

30 Migault, *A Narrative of the Sufferings*, p. xvii.

31 The lower figure is provided by Anne Kershen, *Strangers, Aliens and Asians: Huguenots, Jews and Bangladeshis in Spitalfields, 1660–2000* (London: Routledge, 2005), p. 37.

32 Raymond Mentzer and Andrew Spicer, 'Epilogue', in Raymond Mentzer and Andrew Spicer (eds), *Society and Culture in the Huguenot World 1559–1685* (Cambridge: Cambridge University Press, 2002), p. 227.

33 Jean Marteilhe, *The Huguenot Galley-Slave: Being the Autobiography of a French Protestant Condemned to the Galley for the Sake of His Religion* (New York: Leypoldt & Holt, 1867), p. 158. This account was originally published in Holland in 1757 and translated into English the following year.

34 Susanne Lachenicht, 'Huguenot Immigrants and the Formation of National Identities, 1548–1787', *The Historical Journal* vol. 50 no. 2 (2007), p. 326.

35 Sermon reproduced in Cottret, *The Huguenots in England*, p. 8.

36 *Ibid.*, p. 267.

37 Jeremy Leigh, *Jewish Journeys* (London: Haus Publishing, 2006), p. 69.

38 Yosef Yerushalmi, *Zakhor: Jewish History and Jewish Memory* (New York: Schocken Books, 1989), p. xxxiv.

39 Carolyn Lougee Chappell, 'What's in a name?: self-identification of Huguenot *réfugiées* in 18th-century England', in Vigne and Littleton (eds), *From Strangers to Citizens*, p. 539.

40 Carolyn Lougee Chappell, '"The Pains I Took to Save My/His Family": Escape Accounts by a Huguenot Daughter after the Revocation of the Edict of Nantes', *French Historical Studies* vol. 22 no. 1 (Winter 1999), pp. 1–2.

41 The account is reproduced in French and English translation in Chappell, '"The Pains I Took"', Appendix A1 and A2.

42 *Ibid.*, pp. 43–4.

43 *Ibid.*, p. 44.

44 Dianne Ressinger (ed.), *Memoirs of Isaac Dumont de Bostaquet: A Gentleman of Normandy* (London: Huguenot Society of Great Britain and Ireland, 2005), p. 169.

45 *Ibid.*, p. 11.

46 *Ibid.*, p. 13.

47 William Minet, *The Huguenot Family of Minet* (London: Spottiswoode & Co, 1892), p. 7.

48 *Ibid.*, p. 24.

49 *Ibid.*, p. 24.

50 *Ibid.*, p. 32.

51 *Ibid.*, p. 34.

52 *Ibid.*, p. 34.

53 Dover Museum, Permanent Exhibition, has a reproduction of the Minet coat of arms. Author visit, 8 July 2011.

54 Minet, *The Huguenot Family of Minet*, pp. x–xii.

55 The tombstone transcription and a monument to the Minet family in the same church are available at www.kentarchaeology.org.uk/Research/Libr/MIs/MIsDoverStMarys/01.htm, accessed 9 July 2011.

56 Derek Watts, 'Testimonies of Persecution: Four Huguenot Refugees and their Memoirs', in J.H. Fox, M.H. Waddicor and D.A. Watts (eds), *Studies in Eighteenth-Century French Literature Presented to Robert Niklaus* (Exeter: Exeter University Press, 1975), p. 321.

57 Migault, *A Narrative of the Sufferings*, p. 136.

58 *Ibid.*; Watts, 'Testimonies of Persecution', p. 331 note 4.

59 'Introduction' in Dianne Ressinger (ed.), *Memoirs of the Reverend Jaques Fontaine 1658–1728* (London: Huguenot Society of Great Britain and Ireland, 1992), pp. 18–19.

60 Chappell, '"The Pains I Took"', p. 3.

61 *Ibid.*, p. 19 and similarly Robin Gwynn, *Huguenot Heritage: The History and Contribution of the Huguenots in Britain* (London: Routledge, 1985), pp. 92–4. For more detailed close readings of this memoir, see Dianne Ressinger, 'Good faith: the

military and the ministry in exile, or the memoirs of Isaac Dumont de Bostaquet and Jaques Fontaine', in Vigne and Littleton (eds), *From Strangers to Citizens*, pp. 451–62 and Derek Watts, 'Testimonies of Persecution', pp. 319–33.

62 Ressinger (ed.), *Memoirs of the Reverend Jaques Fontaine*, p. 111.

63 *Ibid.*, p. 113.

64 *Ibid.*, p. 119.

65 *Ibid.*, p. 120.

66 *Ibid.*, pp. 121, 122.

67 *Ibid.*, p. 123.

68 For his loyalty to the British cause in Ireland see National Archives, SP 41/5/149, letter from Lord Galloway, 20 April 1719.

69 Samuel Smiles, *The Huguenots: Their Settlement, Churches, and Industries in England and Ireland* (second edition: London: John Murray, 1868 [1867]).

70 Gwynn, *Huguenot Heritage*, p. 93.

71 Ressinger, *Memoirs of the Reverend Jaques Fontaine*, p. 11.

72 *Ibid.*, p. 5, comments by Randolph Vigne, Huguenot Society.

73 Raphael Samuel and Paul Thompson, 'Introduction', in Samuel and Thompson, *The Myths We Live By* (London: Routledge, 1990), p. 10.

74 Gallway to Sunderland, November 1708, in National Archives, SP 89/20.

75 For a sober analysis of the Huguenot impact on the paper industry which does not exaggerate its significance, see D.C. Coleman, *The British Paper Industry 1495–1860: A Study in Industrial Growth* (Oxford: Clarendon Press, 1958), Chapter 3.

76 A. Stirling (ed.), *The Diaries of Dummer: Reminiscences of an Old Sportsman, Stephen Terry of Dummer* (London: Unicorn Press, 1934), p. 125.

77 Smiles, *The Huguenots*, p. 333.

78 Stirling, *The Diaries of Dummer*, p. 125.

79 Pierre de Portal, *Les Descendants des Albogeois et des Huguenots, ou Memoires de la Famille de Portal* (Paris: Ch. Meyrueis et Cie, 1860). The English Portals clearly valued their deep aristocratic origins in the French past and Henry Portal's papers include ancient documents and recent histories of his family. See Hampshire Record Office, Portal papers, 5M52 F1 and F4.

80 Sir William Portal, *Some Account of the Settlement of Refugees (L'EgliseWallone) at Southampton* (Winchester: Jacob and Johnson, 1902).

81 Andrew Spicer, *The French-speaking Reformed Community and their Church in Southampton 1567–1620* (London: Huguenot Society of Great Britain and Ireland, 1997).

82 Portal, *Some Account of the Settlement of Refugees*.

83 Lachenicht, *Huguenot Immigrants*, p. 327.

84 See Charles Marmoy, 'The Historical Novel and the Huguenots', *Proceedings of the Huguenot Society of London* vol. 23 no. 2 (1978), pp. 69–78.

85 *Ibid.*, pp. 327–8.

86 Robert Liberles, 'Postemancipation Historiography and the Jewish Historical Societies of America and England', in Jonathan Frankel (ed.), *Reshaping the Past: Jewish History and the Historians* vol. 10 *Studies in Contemporary Jewry* (New York:

Oxford University Press, 1994), pp. 45–65.

87 Smiles, *The Huguenots*, p. 185.

88 *Ibid.*, p. 191.

89 Charles Weiss, *History of the French Protestant Refugees, from the Revocation of the Edict of Nantes to Our Own Days* (New York: Stringer & Townsend, 1854), p. 110.

90 *Ibid.*

91 Marteilhe, *The Huguenot Galley-Slave*, p. x; Smiles, *The Huguenots*, p. 201.

92 Smiles, *The Huguenots*, p. 201.

93 The play was first performed at the National Theatre on 4 February 2009. For the script, see Richard Bean, *England People Very Nice* (London: Oberon Books, 2009), p. 19.

94 Worshipful Company of Goldsmiths, *The Courtauld Family: Huguenot Silversmiths* (London: Worshipful Company of Goldsmiths, 1985), introduction, no page.

95 Townsman, 'The Mills of Southampton', *Southern Daily Echo*, 29 July 1939.

96 His naturalisation certificate is in Hampshire Record Office, Portal papers, 5M52 F3.

97 Elsie Sandell, *Southampton Through the Ages: A Short History* (Southampton: G.F. Wilson, 1960), p. 93.

98 Elsie Sandell, *Southampton Cavalcade* (Southampton: G.F. Wilson, 1953), p. 137.

99 Robert Wood, *Walks into History: Hampshire* (Newbury: Countryside Books, 2009), pp. 6, 50.

100 Lachenicht, 'Huguenot Immigrants', p. 330.

101 Robin Gwynn, 'Patterns in the Study of Huguenot Refugees in Britain: Past, Present and Future', in Irene Scouloudi (ed.), *Huguenots in Britain and their French Background, 1550–1800* (Basingstoke: Macmillan, 1987), pp. 220, 224.

102 Ziauddin Sardar, *Balti Britain: A Provocative Journey through Asian Britain* (London: Granta, 2008), p. 248 and Chapter 9 *passim*.

103 Robin Gwynn, *Huguenot Heritage: The history and contribution of the Huguenots in Britain* (second edition. Brighton: Sussex Academic Press, 2001), p. xii.

104 Mayerlene Frow, *Roots of the Future: Ethnic Diversity in the Making of Britain* (London: Commission for Racial Equality, 1996), pp. 13–14.

105 'Galleries of Modern London', Museum of London, visit by author, 14 July 2010.

106 Max Hebditch, foreword to Tessa Murdoch (ed.), *The Quiet Conquest: The Huguenots, 1685 to 1985* (London: Museum of London, 1985), no page. The exhibition took place from 15 May to 31 October 1985.

107 Prince Charles, 'Foreword', in Vigne and Littleton, *From Strangers to Citizens*, p. xix.

108 Robert Winder, *Bloody Foreigners: The Story of Immigration to Britain* (London: Little, Brown, 2004), pp. 60–2.

109 Coleman, *The British Paper Industry*, pp. 68, 79–80.

110 'Townsman', *Southern Daily Echo*, 29 July 1939.

111 Minet, *The Huguenot Family of Minet*, pp. 21, 24. For a more problematic version of the family's connection to Dover, see Minet v Dover (1730) in National Archives, C11/2428/46.

112 Kershen, *Strangers, Aliens and Asians*, p. 11.
113 *Ibid.*, p. 36.
114 Isaac Minet narrative, 1737, reproduced in Minet, *The Huguenot Family of Minet*, p. 24.
115 *Ibid.*, pp. 6, 74–5.
116 Chappell, "'The Pains I Took'", p. 16 who criticises such tendencies within the work of scholars such as Jon Butler and Gregory Hanlon.
117 Kershen, *Strangers, Aliens and Asians*, p. 35.
118 William Cunningham, *Alien Immigrants to England* (London: Swan Sonnenshein, 1897).
119 *Ibid.*, p. 249.
120 *Ibid.*, pp. 264, 266.
121 *Ibid.*, p. 267.
122 Royal Commission on Alien Immigration, *Report* (London: HMSO, 1903), pp. 2–3.
123 See, for example, William Evans Gordon, *The Alien Immigrant* (London: Heinemann, 1903), pp. 6–8.
124 *Hansard* (HC) vol. 148 col. 795, 3 July 1905, comments by Gibson Boules, MP for Lyme Regis.
125 Dorothy Buxton, *The Economics of the Refugee Problem* (London: Focus, 1939), pp. 24, 27.
126 Anthony Browne, *Do We Need Mass Immigration?* (London: Civitas, 2002), p. 27.
127 A. Temple Patterson, *A History of Southampton 1700–1914* vol. 1 (Southampton: Southampton University Press, 1966), p. 10.
128 Robin Gwynn, 'Huguenots and Walloons in Dorset, Hampshire and Wiltshire', *Hatcher Review* vol. 2 (1984), pp. 365–6; 'Church Meeting, 13 March 1711/12' in Edwin Welsh (ed.), *The Minute Book of the French Church at Southampton 1702–1939* (Southampton: University of Southampton Press, 1979), pp. 52–3.

Notes to Chapter 4

1 *Southampton Times*, 13 December 1879.
2 A. Temple Patterson, *A History of Southampton*, 3 vols (Southampton: University of Southampton Press, 1975), vol. 3 *Setbacks and Recoveries, 1868–1914*, pp. 64–70.
3 *Southampton Times*, 13 December 1879.
4 *Hampshire Advertiser*, 13 December 1879.
5 *Southampton Times*, 20 December 1879.
6 Description by a Mr Dixon, a local ship designer, who first befriended them, reported in *Southampton Times*, 13 December 1879.
7 *Hampshire Advertiser*, 21 January 1880.
8 Richard Bean, *England People Very Nice* (London: Oberon Books, 2009), p. 17.
9 *Hampshire Independent*, 20 December 1879.

10 In Southampton Record Office, SC/AG 14/15. Thanks are due to my colleague, Dr James Jordan, for originally coming across this entry in the catalogue of the record office.

11 Details of their origins given to Local Government Board by the Mayor of Southampton, reported in *Southampton Times*, 20 December 1879.

12 See Karl Stumpp, *The German-Russians: Two Centuries of Pioneering* (Bonn: Edition Atlantic-Forum, 1971) and his *The Emigration from Germany to Russia in the Years 1763 to 1862* (Lincoln, NE: American Historical Society of Germans from Russia, 1973–78) for general accounts of this movement and, from a more specific and critical historical perspective, Fred Koch, *The Volga Germans in Russia and the Americas, from 1763 to the Present* (University Park, Pennsylvania, PA: Pennsylvania State University Press, 1977), Chapter 1; James Long, *From Privileged to Dispossessed: The Volga Germans, 1860–1917* (Lincoln, NE: University of Nebraska Press, 1988), pp. 87–102 on the early settlement and economics of the Samara Province.

13 Edith Frankel, 'Introduction', in Ingeborg Fleischhauer and Benjamin Pinkus (eds), *The Soviet Germans: Past and Present* (London: C. Hurst, 1986), p. 2.

14 Ingeborg Fleischhauer, 'The Germans' Role in Tsarist Russia: A Reappraisal', in Fleischhauer and Pinkus (eds), *The Soviet Germans*, pp. 19, 20.

15 Long, *From Privileged to Disposed*, p. xii.

16 This complexity partly explains, although it does not of course justify, some of the exasperation that these migrants confronted from local and national bureaucrats, politicians, media and public.

17 Thus in the preface to Karl Stumpp's, *The Emigration from Germany*, p. 7, Professor Dr Kunzig argues that the author's work was of 'especial significance even today, not only for the history of the local and ancestral origins of the emigrant people but also for the former colonists who are scattered today in many parts of the world'.

18 Long, *From Privileged to Dispossessed*, p. 33.

19 On Russification and ethnic/national/religious groupings within the empire, see Geoffrey Hosking, *Russia and the Russians: A History from Rus to the Russian Federation* (London: Allen Lane, 2001), pp. 333–44; Andreas Kappeler, *The Russian Empire* (Harlow: Pearson Education, 2001), Chapter 7; and Theodore Weeks, 'Managing Empire: tsarist nationalities policy' in Dominic Lieven (ed.), *The Cambridge History of Russia* vol. II *Imperial Russia, 1689–1917* (Cambridge: Cambridge University Press, 2006), pp. 27–44.

20 This was the figure given by F.C. Ford, British Minister in Rio to the Marquis of Salisbury, quoted in an editorial of *Southampton Times*, 7 February 1880. There are no definitive figures for the total number of 'Volga Germans' who went to Brazil. Koch, *The Volga Germans*, p. 226 rejects as 'somewhat incomprehensible', the estimate of 250,000 as late as 1940. The figure was probably one fifth of that total.

21 T. Lynn Smith, *Brazil: People and Institutions* (Baton Rouge, LA: Louisiana State University Press, 1963), p. 407.

22 *Ibid.*, pp. 407–8, 410.

23 Frederick Luebke, *Germans in Brazil: A Comparative History of Cultural Conflict During World War 1* (Baton Rouge, LA: Louisiana State University Press, 1987), p. 10.

24 *Ibid.*, p. 24.
25 A copy of the letter is in National Archives, FO 181/595. It is partly quoted by the Mayor of Southampton to the Local Government Board quoted in *Southampton Times*, 20 December 1879.
26 *Southampton Times*, 7 February 1880.
27 Letter signed by the 'Volga Germans', 9 February 1880 in Southampton Record Office, SC/AG 14/15.
28 Quoted in *Southampton Times*, 7 February 1880.
29 Luebke, *Germans in Brazil*, p. 11.
30 See the statement of the Mayor of Southampton to John Lambert of the Local Government Board, 13 December 1879 in National Archives, FO 181/595.
31 Smith, *Brazil*, p. 410.
32 *Ibid.*, p. 408.
33 *Hampshire Independent*, 4 February 1880.
34 Koch, *The Volga Germans*, p. 228; Smith, *Brazil*, p. 408.
35 *Southampton Observer*, 7 February 1880.
36 Letter from the emigrants to the people of Southampton, 5 January 1880 in National Archives FO 181/595.
37 Mr Cooksey, JP and Councillor, quoted in *Southampton Times*, 13 December 1879.
38 *Hampshire Independent*, 10 January 1880.
39 More generally on these issues, see Tony Kushner and Katharine Knox, *Refugees in an Age of Genocide: Global, National and Local Perspectives during the Twentieth Century* (London: Frank Cass, 1999).
40 M. Bartholomei to the Foreign Secretary, 20 December 1879 in Southampton Record Office SC/AG 14/15.
41 *Ibid.*
42 Bartholomei to Salisbury, 17 December 1879, in National Archives FO 181/595.
43 Bartholomei to Salisbury, 26 December 1879, in *ibid.*
44 The diplomatic correspondence can be followed in *ibid.*
45 See the letter of John Lambert of the Local Government Board to the Foreign Office, 7 January 1880, in *ibid.*
46 See the correspondence in Southampton Record Office SC/AG 14/15 for January 1880. See also correspondence in National Archives FO 181/595 and 634 and FO 183/15.
47 See *Southampton Times*, 20 December 1879 for an account of Lungley's career and approval of his suitability to help the Southampton Board of Guardians with these problem people.
48 Mr Lungley, 'Report on Conveying German Russian Immigrants From Southampton to Wir Ballen in Russia', in Southampton Record Office SC/AG 14/15 (hereafter 'Lungley Report'). The report is partially reproduced in *Southampton Times*, 6 March 1880.
49 *Southampton Times*, 13 December 1879.
50 'Lungley Report'.
51 *Ibid.*

52 There is no mention, for example, of such early facilities in the Hamburg Emigration Museum, situated in Hamburg Auswandererhallen, BallinStadt. Site visit by author, 3 September 2008.

53 'Lungley Report'.

54 *Ibid.*

55 I am grateful to Tobias Brinkmann for this information on Rheinbek's important place in migration history.

56 'Lungley Report'.

57 *Ibid.*

58 *Hampshire Advertiser*, 27 December 1879.

59 Editorial in *Southampton Times*, 7 February 1880.

60 Editorial in *Southampton Times*, 31 January 1880 which refers to them simply as 'Russian immigrants'. A letter from a 'Ratepayer' published in the same paper, 10 January 1880 labelled them as 'foreigners' who should be got rid of, claiming that they were wealthier than they had made out. A similar letter from a Mr Pearce appeared in the *Hampshire Independent*, 24 December 1879 referring to a 'French lunatic' a few years earlier who had become a charge on the local ratepayers.

61 *Hampshire Independent*, 10 January 1880.

62 Editorial in *Southampton Times*, 31 January 1880.

63 Editorial in *Southampton Times*, 17 January 1880.

64 *Hampshire Advertiser*, 20 December 1879.

65 'District News', *Preston Guardian*, 20 December 1879.

66 'Summary of the Morning's News', *Pall Mall Gazette*, 12 December 1879.

67 *Hampshire Independent*, 17 and 21 January 1880.

68 *Hampshire Advertiser*, 21 January 1880.

69 *Hampshire Advertiser*, 27 December 1880.

70 See, for example, *Hampshire Independent*, 3 and 10 January 1880.

71 *Hampshire Advertiser*, 13 December 1879.

72 For its history as a gaol, before being requisitioned by the Southampton Harbour Board, see Philip Peberdy, *God's House Tower, Southampton* (Southampton: Southampton Museums, 1960).

73 For the use of the old gaol, see *Southampton Times*, 13 December 1879 and letter in same newspaper, 27 December 1879, from a man of German origin, F.E. Fahrig, who tried (unsuccessfully) to visit them there. For Atlantic Hotel and concerns about immigrant health at a local, national and global level, see Tony Kushner, *Anglo-Jewry since 1066: Place, Locality and Memory* (Manchester: Manchester University Press, 2009), Chapter 7.

74 Kushner, *Anglo-Jewry since 1066*, Chapter 7.

75 Report of the delegation in *Southampton Times*, 13 December 1879.

76 More generally, see K. Marchlewicz, 'Continuities and Innovations: Polish Emigration after 1849' in S. Freitag (ed.), *Exiles from European Revolutions: Refugees in Mid-Victorian England* (New York: Berg, 2003), pp. 103–20.

77 The story can be followed in National Archives, HO 45/3720.

78 S. Freitag, 'Introduction' in Freitag(ed.), *Exiles from European Revolutions*, p. 2.

79 General George Ruthgaryn to Sir George Grey, 30 July 1851, in National Archives, HO 45/3720.
80 See correspondence between the Foreign Office and the Mayor of Southampton, R. Andrews, in National Archives, HO 45/3720.
81 For diplomatic tension, see correspondence in National Archives, FO 83/294.
82 Bernard Porter, *The Refugee Question in Mid-Victorian Politics* (Cambridge: Cambridge University Press, 1979), p. 126.
83 *Ibid.*, p. 1.
84 Andrews to Treasury, 2 August 1851 in National Archives, HO 45/3720.
85 See Paul Weindling, *Epidemics and Genocide in Eastern Europe, 1890–1945* (Oxford: Oxford University Press, 2000), pp. 56–70.
86 *The Standard*, 2 January 1906.
87 Lungley at the Southampton Board of Guardians, reported in *Southampton Times*, 6 March 1880.
88 Weindling, *Epidemics and Genocide in Eastern Europe*, chapter 3.
89 On the Jewish case, in which return migration was as much as five times smaller than for other groups, but still between 5 and 10 per cent of those departing from Eastern Europe, see Jonathan Sarna, 'The Myth of "No Return": Jewish Return Migration to Eastern Europe, 1881–1914', *American Jewish History* vol. 71 (1981), pp. 256–68.
90 Koch, *The Volga Germans*, p. 222.
91 Long, *From Privileged to Dispossessed*, Introduction.
92 For the most detailed analysis of this phenomenon, see Nicholas Evans, 'Aliens *En Route*: European Transmigration Through Britain, 1836–1914' (unpublished Ph.D. thesis, University of Hull, 2006).
93 Collective letter of 9 February 1880 in Southampton Record Office SC/AG 14/15.
94 Smith, *Brazil*, pp. 12–13.
95 Andreas Kappeler, 'The Ambiguities of Russification', *Kritika: Explorations in Russian and Eurasian History* vol. 5 no. 2 (2004), pp. 291–7.
96 Long, *From Privileged to Dispossessed*, p. 246.
97 Letter of 9 February 1880 in Southampton Record Office SC/AG 14/15.
98 Telegram from Dufferin to Salisbury, 28 January 1880 in National Archives FO 181/601.
99 Stumpp, *The German-Russians*, p. 15.
100 Kushner, *Anglo-Jewry since 1066*, Chapter 7.
101 On the death in the local workhouse of a young girl of consumption, see *Southampton Times*, 20 December 1879. The father of the child expressed gratitude at the treatment she had received and the generosity of the English people. See *Southampton Observer*, 20 December 1879. On the birth, also in the workhouse, see *Southampton Times*, 13 December 1879.
102 J. Aston Whitlock, *The Hospital of God's House Southampton* (Southampton: Henry March Gilbert, 1894), p. 50.
103 *Ibid.*, p. 56.
104 *Hampshire Independent*, 3 January 1880.

105 Whitlock, *The Hospital of God's House*, p. 50.

106 *Ibid.*, pp. 57–8.

107 Mary Douglas, *Purity and Danger: An Analysis of the Concepts of Pollution and Taboo* (London: Routledge, 1996 [1966]), p. 41 and utilising this concept with regard to refugees, Liisa Malkki, 'National Geographic: The Rooting of Peoples and the Territorialization of National Identity among Scholars and Refugees', *Cultural Anthropology* vol. 7 no. 1 (1992), p. 34.

108 Evans, 'Aliens *En Route*', p. 108.

Notes to Chapter 5

1 William Shaun (ed.), *Mollie Panter-Downes: London War Notes 1939–1945* (London: Longman, 1972).

2 Mollie Panter-Downes, 'Amid the Alien Corn', *New Yorker*, 15 July 1939.

3 Nicola Beauman in *Guardian*, 31 January 1997.

4 Anthony Bailey in *The Independent*, 3 February 1997.

5 Obituary in *The Times*, 23 May 2011.

6 'The Love that Pays the Price', *Upstairs Downstairs* (BBC1, 26 February 2012).

7 Panter-Downes, 'Amid the Alien Corn'.

8 *Ibid.*

9 *Ibid.*

10 For some examples of press responses to the first arrivals, see Barry Turner, ... *And the Policeman Smiled. 10,000 Children Escape from Nazi Europe* (London: Bloomsbury, 1990), pp. 52–3.

11 Nicholas Winton, open letter, 4 May 1939 on behalf of the British Committee for Refugees from Czechoslovakia, Winton papers, File 10236, Wiener Library, London.

12 Panter-Downes, 'Amid the Alien Corn'.

13 Quoted by Turner, ... *And the Policeman Smiled*, p. 53. See also her testimony in Bertha Leverton and Shmuel Lowensohn (eds), *I Came Alone: The Stories of the Kindertransports* (Lewes: The Book Guild, 2000 [1990]), pp. 286–9.

14 Richard Breitman and Alan Kraut, *American Refugee Policy and European Jewry, 1933–1945* (Bloomington, IN: Indiana University Press, 1987), pp. 73–4.

15 Panter-Downes, 'Amid the Alien Corn'.

16 *Ibid.*

17 *Ibid.*

18 Earl Granville to Ministers in Vienna, St Petersburg, Paris and Frankfurt, 13 January 1852 in National Archives FO 83/294.

19 *Aliens Act, 1905* (11 August 1905), 5 EDW.7.

20 Sir Edward Troup, *The Home Office* (London: G.P. Putnam& Sons, 1925), p. 143.

21 Letter from Holness to Members of the Immigration Boards, 9 March 1906 in National Archives HO 45/10326/131787/9.

22 Donald Rumbelow, *The Houndsditch Murders & the Siege of Sidney Street* (London:

Penguin Books, 1990) and the exhibition, 'London Under Siege: Churchill and the Anarchists', Museum of London Docklands, December 2010 to April 2011.

23 Clynes to D'Avigdor Goldsmid, 26 February 1929 in London Metropolitan Archives, Board of Deputies of British Jews papers, E3/80.

24 JJRS minute, 18 June 1929 in National Archives HO 382/7.

25 Pedder minute, 18 June 1929 in National Archives HO 382/7.

26 For general policy, see Louise London, *Whitehall and the Jews 1933–1948: British Immigration Policy and the Holocaust* (Cambridge: Cambridge University Press, 2000).

27 See, for example, *Hansard* (HC) vol. 341 cols 1473–4, 21 November 1938.

28 Eagleston report, written in Second World War, in National Archives HO 213/1772.

29 Mr Butcher in *Hansard* (HC) vol. 341 col. 1452, 21 November 1938.

30 Sir Samuel Hoare in *Hansard* (HC) vol. 341 col. 1774, 21 November 1938.

31 See National Archives HO 45/19882/344019 for the Repatriation Committee.

32 See Turner, ... *And the Policeman Smiled*, pp. 90–2.

33 Jennifer Norton, 'The *Kindertransport*: History and Memory', (unpublished M.A. thesis, California State University, 2010), pp. 161–2. See also Doreen Warriner, 'The Winter in Prague', p. 15, Imperial War Museum, Department of Documents and more generally William Chadwick, *The Rescue of the Prague Refugees 1938–39* (Leicester: Matador, 2010). This thoughtful and beautifully constructed study highlights especially the neglected roles of Warriner, Chadwick, and Wellington in contrast to the overstated role of Winton.

34 Chadwick, *The Rescue of the Prague Refugees 1938–39*, p. 136. Susan Cohen is at the early stages of researching the role of women in the rescue of refugees during the Nazi era. See her earlier study, *Rescue the Perishing: Eleanor Rathbone and the Refugees* (London: Vallentine Mitchell, 2010).

35 Memorandum from Schmolka, Steiner and Blake to Skelton, 22 December 1938, in Winton papers, File 10236, Wiener Library, London.

36 See Tony Kushner, *Remembering Refugees: Then and Now* (Manchester: Manchester University Press, 2006), Chapter 4.

37 Elaine Blond with Barry Turner, *Marks of Distinction* (London: Vallentine Mitchell, 1988), p. 73.

38 Primo Levi, *The Drowned and the Saved* (London: Michael Joseph, 1988), Chapter 2.

39 Edith Milton, *The Tiger in the Attic: Memories of the Kindertransport and Growing Up English* (Chicago: University of Chicago Press, 2005).

40 Hugo Gryn, 'A Moral and Spiritual Index', (Refugee Council leaflet, 1996).

41 Milton, *The Tiger in the Attic*, pp. 2, 3.

42 *Ibid.*, p. 14.

43 Testimony in Leverton and Lowensohn (eds), *I Came Alone*, p. 33.

44 *Jewish Chronicle*, 18 June 1999.

45 John Presland [Gladys Bendit], *A Great Adventure: The Story of the Refugee Children's Movement* (London: Refugee Children's Movement, 1944), pp. 5, 16.

46 Mark Harris and Deborah Oppenheimer (eds), *Into the Arms of Strangers. Stories of*

the Kindertransport (London: Bloomsbury, 2000).

47 In Leverton and Lowensohn (eds), *We Came Alone*, p. 33.

48 Norman Angell and Dorothy Buxton, *You and the Refugee* (Harmondsworth: Penguin, 1939), p. 11.

49 Winton open letter, 4 May 1939, in Winton papers, File 10236, Wiener Library, London.

50 Hannele Zurndorfer, *The Ninth of November* (London: Quartet Books, 1989 [1983]), p. 71.

51 *Ibid., passim.*

52 London, *Whitehall and the Jews*, p. 13.

53 Chadwick, *The Rescue of the Prague Refugees*, p. v.

54 Karen Gershon (ed.), *We Came as Children: A Collective Autobiography of Refugees* (London: Papermac, 1989 [1966]), p. 55.

55 *Ibid.*, p. 43.

56 Script reproduced in London, *Whitehall and the Jews*, pp. 118–9.

57 Leslie Baruch Brent, *Sunday's Child? A Memoir* (New Romney: Bank House Books, 2009), p. 40.

58 Zurndorfer, *The Ninth of November*, p. 71.

59 Movement for the Care of Children from Germany, *First Annual Report November 1938 - December 1939* (London: Bloomsbury House, 1940), pp. 7,9.

60 Winton diary, 12 January 1939 in Winton papers, File 10236, Wiener Library, London.

61 See Phyllis Lassner, *Anglo-Jewish Women Writing the Holocaust: Displaced Witnesses* (Basingstoke: Palgrave Macmillan, 2008), Chapter 2.

62 *Jewish Chronicle*, 19 September 2003.

63 Henry Feingold, *The Politics of Rescue: The Roosevelt Administration and the Holocaust, 1938–1945* (New Brunswick, NJ: Rutgers University Press, 1970), pp. 148–53.

64 Vera Fast, *Children's Exodus: A History of the Kindertransport* (London: I.B. Tauris, 2011), p. 193.

65 Author site visit, 15 September 2007.

66 Irene Schmied, 'Fur das Kind, London, September 16th 2003', in Nushin Arbabzadah (ed.), *From Outside In: Refugees and British Society* (London: Arcadia Books, 2007), pp. 40–1.

67 Jenni Frazer, 'Kindertransport sculpture arrives at Liverpool Street', *Jewish Chronicle*, 6 October 2006.

68 The Berlin memorial was unveiled in November 2008 to mark the seventieth anniversary of the *Kindertransport*. See htpp://jta.org/news/article/2008/10/23/110 845/kindertransportmeisler, accessed 28 July 2009.

69 Imperial War Museum Holocaust Exhibition, visited 1 April 2010.

70 Susan Soyinka, *From East End to Land's End* (Derby: Derby Books, 2010), p. 9.

71 Edmund de Waal, *The Hare With Amber Eyes: A Hidden Inheritance* (London: Vintage, 2011 [2010]), p. 283.

72 *Ibid.*, pp. 268, 272.

73 Harris and Oppenheimer, *Into the Arms of Strangers*, p. 99.
74 Panter-Downes, 'Amid the Alien Corn'.
75 Turner, *... And the Policeman Smiled*, pp. 103–5; Blond and Turner, *Marks of Distinction*, pp. 76–7.
76 Fast, *Children's Exodus*, p. 31. Zurndorfer, *Ninth of November*, p. 71 was told later that her father accompanied her and her sister on the train from Dusseldorf to the Dutch border without them being aware of his presence.
77 Obituary of Arieh Handler in *The Times*, 23 May 2011.
78 Brent, *Sunday's Child?*, p. 31. It is reproduced in the frontispiece of his volume.
79 Zurndorfer, *The Ninth of November*, p. 72.
80 Walter Kammerling testimony in Eve Cowan (ed.), *Emet: A collection of Members' true life stories* (Bournemouth: Bournemouth Reform Synagogue, 1999), p. 122.
81 Marcus Dysch, 'Rail evacuees retrace their Shoah escape', *Jewish Chronicle*, 4 September 2009.
82 Quoted by Turner, *... And the Policeman Smiled*, pp. 52–3.
83 Panter-Downes, 'Amid the Alien Corn'.
84 Marianne Elsley, *A Chance in Six Million* (Banbury: Kemble Press, 1989). This is a powerful account of not just re-making a life in Britain but what happened to her parents during the war and her knowledge of their fate.
85 See, for example, the obituary of artist Harry Weinberger in *The Guardian*, 26 September 2009.
86 Blond, *Marks of Distinction*, p. 75.
87 *Ibid.*, p. 68.
88 *The Times*, 12 January 1939.
89 Elsley, *A Chance in Six Million*, p. 41.
90 *Ibid.*
91 *Ibid.*, p. 42.
92 Lilian Levy, analysis of *Kinder* registration cards, communication to the author, 10 February 1997.
93 David Kent, letter to *Jewish Chronicle*, 21 April 2006; *Upstairs Downstairs*, BBC1, 26 February 2012.
94 Dysch, 'Rail evacuees retrace their Shoah escape'.
95 Chadwick, *The Rescue of the Prague Refugees*, p. 138.
96 Daniel Snowman, *The Hitler Emigres: The Cultural Impact on Britain of Refugees from Nazism* (London: Pimlico, 2003 [2002]), pp. 91–5.
97 See his obituary by James Morton in *The Guardian*, 23 July 2009.
98 National Archives HO 213/1772.
99 Jonathan Jones, 'Liquid crystal revolutionary', *Guardian*, 29 September 2009.
100 Kerry Brougher, 'A world on the edge of destruction: setting the stage for Gustav Metzger' in Kerry Brougher and Astrid Bowron (eds), *Gustav Metzger* (Oxford: Museum of Modern Art, 1998), p. 12. I am grateful to my friend Colin Richmond for this catalogue.
101 Norman Rosenthal, 'Gustav Metzger - The Artist as a Wanderer', in Brougher and Bowron (eds), *Metzger*, p. 81.

102 Statement of 2 November 1959 reproduced in Brougher and Bowron (eds), *Gustav Metzger*, p. 30.
103 James Young, *The Texture of Memory: Holocaust Memorials and Meanings* (New Haven, CT: Yale University Press, 1993), Chapter 1.
104 Author visits to the National Maritime Museum, Falmouth, 27 December 2003 and National Museum of Scotland, 23 February 2010.
105 See the plaques at Paragon Station, Kingston upon Hull and in the dock area, the latter labelled 'Immigration'. A plaque was also unveiled in 2003 at Harry Lazarus's Hotel, 32–33 Posterngate, which was used during the 1870s and 1880s 'to feed European Transmigrants En Route to America and Canada'. I am grateful to Nick Evans for a walking tour of these sites, 10 December 2009.
106 Stephen Moss, 'Captive audience', *Guardian*, 8 July 2008.
107 Telephone interview with Mr Golden, 4 May 1937 and statement of the Council of the Save the Children Fund, 10 May 1937 in National Archives, HO 213/287.
108 *Daily Worker*, 24 May 1937.
109 *Ibid*. For descriptions of the journey and early days in England see Oliver Marshall (ed.), *Los ninosvascos* (London: Ethnic Communities Oral History Project & North Kensington Archive, 1991).
110 Dr Ellis quoted in Adrian Bell, *Only For Three Months: The Basque Children in Exile* (Norwich: Mousehold Press, 1996), p. 45.
111 *Ibid.*, p. 188.
112 Jim Fyrth, *The Signal Was Spain: The Spanish Aid Movement in Britain 1931–39* (London: Lawrence &Wishart, 1986), p. 242.
113 See *Southern Daily Echo*, 26 May 2007 for events to mark the fiftieth anniversary of the arrival of the *Habana* and the unveiling of a plaque outside Southampton Library and Art Gallery. More generally see Susana Sabin-Fernandez, 'The Basque Refugee Children of the Spanish Civil War in the UK: Memory and Memorialisation' (unpublished Ph.D. thesis, University of Southampton, 2011).
114 Rachel Fletcher, 'Kindertransport monument derailed at Liverpool Street', *Jewish Chronicle*, 9 December 2005.
115 *Jewish Chronicle*, 6 October 2006.
116 Louise London, 'Whitehall and the Refugees: The 1930s and the 1990s', *Patterns of Prejudice* vol. 34 no. 3 (2000), p. 17.
117 Walter Kammerling testimony in Cowan (ed.), *Emet*, p. 122.

Notes to Chapter 6

1 See, for example, Mass-Observation Archive (M-O A): DR C3092 (Summer 2006), a forty-year-old male antique auctioneer from Chester.
2 M-O A: DR H2634 (Summer 2006).
3 M-O A: DR R2247 (Summer 2000) a retired museum historian from London.
4 M-O A: DR H1543 (Summer 2000) a retired local government officer in Sussex, describing himself as an 'Anglo-Saxon male'.

5 M-O A: DR M1593 (Summer 2000), a middle-aged professional based in London and Aberdeen.

6 Louise London, *Whitehall and the Jews, 1933–1948: British Immigration Policy and the Holocaust* (Cambridge: Cambridge University Press, 2000), p. 13.

7 M-O A: DR V3091 (Summer 2006).

8 See, for example, *Britain's Secret Schindler: Revealed*, Channel 5, 27 January 2011 and more generally on this theme, Tony Kushner, 'The Search for Nuance in the Study of Holocaust "Bystanders"', in David Cesarani and Paul Levine (eds), *'Bystanders' to the Holocaust: A Re-evaluation* (London: Frank Cass, 2002), pp. 70–1.

9 William Chadwick, *The Rescue of the Prague Refugees 1938–39* (Leicester: Matador, 2010), p. 59.

10 First in Gordon Thomas and Max Morgan-Witts, *Voyage of the Damned: The Voyage of the St Louis* (London: Hodder and Stoughton, 1974) and then in Stuart Rosenberg's 1976 Rank Films version of the journey.

11 Arthur Morse, *While Six Million Died* (London: Secker & Warburg, 1968), Chapter 15, esp. p. 283.

12 Shari Segel, 'Voyage of St.Louis Remembered on 50th Anniversary', Museum of Jewish Heritage, 1989.

13 Wiesel on front cover of Kim Ablon Whitney, *The Other Half of Life* (New York: Laurel-Leaf, 2009).

14 *Bound for Nowhere* (American Jewish Joint Distribution Committee, 1939) has been re-released by the National Center for Jewish Film, Brandeis University, Boston, MA, 2007.

15 Hugo Gryn, 'A Moral and Spiritual Index' (London: Refugee Council, 1996).

16 *Jewish Chronicle*, 6 October 2006.

17 Morse, *While Six Million Died*, p. 287.

18 Gryn, 'A Moral and Spiritual Index'.

19 Sarah Ogilvie and Scott Miller, *Refuge Denied: The St. Louis Passengers and the Holocaust* (Madison, WI: University of Wisconsin Press, 2006), esp. pp. 174–5.

20 Quoted by 'Caroline Woods', 'The house of despair', *Guardian*, 30 July 2009.

21 Liane Reif-Lehrer, 'Memory's Edge', *Boston* vol. 80 no. 4 (April 1988), pp. 88–95.

22 Richard Breitman and Alan Kraut, *American Refugee Policy and European Jewry, 1933–1945* (Bloomington, IN: Indiana University Press, 1987), pp. 72–3.

23 Irving Abella and Harold Tropper, *None is Too Many: Canada and the Jews of Europe 1933–1948* (Toronto: Tester & Orpen Dennys, 1982), pp. 63–4.

24 Ogilvie and Miller, *Refuge Denied*.

25 Including the Canadian, Maziar Bahari's 1996 documentary, *The Voyage of the St Louis* first shown on Channel 4, 1 August 1996.

26 Edward Linenthal, *Preserving Memory: The Struggle to Create America's Holocaust Museum* (New York: Viking, 1995), p. 189.

27 Michael Berenbaum, *The World Must Know: The History of the Holocaust as Told in the United States Holocaust Memorial Museum* (Boston, MA: Little, Brown, 1993), p. 58.

28 See, for example, the guide *The Holocaust: The Holocaust Exhibition at the Imperial*

War Museum (London: Imperial War Museum, 2000), p. 15.

29 Imperial War Museum Holocaust Exhibition, 'Thousands Seek Refuge', author visit 1 April 2010.

30 Translation of telegram in National Archives, FO 371/24101.

31 Ernest Cooper (?), memorandum, 12 June 1939 in National Archives, FO 371/24101.

32 In a Cabinet Committee on the Refugee Problem, 8 December 1939 in *ibid.*

33 Cooper (?) memorandum of meeting with Otto Schiff, 9 June 1939 in National Archives, FO 371/24101.

34 Reilly minute, 16 June 1939, National Archives, FO 371/214101.

35 Osbert Peake, Under-Secretary of State for the Home Office, in *Hansard* (HC) vol. 348 cols 1111–12, 13 June 1939.

36 Nicholas Evans, '"A Strike for Racial Justice"? Transatlantic Shipping and the Jewish Diaspora, 1882–1939' in James Jordan, Tony Kushner and Sarah Pearce (eds), *Jewish Journeys from Philo to Hip Hop* (London: Vallentine Mitchell, 2010), pp. 39–40.

37 Bryan Connon, *Beverley Nichols: A Life* (Portland, OR: Timber Press, 2009), pp. 206–7. For more general comment, see Evans, '"A Strike for Racial Justice"?', p. 39.

38 Andrew Sharf, *The British Press & Jews Under Nazi Rule* (London: Oxford University Press, 1964), pp. 158–9.

39 *Daily Express*, 19 June 1939. The equally anti-alien London *Evening News* totally objected to their admittance. See *Zionist Review*, 22 June 1939 for comment.

40 *Southern Daily Echo*, 20 June 1939.

41 *Southern Evening Echo*, 21 June 1939.

42 'Refugees Land At Last', *Southern Evening Echo*, 21 June 1939.

43 *The Times*, 22 June 1939.

44 Gisela Feldman, 'It was like a cruise, then the suicide attempts began', *Jewish Chronicle*, 11 December 2009.

45 *Southern Evening Echo*, 21 June 1939.

46 Thomas and Morgan-Witts, *Voyage of the Damned*, p. 294.

47 Bahari, *Voyage of the St Louis*; Thomas and Morgan-Witts, *Voyage of the Damned*, p. 294.

48 Testimony in Bertha Leverton and Shmuel Lowensohn (eds), *I Came Alone: the Stories of the Kindertransports* (Lewes: The Book Guild, 2000), p. 43.

49 Both in its narrative and in the images selected, *Bound for Nowhere* also emphasised women (including with babies), children and the elderly.

50 Only recently have efforts been made to research the importance of the Kitchener camp and to develop local memorialisation. Clare Ungerson is carrying out a detailed and multi-layered history of the camp and its wider significance.

51 Copy of passport in author's possession.

52 Gisela Feldman, testimony in Menorah Synagogue, Cheshire, 'Shoah Seminar', 26 January 2001.

53 Tony Hare, *Spanning the Century: The Story of an Ordinary Man in Extraordinary Circumstances* (Spennymoor, County Durham: Memoir Club, 2002), p. 84.

54 A television play, *Skipper Next to God* was broadcast on BBC, 7 October 1951.

Written during the war by the Dutch writer, Jan de Hartog, it has strong echoes of the *St Louis* story. It is significant, however, that no reviews or responses at the time made the connection to the 1939 journey. I am grateful to Dr James Jordan for information on this broadcast.

55 Julian Barnes, *A History of the World in 10 ½ Chapters* (London: Picador, 1990 [1989]), Chapter 7.

56 *Ibid.*, p. 242.

57 See Ruth Whelan, 'Writing the self: Huguenot Autobiography and the Process of Assimilation', in Randolph Vigne and Charles Littleton (eds), *From Strangers to Citizens: The Integration of Immigrant Communities in Britain, Ireland and Colonial America, 1550–1750* (Brighton: Sussex University Press, 2001), p. 468.

58 Thomas and Morgan-Witts, *Voyage of the Damned*, p. 294.

59 Barnes, *A History of the World*, p. 188.

60 *Ibid.*, p. 181.

61 Matthew Pateman, *Julian Barnes* (Tavistock, Devon: Northcote House, 2002), p. 44.

62 *Zionist Review*, 22 June 1939.

63 *Jewish Chronicle*, 23 June 1939.

64 Barnes, *A History of the World*, p. 188.

65 *Ibid.*, p. 182.

66 *Ibid.*, p. 185. Here Barnes echoes the script of *Bound for Nowhere*: 'What is the life of a German Jew worth today?'

67 Liisa Malkki, 'Speechless Emissaries: Refugees, Humanitarianism and Dehistoricization', *Cultural Anthropology* vol. 11 no. 3 (1996), p. 388.

68 Hare, *Spanning the Century*, p. 80.

69 Julian Barnes, *England, England* (London: Jonathan Cape, 1998).

70 *The Voyage of the St Louis*, Channel 4, 1 August 1996.

71 Imperial War Museum, Holocaust Exhibition, author visit 1 April 2010.

72 'Refugees in the 1930s', Holocaust Memorial Day Trust, London, 2001.

73 Ogilvie and Miller, *Refuge Denied*, p. 174.

74 Deborah Lipstadt, 'Foreword' in Ogilvie and Miller, *Refuge Denied*, pp. xi–xii.

75 *Ibid.*, p. xi.

76 Michael Marrus, *The Holocaust in History* (London: Weidenfeld & Nicolson, 1988), p. 157.

77 William Rubinstein, *The Myth of Rescue* (London: Routledge, 1997), pp. 61–2.

78 *Ibid.*; Berenbaum, *The World Must Know*, p. 58.

79 London, *Whitehall and the Jews*, p. 12.

80 Holocaust Memorial Day (Trust), 'Refugees in the 1930s' study pack.

81 Whitney, *The Other Half of Life*, no page, questions prepared by Susan Geye, Librarian, Fort Worth, Texas.

82 The importance of paperwork *is* recognised in another American pedagogic exercise based on the *St Louis* – that provided on the website of the United States Holocaust Memorial Museum, 'Incorporating the *Voyage of the St Louis* Website into a unit of study' aimed at High School students. Amongst the questions is 'What

documents did a refugee need in order to enter the United States, and what did he or she need in order to leave countries in Europe?' www.ushmm.org/museum/exhibit/online/stlouis/teach/lesson.htm, accessed 30 July 2009.

83 Lilli Palmer, *Change Lobsters – and Dance: An Autobiography* (London: W.H. Allen, 1976), p. 92.

84 *Ibid.*, pp. 93–4.

85 *Ibid.*, p. 93.

86 Emeric Pressburger, interview with Kevin Gough-Yates, 30 August 1970, quoted in Kevin Gough-Yates, *Michael Powell in Collaboration with Emeric Pressburger* (Brussels: Europalia, 1973), no page and in Kevin Gough-Yates, 'The British Feature Film as a European Concern: Britain and the Emigre Film-Maker, 1933–45', in Gunter Berghaus (ed.), *Theatre and Film in Exile: German Artists in Britain, 1933–1945* (Oxford: Berg, 1989), p. 156.

87 Barry Turner, … *And the Policeman Smiled. 10,000 Children Escape From Nazi Europe* (London: Bloomsbury, 1990).

88 Marianne Elsley, *A Chance in Six Million* (Banbury: Kemble Press, 1989), p. 42.

89 Quoted in Marian Malet, 'Departure and Arrival' in John Grenville and Marian Malet (eds), *Changing Countries: The Experience and Achievement of German-Speaking Exiles from Hitler in Britain, from 1933 to Today* (London: Libris, 2002), p. 81.

90 J.L. Salter minute, 21 March 1937 in National Archives, HO 405/206669.

91 J.H. Hall to Sir John Simon, 23 March 1937 in *ibid.*

92 Michael Crick, *In Search of Michael Howard* (London: Simon & Schuster, 2005), Chapter 1.

93 *Ibid.*, pp. 408–9.

94 Paul Gilfeather, 'Michael Howard's Father: Verdict', *Sunday Mirror*, 20 February 2005.

95 Jonathan Freedland, 'Did Michael fall out of his family tree?', *Jewish Chronicle*, 25 February 2005. See Jonathan Freedland, *Jacob's Gift: A Journey into the Heart of Belonging* (London: Penguin, 2005), pp. 46–7.

96 Edmund de Waal, *The Hare With Amber Eyes: A Hidden Inheritance* (London: Vintage, 2011 [2010]), p. 261.

97 *Guardian*, 30 July 2009.

98 Deborah Dwork and Robert Jan Van Pelt, *Flight from the Reich: Refugee Jews, 1933–1946* (New York: W.W. Norton, 2009), p. 148.

99 Hoare to a delegation from the Board of Deputies of British Jews, 1 April 1938 in National Archives, HO 213/42.

100 Otto Schiff, Chairman of the German Jewish Aid Committee, at a meeting between the Home Office and the Board of Deputies of British Jews, 1 April 1938, National Archives, HO 213/94.

101 London, *Whitehall and the Jews*, p. 80. See also National Archives, HO 372/26 for deportation registration books for the period from 1933 to 1943.

102 See, for example, Holocaust Memorial Day Trust, education work pack, 'Refugees in the 1930s' which asks students to 'find a recent incident when refugees have been

found on a boat and not allowed entry to a country'.

103 Hare, *Spanning the Century*, p. 77.
104 *Ibid.*
105 Dwork and Van Pelt, *Flight from the Reich*, p. xiii.
106 Elaine Blond with Barry Turner, *Marks of Distinction* (London: Vallentine Mitchell, 1988), p. 84 on the former *Kinder* deportees.
107 Eugen Spier, *The Protecting Power* (London: Skeffington and Sons, 1951), p. 180.
108 *Ibid., passim* and p. 251.
109 Ogilvie and Miller, *Refuge Denied*, p. 35.
110 Walter Igersheimer, *Blatant Injustice: The Story of a Jewish Refugee from Nazi Germany Imprisoned in Britain and Canada during World War II* (Montreal: McGill-Queen's University Press, 2005), p. 109.
111 London, *Whitehall and the Jews*, p. 12.
112 Chadwick, *The Rescue of the Prague Refugees, passim*, discusses who was responsible for these forgeries, suggesting that it was probably his father, Trevor.
113 Palestine Police translation, 21 July 1947: 'Listen to the voice of the refugees' ship "Exodus 1947"', National Archives, FO 371/61822 E7699.

Notes to Chapter 7

1 Bill Schwarz, 'Crossing the seas', in Bill Schwarz (ed.), *West Indian Intellectuals in Britain* (Manchester: Manchester University Press, 2003), pp. 14–16.
2 Donald Hinds, *Journey to an Illusion: the West Indian in Britain* (London: Bogle-L'Ouverture, 1966), Chapter 1.
3 *Ibid.*, pp. 29–30.
4 *Ibid.*, p. 33.
5 The patterns of their journeys can be charted in the passenger lists now in the National Archives. See BT 26/1338/62 and 26/1342/53 for two of SS *Auriga*'s journeys in 1955, including that of Donald Hinds'.
6 Mike and Trevor Phillips, *Windrush: The Irresistible Rise of Multi-Racial Britain* (London: HarperCollins, 1999 [1998]).
7 BBC, 'The BBC *Windrush* Season Briefing' (1998), copy in possession of the author. More details of the four-part documentary, 'Windrush', shown on BBC2, 30 May, 6, 13 and 20 June 1998, made by Pepper Productions, can be found in Black Cultural Archives, BCA 6/13/1. For a wider exploration of the mythology associated with the ship, see Matthew Mead, '*Empire Windrush*: The cultural memory of an imaginary arrival', *Journal of Postcolonial Writing* vol. 45 no. 2 (2009), pp. 137–49.
8 Hinds, *Journey to an Illusion*, p. 52.
9 *Ibid.*, pp. 52–3.
10 Joyce Egginton, *They Seek a Living* (London: Hutchinson, 1957), Chapter 4.
11 *Ibid.*, p. 55.
12 See, however, John Ezard, 'Columbus of Brixton reflects on 40 winters', *Guardian*, 31 May 1988. There is mention of these commemorations in Sam King, *Climbing*

up the Rough Side of the Mountain (London: Minerva Press, 1998), pp. 231–3. There was also a brief mention in a BBC Schools Television Programme entitled 'Scene', broadcast in the summer of 1968. See BBC Television archives, T57/270/1. I am grateful to Gavin Schaffer for this reference. At this time, Sam King was also interviewed in Dick Adler, 'Voyage to the Promised Land', *Sunday Times*, 30 June 1968.

13 There is no mention in R.B. Davison, *West Indian Migrants* (London: Oxford University Press, 1962) and a few sentences in Ruth Glass, *London's Newcomers: The West Indian Migrants* (Cambridge, MA: Harvard University Press, 1961), pp. 46–7 based on Egginton's *They Seek a Living*; Sheila Patterson, *Dark Strangers: A Study of West Indians in London* (Harmondsworth: Penguin, 1965 [1963]), p. 45 and Edward Scobie, *Black Britannia: A History of Blacks in Britain* (Chicago: Johnson Publishing, 1972), p. 194. Michael Banton, *The Coloured Quarter: Negro Immigrants in an English City* (London: Jonathan Cape, 1955), p. 60 also provides an extremely brief reference.

14 Briefing paper, Pepper Productions, 1997?, Black Cultural Archives, BCA 6/13/1.

15 Adler, 'Voyage to the Promised Land'.

16 James Walvin, *Passage to Britain: Immigration in British History and Politics* (Harmondsworth: Penguin, 1984).

17 Leslie Thompson, *An Autobiography as told to Jeffrey P. Green* (Crawley: Rabbit Press, 1985), p. 118.

18 Robert Winder, *Bloody Foreigners: The Story of Immigration to Britain* (London: Little, Brown, 2004), pp. 257–62.

19 *Guardian*, 9 January 2006.

20 Hugh Williams, *Fifty Things You Need to Know about British History* (London: HarperCollins, 2009 [2008]), Chapter 10.

21 Stephen Pollard, *Ten Days that Changed the Nation: The Making of Modern Britain* (London: Simon & Schuster, 2009), Chapter 1.

22 Stuart Maconie, *Hope & Glory: The Days that Made Britain* (London: Ebury Press, 2011), Chapter 5.

23 From the back page of the paperpack versions of Pollard, Williams and Maconie respectively.

24 Williams, *Fifty Things*, p. 233.

25 Paul Carter, *The Road to Botany Bay: An Exploration of Landscape and History* (New York: Knopf, 1988), p. xiv quoted by Matthew Mead, 'Empire Windrush: Cultural Memory and Archival Disturbance', *Moveable Type* no. 3 (2007), p. 112.

26 Mike and Trevor Phillips, *Windrush*, p. 6.

27 Neil Spencer, 'Lord Kitchener steps off the Empire Windrush', *Guardian/Observer History of Modern Music* (London: Guardian/Observer, 2011), Part 6, p. 7.

28 *Ibid.*

29 For one of the most detailed descriptions of the journey itself, see the autobiography of one of the *Empire Windrush*'s most prominent passengers – King, *Climbing up the Rough Side of the Mountain*, Chapter 7. See also National Archives, BT 26/1237/91. Mead, 'Empire Windrush: the cultural memory', p. 142 also comments on its complex route to Britain.

30 Adler, 'Voyage to the Promised Land'.
31 Egginton, *They Seek a Living*, p. 59.
32 Lesley Downer, 'The ship that became an icon of black history', *Financial Times*, 30 May 1998.
33 *Daily Express*, 21 June 1948. Mead, '*Empire Windrush*', pp. 142–3 comments on the complex mix of passengers.
34 Tony Sewell, *Keep on Moving. The Windrush Legacy: The Black Experience in Britain from 1948* (London: Voice Enterprises, 1998), p. 39.
35 See Kenneth Lunn, 'The British State and Immigration, 1945–51: New Light on the Empire Windrush', in Tony Kushner and Kenneth Lunn (eds), *The Politics of Marginality: Race, the Radical Right and Minorities in Twentieth Century Britain* (London: Frank Cass, 1990), pp. 161–74.
36 Mead, '*Empire Windrush*', p. 118.
37 King, *Climbing up the Rough Side of the Mountain*, pp. 92–3.
38 Colonial Office report, 'Empire Windrush', 30 June 1948, in National Archives, HO 213/244.
39 See Cabinet discussions, 18 June 1948 in National Archives, CAB 129/28 CP (48) 154.
40 For the substantial literature on the *Empire Windrush*, see the major studies by Sewell, *Keep on Moving*; Mike and Trevor Phillips, *Windrush*; and Vivienne Francis, *With Hope in their Eyes: the compelling stories of the Windrush generation* (London: Nia, 1998). On the demand for tickets, see Adler, 'Voyage to the Promised Land'.
41 See Mead, '*Empire Windrush*', p. 144.
42 Levy at Guardian Book Club discussion, 24 January 2011, quoted in John Mullan, '*Small Island* by Andrea Levy', *Guardian*, 29 January 2011.
43 Powell's Birmingham speech reproduced in Bill Smithies and Peter Fiddick (eds), *Enoch Powell on Immigration* (London: Sphere, 1969), p. 41.
44 See the commentary in *ibid.*, p. 59 and Anne Dummett, letter to *The Times*, 24 April 1968.
45 Andrea Levy, *Small Island* (London: Review, 2004), pp. 470, 525–6.
46 Mike and Trevor Phillips, *Windrush*, pp. 6–7.
47 Roy Porter, *London: A Social History* (Harmondsworth: Penguin, 1996), p. 354.
48 *Small Island*, BBC1, 6 and 13 December 2009, directed by Paula Milne.
49 Sewell, *Keep on Moving*, p. 1.
50 Mike and Trevor Phillips, *Windrush*, p. 6.
51 Sewell, *Keep on Moving*, p. 1. The latter part of this quote reproduces exactly Stuart Hall's 'Introduction' in *Forty Winters On: Memories of Britain's post war Caribbean Immigrants* (London: Lambeth Services, The Voice and South London Press, 1988), p. 4.
52 Mike and Trevor Phillips, *Windrush*, p. 6.
53 *Ibid.*, pp. 2, 6.
54 In Sam Walker and Alvin Elcock (eds), *The Windrush Legacy: Memories of Britain's post-war Caribbean Immigrants* (London: Black Cultural Archives, 1998), p. 66.
55 In Black Cultural Archives, BCA 5/1/17.

56 'Poet of the Tides', http://homepages.which.net~panic.brixtonpoetry/poetoftides.htm, accessed 1 July 2011.

57 The title of a literary evening held on 25 June 1998 in London. See Black Cultural Archives, BCA 6/13/5.

58 Editorial, *Black and Asian Studies Association Newsletter* no. 22 (September 1998), p. 2.

59 By Winder, *Bloody Foreigners*, p. 258. See Cy Grant's autobiographical fragments in Imperial War Museum archive, 05/68/1.

60 Speech to the University of London reproduced in *Black and Asian Studies Association Newsletter* no. 24 (April 1999), p. 8.

61 Report, 23 October 1948 in National Archives, HO 213/716.

62 *Ibid.*

63 *Ibid.*

64 Colonial Office report, 1949?, in National Archives, MT 9/5463.

65 Peter Fryer, *Staying Power: The History of Black People in Britain* (London: Pluto Press, 1984), p. 372.

66 Letter of MPs to the Prime Minister, 22 June 1948 in National Archives, HO 213/244.

67 Draft letter, June 1948, in National Archives, HO 213/244.

68 *Ibid.*

69 *Hansard* (HC) vol. 452 col.422 (16 June 1948).

70 Fryer, *Staying Power*, p. 372.

71 Testimony in Robert Murray, *The Experiences of World War II. Westindian Ex-Service Personnel* (Nottingham: Nottingham Westindian Combined Ex-Service Association, 1996), pp. 147–8.

72 G. Wilson minute, 27 May 1948 in National Archives, LAB 8/1499.

73 Arrangements can be followed in National Archives, LAB 8/1499.

74 Address reproduced in National Archives, LAB 8/1516 and HO 213/244.

75 Mike and Trevor Phillips, *Windrush*, pp. 68,84.

76 *Ibid.*, pp. 65–6.

77 Pathe News, reproduced in 'From War to Windrush' exhibition, Imperial War Museum, author visit 1 April 2010.

78 Hugh Hodges, 'Kitchener invades England: The London Calypsos of Aldwyn Roberts', *Wasafari* vol. 20 no. 45 (2005), p. 26.

79 Pathe Newsreel on the arrival of the *Empire Windrush*.

80 Hodges, 'Kitchener invades England', p. 30, utilising Paul Gilroy's concept of the 'Black Atlantic'.

81 Paul Gilroy, *Black Britain: A Photographic History* (London: Saqibooks, 2007), p. 144.

82 Paul Gilroy, *The Black Atlantic: Modernity and Double Consciousness* (London: Verso, 1993).

83 See www.lambeth.gov.uk/Services/Environment/Regeneration/FutureLambeth/Brixt … , accessed 15 February 2011.

84 Hodges, 'Kitchener invades England', pp. 28–9.

85 *Evening News*, 17 June 1948; Driberg in *Hansard* (HC) vol. 452 col. 1336 (23 June 1948). As a ship opportunistically looking for passengers on an international level, the *Empire Windrush* would indeed have been a familiar ship in the port of Southampton. Even modern histories have thus mistakenly placed its arrival in June 1948 into Southampton. See Don John and Stella Muirhead, *A Black History of Southampton: 16th Century to 21st Century* (Southampton: Positive Message, 2010), p. 40 – an important pioneer local study.

86 Sukdev Sandhu, *London Calling: How Black and Asian Writers Imagined a City* (London: HarperCollins, 2003), p. 141. For the passenger list of this ship which arrived in Southampton on 21 December 1947 see National Archives, BT 26/123/141.

87 *Southern Daily Echo*, 22 December 1947. The story dominated the front page of the news.

88 'Happy Sequel to Stowaway's Trip: Young West Indian Finds Friends in Southampton', *Southern Daily Echo*, 23 December 1947.

89 Wilmot testimony in www.metro.co.uk/newsfocus/233667-britains-first-caribbean-immigrants, accessed 3 January 2010.

90 Mead, '*Empire Windrush*: the cultural memory', p. 144.

91 Charlotte Williams, *Sugar and Slate* (Aberystwyth: Planet, 2002), pp. 98–9.

92 Adler, 'Voyage to the Promised Land'.

93 Egginton, *They Seek a Living*, p. 59.

94 Neither Maisie Simpson nor any other female Caribbean from the *Windrush* feature in Phillips and Phillips, *Windrush*, for example.

95 Egginton, *They Seek a Living*, p. 61.

96 Levy, *Small Island*; Caryl Phillips, *The Final Passage* (London: Vintage, 2004 [1985]).

97 Maya Jaggi, 'The Final Passage: An Interview with writer Caryl Phillips', in Kwesi Owusu (ed.), *Black British Culture and Society: A Text Reader* (London: Routledge, 2000), pp. 157–68 (p. 165).

98 'Time and Place', Brighton Museum, October 2009.

99 Palorine Williams, 'Introduction', Chapeltown Black Women Writers' Group (eds), *When Our Ship Comes In: Black Women Talk* (Castleford: Yorkshire Art Circus, 1992), p. 5.

100 *Ibid.*, p. 66.

101 Jannett Creese, *My Windward Side* (Stockport: Stockport Libraries, 2002), pp. 45–6.

102 Egginton, *They Seek a Living*, pp. 136–7; Glass, *Newcomers*, p. 9.

103 By Patrick Vernon of the Afiya Trust. See *The Guardian*, 25 January 2010.

104 Quoted in www.london.gov.uk/media/press_releases_mayor-unveils-new-bigger-… , accessed 10 June 2011.

105 Maconie, *Hope & Glory*, p. 155.

106 *Ibid.*

107 Egginton, *They Seek a Living*, p. 99.

108 Glass, *Newcomers*, p. 29.

109 Egginton, *They Seek a Living*, Chapter 8.
110 Mass-Observation Archive, University of Sussex, Directive Respondent R470, Summer 2006.
111 Pollard, *Ten Days that Changed Britain*, p. 13.
112 *Ibid.*, Chapter 9, esp. p. 195.
113 Maconie, *Hope & Glory*, p. 164.
114 *Ibid.*, p. 180.
115 *Ibid.*, p. 164.
116 *Ibid.*, p. 152.
117 Lola Young, 'After Windrush', in Walker and Elcock (eds), *The Windrush Legacy*, p. 64.
118 First published as *Old Man Trouble* in 1975 and republished and expanded as *In Troubled Waters: Memoirs of Seventy Years in England* (London: Karia Press, 1986). For a complex reading of this life story, see Gemma Romain, *Connecting History: A Comparative Exploration of African-Caribbean and Jewish History and Memory in Modern Britain* (London: Kegan Paul, 2006), Chapter 2.
119 Roy Kerridge, *The Story of Black History* (London: The Claridge Press, 1998), p. 10.

Notes to Chapter 8

1 Onyekachi Wambu, 'Introduction' in Onyekachi Wambu (ed.), *Hurricane Hits England: An Anthology of Writing about Black Britain* (New York: Continuum, 2000 [1998]), p. 21.
2 Jon Newman, *Windrush Forbears: Black People in Lambeth 1700–1900* (London: Lambeth Archives/Department of Education and Skills, 2002), p. 7.
3 In National Archives, HO 213/244.
4 Notes of a meeting held by the Colonial Office in National Archives, HO 213/714.
5 *Ibid.*
6 Draft Memorandum for Ministers, 'Immigration of British Subjects into the United Kingdom', April (?) 1950 in National Archives, MT 9/5463.
7 *Ibid.* See also Cabinet discussion, 24 July 1950 in National Archives, FO 369/4365.
8 Colonial Office memorandum, 'British Travel Certificates', 5 April 1950, in National Archives, FO 369/4364.
9 Ian Spencer, *British Immigration Policy since 1939* (London: Routledge, 1997), pp. 36–7.
10 Prince Monolulu, *I Gotta Horse: The Autobiography of Ras Prince Monolulu, as told to Sidney H. White* (London: Hurst & Blackett, 1950), p. 9.
11 Stephen Bourne, *Black in the British Frame: Black People in British Film and Television 1896–1996* (London: Cassell, 1998), p. 62.
12 Ernest Marke, *In Troubled Waters: Memoirs of Seventy Years in England* (London: Karia Press, 1986), pp. 98–109.
13 Monolulu, *I Gotta Horse*, p. 177.
14 Neil Evans, 'Regulating the Reserve Army: Arabs, Blacks and the Local State in

Cardiff, 1919–45', *Immigrants and Minorities* vol. 4 (July 1985), pp. 68–106.

15 See testimony in John Akomfrah's film *A Touch of the Tar Brush* (Black Audio Film Collective for BBC, 1991).

16 Rozina Visram, *Asians in Britain: 400 Years of History* (London: Pluto Press, 2002), p. 216.

17 Abdullah Karim application to the Home Office received 31 May 1937 in National Archives, HO 382/67.

18 Constable Stanley Cooper, Skegness Police Station to Lincolnshire Constabulary, 15 June 1937 in *ibid.*

19 Letter of 21 June 1937 in *ibid.*

20 CID letter, 14 February 1938 in *ibid.*

21 Information from Glasgow police, 15 November 1937 in *ibid.*

22 Letter from Skegness police, 15 June 1937 in *ibid.*

23 Police report, 15 November 1937 in *ibid.*

24 Office of High Commissioner for India, 25 April 1938 to Jagelman, Home Office in *ibid.*

25 Police report, 15 November 1937 in *ibid.*

26 On Blackpool, see Mass-Observation Archive, University of Sussex, Worktown Collection, Box 60, File E.

27 Testimony in Irna Imran, Tim Smith and Donald Hyslop (eds), *Here to Stay: Bradford's South Asian Communities* (Bradford: Bradford Heritage Recording Unit, 1994), pp. 34–5.

28 *Radio Times*, 7 July 1939.

29 William Goldman, *East End My Cradle* (London: A&E, 1947 [1940]), p. 98.

30 The script and research for it is found in Mass-Observation Archive: Topic Collection 'Anti-Semitism', Box 1, File E. The programme was broadcast on 12 July 1939.

31 Visram, *Asians in Britain*, p. 254.

32 *Ibid.*, p. 299 and pp. 269–73 for the Indian Workers' Association.

33 Caroline Adams, *Across Seven Seas and Thirteen Rivers* (London: THAP Books, 1987), p. 30.

34 *Ibid.*, p. 28.

35 *Ibid.*, p. xiii.

36 Mr McGuirk, Liverpool Ministry of Labour official, 20 January 1949 in National Archives, LAB 26/226.

37 On Liverpoool and stowaways, see National Archives, HO 344/35.

38 Ministry of Transport notes, no date in National Archives, HO 344/3.

39 Sam King, *Climbing up the Rough Side of the Mountain* (London: Minerva Press, 1998).

40 See the statistics for 1946, 1947 and 1948 in National Archives, HO 344/36.

41 National Archives, FO 369/4364.

42 National Archives, HO 344/35.

43 Report, 26 January 1950 in National Archives, FO 369/4364.

44 Olalekau letter, no date, in Black Cultural Archives, Michael Banton papers, 1/1.

45 Gayatri Chakravorty Spivak, 'Can the Subaltern Speak?', in G. Nelson (ed.), *Marxism*

and the Interpretation of Culture (Basingstoke: Macmillan, 1988), pp. 271–313.

46 Michael Banton, *The Coloured Quarter: Negro Immigrants in an English City* (London: Jonathan Cape, 1955), p. 9.

47 Olalekau letter, Black Cultural Archives, Banton papers, 1/1.

48 Banton, *The Coloured Quarter*, pp. 51–5.

49 *Ibid.*, p. 55.

50 *Ibid.*, p. 238.

51 Spivak, 'Can the Subaltern speak?', p. 308.

52 Olalekau letter, Black Cultural Archives, Banton papers, 1/1.

53 National Archives, MT 9/5463.

54 National Archives, HO 344/36.

55 Kester Aspden, *The Hounding of David Oluwale* (London: Vintage, 2008 [2007]), p. 19.

56 *Ibid.*, p. 20.

57 Kester Aspden, 'Legacy of hate', *Guardian*, 30 May 2007.

58 Aspden, *The Hounding of David Oluwale*, p. 168.

59 *Ibid.*, p. 195.

60 Caryl Phillips, *Foreigners: Three English Lives* (London: Vintage, 2008 [2007]).

61 'HH' review in *Observer*, 19 October 2008.

62 Jeremy Sandford, *Smiling David: The Story of David Oluwale* (London: Calder & Boyars, 1974). It was originally performed at the Brighton Festival in May 1972 and broadcast on BBC Radio Brighton.

63 Linton Kwesi Johnson, *Dread Beat and Blood* (London: Bogle-L'Ouverture, 1982 [1975]), pp. 34–5.

64 Aspden, *The Hounding of David Oluwale*, pp. 8–9.

65 Oladipo Agboluaje, *The Hounding of David Oluwale* (London: Oberon Books, 2009). The play, by theatre company Eclipse, started its tour at the West Yorkshire Playhouse, 31 January 2009. See *Guardian*, 6 February 2009.

66 See the website www.leedsmet.ac.uk/oluwale, accessed 22 September 2009.

67 Aspden, *The Hounding of David Oluwale*, p. 165.

68 *Ibid.*, pp. 8–9.

69 Phillips, *Foreigners, passim*; Aspden, *The Hounding of David Oluwale*, p. 9.

70 'Introduction', in Agboluaje, *The Hounding of David Oluwale*, pp. 17–18.

71 *Ibid.*, p. 18.

72 Aspden, *The Hounding of David Oluwale*, p. 9.

73 Aspden, 'Legacy of Hate'.

74 Phillips, *Foreigners*, p. 260.

75 P. H. note, 16 June 1948 in National Archives, LAB 8/1499.

76 The exhibition ran from June 2008 to March 2009.

77 BBC1, *EastEnders*, 24 February 2009.

78 Hannah Pool, 'All-black EastEnders makes soap history – as in lesson', *Guardian*, 25 February 2009. Pool's own background, adopted from an Eritrean refugee camp, partly explains this sceptical perspective. See Hannah Pool, *My Father's Daughter* (London: Hamish Hamilton, 2005) for an exploration of her roots.

79 See www.lambeth.gov.uk/Services/Environment/Regeneration/FutureLambeth/Brixt ...,
accessed 1 December 2009.

80 Referred to by Deborrah Orr, 'Diversity and equality are *not* the same thing',
Guardian, 22 October 2009.

81 Roy Kerridge, *The Story of Black History* (London: The Claridge Press, 1998).

82 Agbolouaje, *The Hounding of David Oluwale*, p. 111.

83 E.P. Thompson, *The Making of the English Working Class* (London: Victor Gollancz,
1963), p. 12.

84 *Picture Post*, 26 November 1956.

85 Neil Sinclair, *Endangered Tiger: A Community under Threat* (Cardiff: Butetown
History & Arts Centre, 2003), p. 191 note 4 comments that although her birth cer-
tificate has been reproduced 'many people still believe that she was not born in Tiger
Bay'.

86 John Williams, *Miss Shirley Bassey* (London: Quercus, 2010), pp. 10, 14–15. Henry
was born in 1895 or 1896 and Eliza in 1901.

87 Ross Cameron, '"The Most Colourful Extravaganza in the World": Images of Tiger
Bay, 1845–1970', *Patterns of Prejudice* vol. 31 no. 2 (1997), p. 61.

88 'M', 'Sweet Tiger Bay', *Western Mail*, 23 August 1902 reproduced in Sinclair,
Endangered Tiger, pp. x–xi.

89 Testimony and commentary in Paul Thompson, *The Edwardians: The Remaking of
British Society* (London: Weidenfeld& Nicolson, 1975), pp. 114–23, esp. p. 120.

90 *Ibid.*, p. 121.

91 *Ibid.*, p. 121.

92 See Diane Frost, 'Racism, Work and Unemployment: West African Seamen in
Liverpool 1880s–1960s', *Immigrants & Minorities* vol. 13 nos 2&3 (1994), pp. 22–33.

93 Ray Costello, *Black Liverpool: The Early History of Britain's Oldest Black Community
1730–1918* (Liverpool: Picton Press, 2001), p. 70.

94 Ian Law and June Henfrey, *A History of Race and Racism in Liverpool 1660–1950*
(Liverpool: Merseyside Community Relations Council, 1981), p. 25.

95 Stephen Bourne and Esther Bruce, *The Sun Shone on Our Side of the Street: Aunt
Esther's Story* (London: Ethnic Communities Oral History Project, 1991), pp. 4–6.

96 David Vaughan, *Negro Victory: The Life Story of Dr Harold Moody* (London:
Independent Press, 1950); Anne Spry Rush, 'Imperial Identity in Colonial Minds:
Harold Moody and the League of Coloured Peoples, 1931–50', *Twentieth Century
British History* vol. 13 no. 4 (2002), pp. 356–83.

97 Peter Fryer, *Staying Power: The History of Black People in Britain* (London: Pluto
Press, 1984), p. 304; Law and Henfrey, *A History of Race and Racism*, p. 30.

98 Jacqueline Jenkinson, *Black 1919: Riots, Racism and Resistance in Imperial
Britain* (Liverpool: Liverpool University Press, 2009) provides the most thorough
overview.

99 National Archives, BT 350 (CR10 1918–21), Microfiche no. 149. The originals of
these index cards are to be found in Southampton City Archive.

100 Williams, *Miss Shirley Bassey*, pp. 16–7.

101 *Ibid.*, pp. 17–18, 29. See also Muriel Burgess, *Shirley: An Appreciation of the Life of*

Shirley Bassey (London: Century, 1998), pp. 7–8.

102 National Archives, ASSI 76/25 and 26 and ASSI 71/68.

103 Katharine Whitehorn, 'Sexy Singer from Tiger Bay', *Picture Post*, 26 November 1956.

104 On official responses to this riot, see National Archives, CO 318/352.

105 'Stop These Race Riots!', *Sunday Express*, 15 June 1919.

106 National Archives, HO 372/10.

107 *Ibid.*

108 National Archives, HO 372/27.

109 Toyin Falola, *The History of Nigeria* (Westport, CT: Greenwood Press, 1999), pp. 51, 68. For demands for Calabar independence in the late 1950s, see National Archives, CO 957/8.

110 Burgess, *Shirley*, pp. 4,9.

111 Williams, *Miss Shirley Bassey*, p. 35; Burgess, *Shirley*, p. 9.

112 Dannie Abse, *A Strong Dose of Myself* (London: Hutchinson, 1983), p. 12. See also Dannie Abse, *Intermittent Journals* (Bridgend: Seren, 1994), pp. 22, 216–17 for self-exploration of his views on black people and more imagining of Tiger Bay.

113 Neil Sinclair, *The Tiger Bay Story* (Cardiff: Butetown History & Arts Project, 1993), p. 114. A television drama, 'Shirley', acknowledged, if only briefly, her ambivalent relationship with 'Tiger Bay' and also why her family had to leave the area. Broadcast on BBC2, 30 September 2011.

114 Whitehorn, 'Sexy Singer from Tiger Bay'.

115 Sinclair, *The Tiger Bay Story*, p. 114.

116 *Ibid.*, p. 58.

117 Colin Holmes, *John Bull's Island: Immigration & British Society, 1871–1971* (Basingstoke: Macmillan, 1988), p. 136.

118 See Paul Rich, *Race and Empire in British Politics* (Cambridge: Cambridge University Press, 1986), pp. 155–60; Hakim Adi, *West Africans in Britain, 1900–1960. Nationalism, Pan-Africanism and Communism* (London: Lawrence &Wishart, 1998), Chapter 2.

119 In minutes of a meeting held under Colonial Office auspices, 27 July 1931, in National Archives, CO 554/86/5.

120 Keith to Davidson, 22 August 1945, National Archives CO 537/1222.

121 Major Shepherd memorandum, 6 February 1947, in National Archives, CO 537/1914.

122 Banton, *The Coloured Quarter*, p. 56.

123 Henri Tajfel and John Dawson (eds), *Disappointed Guests* (London: Institute of Race Relations, 1965), pp. 136–7.

124 Chikwenda Nwariaku, 'The Paternal Posture', in *ibid.*, p. 75.

125 Andrea Levy, *Small Island* (London: Headline, 2004), Chapter 50.

126 Nwariaku, 'The Paternal Posture', p. 81.

127 *Ibid.*, p. 82.

128 *Ibid.*, p. 84.

129 *Ibid.*

130 Phil Frampton, *The Golly in the Cupboard* (Manchester: Tamic, 2004).

131 See, respectively, Phil Frampton, 'This is my life. The one I never knew', *Guardian*, 2 June 1999 and Alison Benjamin, 'Growing Pains', *Guardian*, 20 October 2004 for the progress he has made in respect of record release.
132 Frampton, *The Golly in the Cupboard*, pp. 15,28.
133 *Ibid.*, p. 28.
134 *Ibid.*, p. 54.
135 *Ibid.*, p. 58.
136 *Ibid.*, p. 36.
137 *Ibid.*, p. 77.
138 Benjamin, 'Growing Pains'.
139 Jackie Kay, *Red Dust Road: An Autobiographical Journey* (London: Picador, 2010), p. 156.
140 *Ibid.*, pp. 192–3.
141 *Ibid.*, p. 193.
142 *Ibid.*, p. 289.
143 Jackie Kay, 'Burying My African Father' in Jackie Kay, *Fiere* (London: Picador, 2011), p. 29.
144 Interviewed by Hannah Pool, 'Black to my roots', *Guardian*, 30 July 2011.
145 Pauline Black, *Black By Design: A 2-Tone Memoir* (London: Serpent's Tail, 2011), pp. 374, 387.
146 Chris Waters, '"Dark Strangers" in Our Midst: Discourses of Race and Nation in Britain, 1947–1963', *Journal of British Studies* vol. 36 (April 1997), pp. 207–38 (p. 229).
147 Phillips, *Foreigners*, p. 172. See similarly, Sandford, *Smiling David, passim*.
148 Buchi Emecheta, *Head Above Water: An Autobiography* (London: Fontana: 1986), p. 68 and *passim* deals with the divisions and unity of Nigerians in Britain through the late 1960s and 1970s.
149 226,000 according to a survey carried out by Experian Mosaic reproduced in *The Observer*, 10 April 2011.
150 Interview in *The Observer Magazine*, 12 February 2011.
151 Emecheta, *Head Above Water*, pp. 28–9. In a fictional version of her journey to Britain, *Second-Class Citizen* (Oxford: Heinemann, 1994 [1974]), p. 33 Emecheta states that if the heroine 'had been Jesus, she would have passed England by. Liverpool was grey, smoky and looked uninhabited by humans.'
152 Black, *Black By Design*, p. 76.
153 *Ibid.*, pp. 387–9.
154 Kay, 'Road to Amaudo', in Kay, *Fiere*, pp. 52–3.
155 *Ibid.*, p. 52.

Notes to Chapter 9

1 Salman Rushdie, *Midnight's Children* (London: Vintage, 2006 [1981]), p. 4.
2 Kathy Burrell, 'Going Steerage on Ryanair: Cultures of Migrant Air Travel between

Poland and the UK', *Journal of Transport Geography* vol. 19 (2011), pp. 1023, 1027, 1029.

3 Kathy Burrell, 'Materialising the Border: Spaces of Mobility and Material Culture in Migration from Post-Socialist Poland', *Mobilities* vol. 3 no. 3 (2008), pp. 353–73 (p. 370).

4 George Lamming, *The Emigrants* (London: Michael Joseph, 1954), p. 36.

5 Caryl Phillips, 'Homeward Bound', *Guardian* (Weekend), 21 June 1997.

6 Letter to *Guardian* (Weekend), 28 June 1997.

7 Joyce Egginton, *They Seek a Living* (London: Hutchinson, 1957), p. 55.

8 Chaim Weizmann, *The Right to Survive: Testimony before the Anglo-American Committee of Enquiry on Palestine* (London: Jewish Agency for Palestine, 1946), pp. 11–12.

9 King quoted in *Forty Winters On: Memories of Britain's post war Caribbean Immigrants* (London: Lambeth Services, The Voice and South London Press, 1988), p. 7.

10 Tony Sewell, *Keep On Moving: The Windrush Legacy: The Black Experience in Britain from 1948* (London: Voice Enterprises, 1998), p. 1.

11 Studs Terkel, *Race* (London: Minerva, 1993 [1992]), p. 145.

12 Brian Klug, *Being Jewish and Doing Justice: Bringing Argument to Life* (London: Vallentine, Mitchell, 2010), p. 215.

13 Colin Palmer, 'The Middle Passage', in *Captive Passage: The Transatlantic Slave Trade and the Making of the Americas* (Washington DC: Smithsonian Institution Press, 2002), p. 75 quoted by Edward Alpers, 'The Other Middle Passage: The African Slave Trade in the Indian Ocean', in Emma Christopher, Cassandra Pybus and Marcus Rediker (eds), *Many Middle Passages: Forced Migration and the Making of the Modern World* (Berkeley, CA: University of California Press, 2007), p. 20.

14 Jan Carew in Onyekachi Wambu (ed.), *Hurricane Hits England: An Anthology of Writing about Black Britain* (New York: Continuum, 2000), p. 305. Gener Martin flew from Jamaica to Britain in 1961 aged 39. She recalls 'When I was on the plane, it was early morning, and when I looked down I saw London with all the lights and it was so beautiful, and I said if this is London what is heaven going to be like?'. In James Barry *et al.* (eds), *Sorry No Vacancies* (London: Notting Dale Urban Studies Centre and Ethnic Communities Oral History Project, 1992), p. 9.

15 Phillips, 'Homeward Bound'.

16 Andrea Schlieker, 'A Million Miles from Home' in idem (ed.), *Folkestone Triennial: A Million Miles from Home* (Folkestone: Cultureshock, 2011), p. 13.

17 Robin Mundill, 'Edward 1 and the Final Phase of Anglo-Jewry', in Patricia Skinner (ed.), *Jews in Medieval Britain: Historical, Literary and Archaeological Perspectives* (Woodbridge: Boydell and Brewer, 2003), p. 70.

18 See Samuel Abrahamsen, 'The Rescue of Denmark's Jews' in Leo Goldberger (ed.), *The Rescue of Danish Jewry* (New York: New York University Press, 1987), p. 10 on memorialisation in Copenhagen and Jerusalem, and the cover of Emmy Werner, *A Conspiracy of Decency: The Rescue of Danish Jews during World War II* (Boulder, CO: Westview, 2002) for a photograph of the relief sculpture of a boat in Helsingborg Town Hall, Sweden. The rescue is at the heart of Daniel Libeskind's design for the

Danish Jewish Museum in Copenhagen. See Henrik Sten Moller (ed.), *The Danish Jewish Museum and Daniel Libeskind* (Copenhagen: Danish Jewish Museum, 2004). A 'Danish Rescue Boat' features in the Holocaust Museum Texas, donated in 2007. See www.hmh.org/ex_show.asp?id=77, accessed 1 September 2009.

19 Laura Varon, *The Juderia: A Holocaust Survivor's Tribute to the Jewish Community of Rhodes* (Westport, CT: Praeger, 1999), pp. 42–3.

20 *Ibid.*, p. 55.

21 See that of Rosa Ferera in Simone Gigliotti, *The Train Journey: Transit, Captivity, and Witnessing the Holocaust* (New York: Berghahn Books, 2009), p. 94 which gives inaccurate details of when these deportation boats left Rhodes.

22 Quoted by Christopher Browning, *The Path to Genocide: Essays on Launching the Final Solution* (Cambridge: Cambridge University Press, 1992), p. 23 and more generally, Chapter 1 *passim* on the Madagascar scheme.

23 Samuel Abrahamsen, *Norway's Response to the Holocaust: A Historical Perspective* (New York: Holocaust Library, 1991), pp. 130–1.

24 *Ibid.*, p. 129.

25 Gigliotti, *The Train Journey*, p. 6.

26 Aviva Halamish, *The Exodus Affair: Holocaust Survivors and the Struggle for Palestine* (London: Vallentine Mitchell, 1998), p. 266.

27 Mr Lu, owner of the *Tu Do*, which left Vietnam in August 1977, quoted in leaflet on the boat, Australian National Maritime Museum, Sydney, 2010.

28 To Minh Dieu, 'Light', *New Homeland*, January 1980.

29 *Ibid.*

30 Tony Kushner and Katharine Knox, *Refugees in an Age of Genocide: Global, National and Local Perspectives during the Twentieth Century* (London: Frank Cass, 1999), Chapter 11.

31 Author site visit, 19 February 2010.

32 Trevor Avery, *From Auschwitz to Ambleside* (Sedbergh: Another Space, 2008).

33 Patricia Skinner, 'Introduction', in Patricia Skinner (ed.), *The Jews in Medieval Britain*, p. 8.

34 Jessica Roitman, 'Sephardic Journeys: Travel, Place and Concepts of Identity' in James Jordan, Tony Kushner and Sarah Pearce (eds), *Jewish Journeys: From Philo to Hip Hop* (London: Vallentine Mitchell, 2010), pp. 179–95.

35 Nadav Kashtan, 'Seafaring and Jews in Graeco-Roman Palestine: Realistic and Symbolic Dimensions', in Nadav Kashtan (ed.), *Seafaring and the Jews* (London: Frank Cass, 2001), p. 25.

36 Donald Hinds, *Journey to an Illusion: the West Indian in Britain* (London: Bogle-L'Ouverture, 1966), p. 45.

37 Sam Selvon, *Moses Ascending* (London: Davis-Poynter, 1975), pp. 43–4.

38 V.S. Naipaul, *The Middle Passage* (London: Picador, 1995 [1962]), p. 23.

39 Gordon Lewis, 'Race Relations in Britain: A View from the Caribbean', *Race Today* vol. 1 no. 3 (1969), p. 79.

40 Jannett Creese, *My Windward Side* (Stockport: Stockport Libraries, 2002), p. 46.

41 Tim Edensor and Mij Kelly (eds), *Moving Worlds: Personal Recollections of Twenty-*

One Immigrants to Edinburgh (Edinburgh: Polygon, 1989), p. 87. Baldev's father had settled in Edinburgh in the mid-1950s, joining his father who had come to Scotland as a pedlar before the Second World War.

42 Tina Jackson, 'Goodness, I'm home!', *Guardian*, 4 December 2010, 'Family' section. See also Sanjeev Bhaskar, *India: One Man's Personal Journey Round the Subcontinent* (London: HarperCollins, 2007), chapter 8 for a return to his family roots. More generally, see Ian Talbot and Shinder Thandi (eds), *People on the Move: Punjabi Colonial, and Post-Colonial Migration* (Oxford: Oxford University Press, 2004) and Ravinder Kaur, *Since 1947: Partition Narratives among Punjabi Migrants to Delhi* (New Delhi: Oxford University Press, 2007).

43 Figures and commentory in E.J.B. Rose *et al.*, *Colour and Citizenship: A Report on British Race Relations* (London: Oxford University Press, 1969), pp. 52, 97.

44 Talbot and Thandi (eds), *People on the Move.*

45 Muhammad Anwar, *The Myth of Return: Pakistanis in Britain* (London: Heinemann, 1979).

46 Irna Imran, Tim Smith and Donald Hyslop (eds), *Here to Stay: Bradford's South Asian Communities* (Bradford: City of Bradford Metropolitan Council, Arts, Museums and Libraries, 1994), p. 42.

47 *Ibid.*, p. 46.

48 A. James Hamerton and Alistair Thomson, *Ten pound Poms: Australia's Invisible Migrants* (Manchester: Manchester University Press, 2005), pp. 114–15, 119.

49 Michel Foucault, 'Different Spaces' in James Faubion (ed.), *Essential Works of Foucault* vol. 2 *Aesthetics, Method, and Epistemology* (London: Allen Lane, 1998), pp. 184–5.

50 Caryl Phillips, *The Final Passage* (London: Vintage, 2004 [1985]).

51 Susanne Lachenicht, 'Huguenot Immigrants and the Formation of National Identities, 1548–1787', *The Historical Journal* vol. 50 no. 2 (2007), p. 326.

52 Bud Flanagan, *My Crazy Life* (London: Four Square Books, 1962 [1961]), p. 13.

53 John Klier and Shlomo Lambroza (eds), *Pogroms: Anti-Jewish Violence in Modern Russian History* (Cambridge: Cambridge University Press, 1992).

54 See http://en.wikipedia.org/wiki/Bud_Flanagan, accessed 28 July 2009. For details of the Weintrop family, see the 1891 Census, for their household in 12 Hanbury Street, Spitalfields.

55 Obituary by Nicholas Watkins, *Guardian*, 26 September 2009.

56 Obituary by Martin Salisbury of Susan Einzig in *Guardian*, 6 January 2010.

57 King, in *Forty Winters On*, p. 8.

58 Mike and Trevor Phillips, *Windrush: The Irresistible Rise of Multi-Racial Britain* (London: HarperCollins, 1999 [1998]), p. 61.

59 *Ibid.*, p. 64.

60 *Forty Winters On*, p. 8. On 22 January 1949 at a Ministry of Labour conference of the regions on 'placing colonial negroes', a Mr McGuirk of Liverpool did ask 'whether it had been found that these coloured workers stood up the vigours of the winter weather'. He himself was 'inclined to think they had'. In National Archives, LAB 26/226.

61 Phillips and Phillips, *Windrush*, pp. 7, 62.
62 Dick Adler, 'Voyage to the Promised Land', *Sunday Times*, 30 June 1968.
63 Irving Howe, *World of Our Fathers: The Journey of East European Jews to America and the Life they Found and Made* (New York: Galahad Books, 1976), p. 39.
64 Flanagan, *My Crazy Life*, pp. 13–14.
65 Vincent Carretta, 'Olaudah Equiano or Gustavus Vassa? New Light on an Eighteenth-Century Question of Identity', *Slavery and Abolition* vol. 20 no. 3 (1999), pp. 96–105 and Vincent Carretta, *Equiano, the African: Biography of a Self Made Man* (Athens, GA: University of Georgia Press, 2005).
66 See Gary Younge, 'Author casts shadow over slave hero', *Guardian*, 14 September 2005.
67 Vincent Carretta, 'Response to Paul Lovejoy's "Autobiography and Memory: Gustavus Vassa, alias Olaudah Equiano, the African"', *Slavery and Abolition* vol. 28 no. 1 (2007), p. 116.
68 For a critique of Carretta's analysis see Paul Lovejoy, 'Autobiography and Memory: Gustavus Vassa, alias Olaudah Equiano, the African', *Slavery and Abolition* vol. 27 no. 3 (2006), pp. 317–47 and Paul Lovejoy,, 'Issues of Motivation – Vassa/Equiano and Carretta's Critique of the Evidence', *Slavery and Abolition* vol. 28 no. 1 (2007), pp. 121–5.
69 Paul Edwards (ed.), *The Life of Olaudah Equiano, or Gustavus Vassa the African* (Harlow: Longman, 1993 [1989]), pp. 23, 25.
70 Elie Wiesel, 'Trivializing Memory', in Elie Wiesel, *From the Kingdom of Memory: Reminiscences* (New York: Schocken Books, 1990), pp. 165–6.
71 Sewell, *Keep on Moving*, pp. 1, 3. See also Adler, 'Voyage to the Promised Land'.
72 Buchi Emecheta, *Head Above Water: An Autobiography* (London: Fontana, 1986), p. 26.
73 Richard Benneman, Cunard executive, 1934 quoted in Nick Evans, '"A Strike for Racial Justice"? Transatlantic Shipping and the Jewish Diaspora, 1882–1939', in Jordan, Kushner and Pearce (eds), *Jewish Journeys*, p. 37.
74 In *St Ives Times*, 11 February 1938, special supplement.
75 Michael Bird, *The St Ives Artists: A Biography of Place and Time* (Aldershot: Lund Humphries, 2008), p. 49.
76 Ze'ev Venia Hadari, *Second Exodus: The Full Story of Jewish Illegal Immigration to Palestine, 1945–1948* (London: Vallentine Mitchell, 1991), chapter 18.
77 *Guardian*, 24 May 2010 provides details and a large colour illustration.
78 Author, site visit, 26 February 2011.
79 Rachel Cooke, interview with Yinka Shonibere, *Observer*, 16 May 2010.
80 Marcus Wood, 'Significant Silence: Where was Slave Agency in the Popular Imagery of 2007?', in Cora Kaplan and John Oldfield (eds), *Imagining Transatlantic Slavery* (Basingstoke: Palgrave Macmillan, 2010), pp. 162–90 (p. 187).
81 *Ibid.*, p. 187.
82 Steven Spielberg, *Amistad* (2007).
83 C.B. Shaw, 'The Huguenot and Flemish Invasion', in Arnold White (ed.), *The Destitute Alien in Great Britain* (London: Swan Sonnenschein, 1892), pp. 15–16.

84 Reverend G.S. Reaney, 'The Moral Aspect', in White (ed.), *The Destitute Alien*, pp. 75–6.

85 Royal Commission on Alien Immigration, *Minutes of Evidence* (London: HMSO, 1903), pp. 39–40. Dr H. Williams, the Medical Officer for the Port of London, provided evidence more to Evans Gordon's liking relating to those migrants travelling on ships from Libau (see pp. 208–9). For a summary of the evidence on this matter see the Royal Commission on Alien Immigration, *Report* (London: HMSO, 1903), p. 11.

86 *Daily Express*, 21 January 1903.

87 'Undesirable Imports', *Daily Express*, 20 November 1901.

88 *This England* vol. 9 no. 3 (Autumn 1976), p. 3. See also Patrick Wright, *The Village That Died for England: The Strange Story of Tyneham* (London: Jonathan Cape, 1995), p. 37 for further comment.

89 *The Voice*, 20–26 July 2009.

90 John Hooper, 'Hundreds of migrants feared drowned off Tunisia', *Guardian*, 3 June 2011.

91 Caroline Moorehead, *Human Cargo: A Journey among Refugees* (London: Chatto & Windus, 2005), pp. 106–10.

92 *Ibid.*, p. 111.

93 Eric Richards, *Destination Australia: Migration to Australia since 1901* (Sydney: University of New South Wales Press, 2008).

94 *Guardian*, 17 December 2010.

95 The postcard of this Eastleigh Carnival float, which won second prize, is in the possession of local postcard collector, Jeff Pain. For further discussion, see Tony Kushner, 'Not That Far? Remembering and forgetting cosmopolitan Southampton in the 20th century', in Miles Taylor (ed.), *Southampton: Gateway to the British Empire* (London: I.B. Tauris, 2007), pp. 185–207, esp. pp. 196–205.

96 *Ibid.*, p. 108.

97 Amon Saba Saakana, *Blues Dance* (London: Amon Saba Saakana, 1985), p. 51.

98 See Tony Kushner, 'Cowards or Heroes? Jewish Journeys, Jewish Families and the *Titanic*', in Jordan, Kushner and Pearce (eds), *Jewish Journeys*, pp. 205–27.

99 Louis Macneice, *The Strings are False: An Unfinished Autobiography* (London: 1965), p. 199.

100 In E.R. Dodds (ed.), *The Collected Poems of Louis Macneice* (London: 1966), pp. 180–1.

101 David Fitzpatrick, *Irish Emigration, 1801–1921* (Dublin: Economic and Social History Society of Ireland, 1984), pp. 1–6.

102 David Fitzpatrick, *Oceans of Consolation: Personal Accounts of Irish Migration to Australia* (Cork: Cork University Press, 1994), p. 525.

103 The most thorough treatment is Nicholas Evans, 'Aliens *en route*: European transmigration through Britain, 1836–1914' (unpublished Ph.D. thesis, University of Hull, 2006).

104 Paul Gilroy, *The Black Atlantic: Modernity and Double Consciousness* (London: Verso, 1993), pp. 16–17.

105 Alan Rice, 'Naming the money and unveiling the crime: contemporary British artists and the memorialization of slavery and abolition', *Patterns of Prejudice* vol. 41 nos 3–4 (2007), p. 330.

106 John Oldfield, *'Chords of Freedom'. Commemoration, Ritual and British Transatlantic Slavery* (Manchester: Manchester University Press, 2007), p. 122. See also the sensitive analysis in Elizabeth Wallace, *The British Slave Trade & Public Memory* (New York: Columbia University Press, 2006), Chapter 1 and pp. 49–50 on Pero.

107 William O'Reilly, History seminar paper, '"Selling Souls". "The Crown" and the 18th-century Atlantic trade in migrants', University of Southampton, 2 February 2010.

108 Per Kristian Sebak, *Titanic's Predecessor: The S/S Norge Disaster of 1904* (Laksevaag, Norway: Seaward Publishing, 2004).

109 Nikolaj Larsen, 'Promised Land', in Andrea Schlieker (ed.), *Folkestone Triennial: A Million Miles from Home*, pp. 84–5.

110 Nikolaj Larsen, *Promised Land*, Folkestone Triennial, Marine Parade, Folkestone, author visit, 7 July 2011.

111 The painting was sponsored by the NSPCC and reproduced in *The Sunday Times Magazine*, 17 April 2011. I have benefited from discussing this image with Aimée Bunting.

112 Caryl Phillips, *The Atlantic Sound* (London: Faber and Faber, 2000), pp. 15–16.

113 From the album *Jimmy Cliff* (Island Records, 1969).

114 Robin Mundill, *The King's Jews: Money, Massacre and Exodus in Medieval England* (London: Continuum, 2010), p. 158.

115 Author site visit, 8 July 2011. Nevertheless, Dover Museum has created a temporary exhibition 'Invaders and Settlers' (September 2010–September 2011) which while not exploring negative responses, does cover settlement in Dover through to contemporary asylum seekers.

116 Quoted in '58 Remembered', in Dimsum, a British Chinese website, www.dimsum.co.uk/viewpoints/58-remembered.html, accessed 4 July 2011.

117 Alan Travis, 'Country houses and white cliffs to portray Britain in new passport', *Guardian*, 26 August 2010.

118 Adler, 'Voyage to the Promised Land'.

119 Emecheta, *Head Above Water*, pp. 114–15.

120 *Ibid.*, pp. 200–1.

121 *Ibid.*, p. 115.

122 *Bound for Nowhere* (American Jewish Committee, 1939).

123 Elinor Brecher, 'SS St.Louis survivors recall voyage from Florida', *Miami Herald*, 14 December 2009.

124 Gisela Feldman, 'It was like a cruise, then the suicide attempts began', *Jewish Chronicle*, 11 December 2009.

125 Patrick Geary, *Phantoms of Remembrance: Memory and Oblivion at the End of the First Millennium* (Princeton, NJ: Princeton University Press, 1994), p. 12.

126 Doreen Massey, 'Places and their Pasts', *History Workshop* no. 39 (spring 1995), p. 186.

127 Sukdev Sandhu, *London Calling: How Black and Asian Writers Imagined a City*

(London: HarperCollins, 2003), pp. 314–15.

128 *Ibid.*, pp. 314–28. *Sweet Thames* was broadcast on BBC2, 3 July 1992.

129 Stuart Maconie, *Hope & Glory: The Days that Made Britain* (London: Ebury Press, 2011), p. 158.

130 *Small Island*, BBC 1, 6 and 13 December 2009. The serialisation ends taking the story up to date, with a positive portrayal of black life in Britain, emphasising rootedness and success.

131 Kesper Aspden, *The Hounding of David Oluwale* (London: Vintage, 2008 [2007]), p. 211.

132 Yasmin Alibhai-Brown, *The Settler's Cookbook: A Memoir of Love, Migration and Food* (London: Portobello Books, 2008), pp. 420–1; Yasmin Alibhai-Brown, *Who Do We Think We Are? Imagining the New Britain* (London: Penguin, 2001 edition), p. xvi on Tebbit's intervention on BBC Radio 4's *Today* programme, September 2000.

133 Alibhai-Brown, *The Settler's Cookbook*, pp. 420–1.

Bibliography

Primary sources

Archives in public collections

BBC Written Archives
BBC Home Service, news transcripts, 1947
BBC North American Service, news transcripts, 1947

Black Cultural Archives
Michael Banton papers
Empire Windrush commemoration papers

British Library Sound Archive
'Living Memory of the Jewish Community' oral history collection

Hampshire Record Office
Portal papers

Imperial War Museum Archives
Cy Grant papers
Doreen Warriner papers

London Jewish Museum
Papers relating to Holocaust survivors

London Metropolitan Archives
Board of Deputies of British Jews papers

Manchester Jewish Museum

Oral history interviews

National Archives

Board of Trade series, BT 26, 350
Cabinet Office series, CAB 37, 128, 129
Colonial Office series, CO 318, 384, 554
Foreign Office series, FO 37, 83, 181, 183, 369, 371, 945
Home Office series, HO 45, 213, 215, 344, 352, 367, 372, 382, 405
Ministry of Labour series, LAB 8, 26
Ministry of Transport series, MT 9
State Papers series, SP 41, 89

Southampton Record Office

Index cards of Colonial Merchant seamen
Papers relating to 'Brazilian refugees'

Tower Hamlets Local History Library

Papers relating to the Jewish East End

University of Cape Town

Cyril Orolowitz papers

University of East London

Refugee Council records:
Vietnamese refugees

University of Southampton

Central British Fund records

University of Sussex

Mass-Observation Archive:
Anti-Semitism Collection, 1939
File Reports, 1947
Summer 2000 directive: 'Coming to Britain'
Summer 2006 directive: 'Core British Values'
Summer 2006 directive: 'History Matters'
Worktown Collection, 1939

Wiener Library, London

Nicholas Winton papers

Bibliography

Printed primary materials

Autobiographical

Abse, Dannie, *A Strong Dose of Myself* (London: Hutchinson, 1983)

Abse, Dannie, *Intermittent Journals* (Bridgend: Seren, 1994)

Alibhai-Brown, Yasmin, *The Settler's Cookbook: A Memoir of Love, Migration and Food* (London: Portobello Books, 2008)

Antin, Mary, *From Plotzk to Boston* (Boston, MA: W.B. Clarke, 1899)

Antin, Mary, *The Promised Land: The Autobiography of a Russian Immigrant* (Princeton, NJ: Princeton University Press, 1969)

Barry, James *et al.* (eds), *Sorry No Vacancies* (London: Notting Dale Urban Studies Centre and Ethnic Communities Oral History Project, 1992)

Black, Pauline, *Black By Design: A 2-Tone Memoir* (London: Serpent's Tail, 2011)

Blair, Tony, *A Journey* (London: Hutchinson, 2010)

Blond, Elaine with Barry Turner, *Marks of Distinction* (London: Vallentine Mitchell, 1988)

Bourne, Stephen and Esther Bruce, *The Sun Shone on Our Side of the Street: Aunt Esther's Story* (London: Ethnic Communities Oral History Project, 1991)

Bragg, Billy, *The Progressive Patriot: A Search for Belonging* (London: Black Swan, 2006)

Brent, Leslie Baruch, *Sunday's Child? A Memoir* (New Romney: Bank House Books, 2009)

Chappell, Carolyn Lougee, "'The Pains I Took to Save My/His Family": Escape Accounts by a Huguenot Daughter after the Revocation of the Edict of Nantes', *French Historical Studies* vol. 22 no. 1 (1999), Appendixes: Escape Accounts by Marie de La Rochefoucauld and Suzanne de Robillard

Chapeltown Black Women Writers' Group (eds), *When Our Ship Comes In: Black Women Talk* (Castleford: Yorkshire Art Circus, 1992)

Chotzinoff, Samuel, *A Lost Paradise: Early Reminiscences* (London: Hamish Hamilton, 1956)

Cohen, Rose, *Out of the Shadow: A Russian Jewish Girlhood on the Lower East Side* (Ithaca, NY: Cornell University Press, 1995)

Cowan, Eve (ed.), *Emet: A Collection of Members' True Life Stories* (Bournemouth: Bournemouth Reform Synagogue, 1999)

Creese, Jannett, *My Windward Side* (Stockport: Stockport Libraries, 2002)

Dieu, To Minh, 'Light', *New Homeland* (January 1980)

Edensor, Tim and Mij Kelly, *Moving Worlds: Personal Recollections of Twenty-One Immigrants to Edinburgh* (Edinburgh: Polygon, 1989)

Edwards, Paul (ed.), *The Life of Olaudah Equiano, or Gustavus Vassa the African* (Harlow: Longman, 1993)

Elsley, Marianne, *A Chance in Six Million* (Banbury: Kemble Press, 1989)

Emecheta, Buchi, *Head Above Water: An Autobiography* (London: Fontana, 1986)

Eshun, Ekow, *Black Gold of the Sun: Searching for Home in England and Africa* (London: Hamish Hamilton, 2005)

Flanagan, Bud, *My Crazy Life* (London: Four Square Books, 1962)

Frampton, Paul, *The Golly in the Cupboard* (Manchester: Tamic, 2004)

Freedland, Jonathan, *Jacob's Gift: A Journey into the Heart of Belonging* (London: Penguin, 2005)

Gershon, Karen (ed.), *We Came as Children: A Collective Autobiography of Refugees* (London: Papermac, 1989)

Goldman, William, *East End My Cradle* (London: A. & E., 1947)

Grade, Lew, *Still Dancing: My Story* (Glasgow: Fontana/Collins, 1987)

Hare, Tony, *Spanning the Century: The Story of an Ordinary Man in Extraordinary Circumstances* (Spennymoor, County Durham: Memoir Club, 2002)

Harris, Mark and Deborah Oppenheimer (eds), *Into the Arms of Strangers: Stories of the Kindertransport* (London: Bloomsbury, 2000)

Harris, Nick, *Dublin's Little Jerusalem* (Dublin: A. & A. Farmer, 2002)

Igersheimer, Walter, *Blatant Injustice: The Story of a Jewish Refugee from Nazi Germany Imprisoned in Britain and Canada during World War II* (Montreal: McGill-Queen's University Press, 2005)

Imran, Irna, Tim Smith and Donald Hyslop (eds), *Here to Stay: Bradford's South Asian Communities* (Bradford: Bradford Heritage Recording Unit, 1994)

Jaggi, Maya, 'The Final Passage: An Interview with Writer Caryl Phillips', in Kwesi Owusu (ed.), *Black British Culture and Society: A Text Reader* (London: Routledge, 2000)

Kay, Jackie, *Red Dust Road: An Autobiographical Journey* (London: Picador, 2010)

King, Sam, *Climbing up the Rough Side of the Mountain* (London: Minerva Press, 1998)

Lambeth Council, *Forty Winters On: Memories of Britain's post war Caribbean Immigrants* (London: Lambeth Services, The Voice and South London Press, 1988)

Leverton, Bertha and Shmuel Lowensohn (eds), *I Came Alone: The Stories of the Kindertransports* (Lewes: The Book Guild, 2000)

Levi, Primo, *The Drowned and the Saved* (London: Michael Joseph, 1988)

Macneice, Louis, *The Strings are False: An Unfinished Autobiography* (London, 1965)

Maric, Vesna, *Bluebird: A Memoir* (London: Granta, 2009)

Marke, Ernest, *In Troubled Waters: Memoirs of Seventy Years in England* (London: Karia Press, 1986)

Marshall, Oliver (ed.), *Los ninosvascos* (London: Ethnic Communities Oral History Project & North Kensington Archive, 1991)

Marteilhe, Jean, *The Huguenot Galley-Slave: Being the Autobiography of a French Protestant Condemned to the Galley for the Sake of his Religion* (New York: Leypoldt & Holt, 1867)

Migault, John, *A Narrative of the Sufferings of a French Protestant Family at the Period of the Revocation of the Edict of Nantes* (London: John Butterworth, 1824)

Mikes, George, *How to be a Brit* (Harmondsworth: Penguin, 1986)

Milton, Edith, *The Tiger in the Attic: Memories of the Kindertransport and Growing Up English* (Chicago: University of Chicago Press, 2005)

William Minet, *The Huguenot Family of Minet* (London: Spottiswoode & Co, 1892)

Mitchel, John, *Jail Journal* (Dublin: University Press of Ireland, 1982)

Monolulu, Prince, *I Gotta Horse: The Autobiography of Ras Prince Monolulu as told to Sidney H. White* (London: Hurst & Blackett, 1960)

Murray, Robert (ed.), *The Experiences of World War II. Westindian Ex-Service Personnel* (Nottingham: Nottingham Combined Ex-Service Association, 1996)

Palmer, Lilli, *Change Lobsters – and Dance: An Autobiography* (London: W.H. Allen, 1976)

Pool, Hannah, *My Father's Daughter* (London: Hamish Hamilton, 2005)

Reif-Lehrer, Liane, 'Memory's Edge', *Boston* vol. 80 no. 2 (1988)

Ressinger, Dianne (ed.), *Memoirs of the Reverend Jaques Fontaine 1658–1728* (London: Huguenot Society of Great Britain and Ireland, 1992)

Ressinger, Dianne (ed.), *Memoirs of Isaac Dumont de Bostaquet: A Gentleman of Normandy* (London: Huguenot Society of Great Britain and Ireland, 2005)

Rice, Alan, 'Exploring Inside the Invisible: An Interview with Lubaina Himid', *Wasafari* no. 40 (Winter 2003)

Shaun, William (ed.), *Mollie Panter-Downes: London War Notes 1939–1945* (London: Longman, 1972)

Smith, William, *An Emigrant's Narrative, or a Voice from the Steerage* (New York: William Smith, 1850)

Spier, Eugen, *The Protecting Power* (London: Skeffington and Sons, 1951)

Stirling, A. (ed.), *The Diaries of Dummer: Reminiscences of an Old Sportsman, Stephen Terry of Dummer* (London: Unicorn Press, 1934)

Tajfel, Henri and John Dawson (eds), *Disappointed Guests* (London: Institute of Race Relations, 1965)

Thompson, Leslie, *An Autobiography as told to Jeffrey P. Green* (Crawley: Rabbit Press, 1985)

Vajda, Albert, *Remade in England: From Her Majesty's Alien to Her Majesty's British Subject* (Edinburgh: Polygon Books, 1981)

Varon, Laura, *The Juderia: A Holocaust Survivor's Tribute to the Jewish Community of Rhodes* (Westport, CT: Praeger, 1999)

de Waal, Edmund, *The Hare with Amber Eyes: A Hidden Inheritance* (London: Vintage, 2011)

Walker, Sam and Alvin Elcock (eds), *The Windrush Legacy: Memories of Britain's post-war Caribbean Immigrants* (London: Black Cultural Archives, 1998)

Whyte, Robert, *The Ocean Plague: A Voyage to Quebec in an Irish Emigrant Vessel* (Boston, MA: Coolidge and Wiley, 1848)

Wiesel, Elie, *From the Kingdom of Memory: Reminiscences* (New York: Schocken Books, 1990)

Williams, Charlotte, *Sugar and Slate* (Aberystwyth: Planet, 2002)

Zurndorfer, Hannele, *The Ninth of November* (London: Quartet Books, 1989)

Politics, travel writing, guides, catalogues, popular history, reports

Alibhai-Brown, Yasmin, *Who Do We Think We Are? Imagining the New Britain* (London: Penguin, 2001 [2000])

Alibhai-Brown, Yasmin, *After Multiculturalism* (London: Foreign Policy Centre, 2000)

Angell, Norman and Dorothy Buxton, *You and the Refugee* (Harmonsworth: Penguin, 1939)

Avery, Trevor, *From Auschwitz to Ambleside* (Sedbergh: Another Space, 2008)

Barker, Ernest, *National Character and the Factors in its Formation* (London: Methuen, 1927)

Barker, Ernest (ed.), *The Character of England* (Oxford: Clarendon Press, 1947)

Berenbaum, Michael, *The World Must Know: The History of the Holocaust as Told in the United States Holocaust Memorial Museum* (Boston: Little, Brown, 1993)

Bhaskar, Sanjeev, *India: One Man's Personal Journey Round the Subcontinent* (London: HarperCollins, 2007)

Brougher, Kerry and Astrid Bowron (eds), *Gustav Metzger* (Oxford: Museum of Modern Art, 1998)

Browne, Anthony, *Do We Need Mass Immigration?* (London: Civitas, 2002)

Bryant, Arthur, *The National Character* (London: Longmans, Green & Co, 1934)

Buxton, Dorothy, *The Economics of the Refugee Problem* (London: Focus, 1939)

Coad, Jonathan, *Dover Castle* (London: Batsford/English Heritage, 1995)

Cohen, Steve, *Deportation is Freedom! The Orwellian World of Immigration Controls* (London: Jessica Kingsley Publishers, 2006)

Conway, David, *A Nation of Immigrants? A Brief Demographic History of Britain* (London: Civitas, 2007)

Costello, Roy, *Black Liverpool: The Early History of Britain's Oldest Black Community 1730–1918* (Liverpool: Picton Press, 2001)

Cunningham, William, *Alien Immigrants to England* (London: Swan Sonnenshein, 1897)

Currer-Briggs, Noel and Royston Gambier, *Huguenot Ancestry* (Chichester: Phillimore, 1985)

Denvir, John, *The Irish in Britain from the Earliest Times to the Fall and Death of Parnell* (London: Kegan, Paul, Trench and Trubner, 1892)

'Dicky Sam', *Liverpool and Slavery: An Historical Account of the Liverpool-African Slave Trade* (Liverpool: Bowker& Son, 1884)

Egginton, Joyce, *They Seek a Living* (London: Hutchinson, 1957)

Foster, Vere, *Work and Wages, or, the Penny Emigrant's Guide* (London: W.F. Cash, 1855)

Frow, Mayerlene, *Roots of the Future: Ethnic Diversity in the Making of Britain* (London: Commission for Racial Equality, 1996)

Gordon, William Evans, *The Alien Immigrant* (London: Heinemann, 1903)

Guardian/Observer, *Guardian/Observer History of Modern Music* (London: Guardian/Observer, 2011)

Harris, Myles, *Tomorrow is Another Country: What is Wrong with UK's Asylum Policy* (London: Civitas, 2003)

Hinds, Donald, *Journey to an Illusion: The West Indian in Britain* (London: Bogle-L'Ouverture, 1966)

Imperial War Museum, *The Holocaust: The Holocaust Exhibition at the Imperial War Museum* (London: Imperial War Museum, 2000)

Jacobson, Howard, *Roots Schmoots: Journeys Among Jews* (London: Penguin, 1993)

Jeanie Johnston Company, *The Jeanie Johnston* (Blennerville, Ireland: Jeanie Johnston Company, no date)

John, Don and Stella Muirhead, *A Black History of Southampton: 16th Century to 21st Century* (Southampton: Positive Message, 2010)

Kerridge, Roy, *The Story of Black History* (London: The Claridge Press, 1998)

Law, Ian and June Henfrey, *A History of Race and Racism in Liverpool 1660–1950* (Liverpool: Merseyside Community Relations Council, 1981)

Lewis, Gordon, 'Race Relations in Britain: A View from the Caribbean', *Race Today* vol. 1 no. 3 (1969)

Mackinder, H.J., *Britain and the British Seas* (London: William Heineman, 1902)

Maconie, Stuart, *Adventures on the High Teas: In Search of Middle England* (London: Ebury Press, 2009)

Maconie, Stuart, *Hope & Glory: The days that made Britain* (London: Ebury Press, 2011)

Mee, Arthur, *The King's England: Kent, the Gateway of England and its Great Possessions* (London: Hodder and Stoughton, 1936)

Modood, Tariq, *Multiculturalism: A Civic Idea* (Cambridge: Polity Press, 2007)

Moorehead, Caroline, *Human Cargo: A Journey among Refugees* (London: Chatto & Windus, 2005)

Movement for the Care of Children from Germany, *First Annual Report November 1938–December 1939* (London: Bloomsbury House, 1940)

Muir, Ramsey *A History of Liverpool* (London: University of Liverpool Press, 1907)

Murdoch, Tessa (ed.), *The Quiet Conquest: The Huguenots, 1685 to 1985* (London: Museum of London, 1985)

Neuberger, Julia, *The Moral State We're In: A Manifesto for a 21st Century Society* (London: HarperCollins, 2005)

Parekh, Bhikhu (ed.), *The Future of Multi-Ethnic Britain* (London: Profile, 2000)

Peberdy, Philip, *God's House Tower, Southampton* (Southampton: Southampton Museums, 1960)

Pennington John (ed.), *The British Heritage* (London: Odhams Press, 1948)

Phillips, Caryl, *The Atlantic Sound* (London: Faber and Faber, 2000)

Pollard, Stephen, *Ten Days that Changed the Nation: The Making of Modern Britain* (London: Simon & Schuster, 2009)

Portal, Pierre de, *Les Descendants des Albogeois et des Huguenots, ou Memoires de la Famille de Portal* (Paris: Ch. Meyrueis et Cie, 1860)

Portal, Sir William, *Some account of the settlement of refugees (L'Eglise Wallone) at Southampton* (Winchester: Jacob and Johnson, 1902)

Presland, John, *A Great Adventure: The Story of the Refugee Children's Movement* (London: Refugee Children's Movement, 1944)

Rees, Jim, *A Farewell to Famine* (Arklow: Arklow Enterprise Centre, 1994)

Rose, E.J.B. (*et al.*), *Colour and Citizenship: A Report on British Race Relations* (London:

Oxford University Press, 1969)

Sandell, Elsie, *Southampton Cavalcade* (Southampton: G.F.Wilson, 1953)

Sandell, Elsie, *Southampton Through the Ages: A Short History* (Southampton: G.F. Wilson, 1960)

Sardar, Ziauddin, *Balti Britain: A Provocative Journey Through Asian Britain* (London: Granta, 2009)

Schlieker, Andrea (ed.), *Folkestone Triennial: A Million Miles from Home* (Folkestone: Cultureshock Media, 2011)

Scruton, Roger, *England: An Elegy* (London: Chatto&Windus, 2000)

Sinclair, Neil, *The Tiger Bay Story* (Cardiff: Butetown History & Arts Project, 1993)

Sinclair, Neil, *Endangered Tiger: A Community under Threat* (Cardiff: Butetown History & Arts Centre, 2003)

Smiles, Samuel, *The Huguenots: Their Settlement, Churches, and Industries in England and Ireland* (London: John Murray, 1868)

Strong, Roy, *Visions of England* (London: Bodley Head, 2011)

Troup, Sir Edward, *The Home Office* (London: G.P. Putnam& Sons, 1925)

Unwin, Peter, *The Narrow Sea: Barrier, Bridge and Gateway to the World – The History of the English Channel* (London: Review, 2004)

Weiss, Charles, *History of the French Protestant Refugees, from the Revocation of the Edict of Nantes to Our Own Days* (New York: Stringer & Townsend, 1854)

Weizmann, Chaim, *The Right to Survive: Testimony before the Anglo-American Committee of Enquiry on Palestine* (London: Jewish Agency for Palestine, 1946)

White, Arnold (ed.), *The Destitute Alien in Great Britain* (London: Swan Sonnenschein, 1892)

Whitlock, J. Aston, *The Hospital of God's House Southampton* (Southampton: Henry March Gilbert, 1894)

Williams, Hugh, *Fifty Things You Need to Know about British History* (London: HarperCollins, 2009)

Wollaston, Sam, Ian Katz and Rick Williams (eds), *Welcome to Britain* (London: The Guardian, 2001)

Wood, Robert, *Walks into History: Hampshire* (Newbury: Countryside Books, 2009)

Worshipful Company of Goldsmiths, *The Courtauld Family: Huguenot Silversmiths* (London: Worshipful Company of Goldsmiths, 1985)

Literature, drama, poetry and music

Agboluaje, Oladipo, *The Hounding of David Oluwale* (London: Oberon Books, 2009)

D'Aguiar, Fred, *British Subjects* (Newcastle: Bloodaxe Books, 1993)

Barnes, Julian, *A History of the World in 10½ Chapters* (London: Picador, 1990)

Bean, Richard, *England People Very Nice* (London: Oberon Books, 2009)

Cliff, Jimmy, *Jimmy Cliff* (Island Records, 1969)

Dodds, E.R. (ed.), *The Collected Poems of Louis Macneice* (London: Faber and Faber, 1966)

Emecheta, Buchi, *Second-Class Citizen* (Oxford: Heinemann, 1994)

Johnson, Linton Kwesi, *Dread Beat and Blood* (London: Bogle-L'Ouverture, 1982)

Kay, Jackie, *Fiere* (London: Picador, 2011)

Lamming, George, *The Emigrants* (London: Michael Joseph, 1954)

Levy, Andrea, *Small Island* (London: Review, 2004)

Mangan, James, *Gerald Keegan's Famine Diary: Journey to a New World* (Dublin: Wolfhound Press, 1991)

Naipaul, V.S., *The Middle Passage* (London: Picador, 1995)

Phillips, Caryl, *The Final Passage* (London: Vintage, 2004)

Phillips, Caryl, *Foreigners: Three English Lives* (London, Vintage, 2008)

Rushdie, Salman, *The Satanic Verses* (Dover, DE: The Consortium, 1992)

Rushdie, Salman, *Midnight's Children* (London: Vintage, 2006)

Saakana, Amon Saba, *Blues Dance* (London: Amon Saba Saakana, 1985)

Sandford, Jeremy, *Smiling David: The Story of David Oluwale* (London: Calder & Boyars, 1974)

Selvon, Sam, *Moses Ascending* (London: Davis-Poynter, 1975)

Whitney, Kim Ablon, *The Other Half of Life* (New York: Laurel-Leaf, 2009)

Newspapers and journals

Black and Asian Studies Association Newsletter
Daily Express
Daily Mirror
Daily Worker
Economist
Evening News
Financial Times
Guardian
Hampshire Advertiser
Hampshire Independent
The Illustrated London News
The Independent
iNexile: The Refugee Council Magazine
Jewish Chronicle
Journal of the '45 Aid Society
Londonderry Journal
Manchester Guardian
Miami Herald
New Yorker
News Chronicle
Observer
Pall Mall Gazette
Picture Post
Preston Guardian
Prospect
Radio Times
St Ives Times

Southampton Observer
Southampton Times
Southern Daily Echo
Southern Evening Echo
The Spectator
The Standard
Sunday Express
Sunday Mirror
Sunday Telegraph
Sunday Times
The Times
The Voice
This England
Zionist Review

Official publications

Aliens Act, 1905

Census returns; 1881, 1891, 1901, 1911

Hansard

Home Office, *Fairer, Faster and Firmer: A Modern Approach to Immigration and Asylum* (London: HMSO, 1998)

Home Office, *Community Cohesion: A Report of the Independent Review Team Chaired by Ted Cantle* (London: Home Office, 2001)

Home Office, *Life in the United Kingdom: A Journey to Citizenship* (London: HMSO, 2004)

Parliamentary papers, 1847/48, 1851

Royal Commission on Alien Immigration, *Report* (London: HMSO, 1903)

Royal Commission on Alien Immigration, *Minutes of Evidence* (London: HMSO, 1903)

Document collections

Arbabzadah, Nushin (ed.), *From Outside In: Refugees and British Society* (London: Arcadia Books, 2007)

Grewal, Shabnam, Jackie Kay, Liliane Landor, Gail Lewis and Pratibha Parmar (eds), *Charting the Journey: Writings by Black and Third World Women* (London: Sheba Feminist Publishers, 1988)

Kampe, Norbert (ed.), *Jewish Immigrants of the Nazi Period in the USA* vol. 4 part 2 (New York: K.G. Saur, 1992)

Kohn, Jerome and Ron Feldman (eds), *The Jewish Writings: Hannah Arendt* (New York: Schocken Books, 2007)

Orwell, Sonia and Ian Angus (eds), *The Collected Essays, Journalism and Letters of George Orwell* vol. II (Harmondsworth: Penguin, 1984)

Poirteir, Cathal (ed.), *Famine Echoes* (Dublin: Gill & Macmillan, 1995)

Salz, Evelyn (ed.), *Selected Letters of Mary Antin* (Syracuse, NY: Syracuse University Press, 2000)

Smithies, Bill and Peter Fiddick (eds), *Enoch Powell on Immigration* (London: Sphere Books, 1969)

Welsh, Edwin (ed.), *The Minute Book of the French Church at Southampton, 1702–1939* (Southampton: University of Southampton Press, 1979)

Other primary sources

Speeches

Brown, Gordon, Annual British Council Lecture, 7 July 2004

Brown, Gordon, 'The Future of Britishness', Fabian Society, 14 January 2006

Cameron, David, speech at Munich Security Conference, 5 February 2011

Denham, John, 'Cry "God for Harry, England and Saint George!": Celebrating England and Englishness', Smith Institute, 2 March 2010

Denham, John, 'Promoting Community Cohesion', Industrial Society and Runnymede Trust, 18 March 2002

Howard, Michael, speech at Conservative Party annual conference, 5 October 2004

Miliband, Ed, speech at Labour Party annual conference, 28 September 2010

Films and documentaries

Amistad (Steven Spielberg, 2007)

Bound for Nowhere (American Jewish Joint Distribution Committee, 1939)

In This World (Michael Winterbottom, 2003)

Refuge England (Robert Vaz, 1959)

A Touch of the Tar Brush (John Akomfrah, 1991)

The Voyage of the St Louis (Stuart Rosenberg, 1976)

The Voyage of the St Louis (Maziar Bahari, 1996)

Television

Britain's Secret Schindler Revealed (Channel 5, 27 January 2011)

East End (BBC, 12 July 1939)

EastEnders (BBC1, 24 February 2009)

The Final Passage (Channel 4, 7 and 8 July 1996)

Garrow's Law (BBC1, 14 November 2010)

The Orphans Who Survived the Concentration Camps (BBC1, 5 April 2010)

Shirley (BBC2, 30 September 2011)

Skipper Next to God (BBC, 7 October 1951)

Small Island (BBC1, 6 and 13 December 2009)

Upstairs Downstairs (BBC1, 26 February 2012)

Who Do You Think You Are? (BBC1, 23 February 2009)

Windrush (BBC2, 30 May, 6, 13 and 20 June 1998)

Museums, exhibitions and site visits

Australian National Maritime Museum, Sydney, 19 February 2010

Brighton Museum, 27 October 2009

Calgarth Estate, Lake Windermere, 18 August 2009
Dover Memorial to 58 Chinese migrants, 8 July 2011
Dover Museum, 8 July 2011
Folkestone Triennial, 'A Million Miles from Home', 7 July 2011
Hamburg Emigration Museum, 13 September 2008
Imperial War Museum, 1 April 2010
Jeanie Johnston, Dublin, 20 November 2010
Kingston upon Hull transmigration sites, 10 December 2009
Liverpool Street station, Hope Square, 15 September 2007
Museum of London, 14 July 2010
Museum of London Docklands, 28 December 2010
National Maritime Museum, Falmouth, 27 December 2003
National Museum of Scotland, 23 February 2010
St Martin's Church, Bowness-on-Windermere, 13 August 2009
Trafalgar Square, Yinka Shonibare's 'Nelson's Ship in a Bottle', 26 February 2011
Windermere Library, 12 July 2011

Websites

Brixton Poetry, http://homepages.which.net~panic.brixtonpoetry/poetoftides.htm, accessed 1 July 2011
BBC, www.bbc.co.uk/news/uk-politics–1142611?print=true, accessed 30 September 2010
Dimsum, www.dimsum.co.uk/viewpoints/58-remembered.html, accessed 4 July 2011.
Guardian, http://politics.guardian.co.uk/conservatives2004/story/0,15018,1320222,00.html, accessed 18 November 2004
Institute of Race Relations, www.irr.org.uk, accessed 2 July 2011
Holocaust Museum Texas, www.ushmm.org/museum/exhibit/online/stlouis/teach/lesson.htm, accessed 30 July 2009
Kent Archaeology, www.kentarchaeology.org.uk/Research/Libr/MIs/MIsDoverStMarys/01.htm, accessed 9 July 2011
Lambeth Council, www.lambeth.gov.uk/Services/Environment/Regeneration/FutureLambeth/Brixt …, accessed 15 February 2011
Leeds Metropolitan University, www.leedsmet.ac.uk/oluwale, accessed 22 September 2009
Refugee Council, www.refugeecouncil.org.uk/news/archive/press/2010/september/280910_pressr, accessed 1 October 2010
UNHCR, www.unhcr.org/pages/49c3646c74-page7.html, accessed 14 July 2009.
United States Holocaust Memorial Museum, www.ushmm.org/museum/exhibit/online/stlouis/teach/lesson.htm, accessed 30 July 2009
Wikipedia, http://en.wikipedia.org/wiki/Bud_Flanagan, accessed 28 July 2009

Miscellaneous primary sources

Australian National Maritime Museum, '*Tu Do*' (2010)
BBC educational guides to accompany *Windrush* series, 1998

Economist, 'Where Do You Stand?' Immigration posters, 2011
English Heritage, 'England's Heritage – Your Heritage' (2003)
English Heritage, 'Sites of Memory: The Slave Trade and Abolition', no date
Gisela Feldman, passport and other contemporary documents
Gisela Feldman, testimony, Menorah Synagogue, Cheshire, 'Shoah Seminar', 26 January 2001
Hugo Gryn, 'A Moral and Spiritual Index', Refugee Council, 1996
Holocaust Memorial Day (UK) study packs, 2001
Lilian Levy correspondence concerning Kindertransport statistics
Leonard Montefiore, 'Address given to the Cambridge University Jewish Society', 18 October 1946
Migration Museum Working Group 'A Moving Story: Is there a Case for a Major Museum of Migration in the UK?' (2009)
Jeff Pain, Southampton postcard private collection
Shari Segel, 'Voyage of St. Louis Remembered on 50th Anniversary', Museum of Jewish Heritage, 1989

Secondary sources

Adams, Caroline, *Across Seven Seas and Thirteen Rivers* (London: THAP Books, 1987)
Adi, Hakim, *West Africans in Britain, 1900–1960. Nationalism, Pan-Africanism and Communism* (London: Lawrence & Wishart, 1998)
Anwar, Muhammad, *The Myth of Return: Pakistanis in Britain* (London: Heinemann, 1979)
Aspden, Kester, *The Hounding of David Oluwale* (London: Vintage, 2008)
Back, Les, 'Falling from the Sky', *Patterns of Prejudice* vol. 37 no. 3 (2003)
Banton, Michael, *The Coloured Quarter: Negro Immigrants in an English City* (London: Jonathan Cape, 1955)
Bar-Yosef, Eitan and Nadia Valman (eds), *'The Jew' in Late-Victorian and Edwardian Culture: Between the East End and Africa* (Basingstoke: Palgrave Macmillan, 2009)
Baucom, Ian, *Spectors of the Atlantic: Finance Capital, Slavery, and the Philosophy of History* (Durham, NC: Duke University Press, 2005)
Bell, Adrian, *Only For Three Months: The Basque Children in Exile* (Norwich: Mousehold Press, 1996)
Belluscio, Steven, *To be Suddenly White: Literary Realism and Racial Passing* (Columbia, MO: University of Missouri Press, 2006)
Bhabha, Homi (ed.), *Nation and Narration* (London: Routledge, 1990)
Bird, Michael, *The St Ives Artists: A Biography of Place and Time* (Aldershot: Lund Humphries, 2008)
Bourne, Stephen, *Black in the British Frame: Black People in British Film and Television 1896–1996* (London: Cassell, 1998)

Boyarin, Jonathan, *Storm from Paradise: The Politics of Jewish Memory* (Minneapolis, MN: University of Minnesota Press, 1992)

Breitman, Richard and Alan Kraut, *American Refugee Policy and European Jewry, 1933–1945* (Bloomington, IN: Indiana University Press, 1987)

Brocklehurst, Helen and Robert Phillips (eds), *History, Nationhood and the Question of Britain* (Basingstoke: Palgrave Macmillan, 2004)

Bullock, Alan, *Ernest Bevin: Foreign Secretary* (London: Heinemann, 1984)

Burgess, Muriel, *Shirley: An Appreciation of the Life of Shirley Bassey* (London: Century, 1998)

Burrell, Kathy, 'Materialising the Border: Spaces of Mobility and Material Culture in Migration from Post-Socialist Poland', *Mobilities* vol. 3 no. 3 (2008)

Burrell, Kathy, 'Going Steerage on Ryanair: Cultures of Migrant Air Travel between Poland and the UK', *Journal of Transport Geography* vol. 19 (2011)

Cameron, Ross, '"The Most Colourful Extravaganza in the World": Images of Tiger Bay, 1845–1970', *Patterns of Prejudice* vol. 31 no. 2 (1997)

Carretta, Vincent, 'Olaudah Equiano or Gustavus Vassa? New Light on an Eighteenth-Century Question of Identity', *Slavery and Abolition* vol. 20 no. 3 (1999)

Carretta, Vincent, *Equiano, the African: Biography of a Self Made Man* (Athens, GA: University of Georgia Press, 2005)

Carretta, Vincent, 'Response to Paul Lovejoy's "Autobiography and Memory: Gustavus Vassa, alias Olaudah Equiano, the African"', *Slavery and Abolition* vol. 28 no. 1 (2007)

Castles, Stephen, 'Towards a Sociology of Forced Migration and Social Transformation', *Sociology* vol. 37 no. 1 (2003)

Cesarani, David, 'The Myth of Origin: ethnic memory and the experience of migration', in A. Newman and S. Massil (eds), *Patterns of Migration 1850–1914* (London: Jewish Historical Society of England, 1996)

Chadwick, William, *The Rescue of the Prague Refugees 1938–39* (Leicester: Matador, 2010)

Chappell, Carolyn Lougee, '"The Pains I Took to Save My/His Family": Escape Accounts by a Huguenot Daughter after the Revocation of the Edict of Nantes', *French Historical Studies* vol. 22 no. 1 (Winter 1999)

Cheyette, Bryan, *Constructions of 'the Jew' in English Literature and Society: Racial Representations, 1875–1945* (Cambridge: Cambridge University Press, 1993), pp. 5–6.

Christopher, Emma, Cassandra Pybus and Marcus Rediker (eds), *Many Middle Passages: Forced Migration and the Making of the Modern World* (Berkeley, CA: University of California Press, 2007)

Clifford, James, *Travel and Translation in the Late Twentieth Century* (Cambridge, MA: Harvard University Press, 1997)

Coleman, D.C., *The British Paper Industry 1495–1860: A Study in Industrial Growth* (Oxford: Clarendon Press, 1958)

Colley, Linda, 'Britishness and Otherness: An Argument', *Journal of British Studies* vol. 31 (October 1992)

Collins, Brenda, 'The Origins of Irish Immigration to Scotland in the Nineteenth and Twentieth Centuries', in Tom Devine (ed.), *Irish Immigrants and Scottish Society in the Nineteenth and Twentieth Centuries* (Edinburgh: John Donald, 1991)

Colls, Robert, *Identity of England* (Oxford: Oxford University Press, 2002)

Connon, Bryan, *Beverley Nichols: A Life* (Portland, OR: Timber Press, 2009)

Cottret, Bernard, *The Huguenots in England. Immigration and Settlement c.1550–1700* (Cambridge: Cambridge University Press, 1991)

Crick, Michael, *In Search of Michael Howard* (London: Simon & Schuster, 2005)

Daniels, Roger, *Coming to America: A History of Immigration and Ethnicity in American Life* (New York: HarperPerennial, 1991)

Davison, Sally and Jonathan Rutherford (eds), *Race, Identity and Belonging* (London: Lawrence and Wishart, 2008)

Douglas, Mary, *Purity and Danger: An Analysis of the Concepts of Pollution and Taboo* (London: Routledge, 1996 [1966])

Dwork, Deborah and Robert Jan Van Pelt, *Flight from the Reich: Refugee Jews, 1933–1946* (New York: W.W. Norton, 2009)

Evans, Neil, 'Regulating the Reserve Army: Arabs, Blacks and the Local State in Cardiff, 1919–45', *Immigrants and Minorities* vol. 4 (July 1985)

Falola, Toyin, *The History of Nigeria* (Westport, CT: Greenwood Press, 1999)

Fast, Vera, *Children's Exodus: A History of the Kindertransport* (London: I.B.Tauris, 2011)

Feldman, David and Gareth Stedman Jones (eds), *Metropolis – London: Histories and Representations since 1800* (London: Routledge, 1989)

Fitzgerald, Patrick and Brian Lambkin, *Migration in Irish History, 1607–2007* (Basingstoke: Palgrave Macmillan, 2008)

Fitzpatrick, David, *Irish Emigration, 1801–1921* (Dublin: Economic and Social History Society of Ireland, 1984)

Fitzpatrick, David, *Oceans of Consolation: Personal Accounts of Irish Migration to Australia* (Cork: Cork University Press, 1994)

Fleischhauer, Ingeborg and Benjamin Pinkus (eds), *The Soviet Germans: Past and Present* (London: C.Hurst, 1986)

Foucault, Michel, 'Different Spaces' in James Faubion (ed.), *The Essential Works of Foucault* vol. 2 *Aesthetics, Method, and Epistemology* (London: Allen Lane, 1998)

Francis, Vivienne, *With Hope in their Eyes: the Compelling Stories of the Windrush Generation* (London: Nia, 1998)

Frost, Diane, 'Racism, Work and Unemployment: West African Seamen in Liverpool 1880s–1960s', *Immigrants & Minorities* vol. 13 nos 2&3 (1994)

Fryer, Peter, *Staying Power: The History of Black People in Britain* (London: Pluto Press, 1984)

Fyrth, Jim, *The Signal Was Spain: The Spanish Aid Movement in Britain 1931–39* (London: Lawrence & Wishart, 1986)

Gainer, Bernard, *The Alien Invasion: The Origins of the Aliens Act of 1905* (London: Heinemann, 1972)

Gartner, Lloyd, 'Notes on the Statistics of Jewish Immigration to England, 1870–1914',

Jewish Social Studies vol. 22 no. 2 (1960), pp. 97–102

Geary, Patrick, *Phantoms of Remembrance: Memory and Oblivion at the End of the First Millennium* (Princeton, NJ: Princeton University Press, 1994)

Gigliotti, Simone, *The Train Journey: Transit, Captivity, and Witnessing in the Holocaust* (New York: Berghahn Books, 2009)

Gillman, Peter and Leni, '*Collar the Lot': How Britain Interned and Expelled Its Wartime Refugees* (London: Quartet Books, 1980)

Gilroy, Paul, '*There Ain't No Black in the Union Jack': The Cultural Politics of Race and Nation* (London: Hutchinson, 1987)

Gilroy, Paul, *The Black Atlantic: Modernity and Double Consciousness* (London: Verso, 1993)

Gilroy, Paul, *Between Camps: Nations, Cultures and the Allure of Race* (London: Allen Lane, 2000)

Gilroy, Paul, *Black Britain: A Photographic History* (London: Saqibooks, 2007)

Glass, Ruth, *London's Newcomers: The West Indian Migrants* (Cambridge, MA: Harvard University Press, 1961)

Gough-Yates, Kevin, 'The British Feature Film as a European Concern: Britain and the Emigre Film-Maker, 1933–45', in Gunter Berghaus (ed.), *Theatre and Film in Exile: German Artists in Britain, 1933–1945* (Oxford: Berg, 1989)

Gray, Peter, *The Irish Famine* (London: Thames and Hudson, 1995)

Gray, Peter and Kendrick Oliver (eds), *The Memory of Catastrophe* (Manchester: Manchester University Press, 2004)

Green, Geoffrey, *The Royal Navy and Anglo-Jewry 1740–1820* (London: Geoffrey Green, 1989)

Groot, Jerome de, *Consuming History: Historians and Heritage in Contemporary Popular Culture* (London: Routledge, 2009)

Gwynn, Robin, 'Huguenots and Walloons in Dorset, Hampshire and Wiltshire', *Hatcher Review* vol. 2 (1984)

Gwynn, Robin, *Huguenot Heritage: The History and Contribution of the Huguenots in Britain* (London: Routledge, 2001)

Hammerton, A. James and Alistair Thomson, *Ten Pound Poms: Australia's Invisible Migrants* (Manchester: Manchester University Press, 2005)

Hathaway, James, 'Forced Migration Studies: Could We Agree Just to "Date"?', *Journal of Refugee Studies* vol. 20 no. 2 (2007)

Hodges, Hugh, 'Kitchener Invades England: The London Calypsos of Aldwyn Roberts', *Wasafari* vol. 20 no. 45 (2005)

Holmes, Colin, *John Bull's Island: Immigration and British Society, 1871–1971* (Basingstoke: Macmillan, 1988)

Holmes, Colin, *A Tolerant Country? Immigrants, Refugees and Minorities in Britain* (London: Faber and Faber, 1991)

hooks, bell, 'Representing Whiteness', in Lawrence Grossberg, Cary Nelson and Paula Treichler (eds), *Cultural Studies* (New York: Routledge, 1992)

Hosking, Geoffrey, *Russia and the Russians: A History from Rus to the Russian Federation* (London: Allen Lane, 2001)

Howe, Irving, *World of Our Fathers: The Journey of East European Jews to America and the Life they Found and Made* (New York: Galahad Books, 1976)

Jackson, Jim, 'Famine Diary: The Making of a Best Sellar', *Irish Review* vol. 11 no. 1 (November 1991)

Jenkinson, Jacqueline, *Black 1919: Riots, Racism and Resistance in Imperial Britain* (Liverpool: Liverpool University Press, 2009)

Jordan, James, Tony Kushner and Sarah Pearce (eds), *Jewish Journeys from Philo to Hip Hop* (London: Vallentine Mitchell, 2010)

Kaplan, Cora and John Oldfield (eds), *Imagining Transatlantic Slavery* (Basingstoke: Palgrave Macmillan, 2010)

Kappeler, Andreas, 'The Ambiguities of Russification', *Kritika: Explorations in Russian and Eurasian History* vol. 5 no. 2 (2004)

Kappeler, Andreas, *The Russian Empire* (Harlow: Pearson Education, 2007)

Kashtan, Nadav (ed.), *Seafaring and the Jews* (London: Frank Cass, 2001)

Kaur, Ravinder, *Since 1947: Partition Narratives among Punjabi Migrants to Delhi* (New Delhi: Oxford University Press, 2007)

Kershen, Anne, *Strangers, Aliens and Asians: Huguenots, Jews and Bangladeshis in Spitalfields 1660–2000* (London: Routledge, 2005)

Kershen, Anne (ed.), *London the Promised Land? The Migrant Experience in a Capital City* (Aldershot: Ashgate, 1997)

Klier, John and Shlomo Lambroza (eds), *Pogroms: Anti-Jewish violence in Modern Russian History* (Cambridge: Cambridge University Press, 1992)

Klug, Brian, *Being Jewish and Doing Justice: Bringing Argument to Life* (London: Vallentine Mitchell, 2010)

Koch, Fred, *The Volga Germans in Russia and the Americas, from 1763 to the Present* (University Park, Pennsylvania: Pennsylvania State University Press, 1977)

Kumar, Krishan, *The Making of English National Identity* (Cambridge: Cambridge University Press, 2003)

Kushner, Tony, *The Holocaust and the Liberal Imagination: A Social and Cultural History* (Oxford: Blackwell, 1994)

Kushner, Tony, *Remembering Refugees: Then and Now* (Manchester: Manchester University Press, 2006)

Kushner, Tony, *Anglo-Jewry since 1066: Place, Locality and Memory* (Manchester: Manchester University Press, 2009)

Kushner, Tony and Katharine Knox, *Refugees in an Age of Genocide: Global, National and Local Perspectives during the Twentieth Century* (London: Frank Cass, 1999)

Lachenicht, Susanne, 'Huguenot Immigrants and the Formation of National Identities, 1548–1787', *The Historical Journal* vol. 50 no. 2 (2007)

Langford, Paul, *Englishness Identified: Manners and Character 1650–1850* (Oxford: Oxford University Press, 2000)

Lassner, Phyliss, *Anglo-Jewish Women Writing the Holocaust: Displaced Witnesses* (Basingstoke: Palgrave Macmillan, 2008)

Laxton, Edward, *The Famine Ships: The Irish Exodus to America 1846–1851* (London: Bloomsbury, 1997)

Lehrer, Erica, Cynthia Milton and Monica Patterson (eds), *Curating Difficult Knowledge: Violent Pasts in Public Places* (Basingstoke: Palgrave Macmillan, 2011)

Leigh, Jeremy, *Jewish Journeys* (London: Haus Publishing, 2006)

Liberles, Robert, 'Postemancipation Historiography and the Jewish Historical Societies of America and England', in Jonathan Frankel (ed.), *Reshaping the Past: Jewish History and the Historians* vol. 10 *Studies in Contemporary Jewry* (New York: Oxford University Press, 1994)

Linenthal, Edward, *Preserving Memory: The Struggle to Create America's Holocaust Museum* (New York: Viking, 1995)

London, Louise, *Whitehall and the Jews 1933–1948: British Immigration Policy and the Holocaust* (Cambridge: Cambridge University Press, 2000)

London, Louise, 'Whitehall and the Refugees: The 1930s and the 1990s', *Patterns of Prejudice* vol. 34 no. 3 (2000)

Long, James, *From Privileged to Dispossessed: The Volga Germans, 1860–1917* (Lincoln, NE: University of Nebraska Press, 1988)

Lovejoy, Paul, 'Autobiography and Memory: Gustavus Vassa, alias Olaudah Equiano, the African', *Slavery and Abolition* vol. 27 no. 3 (2006)

Lovejoy, Paul, 'Issues of Motivation – Vass/Equiano and Carretta's Critique of the Evidence', *Slavery and Abolition* vol. 28 no. 1 (2007)

Luebke, Frederick, *Germans in Brazil: A Comparative History of Cultural Conflict During World War I* (Baton Rouge: Louisiana State University Press, 1987)

Lunn, Kenneth, 'The British State and Immigration, 1945–51: New Light on the Empire Windrush', in Tony Kushner and Kenneth Lunn (eds), *The Politics of Marginality: Race, the Radical Right and Minorities in Twentieth Century Britain* (London: Frank Cass, 1990)

MacDonagh, Oliver, 'The Regulation of Emigrant Traffic from the United Kingdom', *Irish Historical Studies* vol. 9 no. 34 (1954)

McGhee, Derek, 'The Paths to Citizenship: A Critical Examination of Immigration Policy in Britain since 2001', *Patterns of Prejudice* vol. 43 no. 1 (2009), pp. 40–64

Malet, Marian, 'Departure and Arrival', in John Grenville and Marian Malet (eds), *Changing Countries: The Experience and Achievement of German-Speaking Exiles from Hitler in Britain, from 1933 to Today* (London: Libris, 2002)

Malkki, Liisa, 'National Geographic: The Rooting of Peoples and the Territorialization of National Identity among Scholars and Refugees', *Cultural Anthropology* vol. 7 no. 1 (1992)

Malkki, Liisa, 'Speechless Emissaries: Refugees, Humanitarianism and Dehistoricization', *Cultural Anthropology* vol. 11 no. 3 (1996)

Mandler, Peter, *The English National Character: The History of an Idea from Edmund Burke to Tony Blair* (London: Yale University Press, 2006)

Manning, Patrick, *Migration in World History* (New York: Routledge, 2005)

Marchlewicz, K., 'Continuities and Innovations: Polish Emigration after 1849', in S. Freitag (ed.), *Exiles from European Revolutions: Refugees in Mid-Victorian England* (New York: Berg, 2003)

Marmoy, Charles, 'The Historical Novel and the Huguenots', *Proceedings of the*

Huguenot Society of London vol. 23 no. 2 (1978)

Massey, Doreen, 'Places and their Pasts', *History Workshop Journal* no. 39 (spring 1995)

Mead, Matthew, '*Empire Windrush*: Cultural Memory and Archival Disturbance', *Moveable Type* no. 3 (2007)

Mead, Matthew, '*Empire Windrush*: The Cultural Memory of an Imaginary Arrival', *Journal of Postcolonial Writing* vol. 45 no. 2 (2009)

Mentzer, Raymond and Andrew Spicer (eds), *Society and Culture in the Huguenot World 1559–1685* (Cambridge: Cambridge University Press, 2002)

Miller, Kerby, *Emigrants and Exiles: Ireland and the Irish Exodus to North America* (New York: Oxford University Press, 1985)

Modood, Tariq, *Not Easy Being British: Colour, Culture and Citizenship* (Stoke: Trentham Books, 1992)

Modood, Tariq, *Still Not Easy Being British: Struggles for a Multicultural Citizenship* (Stoke: Trentham Books, 2010)

Morash, Christopher, *Writing the Irish Famine* (Oxford: Oxford University Press, 1995)

Morse, Arthur, *While Six Million Died* (London: Secker & Warburg, 1968)

Neal, Frank, *Black '47: Britain and the Famine Irish* (Basingstoke: Macmillan, 1998)

Newman, Jon, *Windrush Forbears: Black People in Lambeth 1700–1900* (London: Lambeth Archives/Department of Education and Skills, 2002)

Ogilvie, Sarah and Scott Miller, *Refuge Denied: The St Louis Passengers and the Holocaust* (Madison, WI: University of Wisconsin Press, 2006)

Oldfield, John, '*Chords of Freedom*'. *Commemoration, Ritual and British Transatlantic Slavery* (Manchester: Manchester University Press, 2007)

Oldfield, John, 'Introduction: Imagining Transatlantic Slavery and Abolition', *Patterns of Prejudice* vol. 41 nos 3–4 (2007)

Olick, Jeffrey and Joyce Robbins, 'Social Memory Studies: From "Collective Memory" to the Historical Sociology of Mnemonic Practices', *Annual Review of Sociology* vol. 24 (1998)

O'Sullivan, Patrick (ed.), *The Irish World Wide: History, Heritage, Identity* vol. 6 (Leicester: Leicester University Press, 1997)

Panayi, Panikos, *The Enemy in Our Midst: Germans in Britain during the First World War* (Oxford: Berg, 1991)

Panayi, Panikos, *Spicing Up Britain: The Multicultural History of British Food* (London: Reaktion Books, 2008)

Panayi, Panikos, *An Immigration History of Britain: Multicultural Racism since 1800* (Harlow: Longman, 2010)

Pateman, Matthew, *Julian Barnes* (Tavistock, Devon: Northcote House, 2002)

Patterson, A. Temple, *A History of Southampton 1700–1914* vol. 1 (Southampton: University of Southampton Press, 1966)

Patterson, A. Temple, *A History of Southampton* vol. 3 (Southampton: University of Southampton Press, 1975)

Patterson, Sheila, *Dark Strangers: A Study of West Indians in London* (Harmondsworth:

Penguin, 1965)

Phillips, Mike and Trevor, *Windrush: The Irrestible Rise of Multi-Racial Britain* (London: HarperCollins, 1999)

Porter, Bernard, *The Refugee Question in Mid-Victorian Politics* (Cambridge: Cambridge University Press, 1979)

Porter, Roy, *London: A Social History* (Harmondsworth: Penguin, 1996)

Rediker, Marcus, *The Slave Ship: A Human History* (New York: Penguin, 2007)

Rice, Alan, 'Naming the Money and Unveiling the Crime: Contemporary British Artists and the Memorialization of Slavery and Abolition', *Patterns of Prejudice* vol. 41 nos 3–4 (2007)

Rich, Paul, *Race and Empire in British Politics* (Cambridge: Cambridge University Press, 1986)

Richards, Eric, *Destination Australia: Migration to Australia since 1901* (Sydney: University of New South Wales Press, 2008)

Roche, T.W.E., *The Key in the Lock: Immigration Control in England from 1066 to the Present Day* (London: John Murray, 1969)

Romain, Gemma, *Connecting History: A Comparative Exploration of African-Caribbean and Jewish History and Memory in Modern Britain* (London: Kegan Paul, 2006)

Rubinstein, William, *The Myth of Rescue* (London: Routledge, 1997)

Rumbelow, Donald, *The Houndsditch Murders & the Siege of Sidney Street* (London: Penguin Books, 1990)

Rush, Anne Spry, 'Imperial Identity in Colonial Minds: Harold Moody and the League of Coloured Peoples, 1931–50', *Twentieth Century British History* vol. 13 no. 4 (2002)

Samuel, Raphael, *Island Stories: Unravelling Britain* (London: Verso, 1998)

Samuel, Raphael and Paul Thompson (eds), *The Myths We Live By* (London: Routledge, 1990)

Sandhu, Sukdev, *London Calling: How Black and Asian Writers Imagined a City* (London: HarperCollins, 2003)

Sarna, Jonathan, 'The Myth of "No Return": Jewish Return Migration to Eastern Europe, 1881–1914', *American Jewish History* vol. 71 (1981)

Schwarz, Bill (ed.), *West Indian Intellectuals in Britain* (Manchester: Manchester University Press, 2003)

Scobie, Edward, *Black Britannia: A History of Blacks in Britain* (Chicago: Johnson Publishing, 1972)

Scouloudi, Irene (ed.), *Huguenots in Britain and their French Background, 1550–1800* (Basingstoke: Macmillan, 1987)

Sebak, Per Kristian, *Titanic's Predecessor: The S/S Norge Disaster of 1904* (Laksevaag: Seaward Publishing, 2004)

Sewell, Tony, *Keep on Moving. The Windrush Legacy: The Black Experience in Britain from 1948* (London: Voice Enterprises, 1998)

Sharf, Andrew, *The British Press & Jews Under Nazi Rule* London: Oxford University Press, 1964)

Sicherman, Barbara, *Well-Read Lives: How Books Inspired a Generation of American*

Women (Chapel Hill, NC: University of North Carolina Press, 2010)

Singh, Amritjit, Joseph Skerrett and Robert Hogan (eds), *Memory, Narrative and Identity: New Essays in Ethnic American Literatures* (Boston, MA: Northeastern University Press, 1994)

Skinner, Patricia (ed.), *Jews in Medieval Britain: Historical, Literary and Archaeological Perspectives* (Woodbridge: Boydell and Brewer, 2003)

Smith, T. Lynn, *Brazil: People and Institutions* (Baton Rouge, LA: Louisiana State University Press, 1963)

Snowman, Daniel, *The Hitler Emigres: The Cultural Impact on Britain of Refugees from Nazism* (London: Pimlico, 2003)

Solomos, John, *Race and Racism in Britain* (2nd edition, Basingstoke: Macmillan, 2003)

Soyinka, Susan, *From East End to Land's End* (Derby: Derby Books, 2010)

Spencer, Ian, *British Immigration Policy since 1939* (London: Routledge, 1997)

Spicer, Andrew, *The French-speaking Reformed Community and their Church in Southampton 1567–1620* (London: Huguenot Society of Great Britain and Ireland, 1997)

Spivak, Gayatri Chakravorty, 'Can the Subaltern Speak?', in G. Nelson (ed.), *Marxism and the Interpretation of Culture* (Basingstoke: Macmillan, 1988)

Stevens, Dallal, *UK Asylum Law and Policy: Historical and Contemporary Perspectives* (London: Sweet & Maxwell, 2004)

Stumpp, Karl, *The German-Russians: Two Centuries of Pioneering* (Bonn: Edition Atlantic-Forum, 1971)

Stumpp, Karl, *The Emigration from Germany to Russia in the Years 1763 to 1862* (Lincoln, NE: American Historical Society of Germans from Russia, 1973–1978)

Talbot, Ian and Shinder Thandi (eds), *People on the Move: Punjabi Colonial, and Post-Colonial Migration* (Oxford: Oxford University Press, 2004)

Thomas, Gordon and Max Morgan-Witts, *Voyage of the Damned: The Voyage of the St Louis* (London: Hodder and Stoughton, 1974)

Thompson, E.P., *The Making of the English Working Class* (London: Victor Gollancz, 1963)

Thompson, Paul, *The Edwardians: The Remaking of British Society* (London: Weidenfeld& Nicolson, 1975)

Turkel, Studs, *Race* (London: Minerva, 1993)

Turner, Barry, *… And the Policeman Smiled. 10,000 Children Escape from Nazi Europe* (London: Bloomsbury, 1990)

Vaughan, David, *Negro Victory: The Life Story of Dr Harold Moody* (London: Independent Press, 1950)

Vigne, Randolph and Charles Littleton (eds), *From Strangers to Citizens: The Integration of Immigrant Communities in Britain, Ireland and Colonial America, 1550–1750* (Brighton: Sussex University Press, 2001)

Visram, Rozina, *Asians in Britain: 400 Years of History* (London: Pluto Press, 2002)

Wallace, Elizabeth, *The British Slave Trade & Public Memory* (New York: Columbia University Press, 2006)

Walvin, James, *Passage to Britain: Immigration in British History and Politics* (Harmondsworth: Penguin, 1984)

Wambu, Onyekachi (ed.), *Hurricane Hits England: An Anthology of Writing about Black Britain* (New York: Continuum, 2000)

Ward, Paul, *Britishness Since 1870* (London: Routledge, 2004)

Waters, Chris, "'Dark Strangers" in Our Midst: Discourses of Race and Nation in Britain, 1947–1963', *Journal of British Studies* vol. 36 (April 1997)

Watts, Derek, 'Testimonies of Persecution: Four Huguenot Refugees and their Memoirs', in J.H. Fox, M.H. Waddicor and D.A. Watts (eds), *Studies in Eighteenth-Century French Literature Presented to Robert Niklaus* (Exeter: Exeter University Press, 1975)

Weeks, Theodore, 'Managing Empire: tsarist nationalities policy', in Dominic Lieven (ed.), *The Cambridge History of Russia* vol. II (Cambridge: Cambridge University Press, 2006)

Weindling, Paul, *Epidemics and Genocide in Eastern Europe, 1890–1945* (Oxford: Oxford University Press, 2000)

Williams, Bill, *Jews and Other Foreigners: Manchester and the Rescue of the Victims of European Fascism, 1933–40* (Manchester: Manchester University Press, 2011)

Williams, John, *Miss Shirley Bassey* (London: Quercus, 2010)

Winder, Robert, *Bloody Foreigners: The Story of Immigration to Britain* (London: Little, Brown, 2004)

Winter, Molly Crumpton, *American Narratives: Multiethnic Writing in the Age of Realism* (Baton Rouge, LA: Louisiana State University Press, 2007)

Wright, Patrick, *On Living in an Old Country: the National Past in Contemporary Britain* (London: Verso, 1985)

Wright, Patrick, *The Village that Died for England: The Strange Story of Tyneham* (London: Jonathan Cape, 1995)

Wood, Marcus, *Blind Memory: Visual Representations of Slavery in England and America 1780–1865* (Manchester: Manchester University Press, 2000)

Yerushalmi, Yosef, *Zakhor: Jewish History and Jewish Memory* (New York: Shocken Books, 1989)

Young, James, *The Texture of Memory: Holocaust Memorials and Meaning* (New Haven, CT: Yale University Press, 1993)

Unpublished

Evans, Nicholas, 'Aliens *En Route*: European Transmigration Through Britain, 1836–1914' (Ph.D. thesis, University of Hull, 2006)

King, Jason, 'Famine Diaries? Narratives About Emigration from Ireland to Lower Canada and Quebec, 1832–1853' (M.A. thesis, McGill University, Canada, 1994)

Norton, Jennifer, 'The *Kindertransport*: History and Memory' (M.A. thesis, California State University, 2010)

O'Reilly, William, "'Selling Souls". "The Crown" and the 18th-century Atlantic Trade in Migrants', University of Southampton History seminar, 2 February 2010

Sabin-Fernandez, Susana, 'The Basque Refugee Children of the Spanish Civil War in the UK: Memory and Memorialization' (Ph.D. thesis, University of Southampton, 2011)

Index